To fellow armenian
Florence
Kindest regards
Samuel [illegible]

America's Adopted Son

The remarkable story of an orphaned immigrant boy

Samuel Nakasian

Edited by Reggie Marshall

BOOKWRIGHTS PRESS
OF CHARLOTTESVILLE

America's Adopted Son: The remarkable story of an orphaned immigrant boy

Published by
Bookwrights Press of Charlottesville
2522 Willard Drive, Suite 108
Charlottesville, VA 22903
Phone: 804-296-0686
Email: Bookwrights.com

Printed in the United States of America
1 2 3 4 5 6 7 8

Bookwrights' books are distributed by
Midpoint Trade Books 816-842-8420
and are available on the Internet through Allbooks at http://AllBooks.com
and through many online bookstores.

Library of Congress Cataloging-in-Publication Data

Nakasian, Samuel, 1915–
America's adopted son : the remarkable story of an orphaned immigrant boy / Samuel Nakasian : edited by Reggie Marshall.
p. cm.
ISBN 1–880404–12–5
1. Nakasian, Samuel, 1915– . 2. Lawyers—United States—Biography. 3. Economists—United States—Biography. 4. Armenian Americans—Biography. I. Title.
CT275.N265A3 1997
973' .0491992'0092
[B]—DC21 96–47365
CIP

The image of Dr. Fosdick is from a painting by Louis Jambor which resides in The Riverside Church. The photograph of Eric Kohler is courtesy of Mr. Jae Yoo. The photo of William Cooper is reproduced courtesy of G.S.B. Multi-media Lab.

I dedicate this book to Patricia, my wife of unfailing support and companionship for almost half a century, and to our four offspring, Stephanie, Stirling, Suzanne and Stacey. They hunger to learn from the life I experienced.

"...Let your light shine before others so that they may see your good works and give glory to your father in heaven."

Mathew 4.22.14

"...Seeist thou a man diligent in his business? He shall stand before kings; He shall not stand before mean men.

Proverbs 22:29

"Seek windows on the world for knowledge; mirrors show little new to the viewer."

Samuel Nakasian

Special thanks to Reggie Marshall, my editor, for his efforts in making the manuscript clearer and more readable. My gratitude also goes to my publisher, Bookwrights Press, for their enthusiasm in accepting these memoirs for publication. And very special thanks to my companion in this venture, Patricia, who accepted the new challenge of mastering our IBM computer to produce this manuscript. Along the way, her observations and advice improved the document by her touch.

—Sam Nakasian

Contents

Foreword

Ameica's Adopted Son makes fascinating reading. In the opening chapters one follows the career of an orphan escaping to the U.S. from the World War I Armenian genocide in Turkey. This path is traced through the depths of the 1930's depression in the U.S. as Sam moves from one attempt at employment and residence to another. With the advent of World War II, however, the path suddenly veers into a new, and ever-changing, world thereafter.

I have personally come into immediate contact with the future in many different dimensions, by virtue of having served as a teacher over many years in several universities. Communication with intelligent young people, passing into adulthood, has made me come to regard World War II as one of the great divides of history. It is hard, if not impossible, to communicate the stagnation as well as the hopelessness of the pre-war 1930s to persons who did not live through these years. Worst of all was the resignation that could be seen on many faces as people adjusted to this state of affairs. The experiences of growing up on farms and in cities during this period are vividly recounted by Sam. These passages are interesting. They are also well worth reading as a reminder of how things were—and how they might have become with a different outcome from the cataclysmic events embodied in World War II.

From these beginnings, Sam traces his career through college, government, law school, private practice, and on into international negotiations in oil (among other things). This covers a large span of years. He then concludes with the purchase of Sunny Brae

Farm, his present home in Virginia, where he has returned to his roots as a farmer, but on a different level and in a different place. At the end of the volume he reproduces a speech he delivered at a ceremony for newly sworn U.S. citizens. He recounts his satisfactions as well as his successes. "I am not a self-made man," he protests. "It is America that made me!—and it can make you, too, if you take advantage of what this country has to offer."

I would say that it is the *changes* in America, or more generally, the *changes* in the world that made possible the opportunities and activities that Sam describes in this volume. How and why these changes came about are described in many different sources, but only in very general ways. This brings me to the topic of some of the "unsung heroes" who were behind these changes. Two of my favorite examples are Harry Hopkins and Paul Hoffman.

The former, Harry Hopkins, as adviser to Franklin D. Roosevelt authored and engineered the Lend-Lease Program which first supplied support to Great Britain when it was on the verge of collapse from attacks by the Nazis, and then to Moscow, where Hopkins flew as a sick (some would say dying) man to retrieve a situation in which Russian armies were collapsing one after another, and Stalin, the Russian dictator, had already fled into hiding. Hopkins brought him back to Moscow and the offer of Lend-Lease, carried by Hopkins in this fateful trip, stiffened Stalin's resolve—not only for the military supplies that this offer carried but also for what it portended in the form of future U.S. support.

These Lend Lease episodes all occurred on one side of the divide represented by World War II. Paul Hoffman is representative of the significantly different events that began to occur on the other side.

Hoffman, as President of the Studebaker Automobile Company, first began to display these heroic aspects in his activities as chairman and organizer of the Committee for Economic Development. Formed as an unusual combination of academic economists and practical businessmen, the CED proved influential in focusing issues for public discussion, with subsequent effects on legislative activities and public policy. Hoffman then went on to become Administrator of the Economic Cooperation Administration (ECA), the agency that administered the "Marshall Plan." There Hoffman played a crucial role in starting the whole post-war world on the road to recovery and self respect, and away from the decline and political despair and desperation toward which it was heading.

There are those who might say that I credit these individuals with too much. Perhaps they are right. For instance, I am not sure who came up with the "idea" of Lend Lease—as a way of circumventing elements of the U.S. Congress who were backed by strong "anti-war" (and other) forces. At least from the vantage point of the Executive Office of the President, where I worked at this time, I do know that it was Harry Hopkins who "carried the ball."

The story recounted by Sam Nakasian in this book on the birth and implementation of Economic Cooperation Administrative (ECA) "Regulation One" is revelatory at a deeper and more detailed level on the way these events occurred. Employed by ECA, Sam was charged by its Controller to ensure that the agency and its programs did not go down into failure from graft and corruption, like that which had engulfed the United Nations Relief and Rehabilitation Administration, under the direction of Fiorello LaGuardia (the ex-mayor of New York), and other international predecessor agencies. In essence, "ECA Reg.1" was designed to protect the government against price discrimination and other forms of graft and corruption represented by "kick-backs," "shipping shy," and other such devices. These anti-corruption activities were built around a certificate (called the Suppliers Certificate) that Nakasian designed, in which suppliers certified that the prices being charged did not exceed the prices charged to private parties. This was accompanied on the face of the certificate by a listing from the supplier of the identities of any agents and commissions paid to them in these transactions. Accompanied by an ever watchful vigilance this Supplier Certificate and ECA Reg. 1 accomplished what was required.

Backed by the Controller's office, where Sam was located, this regulation was debated in often bitter disputes within (and outside) the agency, prior to issuance. The chief antagonist was Richard Bissell, Assistant Administrator and Chief of the Industries Division, who saw the ECA mainly as a "bank" intended only to facilitate international transactions and argued strongly that the proposed regulation would be an impediment. The chief protagonist, fearlessly opposing Bissell, was Sam Nakasian, who supplied the requisite persistence, determination and imagination, as I can testify from direct observation as consultant to the Agency. The differences between antagonists and protagonists is where Hoffman came into the act, as he responded first negatively and then positively to the very strong arguments on either side. Fortunately for all concerned, the regulation was finally approved by Hoffman, after which its day-to-day supervision became the duty of Sam and his staff in the Price Analysis section of the Controller's office in the ECA. The result was remarkable. In many thousands of business transactions conducted over many time periods in many different regions of the world the agency was nevertheless able to avoid the corruption that had blemished the actions of earlier agencies.

We can perhaps better appreciate the vivid portrayals supplied by Nakasian if I recall that Bissell, his antagonist, subsequently joined the CIA where he directed the disastrous "Bay of Pigs" invasion of Cuba. We can then appreciate Hoffman's role even better if we recall that Bissell secured the requisite approval for the Bay of Pigs misadventure from Bobby Kennedy, then Attorney General and adviser to his brother, President Kennedy.

What was the difference that led Paul Hoffman down one path and Bobby Kennedy down another in their dealings with the very persuasive Richard Bissell? One way to explain this is to say that each of them responded differently because of character, wisdom, inner motivation, or whatever. Another explanation might refer to the way Hoffman and Kennedy designed and operated their organizations. One set of operations was clandestine; the other was conducted in a manner, emphasized by Hoffman and his Controller, that was open to public view. I think that something more was also involved. Lawyer-investigator-politician Kennedy, inexperienced in managing large organizations, was guided by his own concept of "realism," whereas Hoffman, the practical businessman, was guided by "idealism." Both in his role as Chairman of the Committee for Economic Development and as Administrator of the Marshall Plan, Hoffman showed that he could bring "idealism" into practical reality. This, too, was a mark of Sam Nakasian in these and the subsequent activities that are described in this book.

Here we have focused on a turning point in an agency which itself represented a turning point in a world coming down one of the many paths it might have taken on this side of World War II. All of this, and more, is vividly described in the memoirs that follow. Where will this all now lead as events seem to move ever faster and ever more out of control? Here, too, these memoirs offer important clues, as Samuel Nakasian describes his experiences in international oil negotiations in the Middle East and elsewhere, and as he examines the worlds that might have been in these very different corners of the planet. The book concludes with the present, more peaceful, life which he and his wife Patricia share at Sunny Brae Farm in Virginia. The world has changed and so has Sam, perhaps, but one can still detect in these memoirs an urge to continue in the "idealistic-practical" character that forms a "leit motif," as Sam comments on the need (and the missed opportunities) for peace and justice everywhere—which are necessary for individual activity to be able to make its contributions to the betterment of humankind!

William W. Cooper
Foster Parker Professor of Finance and Management (Emeritus)
Austin, Texas
1996

1

The Forgotten Life

I MUST HAVE LOOKED EVERY bit the vagrant as I stared at the imposing Upper West Side Gothic apartment adjoining Riverside Church. What was I—a 21 year-old poor, undereducated, orphaned immigrant—doing in front of the home of America's most influential clergyman, whose weekly sermons were broadcast nationwide on the radio? I reread the handwritten note I was holding: "Dear Mr. Nakashian; Miss Comstock has told me that you attend our church, and I would be delighted to make your acquaintance. Please visit me at my home at 8 PM Thursday. Suggest another time if this is not convenient. Otherwise I will expect you then...H.E.F.." It was clear. I had been invited and it would be inexcusable to turn back now. Swallowing the lump in my throat, I strode up to the door of Dr. Harry Emerson Fosdick and rang the bell.

Dr. Fosdick himself opened the door. It was 1936, and he was then about fifty years old, of medium stature, with stentorian voice and emphatic gestures. I especially noticed his small and uncalloused hands_so different from my own brutish farm boy's hands. He greeted me cheerily. "Hello Nakashian," pronouncing each vowel and consonant, "How good to meet you. Let me help you out of your coat."

I couldn't believe my ears. Never had anyone offered to assist me in shedding my coat. Up until now my encounters with those of higher social status—in the Children's Aid Society, the schools and farm families I had known—had been for the most part pleasant, but never had I received such an enthusiastic welcome as this. Dr. Fosdick was treating me as though I were special! The shock of Dr. Fosdick's outreach to me was not relieved as he ushered me into the loveliest and most comfortable living room I had ever seen. It was lined with shelves filled with books. Only in public libraries had I ever seen so many volumes in one room. Inviting me to sit down next to him, he asked if I would like some tea or a soft drink. In my nervousness, my mouth was so parched I could have drunk a gallon, but I politely declined in a barely audible voice.

Thankfully Dr. Fosdick took over, and for the next hour I did little more than shake my head yes or no. "I understand you have been attending our Church." I nodded. "How wonderful to have you with us! It might surprise you, but I know all about your race; it is one of the world's greatest. You see, Armenians mean a great deal to me. Before Herbert Hoover became President, one of his jobs was administering the American Armenian Relief Program. I spent two years in the Middle East working under him, and I know firsthand the suffering and dislocation of your people and what it has meant to your own family with the massacre of your father."

I was stunned. I knew nothing about "my people." Other than my two sisters, I had never known any other Armenians.

"But all that is now behind us," he continued. "Let's talk of the future. First, have you been baptized?"

"Not that I can remember," I mumbled.

"Your people are among the earliest Christians, going back to Gregory in the third century. Obviously, you were born a Christian and baptized, but you must also knowingly be baptized...and with your baptism become a member of our church. I will personally arrange this. Now, tell me, how do you spend your day?" He forced me to respond, focusing on me with piercing eyes, magnified by his glasses.

"I work in a cafeteria during the day and attend McBirney High School in the evening. I hope to graduate next February."

He pressed on. "What do you plan as a career? You are obviously very bright, so you must have a career in mind."

"I - I have thought of becoming a lawyer," I replied hesitantly.

"Splendid, splendid. We have funds available to help you." Impulsively I answered, "Oh, I don't need any help. I make enough to pay my rent and my tuition, and I take my meals at the cafeteria. I can manage." My fierce and unyielding pride, that even I didn't understand at the time. Dr. Fosdick smiled.

"Very well. But I want a commitment from you. Will you come to see me privately, every fall and every spring, and bring me up-to-date on your progress? I will instruct my secretary of this arrangement, and she will await your call." I nodded in assent.

Finally, my head still spinning as in a whirlpool, I made my way to the door, taking leave of Dr. Fosdick and his world to return to mine. Uncomfortable and disquieted, I felt the stimulation of his powerful intellect. More than anything, I suddenly felt a great curiosity about my ethnic heritage. Being Armenian accounted for my darker skin, which had made me stand out in the farm communities of upstate New York, but that was all it had meant to me until today. My sister Vera was ashamed of being Armenian and had tried to talk me into changing my name, but Dr. Fosdick had spelled and pronounced it the Armenian way (the orphanage had dropped the "h") and invited me to take pride in it. I knew very little about my family, only that my father had been a successful merchant in Marsavon, Turkey—near Samsun, a major port on the Black Sea, where the Nakashians had lived for several generations. Vera, eight years older than I, had told me that our home was one of the most spacious in the town. We had our own horses and carriages. In addition to Turkish and Armenian, French (then the international business language) was fluently spoken and written. Then, late one spring night in 1915, the police pounded on the door, waking my father. When he let them in, they arrested him without explanation. That night he and one million other Armenian men were taken to the desert, away from populated areas, and murdered. I was still in my mother's womb.

Leaving Fosdick's, I was full of questions. Why, if Armenians were one of "the world's great races," had this happened? Who would want to exterminate us? Vera had never ventured an explanation and seemed to want to forget the whole thing. So at my first opportunity I went to the massive Public Library at 5th Avenue and 42nd Street and began my search.

I discovered that I was one of millions of ethnic Armenians dispersed across the globe. Our land of origin is the landlocked, mountainous and earthquake-prone area west of the Caspian Sea and northeast of the Black Sea. The biblical Mt. Ararat is in the middle of this region. The Armenian language, one of the first put to alphabet and script, is Indo-European—not Semitic—evidence that, contrary to popular belief, we are neither Jews nor Arabs. Armenia was within range of the earliest Christian missionaries, whose efforts culminated in St. Gregory establishing Christianity as the national religion in 200 A.D. Neighboring Georgians were also converted, but Azerbaijan and Iran to the east and the Arabs to the south later accepted the Islamic faith.

Armenia's mountains and valleys were insufficiently endowed with natural resources to support their growing population. From the earliest times the human surplus emigrated to its Eastern Mediterranean neighbors. One whole village of several thousand accepted the invitation of Shah Abbas to settle in Iran, where they now make up a large portion of the population of Isfahan. Another colony of several hundred families settled in the Bekaa Valley of Lebanon, where they still live and work communally and provide for their own defense through a modern militia. (Years later I was privileged to visit both of these communities). But the largest numbers migrated to Anatolia, which is now a part of Turkey.

In Anatolia the indigenous people and the descendants of the Romans accepted my ancestors, along with Greeks, Jews, Egyptians, and other Middle Easterners. In a world characterized by tribal and ethnic isolation and interracial wars, this area demonstrated a remarkable ethnic and professional diversity. Moreover, it proved ethnic integration could elevate a community to higher levels of human achievement. Its capital, Constantinople, was a cultural and religious center, a metropolis of grandeur rivaling that of ancient Rome.

Armenians, for the most part, continued to thrive under the hegemony of the Turks, following the fall of Constantinople in 1454. A tribal nomadic people, excelling in horsemanship and brandishing the Sword of Islam, the Turks extended their domination north to the Ukraine, east to the Persian Gulf, south into Egypt, and west almost to Vienna, including my homeland and all other countries within these boundaries. Christian Constantinople became Moslem Istanbul, capital of the Ottoman Empire, its Islamification symbolized by the conversion of the ancient cathedral of St. Sophia to a mosque. Still, the warrior Turks needed the skills of minorities within their borders: Jews, Greeks and especially the numerous Armenians. We provided medical doctors, engineering and business acumen, diplomacy, and general administration.

Wherever Armenians settled, we built our own churches and schools, preserving our language and culture while blending into the economic and professional life of the community. Rarely were we politically active, and we virtually never got into trouble because our numbers were so small as to be no threat to the ruling forces. This remained true until the 20th Century.

The discovery of oil in the late 19th Century changed the course of history in the Middle East, and set the stage for the genocide of my people. Petroleum production in the Baku fields of Azerbaijan, then under Russian control, reached 200,000 barrels per day by the turn of the century, and shortly thereafter a British company, Anglo-Iranian Oil, discovered the vast Majid Sulieman Field in Iran. The British Admiralty, under Winston Churchill, declared the Sulieman Field a national treasure for the British Empire, and moved quickly to fund its development. Soon the British navy would be running on efficient oil instead of cumbersome coal, whose transport required manual handling.

Suddenly the European powers were strategically interested in the region, particularly as World War I approached.

Germany eagerly sought Turkey as an ally in their military campaign against the colonial powers of Europe. Turkey saw the war as an opportunity to regain its formerly occupied territories. Over the previous hundred years the Turks had been driven out of the Ukraine, the Balkans, Georgia, Azerbaijan, and Armenia by the Russians. Now Russia, under seige from Germany and Austro-Hungary, its monarchy crumbling, seemed incapable of defending these areas. The Turkish military and the German high command were particularly interested in capturing the oil fields at Baku.

Having recently invested heavily in developing the Iranian oil fields to modernize its industry and navy, Britain was keenly aware that German and Turkish control of Baku oil would inestimably strengthen their adversaries and threaten its own source in Iran. Quickly Britain moved a large segment of its navy into the Bosporous Straits and north into the Black Sea, in restraint of possible Turkish attack against the Balkans. In addition, and with the diplomatic support of its American ally, the British sought to weaken the Turkish government from within by fomenting insurrection among the minorities, especially the Armenians.

While there were interracial marriages between Armenians and Turks, as a society we did not integrate into Turkish communities. The conflict was endemic: Moslem vs. Christian, with our disparate societal traditions and family values—in particular the role of women and mothers in the family. Armenian mothers and wives were highly respected and often educated. Prearranged marriages were not the rule. In Moslem society the women were decidedly subservient, treated as little more than pets in the best of circumstances. Men could have multiple wives, and older wives were regularly shunted aside to make room for younger and prettier ones. And aside from religious and social differences, although Armenians had prospered in peacetime, we harboured a latent hostility to the Turks based on Turkish subjugation of our homeland.

Long experienced in the strategic uses of minorities vis-a-vis local rulers in its colonies, Britain effectively appealed to Armenian community leaders to agitate against Turkey's alliance with Germany. As a reward the British promised the restoration of independence to the ancient homeland. As word spread through our churches, many Armenians took the British appeal seriously. After all, the powerful British navy was anchored just off the coast of Turkey, as assurance of protection and the fulfillment of their promise.

The genocide of the Armenians was completed on a national scale with ruthless efficiency. It clearly bespeaks of German methodology, and in fact was the brainchild of the German high command. Its execution by the Turkish army and police was, however, characteristically Turkish in its barbaric brutality. To the surprise of Turkish and German military commands, the British navy observed but did not act, and the American presence was also silent, duped by the diplomatic prospect of keeping Turkey from overt support of the Germans. America's folly is well documented by our then Ambassador to Turkey, Henry Morganthau, Sr., in his autobiograpy, in which he confesses his own guilt and remorse for not acting to stop the slaughter. Although woefully naive about the execution of the genocide, America responded magnificently in humanitarian aid under the guidance of Herbert Hoover..

British accounts fail to recognize any guilt for the genocide. Although this sacrifice of a minority reached unprecedented numbers, the use of minorities as pawns was a regular feature of British colonial rule. After the war, at the peace table at Versailles, the British promise of independence for ancient Armenia was pursued. The eventual outcome was the retention by Turkey of a large part of Armenia, with the other part going to the Soviet Union as one of its sixteen regions. No punishment was pursued for those guilty of the slaughter of my father and one million other innocent people.

Despite irrefutable evidence and the condemnation of the Armenian genocide by the U.S. Senate, our State Department still, after eighty years, refuses to acknowledge that it even took place. Off the record, State insists that diplomatic comity with Turkey, Germany, and Britain outweigh the importance of condemning the genocide. Recently, however, the Germans produced a television documentary explicitly identifying the Turks as executioners. I suspect that the motive behind this documentary was primarily political, since the large population of Turkish immigrants is very unpopular in Germany.

After WWI, hostility between Turks and Armenians continued unabated. Stripped of its empire, its economy in tatters, employment had drastically shrunk for Turks as well as for us and other minorities. Under these circumstances, a massive emigration of all minorities was encouraged under a deliberate Government policy of Turkification. Minorities abandoned rural areas and cities to the Turkish population. Today, only in cosmopolitan Istanbul are there any remnants of the once thriving minority communities.

After my father's extermination, it took my mother six years and most of the family's resources to obtain an exit visa to emigrate, as government officials demanded one payoff after another for "security" and permission to leave. Little was left after the cost of passage on a French freighter destined for France, and a second freighter bound for New York.

Once in America, my mother made the mistake of marrying a janitor named Baptiste Miller, an earlier Armenian immigrant who had changed his name and was now a naturalized citizen. In return for entrusting him with what remained of her money and jewels, she received citizenship for herself and her children. The brief union was a disaster and probably contributed to the nervous breakdown she suffered shortly thereafter. After placing my two sisters in an orphanage and me with the Children's Aid Society, she entered a hospital, where I'm told she died some years later. I have only the vaguest memories of her.

I have to think that my mother's experience was atypical. There were no other Armenians at the Children's Aid Society. Although Armenians in those days were mostly newly-arrived immigrants themselves, struggling to care for their own families,

I'm sure my mother would have found someone in the Armenian community to care for us were it not for her distrust bred by experience.

As I consider the genocide of my people I must place it in perspective. Since 1915, genocide has continued to be practiced throughout the world, even on a larger scale than that of the Armenian. Since the Holocaust we have seen genocidal campaigns waged against Ethiopians, Biafrans, Cambodians, Kurds and, most recently, the Bosnian Moslems and the Tutsi tribe of Rwanda. Now, as in past eras, the principal victims of genocide are minorities within their countries of residence, and are often exploited, as were we, by outside powers for their own purposes. At the very least, those waging genocide have been massively armed by outside powers.

Yet, in spite of international complicity in these savage incidents, they are generally regarded as internal affairs, condemned on moral grounds but beyond the responsibility of civilized nations to intervene or employ deterrent measures to prevent such future happenings. I have to question the morality of a foreign policy that does not allow one country to attack another, but does allow a ruling group within a country to massacre its own citizens with impunity. Yet I cannot avoid the irony that were it not for the genocide of my people I would never have enjoyed the freedom and opportunity I have found as an American. For although I was born Armenian in Turkey, Certainly I was "Made in America."

The surviving Nakashian family members before leaving Turkey

2

An Orphan on the Farm

IN 1977 MY WIFE PATRICIA and I moved from suburban Westchester County, New York, to rural Albemarle County in Virginia. When word of our impending move circulated, many of our friends were puzzled and a few outraged that I would take Pattie (a city girl) to a farm. One even offered to buy our Oriental rug, not wanting to see it ruined by "the chickens and pigs running about."

Not long after the move one of our Bronxville neighbors, the former CEO of an important Wall Street firm, paid us a visit at our "Sunny Brae Farm." I was proud of our large, slate roof house, with its panoramic view of the Blue Ridge Mountains, the rolling hills pasturing my Charlois cattle. He seemed impressed—at least I thought so. Then he turned to me and said, "Sam, this is an ideal vacation spot, but…living here? I just can't understand how you could leave behind the power and prestige you had in New York."

It was true that, as a lawyer, my clients were some of the largest corporations in the country; and 80,000 people had voted for me in my bid for a seat in Congress. Still, remembering the pale, pinched faces of many of my former colleagues on my last visit to the city, I had no regrets. Smiling, I sought to reassure my friend. "Oh, don't worry about us. Pattie and I waited two years for this place to come up for sale. We love it here!"

A lifelong city dweller, my friend could not possibly understand. Memories of farm life were my earliest and remain some of my fondest. Moreover, it was clear to me that I owed much of my success to my farm upbringing. I had been cast in the mold of an individualist, as most farmers are, who could fix most anything that needed fixing. Farmers could not afford specialists to repair equipment, tend to sick cattle, or anything else. Problems arose, and they solved them as a matter of survival. By the time I left for the city I held the attitude that any problem could be solved by ingenuity and determination, conditioning that has served me well throughout my life.

As much as I grew to love farm life, my introduction to it could not have been more traumatic. In 1922, at age seven, I remember being seated next to a lady on a train as it slowly moved away from the platform in New York's Grand Central Station. Something major was happening, I realized, as the train gained speed through the tunnel, headed north.

The lady holding my hand spoke to me in English, perhaps not realizing that I spoke only Armenian. I suppose she was trying to explain to me what was happening and reassure me. I understood nothing she said. All I knew was that I was alone and headed for some strange place. Life with my family had ended, and life as an orphan was about to commence.

The train stopped several times along the way. Some people rushed off while others remained on the train. Finally, at Valhalla, New York, the train stopped again. As I tightly clutched my small package of belongings, the lady took my other hand and led me off. We boarded a waiting motor vehicle, which drove up a hill and, after a mile or two, entered the gateway of the Brace Farm School for Boys.

At the main house I was checked in, given a numbered tag, and shown a cot in a large dormitory, bedding some 20-30 boys in rows of cots two or three feet apart. I was taken for lunch to a dining hall of fifty or so boys—gulping their food as they generated a deafening and incomprehensible babble. To me the scene appeared hostile, beyond anything I had ever imagined and nothing I could possibly relate to. Without eating, I sneaked unnoticed out of the dining room and into a nearby field, where I hid under a tree.

What was worse, being alone or being thrown in with strangers speaking a strange language? I wanted no part of either. What I wanted was to return home to the life I had known, but that was impossible. So I cried and cried for hours till I fell into sleep, the ultimate refuge from despair. It was after dark when the same lady tapped me, gently waking me, and gave me a warm embrace. It was the first sign of hope—someone cared. That unknown lady, now long dead, will never know how much that small gesture meant to me.

The Children's Aid Society was supported by affluent Protestant families to care for homeless boys. As the principal port of entry for immigrants, New York had by far the greatest number of families in the process of permanent settlement. Many went west to work in the coal mines of Appalachia or the Midwestern steel mills; others went north to work in the textile mills of New England. Large numbers remained in New York to swell its population. In addition to foreign immigration, a great domestic migration was underway from rural areas to the big cities. In a city with as many new arrivals as New York, it was inevitable that some of these families would break up, leaving many boys with no homes and no skills.

Until Roosevelt's New Deal programs of the late 1930s, state and federal assistance was all but non-existent. The Catholic and Jewish Charities provided shelter and aid to their own homeless, but while they did not overtly exclude those outside their confessional ranks, neither was able to absorb the large numbers of Protestant homeless. To address this void, the Children's Aid Society was founded on a non-sectarian basis. Its support came entirely from private donors.

The Brace Farm School, one of three projects of the CAS, was founded at the turn of the century by Robert Loring Brace to achieve two goals—take homeless boys off the streets of New York and teach them the Protestant Ethic. After learning the needed skills, a boy would be placed with a family in the area, working on their farm in exchange for his room and board. If he was lucky, they might adopt him. It was a simple process, involving a single

Young Sam on the farm

court appearance—not like today, when adopting parents must wend their way through a costly maze of federal, state, and local rules and regulations, enriching lawyers and clogging the domestic relations courts.

Brace Farm was equipped with a large dairy and enough land and equipment to feed the herd. The boys, ranging in age from seven to eighteen, did most of the work. Days were long and leisure minimal. The wake-up bell rang at six, beds were made and the dormitory tidied up before breakfast at seven. Housekeeping and meals were the responsibilities of the boys themselves. Some, as assigned, went directly from bed to the kitchen to work under a chef's supervision, while others fed the livestock—chickens, hogs, horses and cows.

After breakfast there were myriad other chores to perform, virtually all of them manual. Livestock quarters had to be cleaned. Cows were milked morning and night, and their manure removed by hand and spread by hand to fertilize the meadows. Hay was gathered, stacked for curing, put on wagons and unloaded into barns. Gardens were planted and weeded. During the school year chores were done before and after school. In the summer the sole break in the workday was a noon dinner. The only time we could call our own was in the evening, after our six o'clock supper.

I recall with great pleasure the outdoor and barn life. As an orphan grappling with a new language, I enjoyed the nonverbal relationships with the livestock. To a city boy, the challenge of getting milk out of a cow and into a pail, without spilling it and without being kicked or knocked down, was exciting.

But the horses were my favorites; in fact, they were really my first friends at Brace Farm. Unlike cows, sheep, and hogs, the horses were always responsive to my hands-on affection. If my commands were in broken English, they didn't seem to care. In those lonely early days, even if no one else understood and appreciated me, I was sure the horses did. In that first summer on the farm, the thrill of taking the reins to direct a team of horses created an ecstacy I remember to this day.

Back in the 1920's, most farm traction was supplied by horses. Henry Ford's first farm tractor was barely an improvement in efficiency over a good team of horses. Brace had one of those Fordsons, a rubberless steel wheeler. It required hand cranking to start, and it would "kick like a mule" in the opposite direction with enough force to break an arm or hand.

Although all of the boys at Brace Farm had been homeless on the streets of New York, they had originally come from many parts of the country. Most boys were blonde. In this Anglo-Saxon world I was an anomaly with my thick black hair almost to my eyebrows and skin easily darkened in summer to that of a Negro. I was often called "Nigger" or "Jew" or half of each. I really didn't know what I was. I knew I was supposed to be an Armenian, but I didn't know what an Armenian was. At Brace Farm there were no Negroes or Jews. In fact, I had never met a Jew or a "Nigger" and yet I knew I wasn't one—the way they made it sound.

My appearance and sparse and broken English made me somewhat ostracized. There were advantages to this. As an all-boy community there was constant peer pressure to rebel against the rules laid down by the supervisors. There was smoking and homosexual activity. Common showers created opportunities for the older boys to prey sexually upon the younger, weaker ones. Fortunately, the rapacious older boys left me alone. The prettier, blue-eyed blonde boys were their targets.

As an outsider amongst the boys, I was befriended by the farm manager's daughter, who was about my age. In my few leisure moments from chores, we would hide away together and cuddle and explore each other, discovering how as boy and girl we were different. Our touching was essentially innocent curiosity, a far cry from the lustful and often brutal encounters I witnessed in the toilets and showers.

I remember my first Christmas at Brace vividly. We decorated a large Christmas tree, sang carols, and put on a Christmas pageant for the local community, who brought gifts and piled them under the tree. Every boy got something. The attention and kindness was so unexpected and welcome. Thereafter Christmas was always a special day of the year for me—all stemming from that first Christmas. (I must have celebrated Christmas in Marsavon, my birthplace, but I have no memories of it, or anything else that happened before I arrived at the orphanage. The trauma of such a sudden and total uprooting from my family and everything familiar to me must have wiped them out).

Sometime after that first joyous Christmas, while working in the laundry room—my assignment for the month—I suffered a devastating accident. While attending the large mangle ironing sheets, I attempted to redirect a skewed sheet. My right hand was drawn in between the two massive rollers up to my wrist, before my screams caused someone to pull the switch. At this point I fainted and was unaware of the struggles made to reverse the rollers and extricate my crushed hand, as the heat from the roller continued to burn the back of my hand—tendons as well as flesh. I awoke in the regional hospital strapped to an operating table, breathing a gas which caused a prickly feeling throughout my body. I visualized myself in space, and all around me were ugly, threatening creatures.

From there I was transferred to New York Hospital in Manhattan, where the hell of ether and its aftereffects was repeated seven times as the medical staff attempted to restore some use to the hand by extensive surgery. As a charity patient, there were no restraints other than the doctor's conscience on what might be tried, and for the next two years they experimented with tendon and skin grafts. The first skin graft, in which flesh was gouged out of my thigh, was aborted for lack of adequate blood circulation. This suggested a graft from my abdomen to provide the circulation. The abdominal graft caused even greater pain and scarring but finally took.

In these two years I never left the hospital, and except for rare, unknown visitors from the Children's Aid Society, my interactions were exclusively with hospital personnel. Doctors and interns were always distressing to me, representing the hell of surgery and anesthesia. It was the nurses who served as my lifeline during this period of gruesome trial. Sensitive to my loneliness, they showered me with love and attention—reading to me, playing games, slipping me a piece of candy—which supported my hope of somehow getting the whole hospital ordeal over with. Thank God for nurses!

Finally, after the seventh operation, they let me go. Naturally I longed to go "home" to Brace, but the Children's Aid Society, figuring that with a crippled hand I was a poor candidate for a farmer, thought otherwise and placed me with a family in the suburbs. Like my first graft, this placement didn't take. I was so miserable that the family contacted Children's Aid after a few days. Desperately I pleaded my case to the worker they sent out, a Miss Clara B. Comstock.

Miss Comstock was only five feet tall, which accentuated her rotund girth. She was not likely to attract any admiration from passersby, but she immediately captivated me with the magnetism of her expression and her musical voice. Her keen yet twinkling blue eyes fixed attentively upon me, I spilled my heart out. If only I was given a chance, I told her, I would prove I could do the farm work. When I finished she smiled reassuringly and said, "Well then, of course you will go back to Brace." I could have kissed her.

A couple of days later she escorted me there on the train herself. Miss Comstock was raised on a farm in Steuben County, New York. After graduating from high school, she taught in elementary schools near her home before joining the Children's Aid Society. Her role at CAS was uncomplicated. She would accompany new boys to Brace Farm, or travel with Brace Farm boys to their new families after placement, carrying the child on her lap,

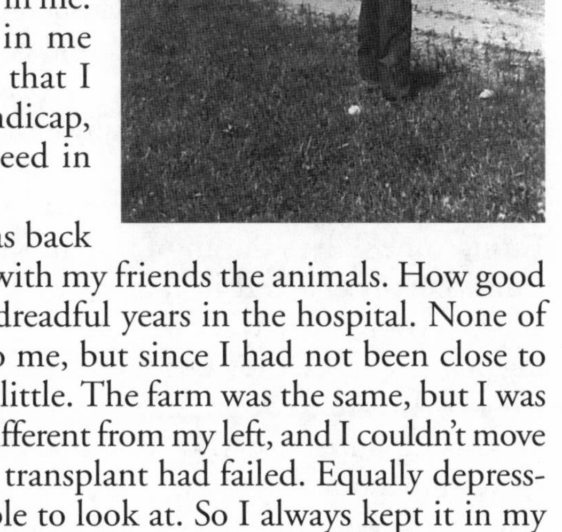
Sam, on the farm, at age 13

or an older boy at her side. In her forty-year career she placed some 2000 boys in foster homes or with adoptive parents as far away as Colorado, and her peak salary was $100 per month.

These days her work brought her to Brace often, and she took a special interest in me. Miss Comstock's faith in me sustained my own faith that I could overcome this handicap, and any others, to succeed in life.

Now age eleven, I was back at Brace Farm, reunited with my friends the animals. How good it looked, after the two dreadful years in the hospital. None of the boys were familiar to me, but since I had not been close to any of them, it mattered little. The farm was the same, but I was not. My right hand was different from my left, and I couldn't move the fingers—the tendon transplant had failed. Equally depressing, the hand was horrible to look at. So I always kept it in my pocket. Given my rough appearance in those years, I could have been taken for pocketing a gun!

(Many years later, after completing my graduate studies at Columbia and serving in the government in Washington, the self-conscious awareness of my hand was overcome. Quite by accident I found that, with the confidence borne of extensive education, I looked people in the eye, with the result that this kept them from noticing my deformity. Henceforth my hand was never hidden, and often an expression of surprise accompanied its discovery after several prior meetings).

I had sworn I would be able to do the farm work. Now I had to figure out how. I confess to a good deal of anxiety. How could I milk the cows? Use only my left hand? That would take twice as long. Who would want a cripple with one hand when other boys had two good hands? What was to become of me? I had to get some use out of my right hand.

Fortunately, while my four fingers were immobilized, my thumb was spared injury. The thumb could reach the first two fingers to provide a grip—not strong, but adequate to hold a pencil and light tools. The grip of the thumb against the side of my hand was strong, and quickly got stronger. I learned that I could milk a cow with my right hand by pressing the teat between my thumb and the side of my hand. The milk stream was about half what I could get using my left hand. With greater effort from both hands, I was not the fastest milker but was better than most. For one-hand tasks I used to perform with my right hand, I learned to use my left. Gradually I regained confidence in my manual skills.

In the society of boys, particularly the rough boys at Brace Farm, some skill in the art of fisticuffs was a necessity for respect from one's peers, and in many situations for survival. As in a chicken coop, there was a pecking order, with the stronger picking on the weaker. Obviously, with one hand I was at a disadvantage. Fortunately my physical handicap caught the attention of one of our supervisors, who happened to have retired from a professional boxing career. Understanding that I wanted to survive on the basis of equality, not sympathy, he secretly gave me boxing lessons at every opportunity.

First my "Jack Dempsey" taught me a nifty left-hand jab—sneaky, fast and jolting. Knowing I could not make a fist with my right hand, he then taught me to combine the jab with a quick shift to the right to deliver a crushing left hook. Then he taught me to shift back to the left and bring the heel of my right hand crashing into the target chin. This training, plus my willingness to endure pain to get in my licks, earned me the highest praise—that of a tough kid. Older kids I couldn't lick avoided taking me on because they learned that victory wasn't worth the punishment they would take. My boxing lessons came in handy many times in those next few years.

Having proven myself that first summer back at Brace, I received my first placement on a farm that fall. The Ackermans were a young couple struggling to pay the debts incurred to buy and equip the farm. Mrs. Ackerman was short and overweight, common in those days on a farm, where the diet was heavy in the saturated fats of whole dairy products and pork. Mr. Ackerman was slight of build, and the work took a physical as well as psychological toll on him. It was truly hard work, long days with no pleasure. As I recall, they made no time for church or social life. Actually, I had a better life than they did. I appreciated the opportunity to work and, unlike them, I had a respite from it—school.

Woodhull School contained in one building both the elementary, which I attended, and the high school. As the new boy my boxing skills were immediately tested. Before, after, and between classes the boys would square off against me. What a blessing my "Jack Dempsey" turned out to be. Even older boys, of greater brawn, were manageable victims of the left jab, the left hook and, if necessary, the heel of my right hand. Almost instantly I received respect and friendship. I had no desire to be a bully, only an intense yearning for comradery. Soon I discovered baseball, and overcame my handicap by gripping the ball between my mobile thumb and stationery fingers. Imagine my exhilaration when asked to join the school team! Farm chores prevented my full participation, but when I could play I enjoyed some of the happiest moments of my life.

The Ackermans were a joyless couple. I never received any praise for my hard work, and I don't think they were capable of showing affection. The more I appeared to enjoy school, sports, and the few books offered me, the more distant they became. After a year there, I expressed my hurt feelings to Miss Comstock upon one of her semi-annual visits. She was horrified to hear that my home was so absent of love. I don't know how she was able to move so quickly, but within days she came to take me to a new farm home—that of the McCarroghers, a senior couple in Jasper, about 8 miles west of Woodhull. It was the fall of 1927.

Sam, dressed to visit a new family

The McCarroghers' home was as full of warmth and love as the Ackermans' had been devoid of it. Mr. McCarrogher was tall, with thinning white hair. Both he and Mrs. McCarrogher were over-weight and in poor health; hence, their farm of several hundred acres was under utilized. In all they had a few cows, some sheep, five or six horses, and enough chickens and hogs to supply the dining table.

Here was an opportunity for me to be useful. My new school was only half a mile away. Instead of staying after to play, I ran home to get the chores done before nightfall. At twelve, I could confidently handle a two or three horse hitch on a harrow, plow, and planter. As the McCarroghers' health worsened they stayed inside the house for days at a time. I was actually running the farm. In gratitude the senior couple showered me with love and attention. At Christmas Mr. McCarrogher bought me presents, and soon afterwards he began letting me drive his Model T on the back roads. Their daughter Alta, a schoolteacher in her mid-thirties who lived at home with them, was pleasant enough. For the first time I had a sense of well-being, of belonging. Every morning I awoke in high spirits.

My elementary school housed all eight grades in one room, taught by one teacher. Since I had attended very little school at Brace Farm, and none at all in the hospital, I was far behind the other children my age. So while I prepared for my own recitals I listened to everything going on in the upper grades. The one-room schoolhouse is a thing of the past, and perhaps deservedly so, but I can testify that it had advantages for the aggressive learner, as I quickly caught up with my age group.

That winter tragedy struck. Mrs. McCarrogher died and I witnessed my first death and funeral service. Her death seemed terribly unfair to me, and the biblical quotations intoned by the minister were wholly inadequate in explaining how this could happen to such a loving, caring person. His wife's passing brought Mr. McCarrogher and me closer together. I persuaded Miss Comstock to let me stay on. After all, Alta was there. Little did I know just how threatened Alta was by the strong paternal interest her father was increasingly showing toward "that strange boy." Thinking back on it now, I feel some sympathy for her. Tall, prim and proper, she had no male suitors, and the diversion of her father's attention must have been painful to her.

The following spring Mr. McCarrogher said, " Sam, you're now a Farmer. That heifer is now yours and that yearling colt is yours. And I want you to grow an acre or two of potatoes to take to market so you will have some money."

So as not to take time from my regular chores, I planted two acres of potatoes in the evenings before dark. Everything was going just great. Alta largely ignored me and I avoided her. Meanwhile, her father's love sustained me through the anxieties—about the weather, sick animals, etc.—that are an everyday part of farm life. With him to watch over me, they just didn't seem to matter that much.

Then, early the next fall, Mr. McCarrogher died suddenly. Paradise had come to an end. For the second time that year I stared into a coffin at the lifeless body of a surrogate parent. Fighting back tears, I honestly doubted I would ever again feel so happy and useful. Attending the funeral, cousins Fred and Margaret White, who had frequently visited the McCarroghers, asked me what I would do. My reply was that Miss Comstock would probably find me another home. They asked if I would like to live with them on their farm about two miles away. They thought I might like to because their son Joe and his wife Maude had three children: two about my age—Francis and Charlotte—and one younger—Josephine.

The White's Home

Knowing the families, I happily accepted. Fred and Margaret White were also in their late years. They owned and operated two dairy farms adjacent to their son's—a total of some 1000 acres. While livestock and horses on their respective lands were kept apart, most work on the three farms was done in concert. Thus, I spent most working days with the young White Family, and returned to the old folks for bed and board.

In many ways my life with the Whites was even more ideal than with the McCarroghers. Immediately I was welcomed as a full member into a supportive extended family with workmates and playmates my own age. Adoption was never contemplated. It would not have added more enrichment to my status.

My memory of the McCarroghers was tarnished when Alta sold off the livestock on her father's farm, including my heifer and my colt, as her inherited property. Despite my pleas that they were her father's gifts to me, she claimed she knew nothing about that, and I was reminded that nothing was in writing. My hurt stemmed less from the loss of what was rightfully mine than the questioning of my honesty. No one bought the two-acre field of undug potatoes. After milking, Joe and Francis White helped me

The cow barn at the White farm

dig up the field and we sold about a hundred bushels of potatoes, the proceeds of which bought me a $20 bicycle. Now I could ride alongside Francis, Charlotte, and Josephine to school.

My new one-room schoolhouse provided eight elementary grades taught by Pamela White, a cousin. All the kids were farm-bred and of British ancestry. About half were Irish Catholics who cherished the Irish tradition of fighting. One of them, the oldest boy in school, found it necessary to demonstrate to me and reaffirm to his fellow schoolmates that he could lick anybody. The time-honored "rules" of the challenge called for the bully to shove his prey and insult him, provoking him to fight or else slink away as a coward. Since I was smaller, younger and different looking, he expected no contest as he sought to humiliate me. When I was shoved the second time, I snapped his head back with my left jab and followed with the left hook. Before I could throw my right he went sprawling and lay dazed.

Hearing the commotion, Pamela White ran to the scene to find the boy laid out. A quick check assured her he was only bruised, whereupon she turned around to find the perpetrator. With the other students' admiring eyes fixed on me, she immediately knew I had done it, and proceeded to give me a tongue-lashing.

"I will have no more fighting in my school!", she steamed.

"I won't be in any more fights, Miss White," I assured her. "I never start a fight." In my two years at that school, no one else started one either.

Both the older and younger White families were "God-fearing Christians"—strict Methodists on one side and strict Baptists on the other. I alternated attending Methodist Church in Greenwood and Baptist Church in Troupsburg. Sunday was the Lord's Day and no work was to be done beyond feeding the animals and milking the cows. This literal interpretation of the Bible occasionally resulted in leaving crops in the fields to be ruined by a Sunday rain. No quarrel with that—it was God's Will. At meals, heads were bowed for grace before a fork or spoon could be lifted. Before entering the house, shoes were removed, as well as any hay or grass clinging to clothing. "Cussing", swearing, or any expression of irreverence brought a swift and severe rebuke. Alcohol, tobacco, and card playing of any kind were strictly forbidden.

The keepers of these moral codes were the senior Mrs. White and her daughter-in-law Maude. Mrs. White, a heavy-set woman of medium height and Scotch ancestry, could be very intimidating without saying a word. A short nod of approval, a sharp glance of disapproval, were all that was necessary to maintain discipline. Maude, tall and lanky but equally taciturn, used the same techniques. Woe be unto the miscreant who let a fly into Mrs. White's spotless home, and greater woe unto the fly, which she would dispatch with an efficient flick of her ever-present fly swatter. Her wrist action was poetry in motion.

Cleanliness was next to Godliness in both homes, and we were expected to keep ourselves clean despite the absence of indoor plumbing. The 50-degree water for the daily washing of our "local parts" was hand carried from a nearby well. For cooking, dishwashing, and our weekly pre-church tub baths, the water was heated on the wood burning stove. With no plumbing, toilet needs were served by a two-seater outhouse over a pit. Instead of soothing, textured toilet paper, old copies of black-and-white Sears

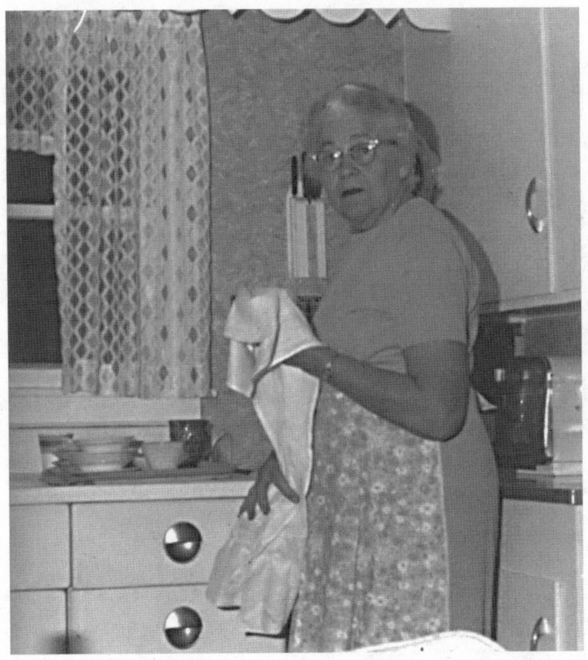

Mrs. White in her kitchen some years later

Roebuck and Montgomery Ward catalogues were kept in good supply to provide both the finality to the exercise and interim reading. Particularly fascinating to me were the models (provocative even in those days) in the corset ads.

Of course we had no electricity either. Oil lamps and candles supplied the minimal light. But with our dawn-to-dusk farm routines, we didn't stay up late. Because we were fifteen miles from the nearest milk processing plant, our milk had to be ready for pick-up at 6 A.M. This meant getting up at 4:30 to complete milking before breakfast. We did our other chores between breakfast and school. In the summer months we were working the fields by 6:30, took a break at noon for dinner and an hour's rest for ourselves and the horses, then returned to the fields for another four hours. Supper would be served at 6 P.M., followed by more milking. By 8 we looked back on the day's work, expressing great pride in our accomplishments.

Inside the White's House

I was always self-driven to prove myself. In my first year at the Whites I undertook to plow a 14-acre field with a team of Morgan horses and a 14-inch plow I held by hand. The field sloped south and could be seen for a great distance by other farmers in the area. In seven plowing days (never on Sunday) I completed the plowing, each day's work turning the dark soil over for all to see. Farmers knew that to turn over that much soil with a 14-inch plow required both horses and driver to move ten hours a day at a near trot. My achievement was the talk of the county. I remember twenty years later, on a visit to the Whites, I met a neighbor from those days, who immediately exclaimed, "You're the boy who plowed that Wykoff field in seven days using a hand plow!" The glow of pride returned, undiminished by two decades of city life.

Two years before I left the Whites, a pure black Morgan mare was born at the farm, and I was allowed to name her. From that day forth "Blackie" was the object of my unstinting affection. First thing in the morning she'd be waiting to nuzzle me as I patted her on the neck and gave her an affectionate tug on the mane. She also knew she could count on a special treat of some sort—perhaps an apple, carrot, or sugar cube.

Sam's pet, "Blackie"

When Blackie was a year old and weighed almost 900 pounds, I crawled on her back one day, held onto her mane, and rode her around the barnyard. It was that simple: no saddle or bridle, no breaking her will. The mutual love we had made all that unnecessary. Before long Blackie would be waiting for me each evening at six o'clock sharp to fetch the cows from pasture. I stayed aloft by wrapping my legs around her ribs, and guided her by pulling her mane left or right. We would gallop a mile or more to get to the cows, then quietly walk them back to the barn so that no milk would be spilled en route by running them.

When I was deciding whether to leave the Whites for the city, Blackie was a major restraint. I worried not only about how she would adjust without me, but how *I* would ever be able to replace her affection. It was only after the Whites promised to send me regular reports on her that I was able to tear myself away.

In spite of my love for Blackie, none of my interactions with the animals matched the short-term intensity of midwifery. With veterinarians frequently too distant and always too expensive for the self-sustaining farm, animal midwifery became an inevitable duty of the family members. It wasn't the most pleasant of chores, but its life-or-death consequences overcame any reluctance to perform it.

Delivering a calf requires the full strength of an adult. As a teenager at the Whites, with smaller hands than the adults, I was frequently called upon to deliver lambs. If the mother was having a difficult delivery I would insert my left hand into her vagina and turn the unborn lamb into the correct position. If she neglected her contractions for one reason or another, I would physically pull the lamb from her—always forelegs first. Nothing is quite as miraculous as the act of birth, and nothing was quite as exhilirating as a successful rescue, with the knowledge that I had saved the life of the ewe or her lamb, or in some instances both.

The White Farms were situated on a plateau, some 2500 feet above sea level. In view nearby was High Up, the highest elevation in Steuben County. In summer, days were cool, rarely reaching 90 degrees, and the nights were chilly. This climate was not conducive to growing corn (though we persisted with poor results), but it was ideal for timothy and clover hay, oats, barley and buckwheat.

The milk-flow of dairy cattle is inhibited by cold temperatures. Thus, soon after Labor Day they were brought inside and not until the following June could they again be turned out to pasture. In the early 1930's mechanical equipment was introduced to dispense feed to the cattle, milk them, and collect and spread their manure, but none of these inventions were available during my time. The manual power of all the Whites—wives and children included—was needed for this mammoth enterprise. Morning and evening everyone helped with the milking. My cow quota was ten, the grandfather and father eleven to fifteen, wives and children six to eight each. Together, seven of us milked sixty cows and collected an average of around a thousand pounds of milk each day.

Cows are essentially processors, converting food and water into milkflesh and manure. To produce milk, each cow was fed ten pounds of grain, ten pounds of silage, and thirty pounds of hay, hand delivered. While we had no running water in the house, we piped water to the barns for each cow to drink at its leisure.

"It was a happy sight when summer came and we could finally turn the cows out to pasture."

Fluid consumption per cow ranged from fifty to seventy pounds daily. Each cow would excrete thirty to forty pounds of manure daily (over a ton for the herd), which was hand shoveled out to keep the barn clean.

In summary, two adult men and Francis and I provided the muscle for the material handling of some three tons per day over eight months, or 720 tons per year. It was a happy day when summer came and we could finally turn the cows out to pasture!

Of course, even with the cows pasturing, there was no shortage of back-breaking work. The economy of a dairy farm involved efficient utilization of all available resources in the orderly, invariable sequence of events dictated by the calendar, and there were no breaks. In the summer the pasture was enriched with manure in order to grow grass for the winter's hay. As fodder for milk cows, hay was supplemented by silage produced from grain and corn (the whole stalk including cobs). Of the tillable land, a quarter was planted in corn, a quarter in oats and barley with grass seed, and about half in hay fields. Every three or four years the hay fields were plowed and the grass turned over with a heavy blanket of manure from the cows wintering in the barn.

The economy of the farm was aimed at self-sufficiency; basic purchases included salt, vaccinations and high protein grain supplements, augmented by whatever labor-saving machinery of the day could be afforded. In those days farmers purchased manure spreaders, a grain binder to cut and tie bundles together, and grass mowers. To separate the grain from the straw, a large and expensive thresher was required, its owner usually servicing area farmers who could not afford their own. The other farmers would "change off", all helping one another haul grain from their fields to the thresher at the barn. The thresher would blow the straw into a nearby stack for bedding the cattle in winter; the grain was carried to the grain bins. Similarly, a silage cutter and blower would cut up the stalks of corn and blow the silage into a silo at the barn, where it was stored for winter feeding.

All the manual labor of pitching corn, grain, and hay into wagons, and pitching it off to the processing machines and into the barn, has now been replaced by machines. Today, corn is cut and simultaneously chopped up in the field, blown into a wagon and blown from the wagon into the silo. Grain is cut and threshed by a single machine, which bags the grain, automatically conveys it to a wagon, and leaves the straw on the field. Hay is cut, bent for fast drying, and windrowed by a machine. Another machine bails the hay and tosses it onto a following wagon for delivery to the barn, or rolls the hay into round half-ton bails.

Until the 1930's, farmers were manual workers, lifting thousands of tons over the course of a year. Today, farmers do little or no lifting, performing essentially as equipment engineers. While the modern farm requires less manual labor, it requires staggering amounts of capital for machinery. Thus, while the farmer of old was largely self-sufficient, today his is a precarious, money/capital economy. He has no choice but to buy from the large, corporate equipment suppliers at their own predetermined prices. Yet he must sell his products as they are produced for what he can get, in a market of uncontrolled supply. It's no wonder that the family farmer is an endangered species.

Sam as a young man at work on the farm

In spite of the heavy workload we all bore, I found time for other pursuits. During the summers Maude's younger brother Clayton, one year older and a little bigger than I was, would come to stay with us and help on the farm. We would play baseball and wrestle with one another. (We avoided boxing: we didn't want to hurt each other). We couldn't play cards, but checkers were acceptable, and I soon became "champ" in the family. I suppose my success came from an ability to see beyond the next move and set up a sequence of plays—my introduction to linear programming.

The reputed checker champ of the county was an itinerant knife-sharpener who visited annually on his horse-drawn cart. On one of his visits he was persuaded to spend the night so that we could play checkers after I finished my milking. Dead tired after a 14-hour day, I beat the knife sharpener two out of three before falling asleep.

Twice a month Grandpa White would take me with him into Greenwood, four and a half miles away, to go shopping. The Greenwood Hardware Store had a pork barrel set up where the idle senior townsmen would meet to play checkers. Not given to undue modesty, lean Fred would stroll up and lay down the challenge: "Fellas, my boy Sam can beat the lot of you." Then he would go shopping, leaving me there as one after another of the old boys would take me on, only to lose. I enjoyed the competition and I enjoyed Grandpa White's pride in me even more.

Thanks to the family environment at the Whites, and the equality of my contact with other members of the community and of the two churches, I had overcome my sense of inferiority and alienation. Instead of feeling vaguely threatened by an outside world I had tried to ignore, I began developing an avid curiosity about it. For the first time, I found an appetite for reading. My one-room school house had only a few prescribed text books, and there was no library, not even in town. My library was the White's Bible, a highly abridged dictionary, a set of Horatio Alger books, and a set of Zane Grey. At this stage of my development, Alger and Grey supplied more satisfying and understandable heroes than the Bible. Nor did I understand the fire-and-brimstone sermons of the Sunday preachers. When you're working

The Whites celebrating their 50th Wedding Anniversary

fourteen hours a day on a farm, and all about you are honest, hard-working families in concert with nature, Sin has little meaning.

After passing the Eighth Grade, I went to town to take the State Regent's Exam, required of all elementary school students. Soon the news spread that I had scored the highest grade in the township on the arithmetic portion of the exam. Proudest of all was Pamela White, who had taught elementary school for ten years and never had a winner. To her it obviously reaffirmed her ability as a teacher. As for me, I wondered what difference it would make to the farmer I thought I would become.

The following fall I entered Greenwood High School. Once again I found myself fighting for self respect and survival. Two or three encounters with underclassmen were painless. But the town jock, held over a second year to earn his degree, was another matter. Six years older, bigger, and familiar with boxing skills, Brundage (I can still remember his name) gave me a full hour's beating. Refusing to give up, I called on every skill my Jack Dempsey had taught me. Finally, with both of us bleeding and near exhaustion, one of the teachers stopped the fight, for which I thanked God, as well as the teacher.

The long trek home by foot seemed endless. Starting late because of the fight, I arrived late, still bleeding. When the Whites saw my cuts and bruises they were horrified that I had become involved in such an incident. I'm sure my opponent went to bed upon arriving home. I went as usual to the barn to milk my ten cows with a broken finger and both hands painfully bruised. Each squeeze and pull on the cow was excruciatingly painful. On a dairy farm, whether sick or crippled, morning and night you milk the cows! Fortunately Brundage never bothered me again.

Classes and sports at Greenwood High were truly exciting for me. In both I was pretty aggressive. The small school had twelve kids who could play ball. I was chosen as catcher because no one else was fearless enough or possibly dumb enough to stand behind the plate. The school provided a face mask and nothing else. Foul tips would bruise my chest, shoulders and, worst of all, my fingers. The finger pain endured throughout morning and evening milking sessions. In spite of my lumps I happily persevered. The team traveled to neighboring towns, giving me a first look at the world beyond the farm.

That winter was one of the coldest on record. Temperatures reached forty below without factoring in the wind chill. The nine mile round trip, on foot in deep snow (country roads were not plowed in those days), was a painful price for the pleasure of schooling. I could not avoid frostbite in spite of plentiful bundling. Still, I finished the year with grades so favorable that continuation of my schooling seemed necessary both to the Whites and Miss Comstock. They were well aware that the nine-mile trek was too much, so other arrangements were made.

An elderly couple known to the Whites had a small farm near Troupsburg and needed a boy. Although they were very nice to me, I missed the presence in the home of children my own age. That fall I enrolled at Troupsburg High School and endured a new round of fights once again. Try as I might to adjust to my new placement, I remained homesick for the Whites. When I turned sixteen in December, I renounced any further school interest in favor of full-time employment as a farm hand.

The Whites were eager for me to come home and generously offered wages of $30 per month with room and board. This was the highest pay amongst the local farm hands. That year, 1932, we milked more cows, raised more horses, put in more crops, and had a bountiful harvest—all the makings of a banner year, except for milk prices! By the end of the summer, dairy farmers in the area were selling their milk for less than one dollar per hundred pounds, or about two cents a quart. That this level of income could hardly justify my monthly wages was clearly understood by me, as well as by the Whites. Farming looked a bleak future. Was there another choice?

Two years earlier, my forgotten older sister Vera, with whom I had had no contact since 1923, traced me to the Whites through the Children's Aid Society, and came to visit. Having been brought up in the city, where she was a practical nurse, she despised the country and berated the life style I had come to love. To her, I was being exploited, and my injured hand was proof of this. She could not see that I enjoyed my work, that I worked no harder than others in the family, and that I benefitted by acquiring their values and discipline. I regarded her in all this as hostile and meddlesome. It was a great relief to me when she left.

When Vera returned to New York she went straight to the Children's Aid Society and threatened a law suit to recover damages for their negligence in permitting an eight-year old boy to operate dangerous laundry machinery. This created a panic at the Society. To prepare for a possible law suit, the Managing Director asked Miss Comstock to visit me at the Whites with a photographer. The photographer took pictures of me throwing a baseball, milking cows and performing my other farm chores. I was very happy to prove that there was nothing wrong with me, and resentful of my sister's further meddling.

Under the circumstances, Vera chose not to pursue the law suit. But since her visit she had written me often, insisting that I leave "farm drudgery" and come to New York to live with her and her husband. Faced with the financial hardships of the Whites, I reluctantly decided to accept her offer. Had I known that in New York's depression, one out of three family bread winners could not find *any* job, and that my sister herself was in desperate financial straits, I probably would have stayed on at the White's for room and board, and might have ended up a farmer after all.

3

New York City: The Depression Years

WITH MY FARM SAVINGS OF one hundred thirty dollars in pocket, I stepped off the Erie Railroad in New Jersey and climbed aboard the Hudson River Ferry. The Manhattan skyline loomed awesome and daunting. "What do people do in those huge blocks of steel and concrete?" I wondered to myself. The fact that I had no idea only added to my confusion and uncertainty about survival. But certainly Vera understood all this, and would help me orient myself and get a job.

The ferry dropped me off in the world's largest city and I took the West Side Subway to 72nd Street, where Vera lived. I went door to door until I found her apartment. Vera was home nursing her infant son, Eddie, and preparing dinner. Her husband, Gustavus Vasa Stoeber, known as "G.V.," had not yet arrived home from work. Her welcome was not as enthusiastic as I had expected after all those letters urging me to come live with her. Soon I learned why.

By 1932 the depression was crushing New York City. Nearly half the buildings in New York were in foreclosure and the banks holding these mortgages were going broke all over the city. (A half century later this pattern of speculation was repeated, the difference being that this time around the $250 billion in Savings & Loan losses were borne by the taxpayers and not the individuals involved). The only investors spared were those who had sensed the unreality of the booming 1920's, and converted their overpriced stocks and real estate holdings to cash before it was too late. G.V. was not one of them.

Born in South Carolina, the handsome G.V. spent a great deal of his time grooming and otherwise cultivating the image of an aristocratic Southern Gentleman. His mellifluous southern accent furthered enhanced his appearance of gentility in a city where spoken English was so influenced by the staccato rhythms of the subway and the guttural patois of Yiddish. G.V. was a very impressive man, probably twenty years older than Vera, and it was easy to see why she had hitched her star to his. An orphan with a high school education, she was no doubt enthralled by his tales of winning and losing fortunes, and believed it was only a manner of time until G.V. was back on top of the heap.

In the meantime, the modest flat on 72nd Street, consisting of one bedroom, a living room and kitchenette, would house the four of us. I slept very comfortably on the living room couch and enjoyed immensely my daily showers, a dramatic step upward from my weekly tub baths on the farm.

Vera acted as if my hundred and thirty dollars would burn a hole in my trousers. We had to go shopping the next day for a pair of city shoes and a decent suit, shirt and tie. This immediately relieved me of fifty dollars. I suspect Vera was afraid that my "country" appearance would reflect negatively on her. Whether being better dressed would help me in getting a menial job was not considered by either of us at the time.

I decided I had better fulfill one of my dreams while I still had some money. So the next day I boarded a subway for the Bronx. It was the end of September and the New York Yankees, in a race for the American League pennant, were playing a double-header at Yankee Stadium against the Philadelphia Athletics. Ever since I had started playing the game, I had heard stories about the legendary Yankees. This adventure didn't set me back too much: the round trip on the subway cost ten cents, a seat in the right field bleachers fifty cents.

I reached my seat after the first game had begun. There in right field, just a few feet away, was Babe Ruth. Further away I spotted Lou Gehrig on first, Bill Dickey behind the plate, and Herb Pennock on the mound. The right side of the infield was covered by Tony Lazzeri at shortstop and Jumping Joe Dugan on third. Never having seen baseball played at a higher level than the country high school games I had participated in, I was entranced by the hitting and fielding skills of these men. The Yankees won two close games and everyone went home happy, especially me. I have seen the Yankees play many times since, but the impression made on me by that first doubleheader has survived more than sixty years.

A few days later, dressed in my new attire, I was walking along 42nd Street when a very polite gentleman asked me for the time. When I replied that I did not have a watch, he seemed genuinely concerned and offered to help. He then ushered me into a nearby auction house where the auctioneer was selling beautiful watches at ridiculously low prices. At least that's what my new friend told me. Soon I was caught up in the bidding and wound up peeling off another fifty dollars for my first watch. My solicitous friend congratulated me on my excellent judgment and disappeared.

That evening, I proudly exhibited my purchase to Vera and G.V. and was met with expressions of consternation. "How much did you pay for it?" G.V. drawled.

"Fifty dollars," I replied anxiously.

G.V. sighed and exchanged a look with Vera, then turned back to me. "It's not worth twenty. We've got to get your money back."

The next morning we went to G.V.'s real estate lawyer, Mr. Godwin. "How old are you?" he asked.

"Seventeen," I replied.

Mr. Godwin picked up the phone and called the manager of the auction house. Without introduction he barked, "You sold a watch to a minor yesterday. I'm sending him right over with the watch and I want you to return his fifty dollars." There was a brief silence and then Mr. Godwin began speaking in Yiddish. I had no idea what he was telling him but it sounded harsh and threatening. When he hung up he said to me, "Young man, let this be a lesson to you. Now go back to the store, ask for Mr. Meyer, and he will give you back your fifty dollars."

This was my first experience with the morality of the city (or lack thereof). Such a scam would never have occurred to the simple farm people I had known. Sometime later, on one of my night jobs, I was befriended by one of these hustlers. He laid a belt on the counter and bent it into several loops, challenging me to put a pencil through one of the loops. It looked easy enough, and I tried several times. But when he straightened out the belt, somehow my pencil was always outside the loops. He showed me the trick, then lectured me: "I work the bars, and I make a good living off suckers who bet they can do it. I showed you this as a lesson: Never think you're so smart that you can beat a hustler at his own game!"

My savings were soon gone anyway. Survival in our household was a day-to-day proposition, creating an underlying anxiety we could not escape. Often we had to pawn personal property to pay for food and rent. Hope sustained us and G.V., like Willy Loman in *Death of A Salesman*, had a fresh plan for success each day. Yesterday's aborted deal was replaced by today's new scheme that could not go wrong. Whether Vera knew G.V. had an alcohol problem when she married him, I don't know, but the problem was acute by the time I arrived on the scene. At times a pint of bourbon took bread and vegetables off the table, but it produced a euphoria for G.V., and he conveyed his optimism to the rest of us.

G.V. was a real estate man, meaning that for the most part he sold property for a commission payable upon sale. From time to time he would purchase a building himself, with little down payment, hoping to sell it at a profit before mortgage and tax payments came due. Soon after I appeared on the scene, G.V. purchased a shabby five-story hotel on 42nd Street between Broadway and 8th Avenue, and I had my first job in the city,—night clerk, working from 6 P.M. to 6 A.M.

A notorious pornography district today, the area had already begun its decline. The hotel was in the midst of "bawdy" houses, shooting galleries and bars. Back then, however, the raciest offerings were at the burlesque theatre across the street, where the girls danced the bump and grind and performed the strip tease, accompanied by a live orchestra. The strip tease generally stopped short of total nudity to avoid a police raid. The police also enforced the adultery laws, not only against the adulterers but also against the hotel management furnishing the venue. Hookers could not work the streets, nor could they ply their trade openly in bars or other public places. Prostitution was dealt with harshly and the John could be charged as well.

My job consisted of checking in guests, operating the only elevator, quelling fights that would break out upstairs, collecting trash, and mopping the lobby. It was a depressing place, and often I would seek escape in one of the twenty-four hour movie houses in the vicinity. The admission was ten cents for a four-hour show including a double feature, cartoons, newsreels, and an occasional travelogue. Once I sat down near a sailor and his girlfriend. Necking and giggling incessantly, they were a distraction. Finally I asked in a loud voice, "Hey, don't you want to see the movie?"

The sailor noticed me for the first time and replied, "What? They got movies in here too?" I laughed and sat elsewhere.

The hotel was clearly on its last legs. The only way G.V. could pay the day man and me our twelve dollars a week was to postpone interest payments on the mortgage and taxes. The bank soon tired of this, and after six months they foreclosed on G.V. before he could sell the place.

In 1933 G.V. made the acquaintance of a five-foot Brooklyn bootlegger. Prohibition had just ended, and the bootlegger was looking for a place to invest his earnings. By now the Manhattan real estate market had deteriorated even further. Apartment house occupancy was shriveling as families doubled up. Office building vacancies were at an all time high as businesses curtailed operations or went broke. Hotels suffered because no one had money to travel. The banks now owned over half the buildings in New York. In spite of all this, G.V. used his tall, regal bearing and soft-spoken Southern manner to convince his client he should invest in real estate.

G.V. directed the man's attention toward the Hotel Alcazar

on West 32nd Street. The eight-story, 150-room hotel was near Herald Square, opposite Macy's and Gimbel's. The Morgan Bank had foreclosed on it and desperately sought a buyer who would operate it, thus sparing Morgan the ignominy of operating it themselves for a questionable clientele, or having to board it up. G.V. assured his client that he could make it profitable. The Bank handed over the keys against a payment that barely covered G.V.'s commission as real estate agent. With G.V.'s agreement to invest half his commission, the deal was done. The ex-bootlegger took pride in his real estate acumen.

The only management change made by G.V. was to fire the night clerk so that I could have the job. Putting me to work at night cleared G.V.'s living room sofa and meant there would be one less body in his cramped apartment. Empty beds were available during the day, so I slept at the hotel.

The night clerk's primary duty was to register as many paying guests as possible. Occasionally the Alcazar was filled, but the requirement of five dollars in advance per night kept the Hotel half empty most of the time. The night clerk was far busier than his counterpart during the day, whose principal chore was to get the overnight guests out by 2 P.M. or see that they paid for another night.

The room clerk also operated the telephone switchboard. With guests calling for more towels, making long distance calls (for which we were to collect in advance), and constantly complaining about leaking pipes, blackouts, and disturbances, switchboard activity justified at least one full time operator, but no money was available. In addition to all this, the hotel's lone elevator was troublesome—always breaking down and stranding passengers between floors. Yet I never thought to complain about the demands on me, and actually relished the challenge of doing two jobs at once.

For most of the Alcazar's clientele, five dollars was a large sum of money, and thwarting attempts at non-payment was the hardest part of my job. Still, some people did have money. Double occupancy was ten dollars per night or any part thereof. For every double occupancy the guest register showed the signatures and address of the married couple. The most common address was Hoboken, N.J.—I never knew why. The most common names were Smith, Jones, and Grant. Occasionally a couple would use an Irish or Italian surname, e.g. McCoy or Martinelli, if that appeared to be their ethnic background.

Most of the women appeared respectable and were cooperative in removing their left gloves to show me their wedding bands. I felt for the nervous novices who could not furnish the required proof. I explained that this was a police regulation and not mine. On several occasions, a couple would depart before dawn, and the man or woman would return with another mate. To keep the record straight, I had to require a new registration, and collect another rental. This business of two wives or two husbands was very puzzling to me at first.

One of the Alcazar's permanent tenants was a young woman named Evelyn Bennett, who worked as a hat check girl in one of the big night clubs. A pretty, blue-eyed redhead with an air of innocence about her, she caught my attention right away. Every morning she came in from work shortly after four, asked for her room key, and being bolder than I, sometimes struck up a conversation. We had a lot in common. Her concessionaire took the lion's share of her tips, so she was almost as poor as I was. She was estranged from her faraway family, and I was an orphan whose reunion with my sister had not resulted in closeness. We were both unattached in the loneliest sense and needed someone who cared.

One morning Evelyn came in shortly before six—late for her. On this occasion she was even friendlier than usual. I suspected she'd had a few drinks after work, but she was far from drunk. When I gave her her key, she suggested continuing our conversation in her room when I got off work. Nervous and excited, I knocked on her door a few minutes later. She answered in her dressing gown, invited me to sit beside her on the sofa, and insisted I join her in a glass of brandy. It was the first drink I had ever had and it went straight to my head. Before I knew what had happened we were in bed and I was no longer a virgin.

After that first time we did not need the encouragement of alcohol to follow our instincts. Our mornings together were something we both looked forward to. All our adversities flew out the window when we fell into bed. It was my first love affair, yet our relationship was never really a romantic one. We were more friends who enjoyed sex than true lovers.

Having sex out of wedlock didn't seem to bother Evelyn, but it did me. I now remembered all those sermons I had heard about Sin and Damnation. And my nightly experience as a desk clerk reminded me of the illegality of what we were doing. Solely to escape my guilt, I proposed marriage, and Evelyn accepted.

After standing in line with other couples, we took our turn before the City Clerk, who performed a brief ceremony in front of two witnesses we recruited from the waiting line. We then went to a window, paid the three dollar fee and received our marriage certificate. Our "honeymoon" consisted of going out to dinner. After that our lifestyle continued as before, except that now Evelyn could share my room and save $25 a week in rent.

The entire seventh floor of the Alcazar was occupied on a monthly basis by a man who I took to be someone high in society. He had so many friends, mostly men, who would appear at the desk or go directly to the elevator asking "to see Joe." The elevator operator, a middle-aged negro retained from the prior management, seemed to know most of these these guests of Joe's, and warmly greeted them. I suspect that my colleague worked this traffic for a tip from each one. A few guests, departing with smiles, would even leave a buck on the counter for me.

One night about midnight, several policemen charged into the lobby. One held the elevator while the others climbed the stairs. A few minutes later they came down with a dozen of Joe's girls and male friends, and loaded them into paddy wagons. Joe was not among them. The sergeant turned to me and the elevator operator and shouted, "You too!" and off we went to the Tombs, the jail downtown near City Hall. A night in the Tombs is a night to remember. First we were finger printed, then taken to a cell shared with a motley crew of prisoners professing their innocence and claiming to be victims of bad luck, revenge, or a double-cross. No sleep was possible.

The next morning G.V.'s attorney, Mr. Godwin, came down and got the elevator operator and me released. A hearing was held and the charges against us were dismissed. Still, my problems were not over. The publicity surrounding the prostitution ring in a hotel legally owned by the Morgan Bank was a death knell for G.V.'s management. The Bank foreclosed on Horn, who was in arrears anyway on his mortgage payments, and boarded up the hotel. That ended my job and my short-lived marriage. I returned to G.V.'s couch, and Evelyn made other arrangements. After the Alcazar I never saw her again.

(A half century later a walk down 32nd Street revealed the Alcazar still standing, with a face lift and a working elevator. The clientele, I suspected, hadn't changed much, nor the city penal code, with respect to prostitution and adultery. But the night clerk's job was no doubt easier, relieved of any obligation to concern himself with evidence of marriage. A couples bar was conveniently located on the first floor. At daily rates of forty dollars for a single room and sixty for a double, the Alcazar was nearly full).

I had heard that room clerks from various hotels would occasionally meet to drink beer and exchange information. Soon after losing my job I attended one of these meetings. My woeful appearance and story apparently triggered the compassion of a well-dressed gentleman named Brown, who introduced himself as the Manager of the Ambassador Hotel, an elegant one on Park Avenue. He inquired whether I would be interested in room-clerking at his hotel. As I stood there dumbfounded he invited me for an interview the next day.

At the appointed time I entered the Ambassador and nervously approached the receptionist, half-expecting to be turned away. When I identified myself she replied without hesitation, "Oh yes, Mr. Brown is expecting you in his suite on the top floor." I felt my fortunes rising with the elevator as we ascended to the top floor.

Mr. Brown received me dressed in a bathrobe. Almost immediately he began touching me and getting very excited. Suddenly I realized I had been deceived: he was interested not in helping me, but in taking advantage of me. I broke free from his ardent but unwanted embrace and bolted out the door. This had never happened to me before. As the elevator began its long descent, I found myself repeating over and over, under my breath, "Pervert! Pervert!" Perhaps I had heard the word used in this context by one of the rural preachers. At any rate this incident has ever since conditioned my feelings toward homosexuals. Despite society's changing attitudes, the word I instantly associate with them is still "pervert."

I searched endlessly for a job in that winter of 1934. From early morning till supper and in the evenings as well, I traveled a pre-arranged route calling on cafeterias, restaurants, hotels—anyplace where someone might not show up for his job and I could fill in. Of course, for this to happen in the Depression, a person had to have been run over on his way to work. "Nothing, sorry," became a familiar refrain. After a month of this, I hit the depths of despair. It was the first time in my life I had been without work of any kind. I would have taken the most menial job for any wages at all.

Then G.V. came up with a great idea. In his youth, he had found work on a tramp steamer. We looked in the newspaper for Ship Departures. The next day, a ship was sailing for Panama from the West 23rd St. Pier. "Get there early," G.V. advised. "Be first in line. If a member of the crew doesn't show up, they might take you."

The next morning I dressed as warmly as I could for the zero temperature outside, and decided to leg it the fifty blocks to save the nickel subway fare. I got to the pier about 4 A.M. to find twenty men—all much older than I, and experienced seamen to boot—hovering over a barrel fire with the same idea I had. Against all odds, I hung around anyway. Listening to their tales of hardship mingled with success in far-off places made me forget my own plight. Around noon the SS Panama let off a blast and one of the men murmured, "That's it." That's as far as I got, and as far as I could have gotten without passport or seamen's papers, neither of which I had even heard of at the time.

So, having struck out again, I walked back to 72nd Street, saving my nickel for more essential things. G.V. and Vera were as depressed as I was over my latest failure. They were having a hard enough time keeping food on the table for the three of them. I was clearly a burden they could not afford.

Finally, in that winter of my nineteenth year, I decided to bite the bullet and go to the Children's Aid Society. I saw no other way. Hunger and desperation will overcome even excessive pride.

The Children's Aid Society had three major projects: a foundling home, for babies and very young children to be adopted, Brace Farm School, and the Newsboy's Home. Instead of sending me back to Brace Farm, the Society placed me in the Newsboys' Home, located at 22 William Street, near City Hall at the foot of the Bowery.

The Newsboys' Home was established soon after the turn of the century, when the subways became operational. Most of New York's daily newspapers—the *Herald*, the *Tribune*, the *Sun*, the *Journal American*, the *Daily News*, and the *Times*—were printed in the area of City Hall. The subway provided quick access to neighborhoods throughout Manhattan, the Bronx, Brooklyn, and Queens. It was only logical that newsstands be located at the subway stations. From early morning on into the night, young boys would line up to take their bundles of newspapers via subway (or ferry to Staten Island) to hundreds of newsstands throughout the five boroughs—an area of fifty square miles.

With newspapers selling for five cents or less, the boys could not possibly earn a living wage. The Newsboys' Home provided food and shelter for some 500 otherwise homeless boys each year—about 150 at any time. The boys were housed in three large dormitories and fed a basic diet in one cafeteria. Even after truckers replaced the newsboys, in the late 1920s, the Newsboys' Home remained in operation to shelter the growing number of homeless youth, referred there by the Police Department, Traveler's Aid Society, and other private agencies.

Although I returned there later as a counselor, this first stint at the Newsboys' Home was thankfully brief. With my Brace Farm background, I was soon placed with another farm family, in Wappinger Falls near Poughkeepsie. The terms of employment were twenty dollars per month plus board until April, then fifty dollars per month through September. At last—work and wages! I can't recall the name of the couple who employed me. Like the Ackerman's, they were struggling dairy farmers, barely producing enough milk to cover operating costs, with little or nothing left over for mortgage payments. The wife was kind and thoughtful; her husband, irritable and sometimes downright mean.

Late one night in early March, I was awakened by animal cries. I rushed outside in my night clothes to see the barn on fire, with several horses and some fifty cows trapped inside. Quickly the husband, wife, and I opened the barn doors and drove out as many of the terror-stricken animals as we could before the blazing hay in the loft, fueled by air from the open doors, collapsed the supporting timbers and brought the inferno down upon the remaining animals. More than half the cattle were dead by the time the fire company arrived. The firefighters' actions spared the rest of the buildings, but the barn was reduced to a smoldering heap of rubbish, emitting a pungent odor of burning flesh.

At the milk station the next day, farmers lingered and gossiped about the fire. Some suggested that the fire might have been deliberately set to collect insurance. I couldn't believe that anyone would burn cows and horses alive for insurance money. But I did wonder about it.

Well into April, I reminded my employer of the raise I was due. He denied any such agreement and insisted on keeping my salary at twenty dollars per month. I was furious.

By now I had a reputation amongst the local farmers as a "high-yield worker." The next day, while delivering milk to the station, I asked a neighbor if he could use a farm hand for the summer. He replied that he was looking for a good hand. He would pay fifty dollars per month until October, and I could start that very day.

When I got back, my employer was not at home. His wife

patiently and sympathetically heard me explain my position: I needed money to return to school, and since her husband was not abiding by our agreement I had accepted a job elsewhere. As I departed, she sincerely wished me well.

I walked the two miles to my new employer's farm. He greeted me warmly and was introducing me to his wife when my former employer drove up in his truck. Flushed with anger, he shouted that I could not leave him. I replied that since he had decided not to honor his agreement I wanted nothing more to do with him. He bellowed, "You'll go back with me whether you like it or not!" opened the truck door and walked menacingly toward me. As he moved within reach, I caught him with a clean left jab, leaving his head nicely positioned for the left hook that sent him sprawling. As I stood ready to hit him again, he got into the truck and drove away. My new employer stood there stunned, shaking his head. "My you have a terrible temper! I don't believe you should work here. My son also has a terrible temper, and the two of you would be fighting all the time!"

I begged and pleaded with him. "Sir, you saw him come after me. I've never started a fight in my life! I don't like to fight. Really, I'm very good natured. Please sir, I need the money to go back to school." He finally relented. Later I learned that his son had seen the whole show from the nearby barn. For the next six months the terrible-tempered son and I worked side by side without so much as a cross word between us.

A week later Miss Comstock arrived on the scene with a complaint filed by my former employer against me. She looked concerned. "I insisted at the Society that I handle this matter directly with you. What happened?" I recounted the agreement, his refusal to honor it, and his attempt to prevent me from taking my new job. She pressed on. "But why did you break his jaw with a club?"

I responded with a surprised frown. "If I broke his jaw, it was with my left hand. I did hit him twice when he got out of his truck and came at me." Miss Comstock looked at me in amazement and then said emphatically, "Sam, you done right!"

Miss Comstock and Sam "sightseeing" in New York

On the first of October I hitchhiked back to Manhattan with more than $200 in my pocket. I found a room for three dollars a week, made the rounds of the cafeterias and landed a job as a busboy, working the nine-hour night shift for twelve dollars per week with meals. Then I located the nearest high school, Haron High on West 59th, and enrolled as a sophomore, determined to get my high school diploma.

I was three or four years older than my classmates, who didn't know what to make of me. I was too big to tangle with and too preoccupied with my schoolwork to pay them any mind. It was all I could do to pay attention in class, having worked most of the night. Still, I completed the fall term.

I don't remember how I found out about McBirney High School. Run by the YMCA, it offered high school courses in the evening for working youths such as myself. The manager of my cafeteria promoted me to assistant short order day cook and that winter I began walking over to West 63rd Street after work to take classes at McBirney in the evenings. Shortly after I began classes I was promoted again, to manager of the storeroom, where the cafeteria kept its groceries, meats, and supplies. I suppose the manager figured that a farm boy was likely to be more trustworthy than a city boy in such a job. (In the depression, thefts of food were common in restaurants). At any rate, this became my daily routine for the next two years—the storeroom by day, McBirney in the evenings.

Once a month or so I would drop by to see Vera and G.V., but more particularly Eddie and their baby girl, Barbara. I still corresponded with the Whites, who kept me up-to-date on Blackie. I remembered my life on the farm fondly, but the memories were growing more distant with time. The city was my home now. It didn't much matter that my three-dollar room was boiling hot during those humid summer nights—I slept soaked in sweat. If you're tired enough, I found out, you can sleep anywhere under any conditions.

Miss Comstock's official visits ended when I turned 20 in December, 1935, but she continued to visit me at least twice a year out of personal interest. I would give her a detailed progress report on school and work, and she would inspire me with Scripture, e.g. "Seest thou a man diligent in his business? He shall stand before kings. He shall not stand before mean men." (Proverbs 22-29). Some time in 1936, on one of her visits, she asked whether I attended church. I admitted shyly that I did go every Sunday to the big church on Riverside Drive. "Oh, then you know Dr. Fosdick!" she said cheerfully.

"No, I never met him," I replied. "I sit up in the balcony. But I love to hear him speak, and the choir is beautiful." Two days later I received my invitation to Dr. Fosdick's house. I never knew what Miss Comstock wrote him. I imagine it was short and to the point, e.g. "One of my boys attends your Church. He's a very good boy, and I think you should meet him....Sincerely, Clara B. Comstock."

As I mentioned, Dr. Fosdick was the first person who had shown any interest in, or knowledge of, my ethnic background. At one point during our one-sided conversation he told me, "We have an elder in the church, a doctor, who is Armenian. I will arrange for you to meet him. You ought to know some of your own people."

Soon afterwards the Armenian doctor, who was well-known in his own right, was ushering one Sunday. I walked up and showed him the new "1A" pew card Dr. Fosdick had given me. Fueled by my new curiosity about my heritage, I introduced myself as he showed me to my seat. "Dr. Fosdick suggested that we meet," I added.

"Oh, yes" he said politely, and those are the only two words I ever heard from him. I surmised that he felt it inappropriate that a country bumpkin such as myself should be seated in the front row with the social elite of the city. Evidently he didn't share Dr. Fosdick's democratic instincts.

No matter. On the Sunday following my initial meeting with Dr. Fosdick, I found myself behind the altar, in line with several others to be baptized. The baptismal font was in full view of the congregation, and as I stood to take my turn, I surveyed the nave, aisles and balcony. Riverside Church was packed—1500 people to see me baptized. In my gown, I stepped into the water and held on to the rails as I dropped to my knees. Dr. Fosdick whispered, "Hold your breath," and dipped me backwards until I was completely submersed. It was a significant moment for me; not in a religious sense, but the ceremony seemed to confer a kind of formal acceptance upon me, an acceptance I had never felt before. (In later years I marvelled at the ministry preserving this ancient ritual of John the Baptist, when Dr. Fosdick otherwise assaulted the dogmas and practices of the Church as irrelevant to urban life in the Twentieth Century).

In my early meetings with Dr. Fosdick I likened him to the heroes I had read about in Zane Grey and Horatio Alger. He kept talking about the future, about striving for goals. He didn't seem to notice my shabby appearance, shyness and crude manners. Why should he be that interested in me? What qualities did he see in me that I should know about?

In hindsight I realize what a natural leader he was, inspiring others to achieve self fulfillment by working towards goals within their reach. Like Shaw's Pygmalion, he demonstrated his belief in the potential of the ordinary person, and by implication disavowed inherent superiority vested in the privileged class. His message of hope and challenge stood in sharp contrast to the earlier sermons I had endured on Sin and the Hereafter. I can't recall him ever using Heaven or Hell as a motivation for doing Good. To Dr. Fosdick, Christianity was the example of Jesus's Life; humanitarian concerns; the worth of the Individual vs. Man's institutions of Privilege, Wealth and Power. He focused on the Individual as a creation of God, inspiring the less fortunate to achieve their potential, and challenging the privileged to use their resources to help others, not as a dole but by enhancing their opportunities.

In February 1937, I finally graduated from high school, at the age of twenty-one. The McBirney graduation ceremony was the first social event I attended in New York. My fellow graduates were all city kids who, like me, worked during the day. As a farm boy, I was unduly shy, talked differently, and even walked differently—the result of all those hours behind the plow. Despite these differences there had been a comradery amongst us, based on our shared quest for an education.

I was more embarrassed than honored to be recognized as the editor of our semi-annual school newspaper. I had written the lead article, drawing fervently expressed conclusions on a subject I knew little about. I would have done better writing about farm life.

Anticipating my graduation, Dr. Fosdick had suggested I attend Columbia University. I had a different plan. Columbia did not offer mid-year entry to freshmen. I was anxious to make up for lost time and in no mood to wait for September to begin college. At New York University I could begin freshman classes immediately, attend summer school, and be a sophomore by September. In addition, NYU offered night classes, allowing me to retain my day job at the cafeteria, whereas Columbia did not. Dr. Fosdick urged me to accept church funds allocated for the educational expenses of needy students. I declined with thanks, explaining that my financial needs were covered. For once my refusal was based on something more than stubborn pride.

During the summer of 1930, when Vera visited me at the

Whites and created such a stir over my injured hand, I had another visitor. Miss Comstock brought Mr. Robert L. Brace himself, then in his twilight years, to see me. I was honored to meet the founder of the school that had meant so much to me. Mr. Brace volunteered to me, in Miss Comstock's presence, that when my accident had occurred he had written a memorandum stating that the Society should provide funds for my higher education, if I chose that route to overcome my disability. This seemed a distant possibility at the time, and I gave it little thought.

As I was about to graduate from McBirney, I remembered that conversation. I also knew that at the time of my injury Vera had spoken with a lawyer, probably Mr. Godwin, and was convinced that I could get a large compensation award from the Society, if I chose to pursue it. After all, they had assigned an eight-year-old boy to a dangerous ironing machine. Perhaps she was right, but I could not bring myself to accept her advice in this regard. I felt only gratitude to the Society that had taken me in off the street. If they would honor Mr. Brace's promise of financial aid toward my education, then I would be entirely satisfied.

And so I paid a visit to the Children's Aid Society. Mr. Brace had since passed away, but I was granted an audience with the Executive Director, Arthur Huck. When I recounted to him Mr. Brace's visit and promise to me, he looked surprised and skeptical. Understandably, he had serious misgivings about my college ambitions. Why would *I* be able to succeed in college when so few CAS wards had even tried, and most of those had failed?

My request was a modest one—only $400 a year to cover my tuition at NYU. I would continue working full time to pay my living expenses. Finally Mr. Huck reluctantly agreed, on the condition that I remained in college "in good standing" and understood that payments would terminate upon graduation. I got the feeling he regarded my wish as a demand, and felt that prudence would suggest accepting it.

In all, a total of $1,600 was granted to me by the Children's Aid Society. I consulted no one before making this arrangement, not even Vera. Although she had encouraged me to finish high school, I recalled her explicitly stating that college was beyond my capacity. No doubt she would have considered the $1600 grossly inadequate compensation for my injuries, and using it for college tuition a total waste.

Armed with my first check from the Society, I entered the maze of the NYU campus and finally located the Admissions Office. Once there, I realized with embarrassment that I had no idea what courses to sign up for. Most entering students had been guided through the curriculum offerings by a parent or relative, but I was totally on my own. I couldn't even answer the question, "Are you enrolling in Commerce or Liberal Arts?" It puzzled the Admissions officer that I was so blank. Finally I blurted out, "I want to become a lawyer!" This broke the impasse.

"Well, in that case, you must enroll in the Liberal Arts Program. That requires you to take English, History, a foreign language, and your choice of either Economics or Government." Rather than take two or three courses at a time, as most night students did, I signed up for a full course load, choosing Economics as my elective. Based on his brief interaction with me, the Admissions officer no doubt thought this unwise, but said nothing to discourage me—the more courses taken, the higher the tuition paid.

Washington Square College of New York University was the Working Man's answer to Columbia. Sustained by tuition and private donations—no public funds, unlike CCNY and the state universities—its overcrowded and underfurnished Greenwich Village facilities reflected the difficult economic times. Its strength lay in its excellent faculty, drawn from the surrounding business and professional communities. Unlike many in academia, these people were not armchair theorists, but successful businessmen, journalists, etc., with a wealth of real world experience to impart. Though the curriculum was strange to me, being largely unrelated to my life up until then, I absorbed their knowledge like a sponge.

At the time of my enrollment, in the spring of 1937, New York was still in the midst of the Depression. One out of four males was unemployed. There were no welfare funds—state or federal. Families were struggling to survive, and the campus reflected these struggles. Protests and rallies were everyday events, organized largely by the day students, who had the time as well as the inclination for such extracurricular activities. Demonstrations would still be in progress as the evening students arrived for classes. Although most of us were preoccupied with personal goals, it was impossible for anyone not to be aware of this unrest, and of the ideological debate behind it.

Pervading the university, both faculty and student body, was the belief that capitalism had failed. Labor leaders such as Eugene Debs and Samuel Gompers were folk heroes. Marx, Engels, and Lenin were required reading; Adam Smith was all but interred during this period.

The Depression was understood to be the result of the unbridled greed of the privileged rich, and nothing within the bankrupt system gave hope for the future. President Roosevelt, then in his second term, was accused of patronizing the poor while protecting the privileges of the upper class. Government ownership and control was seen as the only solution. If there were any advocates for free enterprise or capitalism on campus, they certainly didn't surface to challenge the Communists and Socialists. Consequently, the primary conflict was between these two groups; and the debate between Earl Browder, head of the American Communist Party, and Socialist leader Norman Thomas, was a huge event at NYU.

The Communists recruited heavily and were the dominant and most articulate force on campus. The Spanish Civil War was the cause celebre. This had become an international conflict, with the elected government, supported by the peasants and workers and aided by the Soviet Union, under attack by Spanish royalists and the Catholic church, allied with Germany. A contingent of American volunteers, the Abraham Lincoln Brigade, went off to Spain to fight against Franco and Hitler. They were vociferously supported by several American universities, NYU being one of the most active.

To me, all this passionate activity was little more than a backdrop against which I relentlessly pursued my education. That first semester at NYU my days began at 4 A.M., as they had on the farm. I prepared for my classes until 8 or so, then went to work at the cafeteria from 9 A.M. until 6 P.M. After eating dinner I went straight to classes, which began at 7 and ended at 11. Then I went home, caught a few hours sleep, and began all over again.

This routine was actually quite practical and manageable for me, so it came as an unpleasant surprise when the cafeteria was sold that summer and the new management fired all the employees. Fortunately, this time my job hunting luck was better than it had been in the past. Before the beginning of the fall semester I found a job working from 6 P.M. to 6 A.M. as night doorman, elevator operator, and porter in an exclusive apartment building of some twenty suites, located on 37th Street off Park Avenue. It was the first of several changes in employment while I was at NYU, and necessitated a switch back to daytime classes. This was not a problem, although of course I had no more time for extracurricular activities than I'd ever had.

The lady on the fifth floor of the apartment building operated a hostess service for the Broadway elite. I saw famous producers and songwriters, and sundry others—all very rich. Having lost my naivete at the Alcazar, I assumed that being a hostess meant submitting to various degrees of intimacy, which could be negotiated. The hostesses were the most beautiful 18-to-25 year olds one could imagine. From their accents, dress, and demeanor, as I observed them on their elevator rides, most seemed to be middle or upper class girls from the South or Midwest. I concluded they were being venturesome rather than fighting poverty. Perhaps because I too was a working person, they treated me with respect—with one notable exception.

On this particular night one of the girls came in alone, well after midnight, obviously intoxicated. Once the elevator doors closed she reached over and pushed the stop button, suspending it between floors. Without warning or introduction she then wrapped herself around me and used me to masturbate, reaching her climax just as the elevator buzzer sounded. A bit frazzled,

I restarted the elevator and took her to her floor as she composed herself. As she exited to her apartment she smiled and handed me a twenty dollar bill—my only proof that the whole thing hadn't been a dream!

Each night at midnight I would lock the entrance door from the outside, mop the lobby floor spotless, and try to catch a nap on a mattress I had spread out in the basement. I had rigged the front doorbell and elevator button to a basement bell that was positively deafening. I felt confident that I would never sleep through the clang's warning. This setup ideally suited my needs. I could count on four to five hours of sleep, although it would be interrupted by the bell of a guest or tenant, coming or going.

A prominent lawyer owned the building's penthouse. One night in December, far past midnight, I awoke with a start to the clanging bell. Rushing upstairs I saw the lawyer outside, furious. As I opened the door he bellowed, "I've been ringing this bell for over five minutes. Where the hell have you been?!" I apologized profusely, explaining that I was in the midst of college exams, and in all likelihood was so exhausted that I'd slept right through the bell. The next day the apartment house superintendent informed me that I was fired. I called the lawyer on the phone and pleaded with him to restore my job. I told him how desperately I needed this job, and apologized again for causing his discomfort. His reply could not have been more curt: "Your problem is none of my concern!"

I couldn't believe my ears. How could a lawyer be so heartless?! Overhearing my conversation, the superintendent sympathized with me and expressed his desire to help. If I would go with him to his Christian Science church, it would strengthen my morale and resolve to carry on. I assured him I was well endowed with both—all I needed was a *job*! Alas, in that regard he could not help me.

Despite these tribulations I earned mostly A's and B's in my first year at NYU. When I stopped by to pick up my tuition check for the second year, Mr. Huck received me and was noticeably more respectful than he had been the preceding year. I was very happy that he was finally comfortable with his contribution to my education. When I told him about losing my position at the apartment building, Mr. Huck surprised me with a job offer—night clerk at the Hotel America on West 47th Street, off Broadway. I learned later that the Society was a creditor-in-possession of the hotel after the owners had defaulted on their mortgage payments.

This hotel was definitely a cut above the Alcazar. To service its 300 rooms it had two elevators, two bellhops, a telephone operator, and a nightshift repairman. I managed the desk. The clientele, more than half registering after 6 P.M. for one night (or less), paid several times the asking price at the Alcazar. Accordingly they were better dressed—some elegantly, especially the Mafia soldiers who were frequent clients.

Located on Times Square, the Hotel was a convenient "home away from home" for many of New York's most respected citizens. Some of them went to great lengths to conceal their identity with dark glasses and false moustaches, as well as false names. Their lady friends always wore the mandatory wedding ring. To its credit, this hotel did not harbor managed prostitution or, as some would say, a "cathouse."

I will never forget my first New Year's Eve on Times Square. As the clock neared midnight on December 31, 1938, one of the bellhops relieved me at the front desk so that I could participate. I walked to the corner of Broadway and looked up at the clock just as the countdown began. The excitement built to a fever pitch, and at the stroke of midnight the massive throng erupted—wild cheering, horns and noisemakers, fireworks, kissing and drinking openly in the streets. I had never experienced anything like it. In the midst of the pandemonium my thoughts went back to the farm. At midnight on New Year's Eve I would have been asleep for hours, and at 4:30 in the morning, when many of these revelers would be going to bed, I would be getting up to milk the cows, just like any other morning.

Unfortunately, the Society's possession of the America was short-lived. Early in the new year it changed hands and I was out of work again. Since this job had been convenient and paid better than any I'd ever had, I regretted the loss deeply. But before I could fret about it too much, I got a lead on an even better job, from an unlikely source—my other sister, Hannah.

I hardly knew Hannah, who was two years older than I was. Separated since early childhood, when I went to Brace Farm and she was placed in the same orphanage as Vera, neither of us had the time to become reacquainted as adults. After I moved to New York she would occasionally come over to Vera's for one of our rare family get-togethers, but other than that I never saw her. As eager to get ahead as I was, Hannah worked all day on her feet as a beautician, then worked at night in a garment factory.

At the beginning of 1939 Hannah was working in a high class beauty salon. One of her customers was Mrs. Earl Honig, daughter of William S. Sussman, who owned a prominent real estate management firm. Hannah spoke favorably of me to Mrs. Honig, who persuaded her husband, then executive vice president at the firm, to hire me as his office boy. Suddenly I was a white collar employee in an executive office. This was an abrupt transition from mopping floors, washing dishes, running elevators and throwing bums out of hotels—to say nothing of my earlier years as a farm hand. Both Mr. Honig and Mr. Sussman were impressive gentlemen: Honig suave and sophisticated but clearly subordinate to his regal, theatrical father-in-law. I was very self-conscious about my presence and deportment. But both men treated me with respect and, as Jewish people tend to do, encouraged me in my pursuit of an education, even giving me some days off to study for exams.

Wm. S. Sussman, Inc. had its offices at 157 Chambers Street, one of the buildings owned by the Trinity Church Corporation. By any standard these were deluxe offices, on the upper floors with a view of the Hudson River and New Jersey to the west, the skyscrapers of Wall Street to the south. Mr. Sussman occupied the penthouse.

Trinity Church Corporation had been the beneficiary of one of two major land grants created by the British Crown after they seized Manhattan from the Dutch in the 1600's. Trinity was granted most of lower Manhattan, and King's College (renamed Columbia University after the American Revolution) was granted an area extending from Midtown north into Harlem.

Over three hundred years later, much of Manhattan is still owned by (and leased from) these two institutions. Rockefeller Center rests on land owned by Columbia. Likewise, Trinity owns the land beneath many Wall Street skyscrapers. Trinity's landmark is the Episcopal Trinity Church at the foot of Wall Street. This elegant edifice, the first grand church built in America, has always been identified with Wall Street. Its bells toll at the opening and closing of the New York Stock Exchange. Yet Trinity also owns some of New York's worst slums (as does Columbia), a source of occasional embarrassment when the mainstream media does one of their periodic "exposés."

With the collapse of the real estate market, particularly the commercial market, Trinity Church Corporation faced a crisis. During the high-flying days of the late 1920's the Corporation participated in construction of a dozen or more buildings—commercial, industrial, lofts and offices—containing hundreds of thousands of square feet. Only partially rented when the stock market collapsed in 1929, they were almost totally vacated in the next several years as tenants went bankrupt. With mortgages and taxes in arrears, the Corporation assumed these obligations from the banks and city and took possession and sole ownership. These debts, taxes, and operating obligations consumed not only revenue from other sources but also borrowed funds, placing the Corporation itself in financial jeopardy.

Vestrymen of Trinity Church were also on the Board of the Corporation. To manage its properties, the Board normally engaged well-known real estate firms, whose owners and management had close relations with the Church and the exclusive English Speaking Union. So it was a bit of a surprise when, in the mid-1930's, the Board entered into a contract with the relatively minor firm of Wm. S. Sussman, a Jewish immigrant who had retained his Hungarian accent, to manage two dozen of its dis-

Dr. Harry Emerson Fosdick

tressed, recently-erected commercial buildings. I suspected that Sussman had a "Godfather" on the Trinity Board.

Mr. Sussman, then around sixty, was extremely active and creative. I deduced this from the industrial development models and the reams of advertising copy that I carried up to Mr. Sussman in his penthouse office. I also deduced a great deal else. An observant office boy, all eyes and ears and no lip, can learn a great deal about the inner workings of an organization. In moving from office to office he overhears what is being said and to whom. He soon learns which subordinates are in favor, by their access to the bosses. One young man in the office, conspicuous by his immaculate dress and polished manners, was pandered to by his superiors, puzzling until I discovered that he was the son of a vestryman. Not infrequently I happened upon one of the big shots making out with a secretary in a staircase or storeroom, which explained why some secretaries dressed more provocatively than others and seemed to have more flexible work schedules.

I also heard rumors that the Anglo real estate establishment was out to get Sussman, that "kike immigrant who ran off with the jewels" of Trinity's downtown property. At the end of 1939 there were some changes in the Vestry's membership. Sussman lost his contract, and I was out of a job...again.

In the meantime Hannah had contracted tuberculosis and entered a sanitarium on Staten Island, where they removed the infected lung. During her hospitalization I would sometimes break my routine to visit her. When she got out she immediately resumed working long hours. Soon afterwards she married and had a child, which only added to her endless labor. By the time I left New York she was out of my life again.

During my NYU days I also experienced a change of residence, courtesy of Dr. Fosdick. Sometime in 1938, during our semi-annual walk along Riverside Drive, he mentioned the International House and what a great idea it was to bring foreign students from all parts of the world to live together, as they pursued their studies at the city's seminaries, colleges, and universities. He spoke of the famous Sunday night buffet suppers where speakers of national prominence lectured and answered questions from the students.

Intrigued, I asked Dr. Fosdick what the requirements were for residence. He replied that Americans were limited to a maximum of twenty per cent of the 400 available spaces. High demand and limited space demanded careful screening of the applicants, to reward academic promise and achieve representation from as many states and foreign countries as possible. Dr. Fosdick also mentioned that he had helped found the IH and was a member of the Board. Then he casually dropped the bombshell on me: "How'd you like to live there?"

"I'd love it!" I replied enthusiastically and without hesitation. Before I knew it I was accepted into residence at the International House, bypassing the rigorous entrance requirements thanks to the sponsorship of Dr. Fosdick.

So it was that I gathered my meager personal possessions, left my walkup hovel with the shared bathroom, and made the leap from poverty to affluence. The International House, built by John D. Rockefeller, Jr., is a magnificent Georgian structure overlooking a park, beyond which lies Riverside Church and, to the southwest, Grant's Tomb. The building was divided vertically with men on the eastern side and women on the west. My private room was already furnished at a level of comfort far beyond anything I had previously experienced.

In those days of racial segregation, IH was uniquely integrated. Whites from the South encountered adjustment problems, since everyone ate in the same dining hall and shared community bathrooms. Although few if any American Negroes were residents, there were substantial numbers from Equatorial Africa. One of those was a handsome giant from Nigeria we knew as Benny, who spoke in a superlative British accent, with comparable charm and intelligence. He attended Columbia's College of Physicians and Surgeons. The international fraternity also included Chinese, Japanese, Southeast Asians, West Indians and South Americans of every conceivable color, and of course Europeans.

The genial IH atmosphere minimized any racial discord, but I couldn't help but notice that the British made their presence distinguishable from the rest. Their traditional attitude toward "colonials" (including Americans)—an air of superiority and patronizing civility—persevered even as the Battle of Britain raged and their government pleaded for American help against the Nazis. (After the War, in my travels to London, I found it amazing how much the British had changed their attitude toward Americans—relating to us finally as social equals).

Given my work and study schedule, my social participation was limited to the Sunday night suppers and regular attendance at Dr. Fosdick's fervent and always inspirational Riverside sermons. Still, on my floor, I made three memorable friends.

Takeuchi from Japan had a Ph.D. from the University of Texas and was allegedly taking some courses at Columbia. Actually, he confided in me, he was preparing speeches for a Japanese prince, who was speaking with U.S. business organizations as a special representative of his Government. Japan's aim was to bring U.S. business into a working relationship with the Zaebatsu, its own organization of industrial giants. By this joint venture, Japan and America could dominate the raw materials and markets of Asia.

Takeuchi believed that the United States had no choice but to cooperate with Japan. Otherwise Japan would simply conquer the entire Pacific as well as Eastern China. My contemptuous laugh was met with a friendly but fervent restatement of his position. Takeuchi wasn't anti-American; he loved America. But he was 1,000% Japanese, which meant America must yield to Japan. On a personal, one-to-one basis, we were friends and enjoyed our debates, as well as playing checkers, a game he ardently relished.

Paul, from Binghamton, New York, was my first upper class friend. His interests were Literature and Theater. I suspect that my roughhewn, overzealous personality intrigued and amused him. On one occasion he asked if I would do him a great favor. He had asked two lovely girls from Long Island to the theater and supper afterwards, but his friend had regretfully bowed out at the last minute. Could I possibly fill in? I protested that I had no money for such purposes and could hardly justify taking the time. He insisted. He would cover all expenses, and would be honored if I would share the evening with him and the lovely girls. Reluctantly I agreed, did the best I could with my modest wardrobe, and together we met the girls at the theater. There was little chance for conversation until we arrived at the Stork Club for supper. The head waiter looked at me as though I were something the cat had dragged in. Fortunately he knew my host; otherwise I never would have slipped through the snob net scrupulously erected by Sherman Billingsley, owner of the famous society club.

My schedule the past few years had left me little time for romance. I was starved for female interaction and quite smitten by the girls. Soon I was telling some pretty earthy jokes and anecdotes drawn from my experience, which unfortunately was light years from theirs. Their laughter was polite but far from enthusiastic. Still I persisted, my personality exploding like a neutron bomb, killing my companions without destroying the table. The climax to this ill-fated evening was my sophisticated acceptance of the suggestion that I try Welsh Rarebit. "I love rabbit!" I blurted out. My friend spared me the embarrassment of correction. I was unaware of my goof until years later.

That same year I met Sidney T. Smith from Winnipeg, Canada, who was studying Sociology at Columbia. Sid and I attended Riverside Church together and were inseparable on those rare occasions when neither of us was busy. He was from a well-to-do family, but his modest, soulful personality broke down the barriers which might have prevented us an equal exchange.

A trained social worker, he was fascinated by my honest responses to his rather direct questions concerning my past. Specializing in intelligence measuring techniques then on the threshold of universal application, he persuaded me to take one of the first IQ tests. Whether I measured moron or genius or somewhere in between, I never found out. He refused to give me the results. All he would say was, "Very interesting." In terms of subject matter, the test was clearly targeted at urban youth from family backgrounds; it was certainly not addressed to a farm boy's thinking and experience. I think Sid understood that.

Sid's father was a grain tycoon—generous with his money but parsimonious with his affection. Although they lived under the same roof, he hadn't spoken to Sid's beloved mother in ten years. At Christmas Sid's father sent him an envelope containing five hundred dollars and a note: "Spend this however you wish."

Sid shook his head. "That old geezer knows how to get at me.... O.K. this is what I want for Christmas—you take half of this and do whatever you want with it."

My reply was, "No way! I can't take your money!" Sid was determined, and questioned the depth of our friendship if I denied him the pleasure of giving at Christmas. Finally I gave in. I spent part of the windfall on a present for Sid and saved the rest for a rainy day.

When I lost my job at Sussman, I waited tables at IH for my room and board, always an option for any resident who needed financial help. Among the other penniless students doing the same was Burl Ives, who led folk-singing at the Sunday Suppers. After entertaining at IH Board Meetings, attended by many persons of influence, he was soon launched on his famous singing career.

Another musician I befriended while waiting tables was an Iowa farm girl, then attending Juilliard, named Jean Browning. Later, known by her married name of Jean Madeira, she became one of the principal soloists at the Metropolitan Opera. From time to time I would meet her backstage after one of her performances and we would go out for a late supper, trading stories about our respective careers and reminiscing about our days at IH.

By carrying a full course load, during summers as well as the school year, I finished my undergraduate work at NYU in three years. Although I had received consistently high marks in my classes, I realize now that I also missed out on a great deal that college had to offer. I needed more time for reflection and digestion (of food *and* ideas) and more interchange with other students. I came out of NYU recognizing fellow students but not really knowing any of them.

In February 1940 I received my B.A. from NYU and immediately entered graduate school at Columbia. My stipend from CAS having come to an end, I continued to wait tables at IH while I looked for a night or weekend job (or jobs) that would cover my tuition.

From the help wanted board at IH, I found parttime employment as a companion to Mr. Francis Higginson Cabot. Both the Higginson and Cabot families were prominent in the Eastern plutocracy, but Mr. Cabot was now in his seventies and confined to a wheelchair. My job was to take him for a walk on days the weather permitted it. I would wheel him from his townhouse in the east sixties over to Central Park and back.

Though frail of body, Mr. Cabot was sharp of mind, and eager to share his thoughts and memories with me. As we walked past the mansions of Carnegie, Harkness, Gould and others, he would share his personal recollections of these families along with his moral evaluations, distinguishing between those "builders who contributed much to the country," and those who had simply manipulated the stock market for their own gain. He especially admired those philanthropists who had made their generous gifts anonymously. Listening to Mr. Cabot shattered my preconceived ideas about the rich. Suddenly they were not so distant—or so heartless—as I'd imagined them. His stories, and Mr. Cabot himself, humanized them.

As the weeks rolled by, he gradually drew me out as to my own life and ambitions. We became such good friends that Mrs. Cabot confided to me that Mr. Cabot eagerly looked forward to our day's walk and talk. She repeatedly pressed me to accept a contribution toward my educational expenses. Finally, since my salary did not begin to pay my tuition, I accepted a gift of two hundred dollars. I fully intended to pay it back, but when I tried to several years later, Mrs. Cabot was adamant in her refusal to accept it, angrily stating that I was attempting to deprive them of "the privilege of giving." I learned my lesson, and visited her occasionally even after Mr. Cabot's death.

In the spring of 1940 the Children's Aid Society, having cut off tuition money, offered me the position of Counselor at the Newsboys' Home. My compensation would be room and board and a modest salary. The job would begin at 6 P.M., after the daytime staff had left. I would conduct intake interviews in the evening and, sleeping in an adjacent room, maintain order overnight amongst the fifty or so boys on my floor.

When I described the position to Sid Smith, he was more enthusiastic than I. To him this represented an opportunity to complement his academic studies at Columbia with some practical experience. I went to the Director of the CAS and told him that Sid was better qualified than I and that he should have the job. The result was that after interviewing Sid, they hired us both. I hated to leave the International House, but I needed the job, and I looked forward to working with Sid. In addition, Dr. Fosdick was positively elated when I told him of my assignment.

Glowing with nostalgia, he described his two years of missionary work in the Bowery following the Seminary. So that spring I returned to the Newsboys' Home.

Sid and I and another counselor conducted interviews with each new boy—some 500 a year, ranging in age from fifteen to twenty-one. The questions were basic: "Where is your home?...What are your reasons for leaving?...Do you have any job experience?...What would you like to do for a living?...Do you have any health problems?... Any police record?"...and the like.

Finding employment would have solved many of the problems these boys faced, but by no means all. There were countless reasons why the boys had left home. Frequently cited were abuse at the hands of their fathers, family feuds, unresolved sibling conflicts, and trouble with the police, or neighborhood gangs. Many second generation immigrants were ashamed of their unassimilated parents. A substantial number of boys had fled small towns with unrealistic dreams of making it in the Big City. And a few boys had actually been encouraged to leave, by families who were simply too poor to provide for them. All stranded in the streets without food or shelter, they would usually be referred to us by either the police or Traveler's Aid, which maintained booths at the bus and railroad terminals.

As counselors, our primary challenge involved gaining the confidence of the boys, each of whom was understandably insecure and uncertain what to do next. Sid's approach represented the best combination of professionalism and heartfelt concern. My approach would not qualify as professional but was equally effective because I had grown up with boys like these and could easily relate to them. Young runaways we tried to convince to call home, or we would call for them and reassure their parents. Frequently we could be helpful in mediating an underlying conflict. One of the most subtle and intransigent problems was the boy ashamed of his parents. In some cases, after hearing the boy's complaints, I wanted to say, "I wouldn't mind having them as my parents! How would you like to be an orphan?"

The most critical day-to-day problem with a hundred and fifty "dead end kids" was maintaining order. Three counselors could not do the job, nor could threatening to call in the police. Much to Sid's chagrin I pursued a practical approach not found in any of his textbooks. I would deliberately befriend one or two of the tougher kids in the pack, pull them aside and ask for their help. Feeling important, they were only too happy to oblige: I mean that literally, as their over-enthusiastic performance sometimes necessitated first aid for the objects of their intervention.

During one period, the toughest bully was as belligerent with the counselors as with the boys. We were ready to have the police take him away, but had no criminal charge to rely upon. As we faced this dilemma, I happened to interview a Scotch boy, a seaman whose ship had been sunk by a Nazi U-Boat off New Jersey. Little more than five feet tall, all sinew, he spoke very mildly in his brogue, thanking us for our hospitality and help in getting him back to sea, and asking if there were anything he could do in return. Following my instincts I asked him if he could help me keep order while he was here.

"No problem for me," he replied. "I can take care of the rowdies."

"Well, there's one tough, twice your size, who is raising hell these days, and he may be too much for you." Scottie just laughed. "If you get noticed he'll go after you," I added.

Less than an hour after the interview I heard a commotion. Rushing out, I saw Scottie duck under the bully's punch and lunge, butting his forehead into the boy's stomach. Then, while his opponent was bent over and gasping for breath, Scottie drove a knee into his head and followed that with a right hand, leaving the bully a motionless heap. As the watching boys applauded, Scottie straightened up and said to me with a wink, "Sorry about that. Mean one, eh?" The Newsboys' Home was never more peaceful than during the month that Scottie stayed with us.

Many of the boys were clearly intelligent, and if given an opportunity could develop into productive citizens. With others it was not so clear. The whole matter of intelligence became more

Sidney Smith

difficult to fathom after meeting one boy who had the appearance and manner of a moron hardly capable of attending to his bodily functions. When asked what he could do, he startled me with his reply: "I can add, subtract, divide, and multiply."

"You did that in school?" I inquired.

"No, in a circus. Against a calculator I can do it faster." To test his claim, I set out a column of figures six digits across and ten down. He looked at it and immediately put down the total. I took five minutes to check it. The answer was correct. Complex division and multiplication came just as easily to him. This encounter with an "idiot savant" fascinated both Sid and myself.

Nearly every day, after hours, Sid and I would walk across nearby Brooklyn Bridge—overlooking the walkup flats of little Italy and the eastside Jewish ghettos, the Manhattan skyline looming in the background—and share our thoughts and reflections about the boys: their backgrounds and problems, any problems we were having with them, and possible solutions to those problems. These regular hour-long dialogues, as we traversed the bridge, filled a void in my process of learning and understanding. How does one digest to comprehension what is taken in through reading and lessons in school? Often, parents and relatives test the student's comprehension. Or perhaps this function is performed by the exchange of views and opinions with fellow students.

Until Sid, I had neither. I had learned in a vacuum. Now, on our walks, we could each test our proffered solutions against the perceptions and intellect of someone from an entirely disparate background. What better test of the validity of a value or practice than its adoption by persons as different as we were? Thanks to Sid, my emerging intellect was continually challenged to probe deeper and wider as I searched for meaning in the world around me.

Sid and I both kept a respectful distance from the day staff of professional social workers, who expressed little curiosity about what happened to the boys after they went home. As long as there were no deaths or serious injuries they seemed satisfied, and left us alone. The boys came and went. But many of them did go back home, did get jobs, and did come back or write Sid and me to say thanks.

For the next two years my life revolved around Columbia and the Newsboys' Home—except during the summers. Within a few weeks after enrolling in graduate school at Columbia, I had to choose a dissertation topic for my Master's Degree. Given my background, the choice was easy—the Milk Industry of New York.

I decided to cover the economics of its production, processing, and distribution to consumers. As the spring term drew to a close, I was attracted by the possibility of spending the summer recess among the dairy farmers.

At that time the major processors—Borden, Sheffield Farms, and the Dairymen's League—determined the prices they paid for raw milk, and that was that. The newly formed Dairy Farmers Union, headquartered in Utica, was attempting to organize farmers to bargain collectively for higher prices. I called the Union headquarters and received an invitation to meet with its President, a farmer from nearby Oswego County. I walked out of the meeting an official Union organizer for Steuben County (where I had lived with the Whites), and adjoining Allegheny County. The Union agreed to advance me $300 to buy a used car, and to pay me ten cents a head for each cow owned by a farmer I signed up. Typically a farmer would have around thirty cows. His signature made him a Union member and put three dollars in my pocket.

About the first of June, I headed west to embark upon my traveling one-man show. Throughout the summer I covered the two counties, convening meetings with the farmers and persuading them to sign up. The Greenwood farmers gave me my start and news spread from there by word of mouth. Each meeting would result in another meeting in an adjoining town. The local press viewed my activities as revolutionary. The status quo was being threatened and I was branded a radical, or worse yet—unAmerican. My unpronounceable foreign name didn't help.

I had been tipped off that there might be trouble in the largely Catholic community of Andover. Father O'Keefe, a prominent priest from Buffalo who happened to be visiting his farmer brother, supported my efforts and accompanied me to the meeting. He was a big man, 250 pounds or so, with a booming voice. Midway through the meeting a group of American Legion members, obviously under orders to disrupt it, charged in shouting, "Communists!" Father O'Keefe tried his best to persuade them otherwise, but they were not about to be influenced by the priest, let alone by me. At the height of the bedlam and apparent futility of the meeting's continuation, Father O'Keefe shouted, "May the curse of God fall upon you!" but that didn't help either.

The next afternoon I was driving through Andover when a car pulled in front of me and forced me to the curb. Three men got out, and I recognized them as legionnaires from the night before. Trying to appear calm, I casually asked, "How can I help you?"

The biggest of the three spoke plainly and quietly: "You can get out of town if you know what's good for you. We won't let you go next time." The three of them then returned to their car and drove off.

News of this encounter spread like wildfire and the farmers organized a second meeting several times the size of the first. This time they were prepared for the legionnaires, who were without exception not farmers but townspeople. The legionnaires never showed up and the farmers joined the Union almost to the man. Instead of killing the membership drive, the legionnaires had sparked it. Several days later the head of the local chapter of the American Legion came to me and apologized, saying that he had been misled, but he didn't volunteer the name of the one who had influenced him.

By the end of the summer I had earned $600, which covered my expenses (including the cost of my car) with a little left over. I drove back to the city, sold the car and paid my fall tuition, and returned to Columbia, where I focused my attention on completing my Master's dissertation on the New York Milk Industry, much the wiser for my experiences that summer.

Thanks to Professor Robert Brady, late that fall my dissertation was completed and accepted toward my Master's Degree. A stocky, forceful man in his late thirties, Brady had a concise, forthright way of expressing himself, and tried to instill the same in his students. His margin notes expressed his frustration with me; e.g. "There's a point here somewhere, I guess. What **is** it?" or "For God's sake come down to earth. Why don't you *say* it instead of beating around the bush?" and so on. He expected better grammar and organization of ideas from a graduate student, but knowing my background, and realizing how well I knew my subject, he patiently worked with me to hone my thesis into acceptable form.

Within the field of Economics, Brady's area of expertise was Industrial Organization. He was convinced that a free enterprise system in a democracy would lead inevitably to a concentration of industrial power married to state power—either the Fascist model of Nazi Germany or the Communist system of the Soviets. Of the two, he preferred the latter. I argued instinctively, and not very persuasively, that in America people were more flexible and self-reliant, and thus could avoid either of these fates. His response: "Where are the leaders who will rally people to oppose their subordination to the Industrial State? They are nowhere to be found!" Brady's concerns about Industrial Fascism in America grew not only from witnessing what Mussolini and Hitler had done, but also from Roosevelt's efforts to harness the private sector under Government control in order to prevent deflation of prices and promote higher wages.

Although he was an avowed atheist, Brady surprised me by accepting my invitation to hear Fosdick at Riverside Church. That Sunday Fosdick was at his inspirational best as he challenged his listeners to achieve their God-given right to self-fulfillment to the best of their abilities. Tough-minded Brady was clearly moved and wondered aloud if he might after all be underestimating Man's ability to resist State control by relying on higher spiritual influences.

(In fact, recent developments may be proving Brady more prescient than we would like to believe. From the end of World War II until the 1980s, antitrust laws discouraged private firms from mergers and acquisitions that would concentrate economic power in fewer and fewer hands. However, the Reagan and Bush Administrations' emphasis on a free market, unencumbered by enforcement of the antitrust laws, encouraged the greatest concentration of industrial power since the beginning of this century. And Clinton, though a Democrat, has not noticeably reawakened the AntiTrust Division of the Justice Department.

Is the groundwork being laid for American fascism? Brady would probably say yes).

Sid and I resumed our friendship and our discussions, which now frequently took place over dinner at Angie's, an Italian Restaurant up the street on the edge of Little Italy. The restaurant was a popular Mafia hangout, thanks to Angie, a swarthy, middle-aged Sicilian who did triple duty as owner, bartender, and superb cook. Realizing that our fare at the Newsboys' Home was as unimaginative as it was cheap, he offered us the run of the menu at bargain prices, an expression of Italian hospitality for which Sid and I were extremely grateful.

Living on the edge of the Bowery gave us a look at an interesting slice of American life. The Bowery was surrounded by Chinatown, Little Italy, and the Jewish ghetto. The inhabitants of these ethnic enclaves lived essentially as they would have in their countries of origin. They observed the traditional feast days and holidays, ate their native dishes, and spoke their native tongues most if not all of the time.

They also took care of their own. You never saw a "Bowery bum" from one of these ethnic groups. I don't recall there being any Negroes, either. Almost exclusively the bums were of Anglo-Saxon origin and more likely than not were at least third-generation Americans. At the time, I dismissed these derelicts as quitters—men (and a few women) who had tried and failed, or perhaps never tried at all, and chose to "drop out" of Society rather than face its condemnation. In the oblivion of the Bowery they found comraderie amongst like-minded others.

The lifestyle of the Bowery bum centered around the pursuit of three things: free food, free shelter during inclement weather, and cheap alcohol—not necessarily in that order. For food and shelter the bum was forced to endure a sermon. Some of the preachers were men of the cloth, sincerely dedicated to breathing life and hope into these lost souls. Others were simply egoists, who enjoyed listening to their own success stories (told under the pretense of inspiration), and feeling superior to their captive audience.

Daisy Gordon was the God Mother of the Bowery—an easy touch for a handout. An aging, bleached blonde with a crusty facade, she had at one time been the girl friend of gangster Maxey Gordon. Maxey had set Daisy up as proprietress of the Bowery Theatre, and she adopted his name out of gratitude.

The Bowery Theatre specialized in third and fourth run movies. Admission was ten cents before 5 P.M. and fifteen cents after, making it an ideal place to get out of the cold, enjoy a drink, and take a "nap." Daisy spent twelve hours a day in the change booth, and knew every bum in the Bowery. She was also good to our newsboys. She kept order in her own way and only rarely called for help, and then somewhat apologetically. A story made the rounds about the time a delegation of women from the local Temperance Union came to the theatre to complain that she was giving money to the bums to buy alcohol. Daisy listened stone-faced, then replied, "Ladies, your guts are growling; what you need is a beer."

On some weekends I was able to travel out of the city to Long Island. Fred Diemer was a boyhood friend of Sid's from Minnesota, where they had attended summer camp together at Lake of the Woods. Now he and his wife Carol had a beautiful home in Bayside. Sid and I alternately had Sundays off and one or the other of us would often visit the Diemers for a sail around Long Island Sound in their twenty-foot yawl. This was my first taste of luxury.

My second taste came courtesy of my brother-in-law. G.V.'s niece was Patty Ortell, daughter of Frank Ortell, the racing authority for the Journal American. Frank was famous for betting on his own picks with amazing success. Patty was well-groomed and drove the latest Buick convertible. G.V. had told her about me, and when she wanted a change of pace from the fast crowd she usually ran with, she would call me for a date. She had plenty of time and plenty of money, and would not accept my lack of either as an excuse. Soon, unable to resist the temptation of her good looks and enthusiasm, I gave in. I didn't spend any money—the gas tank was always full when she arrived to pick me up.

After a few dates I received a call from her father, who amiably suggested that I not get hooked on Patty, because I could never afford to support her. Any idle fantasies I had in that direction were effectively squelched by Frank's advice. Shortly after that she stopped calling. Patty later married into a rich, prominent New York family that went broke. Her parents died and she fell on hard times, having developed neither the discipline nor useful skills to escape them on her own—a cruel fate.

In June of 1941, just after the close of the spring semester, I received a call from the Dairy Farmers Union. Impressed with my performance the previous summer, they asked me to come and help with a crisis that was developing. A serious spring drought threatened to ruin the farmers. Instead of pasturing their cows as they usually did this time of year, they were forced to purchase feed at skyrocketing prices; yet the price paid for their milk remained the same. By law, a minimum price was set by the Federal Milk Marketing Administration. The major processors had never paid more than this minimum, and refused to even now, in spite of the circumstances.

One by one the county chapters of the Union had voted to strike. With the strike date rapidly approaching, I arrived in Utica and met with the board members—all dairy farmers, none with any strike experience. Of course I didn't have any either. Still, they looked to me for advice.

I immediately identified two problems. First, the drought was affecting costs but not production. Hence, with milk in adequate supply, no consumer pressure could be brought to bear on the state and federal agencies. The strike had to be widespread throughout the milk shed or it would fail. Second, the prospects of a successful strike were reduced by the political climate of the day. The Battle of Britain had begun and, with the impending national emergency, it was essential that the strike be viewed as respectable by the press and the public.

If we could win the support of a major public figure, we could perhaps overcome our anonymity and public suspicion of our motives. It occurred to me that we had just such a person "down the road apiece" in Owen D. Young, Chairman Emeritus of

General Electric, who happened to own several dairy farms. Taking a shot in the dark, I asked the farmers present whether any of them happened to know Mr. Young. Three said they knew him personally. Without hesitation I suggested that if Owen D. Young could be persuaded to strike along with the other farmers, we had a good chance of success. Obviously, it was a big "if," because normally a major industrialist would be against resolving disputes by striking. But if we could somehow win Mr. Young's support, it would give us the attention and credibility we needed. It was well worth the try.

A delegation of three farmers, led by Frank Brill, one of the Union's executive committeemen, called Mr. Young and requested a meeting. They were invited to come to Young's home in Van Hornsville, about twenty miles away, that same afternoon. I remained in Utica. The strike was scheduled for the next day.

Late that afternoon a *New York Times* reporter, Seymour Raskin, entered Union headquarters and asked if there was going to be a strike. My reply was, "Our board members are in an important meeting right now. We expect them back here by seven, and I can give you some information then."

A little later Brill and the others rushed in with broad grins and raced past Raskin into my office. "Owen D. Young will hold his milk!!" they shouted with glee.

I left the room and said to Raskin, "There will be a general dairy farmers' strike beginning tomorrow. Owen D. Young will strike his dairy farms along with everyone else..." As I sought to elaborate, Raskin quickly interrupted me.

"No! Don't *tell* me anything. Just answer my questions." For about a minute and a half he fired questions at me nonstop. Then he asked, "Can I use this typewriter?" I nodded and he typed furiously, then picked up the phone and called in his story to the *Times*. When he was all finished he turned to me and asked with genuine curiosity, "What the hell is going on?!"

I couldn't help but laugh at this first-hand lesson in the superficiality of news reporting. At any rate, the next morning the

New York Times headline read in bold letters, "**OWEN D. YOUNG STRIKES**," and the article Raskin had called in filled two columns on the front page.

With sensational newspaper and radio coverage throughout the state, the strike was on, and all hell broke loose. The president of the Dairymen's League, the heads of the milk companies, as well as Herbert Lehman, the Governor of New York, all pounced on Owen D. Young by telephone. He refused to budge from his position and issued a long statement to the press, saying among other things that, "I am and always have been opposed to strikes, and yet if it is the only redress for clearly evident wrongs, then yes, I will strike!"

Owen D. Young, then in his late 60's, had been born and raised in Van Hornsville. The son of a dairy farmer, he received his early education, as I did, in a one-room school house. Following law school he began his career at General Electric, whose original manufacturing plant was located in nearby Schenectady. Although he was largely responsible for developing and structuring the expanding company, he never lost touch with Van Hornsville, preserving the homestead farm and in later years acquiring additional farms nearby. He was a large volume milk producer, but he hardly looked the part of a dairy farmer. He was tall and erect, with an air of competence that inspired confidence, balanced by a modesty which encouraged his farm neighbors and townspeople to call him Owen.

Van Hornsville, a hamlet of only thirty or forty people, had a church, a country store, and a new high school built by none other than Owen D. Young. Assisted by his son-in-law Everett Case, Young convened a meeting at the high school—a meeting attended by the Presidents of Borden Company, Sheffield Farms and the Dairymen's League. The company VIP's arrived in chauffeured limousines. Three representatives of the Dairy Farmers Union, including myself, stepped out of a dust-covered, five-year old Ford. This was my first encounter with the upper echelon of the business world. The dairy farmers of the Union, knowing Mr.

Young personally, addressed him as Owen. Everyone else addressed him as Mr. Young.

The meeting began with the milk company spokesmen attempting to persuade Mr. Young to discontinue his participation in the strike. The President of the Dairymen's League claimed his organization represented dairy farmers and opposed the strike. Although a farmer's cooperative, the Dairymen's League performed the same processing and distribution functions as Borden and Sheffield, with the attendant revenue possibilities; hence its official policies were kindred to the private companies and hostile to the Union. Since many farmers of the League were members of the Union and on strike, the League felt threatened.

Young made it clear that this was not his strike but one in which he was participating . . . and that he would use his influence to end the strike only if the farmers' grievances regarding milk prices were addressed. His next statement I'm sure sent a chill down the executives' spines: "It is not up to you to decide the issue of striking; it's up to the Union, and I will abide by their judgment."

In taking this position, Mr. Young put the ball in our court. The Union had given me no clear guide lines as to what initiatives I might suggest at this meeting, but my dairy farmer colleagues, perhaps a bit intimidated by the bigwigs, kept looking at me to say something. I was no more prepared than they to play the role of spokesman and asked Mr. Young if we might have a brief recess. We were given a private room where we huddled and discussed what course of action we should take in light of Mr. Young's eagerness to help. It was clear that he was our trump card. Without him the strike might go on, but we were destined to lose it.

When the meeting reconvened, I set forth the stance we had agreed upon: if we could be assured that the State and Federal Governments would seriously address the problem of inadequate prices, the Utica headquarters would encourage farmers to return their milk to market. Mr. Young proposed that he arrange a meeting with Governor Lehman and Claude Wickard, Secretary of Agriculture, and offered to represent the dairy farmers at the meeting. The milk companies embraced the proposal, declaring that this represented sufficient progress to justify calling off the strike. I immediately responded that the issue was not Mr. Young's intentions, but tangible evidence that the Governor and Secretary of Agriculture would act on the problem. I emphasized that we had no control over the local organizations and therefore such evidence must be convincing not only to the farmers present at this meeting, but also to the rank and file throughout the state. The meeting was adjourned with the understanding that we would meet again following Mr. Young's conversations with the Governor and the Secretary of Agriculture. In the meantime, the strike continued.

That evening the dairy farmers of Oswego County were meeting at the fairgrounds in Boonville, and the Union leaders asked if I would go up and make a speech. This was my first appearance at a strikers' meeting and a strange experience indeed. The atmosphere was highly charged—one could feel it—for the farmers were fed up, desperate, and eager to unite in demonstration of their strength. Their emotion was contagious and it inspired me to make an impassioned plea for solidarity, recalling Benjamin Franklin's famous admonition: "We must all hang together or we will surely hang separately!" The climax came when, after a dramatic crescendo, I thundered at the top of my lungs, "Boonville will be bone-dry tomorrow!!" Tumultuous cheering and applause greeted my proclamation and continued as I sat down, flushed with an odd mixture of pride and embarrassment.

The next day I was asked to meet an even greater challenge. In a Fourth of July address the Federal Milk Marketing Administrator had charged that the strike was fomented by left-wing agitators and communists, and had urged the farmers not to be led astray by these unpatriotic radicals. Of course similar charges had been leveled against the Union since its inception the summer before, but never by a high government official. The Union leaders asked if I would make a radio address countering these charges. Utica's radio station served most of Central New York, and my speech would be widely heard and discussed. I had never been to a radio station before and was very nervous.

Since I had no training or guidance from anyone, I spoke without sophistication, and simply told the truth in the language of the farmers themselves. At the end of my speech I blasted the administrator: "When someone refuses to address the problem at hand, that of the unfair price of milk, and instead launches into a personal attack against the integrity of the farmers, this is an attempt to deceive. How can a federal official stoop to such tactics? Is he a spokesman for the milk companies? How can a federal official accuse farmers of being unpatriotic? Perhaps we should recall the great Englishman, Samuel Johnson, who defined patriotism as 'the last refuge of a scoundrel'." News accounts of my speech highlighted the term "scoundrel" placed on a high Government official by an ex-farm boy. Again I was congratulated by the farmers for a job well done.

On the third day of the strike I accompanied Frank Brill to a meeting of the farmers in Oswego. A big, muscular man in his mid fifties, Frank was uncomplicated, honest and direct in his dealings with people, and a natural leader in spite of his lack of training. At the meeting we were joined by John Johnson, a local resident with some experience in organizing labor unions, who had been asked by the Oswego chapter to help them.

I spoke first, bringing the farmers up to date on the progress of the strike and explaining Owen D. Young's role in it. Frank spoke next, explaining why he supported the strike from his own experience as a farmer. As he spoke, an elderly woman in the front row turned to her nearly-deaf husband and said loud enough for us to hear, "Look at his hands, George! Frank has *huge* hands, and any man who works with his hands must be honest!" I felt good because I too had large, working man's hands. But Johnny Johnson, a non-farmer, looked pained as he rose to speak, self-consciously sticking his undersized hands in his pockets.

The strike was picking up momentum, but farmers were getting restless and more belligerent by the day. We at headquarters deplored violence as counter-productive, but the farmers were beginning to take matters into their own hands. In some areas, the milk of non-striking farmers was being intercepted and dumped en route to milk stations. Many of the large thermal trucks, perforated by rifle shots, squirted milk on the road and on passing cars as they sped down the highway.

A week after the first meeting in Van Hornsville, the original attendees convened for a second. The strike had escalated and public attention was focused on the farmers' plight. Mr. Young reported that two meetings were scheduled within the next week: one with the Governor in Albany and another with the Secretary of Agriculture in Washington. The Secretary would then convene a hearing by the Federal Milk Marketing Administration to review the farmers' economic situation and possibly adjust prices—there was no promise they would do so. Then Mr. Young tossed the ball back into our court. Did this response constitute sufficient justification for the Union to call off the strike?

I requested a recess so that we could discuss it privately. During the recess we evaluated our situation. This seemed to represent the tangible evidence of progress we had demanded. If the strike went on, the increasing violence might turn public opinion against us. On the other hand, if we called off the strike now, and the government ruled against the farmers, where would we be then? I suggested we announce that we would "suspend" the strike, pending results of the upcoming meetings, rather than "terminate" it. This was accepted by all parties, including the county Union leaders, and milk deliveries resumed the next day.

A few days later we all met with Governor Lehman in Albany. Company executives continued their argument for the status quo, assuring the Governor milk supply was more than adequate for consumer needs. In condemning the strike they stopped short of denouncing its leaders as "radicals and troublemakers," as they undoubtedly would have, had Owen D. Young not been one of them.

Again, I was asked to make the case for the farmers. They were impressed with my performance thus far and I think they thought that, with my college education and urban experience, I was less likely to be intimidated by "the Governor's Mansion." In reality

I was as overawed as they, but after stuttering through my opening sentences, I settled down and made an impassioned plea for the Governor's help.

Knowing he had been reared in New York City, I assumed he knew very little about dairy farming. I was certain he was outraged by news reports and pictures of farmers dumping milk on the ground and shooting holes in the milk trucks. I cited these actions as evidence of the farmers' desperation. Here it was July; normally the cows would be grazing in green pastures, but with the pastures burned up by the drought, farmers now had to buy expensive fodder shipped from far away. The cost of the fodder was much higher than the price of milk. This tragic hardship appeared to be of no concern to the milk companies, and authorities of the Federal Milk Marketing Administration had refused to address the crisis, leaving the farmers no recourse but to strike.

"Your Honor, Mr. Governor, I am delegated to make the dairy farmers' position clear to you. The strike is not terminated; it is only suspended. If price relief is not granted, the strike will resume. Farmers will continue to dump their milk on the ground, and will soon begin selling their cows for beef. That last resort is a great financial sacrifice, but no more so than producing milk at a loss. As a former businessman, I'm sure you can appreciate circumstances in which one has to choose between the lesser of two evils."

The Governor thanked me politely for my statement, but I was not sure it had moved him. Next Mr. Young, underscoring what I had said, declared that despite his previous, publicly declared opposition to strikes, he felt compelled to "join the farmers' strike because their economic situation was so desperate. It was the only recourse to get the attention of the governmental authorities." At the conclusion of the meeting Governor Lehman promised to appeal to Secretary of Agriculture Wickard for appropriate action. Mr. Brill and others applauded my efforts and I was exhilarated at having performed my assignment to the farmers' satisfaction.

A day or two later Mr. Young flew to Washington and met with Secretary Wickard. The meeting went well and, as promised, the Secretary then set a date for a formal hearing by the Federal Milk Marketing Administration to determine the adjustment, if any, in milk prices. Our chances of success were looking better and better.

The Federal Milk Marketing Administration held the hearing in Brooklyn, New York. At first this struck me as an odd choice, but then I realized that the Administrator no doubt wanted a hearing room packed with consumers rather than farmers. By coincidence I met Fred Sexauer, President of the Dairymen's League, en route to the meeting. In the din of the subway he said, "Sam, when you finish at Columbia, we'd like you to come to work for us." I could not say thank you. In fact, I was so taken aback and angered—by my impression that he was trying to buy me off with a promise—that I just stared at him.

Our efforts finally bore fruit, in the form of an emergency increase in the price paid farmers for their milk. Fortunately the rains fell again that fall. With the milk strike over, Mr. Young made an unsuccessful run for Governor, and his son-in-law Everett Case became President of Colgate University. I returned to Columbia and the Newsboys' Home.

On Sunday, December 7, 1941, I was reading in the stacks of South Hall Library at Columbia. Around 4 P.M., just as I was about to leave for the Newsboys' Home, a student rushed in out of breath and shouted, "The Japs' Air Force and Navy are bombarding Pearl Harbor!" Although Takeuchi had warned me that Japan would go to war if no deal was struck with the United States, the attack on Pearl Harbor still came as a shock to me. I soon learned that the FBI had rounded up Takeuchi, and a dozen other Japanese students at the International House, for internment.

The Newsboys' Home was abuzz with talk of war. In earlier discussions, opinions were divided over whether the U.S. should go to war or not. Hitler's full employment and race purification programs appealed to many of these jobless Anglo-Saxon boys. All that was now forgotten as the boys buried their differences and united in patriotism. Suddenly they couldn't wait to fight the Japs and her allies, Germany and Italy. Unwittingly, by attacking

Pearl Harbor the Japanese had created job opportunities for millions of the nation's unemployed youth, including our newsboys. The ten-year U.S. depression was over, and a new era had begun in which everyone would be gainfully employed either in industry or the Armed Forces.

Immediately the newsboys rushed to enlist, too impatient to wait to be drafted. The number of homeless boys seeking shelter began to shrink. Daily the building was noticeably emptying out. (By war's end the building was almost empty, and the Newsboys' Home was boarded up and later demolished for an urban renewal project. Today, no plaque or other marker commemorates nearly half a century of service by the Children's Aid Society to the thousands of boys who were sustained at a critical time of their lives).

Having struggled to support myself these past ten years in the city, I was highly critical of our free enterprise system that had stranded millions in poverty and hardship. But that seemed of little importance now, as I concentrated on serving my country along with everyone else. I rushed to the nearby enlistment station with several of the newsboys, and stood in line anxiously awaiting my turn. My fears were confirmed when the enlisting officer glimpsed my right hand, immediately stamped me 4-F, and called out, "Next!"

If the army wouldn't take me, perhaps the Red Cross would, and I could still serve at the front with the troops. Impressed with my work at the Newsboys' Home, a Red Cross recruiter fancied me on the fast track to join the first overseas unit—until he got to the next question in his interview: "Do you have any physical defects?"

Reluctantly I answered, "Well, I hurt my hand some years ago, but it's no problem now. Anything I can't do with my right hand, I can do with my left."

He looked at it and shook his head. "You'll never pass the physical. You must be able to bear and use firearms if necessary."

"I'm a good shot," I replied with some exaggeration. "I had a lot of practice on the farm."

Being in a hurry, he said, "Forget the field service. We'll gladly put you on the Red Cross team in headquarters."

"No thanks," I sighed, and I excused myself.

In the next week or two, I finished the two-year residency requirement for my Ph.D. in Economics, postponed writing my dissertation, and made plans to go to Washington and join the war effort there. Sid returned to Canada, where all three of its services—Army, Navy, and Air Force—commissioned him to structure their respective recruitment procedures.

Less than a month after Pearl Harbor I went to Penn Station and boarded one of the hourly trains to Washington. I grabbed the last window seat in a jammed passenger car and for the next four hours stared out the window, transfixed by the passing sights as the train carried me toward a new life.

4

The War Years: Washington, D.C.

IN ALL HONESTY I WAS ANXIOUS about what lay ahead. Most of my work experience had little relationship to the operations of government. What did I have to offer that would justify a position of responsibility in the war effort?

I pondered this as the train sped southward. Today the entire route is part of the "urban corridor," but in those days, after Newark and New Brunswick, industrial and commercial buildings abruptly gave way to open fields of lush farmland. Soon New Jersey's famous Walker-Gordon dairy farms came into view. In those days prior to government inspection, Walker-Gordon, which produced, bottled, and delivered premium milk to consumers over a wide area, was the standard by which dairy farms were measured. Although the silos and barns were larger than any I had ever seen, I found my anxiety immediately calmed by the familiar sight. Perhaps I could find some similar continuity between my education and employment in New York City and what was to come in Washington.

I realized I *did* have one work experience that might be akin to Government control of Housing: namely the real estate operations of Sussman's Trinity Church properties. And my two college degrees should garner some respect. With this in mind, I determined to go first to the Rent Department of the Office of Price Administration.

When I walked out of Union Station in Washington I was awed by my first glimpse of the Capitol building. I had of course seen pictures of it, but nothing had prepared me for its actual size and grandeur. From Union Station I went directly to the OPA offices on the Mall, between the Capitol and the Washington Monument. The offices, housed in two-story buildings hastily erected during World War I and still referred to as "tempos," were anything but grand.

After waiting for a long time I was finally interviewed by Frank Manuel, head of Residential Rents. Within an hour, he hired me as a Grade P-2 Economist—salary $2100—and invited me to start right away. Thus I was immediately thrust into an intensive work schedule which I maintained throughout the war years. It would be several weeks before I could even think of seeing any of Washington's many sightseeing attractions.

My new job called into use some of the training in Economics that I had received at NYU and Columbia. I was assigned to draft position papers, which were to be incorporated into regulations that fixed rents for urban housing. After Pearl Harbor the Roosevelt Administration had quickly concluded that "inflation must be contained for the duration of the War to avoid the cost of Defense increasing out of control." Consumable products, agricultural and industrial materials, and housing were price-fixed, as were wages. Leon Henderson, the academic economist who headed the Agency, masterminded the fight against inflation and also possessed the dramatic flair to rally public support for it through a dynamic ad campaign.

Working conditions at OPA were barely tolerable. Only Manuel and his supervisors had private offices and secretaries. The rest of us worked in large rooms with our desks crowded together as closely as possible, sharing telephones and a secretarial pool serving us on a one-to-five ratio. The building was over-ventilated during the winter and absorbed heat and humidity during the extremely hot summer of 1942. Air conditioning was of course non-existent and fans were scarce.

Everyone had more work than could be accomplished in long, overtime days. The lights burned late into the night, even for those of us who came in early in the morning.

Despite these conditions a high morale sparked the staff. We all felt we were serving our country in an important way at a critical time. Almost everyone that I saw willingly accepted the extra work and longer hours, but to my shock there were a few "freeloaders" who whiled away the workday and left promptly at five. If these government employees existed even then, in a desperate war situation, imagine how many there are in the tranquility of peacetime, with union power virtually guaranteeing their jobs regardless of performance. (It is not only the taxpayers, but also the truly dedicated public servants, who are victims of these freeloaders.)

Quite to my surprise I found that I did not feel inadequate or strange amongst my fellow workers, in spite of my plain clothes, bucolic gait, and eager manner (which some of them took as "aggressive"). Many of my new colleagues were talented people from impressive backgrounds, destined for future fame. For example, my immediate desk-neighbor was Richard Neustadt, who went on to a distinguished teaching career at Harvard. Others at the Agency included John Kenneth Galbraith, who also enjoyed a prestigious career at Harvard; Lester Chandler of Princeton; Chester Bowles, who became Ambassador to India; Paul A. Porter, later of the Arnold Fortas and Porter Law Firm; Saul Linowitz, who became a prominent DC lawyer; and Jim Brownlee, Senior Partner at J. H. Whitney. At one time or another during my government tenure, I worked with all of these people.

Although I did not feel I was in over my head, I did approach my job a bit differently than my colleagues from middle and upper income families. They frequently engaged in office philosophizing, discussing the underlying complexities of the issues we were dealing with. I did not participate in these discussions, preferring instead to concentrate on the specific task in front of me. As a result, I got more work done. I felt more natural affinity with my supervisor Frank Manuel. Like me, he lacked polish and was a hard worker. We became friends, and stayed in contact even after I left the Agency. One incident in particular stands out in my mind and illuminates his personality.

Frank's effective management of rent control earned him the enmity of the Real Estate Owners, who decided to try and force him out. They found a champion for their cause in senior Congressman Howard Smith of Virginia, who was Chairman of the House Rules Committee. Smith hired a tough New York trial lawyer to conduct hearings. I attended one hearing when Manuel was scheduled to testify.

Frank was short, overweight, and clearly Jewish, hardly the type to compete with the forceful, well turned out executives at the hearings. The lawyer proceeded as though he had a criminal in the dock, and Frank was obviously nervous. "State your name!" the lawyer barked.

"Frank Manuel."

"Where were you born?"

"Brooklyn."

"Did you go to college, and if so where?"

"Harvard."

"And did you get a degree?"

Frank answered meekly yet with obvious pride, " Yes, an A.B. and a Ph.D."

"What was the topic of your dissertation?"

"Spanish History." Frank looked worried; he could see where this was headed.

The lawyer raised his voice contemptuously. "And after that, did you go to work, and if so, where?"

Frank's answer was almost inaudible. "The WPA—Works Progress Administration."

The lawyer quickly moved in for the kill. "By what right are YOU, a Spanish History major and a WPA job-holder, BY WHAT RIGHT do you control this billion dollar housing industry?" he demanded.

Frank shrunk in his chair. He appeared a beaten man. The lawyer leered triumphantly at him. After what seemed an endless silence, Frank finally came up for air, looked the lawyer in the eye, and asked in his plaintive, Yiddish accent, "Do you have to be a lion to be a lion tamer?"

The roomful of observers, most of them hostile rental property owners, exploded in laughter as Chairman Smith futilely banged his gavel until he could be heard. He announced the hearing adjourned, and Frank survived the inquest.

Housing in the District of Columbia, and across the Potomac in Alexandria, was wholly inadequate for the flood of new government employees. Emergency housing, quickly thrown together on vacant lots everywhere, helped with the shortfall, and private home owners, renting out space in basements and attics, provided the rest. Also, there was widespread doubling up. The roof over *my* head was in a basement which I shared with a young Harvard economist, Gerald Alter. We had one room and a bath, in all not more than 12 feet square. Ventilation was supplied by a single small window. That summer I returned from sweating all day at the office to a night of tossing in wet sheets. Still, it mattered little. I was so exhausted I slept anyway. My room was merely a place to sleep, shower, and change clothes.

When I got to Washington I was surprised to find that OPA, along with other government agencies, had racially segregated toilets and cafeterias. The main dining room at OPA was marked "For Whites Only" and Negroes, who worked as messengers, file clerks, and secretaries, were relegated to a back room off the kitchen to take their meals. I did not have any friends amongst them; nevertheless, I personally found this situation repugnant.

I was further surprised when an ad hoc group of white employees asked me to be their spokesman in an effort to eradicate this policy. I suspected that Sylvia Prager, an attractive Jewish girl from Brooklyn with whom I had become friendly, had spread the word of my role in the New York Milk Strike. I immediately accepted, before I gave any thought to what my argument should be. Mindful of the weight of the "Jim Crow" tradition, institutionalized since Colonial times, I wondered what case could now be made to eliminate it in government agencies. If I got into the issue of equality, we would no doubt engender forceful opposition from hardnosed advocates of the racial status quo, and in all likelihood we would fail. It was, after all, another twenty years before Congress passed a Civil Rights Bill.

It was clear that the war gave us a unique opportunity. Already Negro support units were part of the Armed Forces. (Later in the conflict the all-Negro "Red Ball Express" would provide a crucial, 1500-mile truck supply link between the Persian Gulf and a Russian terminal near the Caspian, enabling the Soviet armies to turn back the German assault and change the momentum of the war). In meetings with OPA officials I dramatized the contribution to the war effort Negroes would make, and the risks they would take, and contrasted that with the unconscionable discrimination their kinfolk faced in our own agency.

Perhaps because they wanted to avoid the publicity that an extended protest would attract, the Agency quickly agreed to make the changes. The dining room and restrooms were integrated, with a minimum of grumbling and no overt hostility from those employees with racist leanings. This first break in "Jim Crow" created a domino effect, and soon other agencies followed suit throughout the Government.

With the success of this initial collective action, leaders of the protest group, including Sylvia, began to unionize federal employees. These leaders, largely from eastern universities, were, in fact, pursuing ideological goals, voicing much of the communist rhetoric I had heard at NYU. Here we parted company. Although I had helped unionize the farmers of upstate New York in their battle against the private milk companies, this was a very different situation, and I made my objections known. I felt that government employees, both management and workers like us, were all civil servants, answerable only to the people. Establishing an adversarial relationship between managers and their employees did not, I believed, serve the public interest. For taking this position I was openly accused of surrendering to the Bourbons of Society and Capitalism. When I look now at the bloated, arrogant, and widely despised bureaucracy we call our government, I feel vindicated by History.

In my job I had the good fortune of conducting field studies in Pittsburgh, Norfolk and Denver. Due to the urgency of the war, air travel was encouraged. Most employees declined that invitation. Others of us, more adventurous or perhaps foolhardy, preferred it, although we were never so confident as to resist the purchase of flight insurance, which was available at all airports. My seat companions were likely to be middle class professionals like myself.

In those days airports, and the sky itself, were uncluttered by traffic. On my trips the most used carrier was a twin-prop DC-3, with a seating capacity under thirty. At 130 miles per hour, flying time from Washington to Denver was longer than the present flying time from Washington to Sidney, Australia. On my first flight, a bird's eye view of landscapes and cities new to me whetted my appetite for travel, and thereafter, unlike some business travelers, I always enjoyed my government and business trips across country and throughout the world.

Near the end of the year I accepted a position as Head of the Fresh and Frozen Fish Section at War Foods Administration. This was a promotion of several notches over my position at OPA, in terms of both money and authority. Moreover, instead of the hardship conditions I'd endured at OPA, I now had a personal secretary and private office at the Department of Agriculture. There I inherited a small staff and reported to a fine gentleman, Maurice Rattray, a major west coast exporter of salmon who was donating his expertise to the government for one dollar a year. Rattray did not hesitate to give me maximum authority to do my job, which primarily consisted of drawing up regulations for the nation's commercial fishing industry. The challenge I faced was how to encourage the supply of fish without unduly inflating prices.

My first crisis was a strike by fishermen in the Boston-Gloucester area of Massachusetts. I flew to Boston to meet with their union leader, Pat McCue. Remembering the Milk Strike, I sought to understand his side of the issue. With a demeaner of humility and sympathy, I related to Mr. McCue my efforts on behalf of the farmers, which immediately established a good rapport between us. He understood he was on thin ice, leading the strike at a time when the nation was in all-out war. I stressed to him that Washington was adamant in its fight against inflation, but if we could agree upon a modest price increase, I would support it as justified in order to increase supply. At the end of the third day we reached such an agreement, and it was accepted in Washington.

I had only been at War Foods for six months when I received a phone call from the Executive Office of the President, Bureau of the Budget. Apparently W. W. Cooper, an old classmate of mine at Columbia who had recently joined the Bureau, had suggested to the Assistant Director, Dr. Stuart Rice, that he interview me as a possible recruit. I remembered Cooper right away, and was flattered that he had remembered me.

Although we had never had the time to become close friends at Columbia, Bill Cooper and I had liked each other from the start. We had a good deal in common. We were both rough-hewn, from working class backgrounds, and highly motivated to succeed. Both of us had tended to be outspoken in class, and both of us were pugilists, although my modest feats growing up paled next to Bill's.

Cooper had grown up in Chicago with his disabled father, a younger brother and sister, and his mother, who was the family's sole breadwinner throughout most of his youth. He did not attend high school, going directly into manual labor to help support the family. At seventeen, he became a professional lightweight boxer, supplementing his regular income by fighting for as little as ten dollars and (when lucky) as much as a hundred dollars per match.

One day in his early twenties, as he hitchhiked from a golf course where he caddied, he was offered a ride by Eric L. Kohler, then professor of accounting at Northwestern University. Noticing the volume of Shakespeare under Cooper's arm, Kohler asked, "Where do you attend College?" Cooper replied that he was not attending college; that he had just caddied at the nearby golf course. Kohler persisted. "So why are you reading Shakespeare?" Bill replied, "Shakespeare seems to be of interest to the college kids waiting in line to caddy. I felt left out because I didn't know what they were talking about, so I thought I better read this Shakespeare and find out why he's so great."

"Would you be interested in going to college?" Kohler asked.

"It's out of the question," said Bill. "I have to support my family."

Then Kohler asked, "If you could make the same amount of money you are now, *and* go to college, would you be willing to try?"

"I'd like nothing better, but I haven't even gone to high school," Bill replied.

Kohler offered him, then and there, a job taking care of his yard in suburban Winetka, and promised to assist him in enrolling at the University of Chicago, assuring him that he did not need a high school diploma to be admitted.

With his pugnacious demeanor and cauliflower ear, Bill hardly looked the college type. When he enrolled in college he had no more idea than I'd had what courses to choose. Fortunately he had Kohler to direct him. According to Bill, Kohler also taught him how to study. (I was a bit jealous when I heard this—I'd had to learn by trial and error).

In the first year, Cooper barely managed to survive academically. His low performance level was tolerated by the university under its program of open enrollment. Chicago's new President, Robert Maynard Hutchins, had publicly excoriated the inadequacy of high school instruction, and defiantly proclaimed that, "The University of Chicago will accept deserving students with or without a high school education." Cooper proved to be one of Hutchins' success stories, graduating Phi Beta Kappa.

Following a two-year stint working under Kohler for the Tennessee Valley Authority, Cooper applied for a PhD fellowship at Columbia, which had one of the most celebrated faculties in the country. The fellowship, one of only two available, was granted, entitling Bill to free tuition and housing and a cash stipend of $1,000 per year. It also made him a very prominent student on campus, and I felt privileged to be one of his friends, however casual.

Cooper's boxing feats furthered distinguished him in the eyes of his fellow students. One day, as he was working out at the Columbia Gym, the college boxing coach cornered him and lamented, "Bill, I've got a kid who's a great prospect. I can teach him to keep his left up, but I can't learn him. Would you go a round or two with him?"

Bill agreed and climbed into the ring with him. The young man, much larger than Bill, appeared overconfident as he squared off with his left hand down, ignoring his coach's shouted admonitions to "KEEP YOUR LEFT HAND UP!" Finally Bill feigned a left jab and then crossed over his young opponent's lowered left with a right hand that sent him sprawling across the canvas. As Bill climbed down out of the ring, the coach smiled and said, "Thanks Bill. You learned him!"

Upon learning that Cooper and I might be reunited at the Bureau of the Budget, I immediately turned my attention to the history and role of the Bureau, in order to prepare myself for the interview with Rice.

The Bureau of the Budget, within the Executive Office of the President, was organized by President Roosevelt in 1939, under the Budget and Accounting Act that had been signed into law by President Harding in 1921. In general terms, the Bureau would prepare a single Annual Budget for the Government, which the President would submit to Congress. Reporting only to the President, the Director would coordinate the various functions of civilian and military agencies and thus eliminate duplication and conflicts among them. The Bureau would also review legislation proposed by agencies and by Congress and recommend to the President whether to accept it, reject it, or amend it.

Unlike OPA and the War Foods Administration, which were newly staffed to perform wartime functions, the Bureau had seasoned professional staff. Still, this staff was too small to cope with the additional burden of a centrally-managed economy. Each new recruit was expected to carry out his assignment under a broad policy directive, with significant decision-making responsibility. The recruits were all equal, each reporting only to one of several

Assistant Directors, who in turn reported to the Director, who reported directly to President Roosevelt.

I must contrast the simplicity and efficiency of this structure with the bloated White House bureaucracy that came into being after World War II. The President's Chief of Staff (a post created after the war) now oversees twelve hundred assistants to the President, most appointed to their prestigious positions as a reward for their role in the President's election campaign. Cabinet officers and Agency heads must filter their initiatives through various "Special Assistants" to the President, whose appointments do not require Senate confirmation. All policies and actions of the federal apparatus, in both Republican and Democratic administrations, are directed by this cadre of twelve hundred, whose interest is not the national interest but the President's popularity. (In spite of their efforts, of nine post-war Presidents, only four were reelected.)

The magnificent old State Office Building, next to the White House, elegantly housed the Bureau of the Budget as well as the State Department. Dr. Rice, a distinguished gray-haired gentleman in his fifties and a Bureau veteran, received me in his office. I was impressed that he made no inquiry into my political affiliation or preference. Instead he focused on my experience within OPA and War Foods, and also on my studies at NYU and Columbia. Satisfied that I had the necessary training and experience in cost/price relationships, Dr. Rice hired me on the spot. I shared a large office with another staff member, and the two of us shared a secretary, who had her own desk in an adjoining room. Working conditions were ideal.

Dr. Rice defined my role in the most general terms. It was my job to resolve intragovernmental conflicts over prices, which meant dealing frequently with OPA and with War Foods Administration, some of whose products were subsidized by the government through the Reconstruction Finance Corporation. Here are two examples of disputes in which I became involved.

The first involved the sugar cane industry. The production of sugar cane was programmed by WFA and its costs subsidized by the RFC. The consumer price of sugar was controlled by OPA. A conflict resulted when WFA wanted increased production, but OPA refused to increase prices and RFC would not increase subsidies. Naturally the growers and refiners balked. I was assigned to resolve this conflict.

First I convened a week-long series of fact-finding meetings in the New Orleans area. I chaired these meetings, at which the sugar cane growers and refiners stated their case. Facts, figures, and opinions were recorded in an official report, which I carefully reviewed over the next week. I concluded that in this instance the growers had not substantiated a case of undue hardship, and that production could be increased by a modest raise in RFC subsidies. Sugar prices were not raised, in spite of the public demands of Louisiana's powerful congressmen. Nor did these legislators try to go over our heads to the President. In those days, the Bureau's decision was final. Also in strong contrast to the way politics is conducted today, I, as point-man for the Bureau, was not approached by any lobbyists!

The second example occurred in 1944, and involved the price of crude oil. Secretary of the Interior Harold Ickes decided that the current price ceiling should be lifted from fifty cents per barrel at the well head, to one dollar. Sumner Pike, Administrator of the Fuels Division at OPA, opposed the increase as unnecessary and inflationary. He challenged Ickes' claim that the producers needed a price increase as relief from the hardship of escalating costs.

This conflict was assigned to me. I had no prior knowledge or experience with the oil industry, so I approached the problem, one might say, in objective ignorance, and carefully listened to the conflicting arguments. Ickes sent his deputy, Abe Fortas, to persuade me of his position. Pike, also prestigous, made his position clear in direct meetings with me.

I trusted Pike's judgment on this one. It was clear to me that Ickes, who was also involved in Roosevelt's campaign for re-election, was under political pressure from the oil industry, and that in sending Fortas to see me he was trying to throw some of this pressure onto me. I had no intention of caving in; yet I understood the difficult position Ickes was in.

My official determination was that we had insufficient data to decide this conflict, and I arranged for a survey of the oil producers' costs and revenues. During this survey, crude prices would remain unchanged.

As I suspected, the survey objectively confirmed Pike's position that the oil industry was not suffering any hardship at current prices, and that there was no substantive reason why production should be threatened. By this time the election was over. The political heat from Ickes subsided, and the producers continued to endure their alleged hardship, at least till War's end. I doubt Ickes ever mentioned to Roosevelt this idea of raising crude prices. If he had, the President's response, I'm convinced, would have been, "Take it up with the Bureau!" Again, it's noteworthy that the oil lobbyists never approached me, even though they knew the survey was being conducted under my aegis.

My colleagues at the Bureau were truly experts in their respective areas, and I felt privileged that they shared with me their knowledge and original thinking. After the war, as with OPA, many of them went on to pursue distinguished careers. To name just a couple: Elmer Staats became Controller General of the General Accounting Office, and Dr. Edward Deming, whose office was next to mine, was later honored by the Japanese government for utilizing his statistical talents to analyze and reform their Industry.

When I was hired by the Bureau, my lifestyle took a sudden turn for the better. Although the government had no authority to requisition housing for its civilian employees, landlords were very impressed with anyone employed by the Office of the President, whether it was in the Bureau of the Budget or within the White House itself. I left my dingy basement quarters when Cooper and I found an apartment on the second floor of a four-story building on Connecticut Avenue, near the Shoreham and Wardman Park Hotels. With two bedrooms, a dining room, living room, kitchen and porch, this represented "high living" to me. Shortly after we settled in, Harry Oshima, a classmate from Columbia, paid us a call. He had just been employed by the War Department, who utilized his familiarity with Japan's Zaibatsu (Harry's thesis topic at Columbia) by assigning him to Japanese Strategy. Harry's manner—restrained, polite, meticulous—and his taste in food were characteristically Japanese, but in allegiance he was 100% American. He was elated with this opportunity to serve in Washington, but much more subdued when he admitted to us, "I have one problem. I can't find a landlord to rent me a place to live. I guess they don't like my Japanese appearance." Hearing that, Cooper and I warmly invited him to share our apartment.

Although Hawaiian-born Japanese such as Harry were not "relocated" during World War II, west coast residents of Japanese origin (including many "nisei"—second generation immigrants with full American citizenship) were rounded up and interned for the duration of the war, in camps scattered throughout the West. This action was taken by the U.S. Army in response to the hysteria engendered in large part by the Hearst publishing empire. (At the end of the war many Japanese-Americans returned home to find their property was now in the hands of Caucasian-Americans, an outrage inadequately rectified by later compensation). Cooper and I soon discovered that Harry published a newspaper called "The Nisei Weekender," with distribution to the relocation camps. Behind his slight frame and thick glasses (poor eyesight had kept him out of the Army), Harry was a fighter, dedicated to eradicating the fear and prejudice directed against his people.

Shortly after Oshima joined us, he asked if he could entertain some of his brethren who would be passing through Washington. Of course we agreed. In preparation for his visitors, Oshima bought whiskey, beer, and packages of native Japanese foods. Aside from the fresh fish, most of the food was strange to me. Harry's dried baby shrimp I jokingly referred to as "dry toenails." In actuality Cooper and I were looking forward to the event with curiosity and a bit of excitement.

That weekend some forty Japanese-American troops arrived at our apartment, causing quite a stir on Connecticut Avenue. They probably would have been attacked had they not been in uniform. Cooper and I spent the evening talking with them. When we asked one of them how they happened to be in the army, he replied, "We are born Americans, but they would not draft us. So we volunteered. We have our own nisei unit, the 100th Infantry Battalion." When I asked where their families were, the reply was invariably, "Back at the camp."

"In view of the shameful treatment of your people," I would ask, "Why did you enlist?"

The answer was always the same: "We want to prove that you Caucasian-Americans have us all wrong."

The nisei were heavy drinkers, but avoided drunken behavior. Toward the end of the evening they asked, "Could we spend the night here? We will be very comfortable on the floor. We can use our knapsacks as pillows."

"Of course" we replied.

"What time do you get up?" they asked.

"About six." The next morning we awoke at six to find our apartment spotless. All the trash had been taken out and there was no evidence of the night before. All that remained was a pile of "thank you" notes. I felt as though we should have thanked *them*.

Over the course of the next few weeks one group of forty nisei soldiers was followed by another. I remember one young man who had volunteered for espionage duty in the Philippines—a behind-the-lines assignment. He was fully aware that if he were caught by either the Japanese or the Filipinos, he would be tortured and put to death. I've often wondered what happened to him.

A year later some of the wounded returned to be treated at nearby Walter Reed Army Hospital. One of these was a Colonel Inouye, who came to our parties on crutches, escorted by a beautiful nisei girl. He later returned to battle and was highly decorated, losing an arm in the process. Now, of course, Colonel Inouye is better known as Hawaii's senior Senator.

Our Connecticut Avenue apartment was also graced by visits from coeds at Smith, Vassar, and Wellesley, enroute through Washington to join the OSS (Office of Strategic Services—predecessor to the CIA) for overseas duty. I suspect that our Columbia backgrounds and Bureau employment were part of our appeal, but whatever the reason, our credentials as hosts appeared highly rated, and our apartment became a pipeline for these girls. One wave of visitors would report to the next and keep them coming. In spite of our busy schedules, Cooper and I found time to entertain them on Saturday nights. Oshima never participated in these parties, as he had a steady girlfriend named Chiyea—a real hotspur, who looked Japanese but was totally American in her vivacious personal style. They made an odd couple but the relationship worked.

No lasting relationship was possible, or sought, with any of the coeds who streamed through our apartment. An evening together was little more than a release of tension—a brief respite from the stresses, magnified in wartime, of everyday life. In many cases all the girls really wanted was the same thing G.I.'s did—a last night to remember before going off to war—and I was happy to oblige them. Anyway, other than an hour or two of tennis a week, these passionate encounters were my only form of exercise!

During the week my roommates and I, totally preoccupied with our own programs, rarely saw each other. I was an early riser, but Harry always beat me to the shower. Cooper, as a night worker, slept as late as he could. Harry put in fourteen to sixteen hours at the office, seven days a week. Cooper and I put in sixteen to eighteen hours daily, but that included additional studies. Cooper concentrated on higher mathematics, while I enrolled at Georgetown Law School in the evenings.

Most of the evening students at Georgetown Law were aides to members of Congress, or other government employees. All in all, it was an exceptionally mature group of law students, with far more real world experience than one would normally encounter.

With my heavy workload at the Bureau, I found I needed to

adjust my study habits. Georgetown Law used the case method in class. When called upon by the professor, the student was expected to recite a case, including the central issue, the parties involved, the essentials of the complaint, the defense, counter claims (if any), the finding of facts, and the decision of the court. Since each case was chosen to illustrate a principle of law, a student's recitation revealed his understanding of the case, the principles involved, and its broader implications.

Since speed reading courses had not yet been invented, I invented my own, flashing through the text and underlining the essentials. (I always bought new books, to avoid the notations made by prior students). Rather than outlining and briefing the case in my notebook, a time-consuming process relied upon by most students, I developed a capacity to commit to memory the important elements of the case. This method cut my preparation time considerably. Relying on my underlinings, I was always ready to recite a case in class. I also developed the capacity to hear the recitals of other students and at the same time review the next case. (Fortunately the professors followed the same order as our law books). Most of my law studies consisted of work done in class.

Enrolling in September 1943, I passed the bar exam in December of 1945, taking two days off from the office to do it. After the last exam I attended a Christmas party at the Bureau. Dr. Rice himself greeted me at the door and commented on my bloodshot eyes. There was a hint in his voice that I had been misbehaving and indulging in alcohol. To clear myself I blurted out, "I have just completed two days of taking the bar exam."

Dr. Rice was astonished. Neither he nor anyone else in the Bureau had had any idea that I was going to Law School. He replied, "I don't see how you could've done it! Our records show you carrying the heaviest workload in your section, and we were thinking of lightening up on you." I assured him that that was not necessary.

Just prior to my graduation in May, Father Lucey, the Rector of the Law School, called me into his office. As I listened in bewilderment he said sternly, "I see you are listed to graduate. I am opposed to it."

"But sir," I pleaded. "My grade average is among the highest in the class. Moreover, I've already passed the bar exam!"

"I know *that*," he retorted angrily, "but *no* one has gone through *this* school at night in three years! Students, working by day, take at least four years, often five or six to graduate. But that is not so important to me as the fact that you have contributed *nothing* to the school itself. You should have been on the Law Review."

Like Dr. Rice, Father Lucey had no inkling of the double life I'd been leading. I had not wanted sympathy or special treatment from either of them. Now I saw little choice but to tell him. "Father Lucey, I am a Senior Economist in the Bureau of the Budget, carrying a heavy program at the office."

Father Lucey was as surprised as Dr. Rice had been, but his reaction was more muted. The only remaining issue seemed to be my contributing to the Law Journal. "I would have been honored to have been on the Law Review," I assured him, "and, hopefully, to have written the lead article."

Father Lucey softened and said. "Well, you still can. Would you *do* it?" After I promised that I would, he said, "Well, I'll take your promise. Give us an article worthy of a lead within ten years."

True to this promise, several years later I submitted an article on the Iranian Oil Nationalization Case before the World Court. It was printed as the lead article in the Georgetown Law Journal.

My most cherished memories of these years were the intellectual sessions with Oshima and Bill. For a while we were comparably well-grounded in economics and political science, and our dialogue was enriched by the diversity of our backgrounds. We also attracted friends to these give-and-take discussions.

Towards the end of the war, we often debated one of the pressing issues of the day: What should we do about Post-War Germany? Do we convert Germany to an agrarian society, as Secretary of the Treasury Henry Morganthau was advocating? As one of the leaders of the Jewish-American community, his was a powerful voice. His argument that the Allies should remove Germany's industrial capacity for the sake of world peace had a great deal of appeal, especially to Holocaust survivors.

Also, many Americans recognized that the Soviets had taken on the lion's share in destroying the German Army, losing much of its own industrial capacity in the process. They were sensitive to Russia's need to be compensated, which could be accomplished by dismantling German plants and shipping them to the Soviet Union. The Russians were already dismantling them in East Germany, where they had total control. As events unfolded, and Stalin's policies revealed themselves as antagonistic to America and Western Europe, the Morganthau plan fell out of public favor. West Germany's industrial capacity was now viewed as probably necessary to secure Europe.

The trio of Cooper, Oshima, and Nakasian disassembled in 1946. Shortly after the end of the war, Harry and I stood in the pouring rain along with hundreds of thousands of Washingtonians, to pay our respects to the 442nd Division, which included the 100th Infantry Battalion. The Battalion had been decimated three times as it fought its way through North Africa, up the boot of Italy, and north to the final battles in Germany. As the Division marched up Pennsylvania Avenue to the White House to be decorated by President Truman, I applauded the survivors and wept for those brave young nisei who had given their lives to prove their patriotism.

From Washington, Harry went home to Hawaii, where he became head of the Economics Department at the University of Hawaii. Years later, on my first trip to the Pacific, I stopped off in Hawaii. Harry took me sightseeing, and reserved for last a visit to Punchbowl National Cemetery, situated dramatically in the mouth of an extinct volcano. There he waved his hand in a semicircle and said, "Many of our friends are out there."

Yes, the nisei had proven conclusively that the Caucasians were wrong. Japanese-Americans hold a place of honor in the mosaic of ethnic America, and since the war I think the American system has been a powerful force in the conversion of Japanese culture, from its ancient racist, militaristic, feudal traditions to a society based more on humanitarian and democratic values.

Immediately following the war Cooper got married. Coincidentally, his bride Ruth had been employed by the War Relocation Authority, the government agency in charge of the Japanese internment camps. The two of them moved to Chicago, where Cooper

joined his Alma Mater, the University of Chicago, as Associate Professor. He had come a long way from his days as a laborer and prizefighter. Now his pugnacity was tinged with a dash of sauvity and gentleness, but he could be as tough as ever when the occasion warranted, as one story illustrates.

The University was located on the south side of Chicago, in the middle of a deteriorating neighborhood, and gangs of young toughs would occasionally come on campus and attack the students and professors as they crossed the lawn from one building to another. Returning home from the library one evening, Bill came upon three toughs whaling away at a young student they had knocked to the ground. Without hesitation he stepped in, shouting for them to stop, whereupon the three thugs stopped beating the boy and charged Bill. Bang...Bang...Bang! The toughs were sent sprawling. The young student-victim looked up from his prone position and exclaimed in amazement, "Why, *Professor Cooper*!" The student, son of a Dean, spread Bill's legend throughout the campus.

During the summer of 1946, after Bill and Harry left Washington and I had completed law school, I made several weekend visits to go sailing with Carol and Fred Diemer on Long Island, as I had done when living at the Newsboys' Home. On the first of these visits they introduced me to a Bayside neighbor of theirs, Patricia Dohrenwend. Pat was an attractive, intelligent, and fun gal, and from then on she was my constant companion whenever I visited.

After the whirlwind of the war years, the prospect of a family life was appealing. The only time I had ever felt a part of a family was during those few short years at the Whites, and that seemed a long time ago. My own family had fragmented upon arrival in this country, and in 1945 my sister Hannah, whom I had not seen since my New York days, had died following a recurrence of tuberculosis in her remaining lung.

At the funeral I learned that her marriage had not been a happy one, and that before her death she had given up her daughter for adoption—just as our own mother had done with us. (I felt relieved when I heard my niece had been adopted by the stable, middle-class family of one of Hannah's beauty salon customers.) Hannah's husband had thrown out as trash the few family heirlooms that she cherished. All that remained were my mother's wedding ring and a family photograph taken in Samsun, both of which I still have. Probably all of this was in the back of my mind when at the end of the summer I proposed marriage to Pat Dowrenwend, and she accepted.

Marrying Pat seemed complex beyond belief, my first marriage having been so ridiculously simple. Pat's mother, a graduate of Barnard, and her father, a mid-level executive at Shell Oil, were both devout Catholics, and wanted a Catholic wedding. Obviously, two obstacles had to be overcome: my Protestantism, and my prior marriage and divorce, which I had revealed to Pat during our courtship.

After the Alcazar, I had made several attempts to find Evelyn, all to no avail. In the process it became clear to me that in spite of my high moral principles, my marriage had been a mistake. Yet without Evelyn, I could not seek a divorce—or so I thought. Around that time I mentioned my concern to Mr. Godwin, G.V.'s lawyer, who told me about New York's "Enoch Arden" law, under which the disappearance of a spouse for seven years is a presumption of death, and entitles the petitioning spouse to dissolve the marriage without divorce proceedings. Years later Mr. Godwin, an affidavit in hand of seven years absence, made a single appearance before the Clerk of the Court and obtained my divorce decree.

My divorce was an unalterable fact; nor did I have any intention of converting to Catholicism. How could I turn my back on the church of Comstock and Fosdick? This created an impasse, until finally a compromise was agreed upon. Pat's much-loved and recently retired family priest would perform a Catholic ceremony at a nearby country-club-style restaurant. Permission was granted by the church and in late 1946 we had a beautiful wedding, with her many and my few relatives attending.

Following a week's honeymoon in Quebec, we settled in a new apartment I acquired on 16th Street in Washington. Patricia took a job as receptionist at the law firm of O. Max Truitt, son-in-law of Alben Barclay, Senate Majority Leader. Although she seemed to enjoy her contact with the firm's big name clientele, she was clearly ill-at-ease with my high-powered colleagues at the Bureau. An only child, Pat also missed her parents, especially her mother, and made it known that she would be much happier in New York.

I myself had never regarded government as a career, and was open to the move. New York was headquarters for Big Business, and its activities held greater appeal for me. Moreover, the New York of 1947 remained much as I remembered it from the thirties and early forties: a delightful place to live with all the highest cultural and intellectual opportunities. And so, having been admitted to the bar in the District of Columbia, I decided to take the New York bar exam, in preparation for private practice in the city.

5

A Lawyer in New York

TO PRACTICE LAW IN NEW YORK, I faced a daunting obstacle: New York's policy of limiting the entry of new lawyers. The tough bar examinations were designed to flunk two-thirds of the applicants, and those who passed were further screened for "character fitness."

The New York Bar was given in two parts, procedural and substantive. I felt I had a good chance to pass the substantive section without additional preparation, since in content it should be comparable to the D.C. exam. However, the procedural differences between New York and D.C. laws were *very* major. I thought that if I could pass half of the exam, and make a trial run at the procedural part, I would be making some progress. It worked out that way: I passed the one and failed the other.

In preparation for repeating the procedural, I enrolled in the "cram course," and took a room at the St. George Hotel in Brooklyn. For one week I closeted myself in that room, emerging only for meals, a daily one-hour walk, and the cram-course lectures. All my energy went into memorizing the voluminous code of civil procedure. This exam was a memory test. Lawyers with poor memories were doomed to fail. My memory was good enough, and I passed.

My final obstacle was the screening for "character fitness". First I had to respond to a massive questionnaire, listing the names of my parents and close relatives, and their addresses; all the places and people I had lived with since birth, with two references for each residence; all the schools I had attended and their addresses, from elementary school through college; all the places I had been employed, their addresses, and the names of my employers, providing two witnesses for each job; any instances in which I was ever under police arrest, and the charges—including misdemeaners; and so on.

Normal applicants had little trouble with the questionnaire, but for me it was a different story. I could not remember anything prior to Brace Farm School, and my memory was, to say the least, fuzzy regarding the many rooming houses I slept in during the thirties. It would have been impossible for me to track down the persons who shared these rooming houses with me, when I couldn't even remember their names. The addresses were suspect ones for aspiring lawyers. I couldn't remember all the numerous menial jobs I had held, and I was sure many of the places where I had worked were no longer in business, or had moved. How could I possibly find the owners, or persons who knew me on-the-job and could vouch for my presence?

Of course I had to list my arrest during the prostitution raid at the Alcazar. I worried that this event alone could be fatal. Felons were automatically denied admission to the bar. Even an arrest, though not followed by conviction, might be taken as evidence of my unfitness to practice law. Or it might arouse suspicion that perhaps there were other incidents, not reported.

Having completed the appropriate documents with more blanks than information, I appeared personally before each of the three lawyers on the Fitness Committee. My application obviously indicated a unique story that signaled "danger" to the committee. I could have been a gangster or a thief; there was no way to absolutely prove my innocence. Could I satisfy these lawyers with my oral explanation? I was seriously in doubt that I could.

The first two interviews followed the same scenario. As I told the extraordinary saga of my early life, the lawyer's skepticism turned into fascination, and by the end he was not only sympathetic but encouraging. America loves an underdog, and once I convinced the lawyers of my sincerity, they were more than willing to help. By the time I met the last examiner in his Staten Island office, I had honed my explanation till it was even more coherent and convincing. He seemed to accept it and I relaxed a bit. Then this lawyer decided to inquire into my knowledge of constitutional law, asking, "Since the Constitution is framed as prohibitions against the use of federal power, and since it contains only specific grants of power to the federal government, wherein are the residual powers of governance?"

My reply, without hesitation, was, "In the states, or the people."

The expression on his face told me that he did not accept my answer as correct. Apparently he believed the federal government had the residual powers. "My God," I thought to myself, "I can't argue with the man and prove him wrong. He just might turn hostile and not approve me fit." Being right, I sensed, is of limited virtue if it is fatal. With this in mind, I hastened to add, "Of course, federal jurisdiction has been greatly expanded in recent years through the commerce clause and the spending power." This deflected the disagreement over residual powers and turned our discussion into one of philosophy about government. I was greatly relieved when he assured me of his support. Formal admission to the Bar followed soon after.

I now turned my thoughts seriously to the practice of law. It was early 1947 and the demand for lawyers was a small fraction of what it is today. I chose not to make the rounds of law firms, where I would be paid at the the bottom of the salary range, and be subordinate to the tenured partners.

I found myself attracted to an ad in the Wall Street Journal. An export firm with an Armenian name—Dadourian Corporation—was soliciting a lawyer. At age 32, I had had virtually no contact with Armenians, and my curiosity was aroused. I contacted the firm in New York and they immediately offered me the job at a salary of $10,000 per year, an increase of $2500 over my Bureau salary. At the time, in both government and private industry, this was top compensation, just below that of the Chief Executive Officer. With six months accumulated vacation time, I would be collecting $17,500 in my first year. For the first time

I could build up savings! In the past I had always avoided debt, but savings under wartime taxation was virtually impossible.

I reported to Dr. Rice my intention to resign and go into practice. He was distraught, and argued that I was foregoing a brilliant government career. "Moreover," he warned, "you are taking the risk that this adventure as a lawyer in New York might prove disappointing." After a pause, he graciously suggested that, rather than resign, I take a leave of absence, at least for the period of my accumulated leave. "That will leave open the option of returning to the Bureau," an option he fervently hoped I would exercise. With nothing to lose, I accepted his offer, and agreed to let him know one way or the other when the six months was up.

The Dadourian Corporation was founded and managed by two Armenian immigrants. Aggressive and imaginative, they had succeeded in carving out a special niche for the company: business too small for larger companies but large enough to produce handsome returns. In addition to the firm's legal matters, my duties included negotiating contracts overseas. Although fascinated by the prospect of working abroad, one early experience I had with a foreign businessman showed me that I had a lot to learn.

One day a Saudi Arabian came to the office to negotiate the purchase of a substantial quantity of goods. I was present in order to prepare the contract. After the deal had been struck, the Arab said to the one of the partners, "You made a big profit on this deal."

The partner shrugged. "When I pay my taxes there will be very little profit."

"I don't understand why you, as an Armenian, would pay income taxes," the Saudi retorted.

"All Americans pay income taxes," replied the partner.

Incredulous, the Arab rejected this statement outright, in effect calling Dadourian a liar. An argument ensued, which reached its climax when the Saudi shouted, "Why do you pay taxes? Don't you keep your *own* books!?" Later the partner explained, a bit enviously, that it was a common practice for businesses in foreign countries to keep three sets of books: one for the banks, one for the government, and an accurate one for themselves.

In the summer of 1947 the firm asked me to make a trip to Venezuela, and invited me to take Patricia along. I happily accepted. It would be the first opportunity for either of us to visit a foreign country and to meet its people—an adventure I had long looked forward to.

We disembarked from our Grace Company luxury liner at Laguira, the seaport closest to Caracas. The trip from the port to the city was by taxi, via a treacherous two-lane road that wound up and over a steep mountain. Along the way we saw thousands of crosses, marking the locations where cars and trucks had gone off the cliffs, usually as a result of collisions on the narrow hairpin turns. Finally, after several harrowing hours, we arrived at the beautiful tropical city of Caracas, situated on a mile-high plateau. (A decade later, Venezuela used its oil exports to tunnel through the mountain, and installed a magnificent four-lane highway from the seashore to Caracas, cutting the travel time to twenty minutes and eliminating countless casualties on the mountain highway).

As a curious visitor, I noticed that much of Caracas was newly built by European immigrants. While Spanish was the official language, Spaniards were a minority. Most of the immigrants were Germans, Italians, English, or Irish. The native Indian population occupied slum housing in the Old City. Notably absent were Negroes, since Caracas did not have a slave tradition.

Reflecting the European influence, Venezuela did attempt democratic rule. However, periodically the military established dictatorships by coup. The European immigrants did not care who governed their adopted country so long as they preserved its convenience for accumulating wealth. And unlike Americans, successful Venezuelans exported their surplus wealth to their countries of origin.

For the first time I observed open corruption in the private sector as well as by public officials. In government, this was a clearly a way of life, permeating all levels down to clerk. I found that it took a gratuity to a clerk to move a document from the incoming box to the outgoing. Native Indians were outside the money-making loop.

As a result, this country, bountifully endowed with oil and other mineral resources, is always in serious international debt. Moreover, most of its native population remains uneducated and condemned to a life of bare subsistence.

On our return voyage, we found ourselves traveling with recently elected President Betancourt, who was on his way to the United States to attempt to negotiate higher royalties for Venezuelan oil. In our conversations he expressed his high hopes for Venezuelan democracy. While he was in the U.S., General Jimenez staged a coup d'etat, and Betancourt went into exile. So much for democracy. Jimenez remained in power for more than a decade, amassing a large fortune, most of which he placed safely outside the country in Swiss and American banks.

Shortly after returning from the month-long trip to Venezuela, I was asked by the firm to go to Europe. This time I traveled alone: by ship to Holland, then by rail to Paris and Geneva. From Geneva I was to travel by plane to Beirut, via Athens and Jerusalem. That summer a cholera epidemic struck Egypt and other Middle Eastern countries. In those days an American traveling abroad had to get vaccinated for smallpox, typhoid, diptheria, and cholera—a very painful procedure which, thankfully, is no longer required today.

The TWA flight from Athens was scheduled to go directly to Jerusalem. Instead, the four-engine prop plane landed in Cairo. There overzealous authorities required all passengers to present their passports to be stamped—even passengers not disembarking in Cairo.

Upon arriving in Jerusalem, equally overzealous health authorities herded us into quarantine, despite our protestations that we never left the aircraft at Cairo. All of us had to be vaccinated, whether previously inoculated or not. In two weeks we were to return for the second shot, and only then would we receive our exit visas. This meant that I would be two weeks late getting to Lebanon for my business meetings.

In spite of this frustration, I looked on the bright side. In effect, I had a two-week vacation to sightsee and learn about the Holy Land. The medical officer who administered my vaccination was an Armenian, most gracious and friendly, who took me aside to give me some useful advice. "Keep away from the British," he warned. "They are being attacked by Zionist terrorists! In public you will be safe if you are with a Palestinian, so hire one with a car and he can show you the sights. When you are in his presence, you will not be in danger. The Zionists are very careful not to harm Palestinians."

He went on to give me some further background on the political situation. "The Zionists want the British out. Most Palestinians feel the same way, but are not engaged in any fighting. The British have agreed to terminate their occupation, and in fact are already evacuating the country, but the Jewish terrorists continue to attack them anyway. They attack British civilians as well as troops, with sniper fire and bombs." As a final admonition he said pointedly, "Do not go out in public without your Palestinian escort. You might be mistaken as British. In that case, you could be shot!"

I was most grateful for the doctor's survival briefing. As soon as I checked in at Jerusalem's best hotel, the King David, I went out and hired a Palestinian driver and car. My driver turned out to be a knowledgeable and congenial companion. He spoke all the languages of the local people—English, Hebrew, and Armenian—as well as his native Arabic, and expressed disappointment when he found I could not converse with him in Armenian. In English he told me that his family had been Roman Catholic for many generations, as were many Palestinians—converts of the Crusaders centuries ago.

As a Christian he knew intimately all the holy places, and mapped out an itinerary for the next two weeks. Among the highlights were the Church of the Nativity in Bethlehem, the Church of the Holy Sepulchre, the Tomb of Jesus, the Rock of Agony, the Garden of Gethsemane in Jerusalem, and the route taken by Jesus to his crucifixion. Seeing all these holy places greatly enlivened the story of the New Testament.

However, I was disappointed to find that in some places Jesus's life and message had been denigrated by his followers. The Nativity, for example, had been transformed beyond recognition. Gold and jewels adorned the manger scene, and over the stable a church had been built, with separate naves and altars for the Armenian, Greek Orthodox, and Roman Catholic denominations. On holy days these groups often fought with one another, requiring the intercession of police and sometimes even the army.

On the other hand, the Tomb of Jesus was preserved in humble simplicity. When I was emerging from the Tomb, I raised my head too soon and cracked it on the outside cornice of the entryway. "Be grateful," said my Arab guide as I tried to rub away the pain, "You will always remember this visit." Even more memorable was my visit to the Garden of Gethsemane, with its knotted and gnarled olive trees the very same ones Jesus gazed upon two thousand years ago.

Equally fascinating to me in its antiquity was the Old City of Jerusalem, with its coexistence, side-by-side, of urban and pastoral lifestyles. By tradition, goats and sheep had the right-of-way over pedestrians and vehicles, and every morning shepherds in the walled city would lead their flocks through the streets and the narrow passageways, lined with small family stalls on both sides, and out the ancient gates to graze in the nearby countryside. Before sundown the flocks would be brought back for milking, and bedded down for the night. (Today the countryside has given way to high density urbanization, and the grazing of sheep and goats from the Old City has passed into History).

In addition to our excursions into the past, my guide and I also visited new settlements near the Sea of Galilee, where recent Jewish immigrants were introducing modern agricultural and irrigation systems, and we spent one night each in the growing industrial cities of Haifa and Tel Aviv. While staying at the International Hotel in Haifa, the Armenian doctor's warning of terrorism was made real when two British engineers, taking a walk after dinner in the gardens, were killed by sniper fire.

A few days later, back in Jerusalem, I was awakened about midnight by a deafening explosion. When I went to my window I saw smoke billowing into the sky from a couple of blocks away. The next day the press reported that grenades had been thrown into a cabaret crowded with British soldiers celebrating their departure for home the next morning. Some twenty Tommies were killed, and many others injured. The Stern Gang, whose leader in exile was Yitzhak Shamir, took credit for the attack. I couldn't help but wonder what purpose was served by these attacks on Tommies, since the British were evacuating the country anyway.

Sensing in me a genuine curiosity about the changes taking place in his country, my driver/guide arranged for me to talk with several community leaders in the Old City, which housed some twenty thousand Jews, Christians (many of them Armenians), and Moslems, all living together in close quarters and remarkable harmony. As my guide explained, the three communities (which were approximately equal in number) had coexisted peacefully since the days of Jesus, trading goods and services, and communicating freely in one another's languages while at the same time preserving their own distinct traditions.

Although an American, I looked Middle Eastern; my appearance was different only in dress and manner. In all three communities I was welcomed as a rarely seen American guest and graciously offered tea and biscuits and a lively discussion.

With my multilingual guide serving as interpreter, I learned that all the residents of the Old City felt threatened by the new wave of Jewish immigrants. Whereas the native Jews spoke Hebrew, wore clothing identifying themselves as orthodox, and were likely to be short, bearded, and dark complexioned—in appearance much like their Arab cousins—the immigrants, many of them blonde-haired and blue-eyed, looked and acted like Europeans. Few attended synagogue or even knew Hebrew, and many were professed atheists. Gregarious, politically ambitious, militaristic, and intent on making money the modern way, they disrespected the beliefs and lifestyle of the native Jews, and were deeply resented by them.

At that time there were rival gangs of Jewish terrorists: Menahem Begin's Irgun, and Shamir's Stern gang. Both were engaged in violence against the British, both claimed to represent the Jewish population, and both were fervently recruiting members and supporters from amongst the immigrants, most of whom shared their Zionist ambitions.

The native residents of the Old City were openly hostile to the Zionist movement—born in England—which they saw as imposing upon them an alien, urban, Western European culture. If the Zionists succeeded in taking over the Jewish community in Palestine, as it looked certain they would, their traditional lifestyle would be wiped out. Beyond that, the militancy and sheer numbers of the immigrants, combined with the scarcity of land and resources, made conflict between them and Palestinian Arabs inevitable.

When pressed about the prospect of war, the Jews in the Old City acknowledged that they saw no alternative but to align themselves with the immigrant Jews, much as they disliked them. The Arabs acknowledged that they would have to fight to protect their land from being taken over. Armenians and other Christians said they would try to keep out of the conflict, from which no good could come.

Nearly half a century has gone by, and I have often thought about these prophetic conversations in light of the developments that followed. In many subsequent trips to the region, I have seen firsthand the impact on neighboring countries of Israel's evolution into a modern, militaristic nation. The Arab-Israeli conflict has been used by demagogic Moslem leaders to foment hostility towards *all* Jews, domestic and foreign, and by extention, other native minorities and foreigners as well.

Large Jewish populations in Baghdad and other Iraqi cities were all but wiped out as native minorities emigrated. With few exceptions, Persian Gulf countries also became hostile to *any* immigration, even that of Palestinian refugees. Ironically, native Arabs lacked the knowledge and skills to build infra-structures and facilities. Instead, flush with oil revenues amounting to tens of billions of dollars annually, the privileged few who coveted Western comforts and conveniences imported contractors from the West and Far East to provide them. The tragedy is that, in the absence of Zionist incursions into Palestine, Arab societies could have turned to their own communities of enterprising, artistic, and professional Jews to supply many of their needs. After all, Jews and Arabs share common ethnic origins and common religious acceptance of the Old Testament.

Unfortunately, decades of conflict have institutionalized the hostility, with deeply entrenched vested interests on both sides. By the 1967 War the Jewish diaspora, especially in the United States, was highly organized to support Israel both politically and financially. The Arab countries, in part due to the exodus of their talented minority populations, lagged behind.

I had a Jewish-American friend, Ludwig Jesselson, major owner and a principal founder of Phillips Brothers, one of the world's largest trading companies. Ludwig was Jewish through and through. Philbro had originated in Holland, and most of Ludwig's trading partners were European Jews. I remember one time at lunch in his private dining room, he said to me, "I've got a new trader in oil. I want you to meet him. His name is O'Malley." Noticing my surprised expression, he quickly added, "Yes, he is Irish. But he *thinks* like a Jew."

(Several years later, after they had parted company and O'Malley had started his own oil business, I asked Jesselson where O'Malley got his financing. "From the stupid bankers!" was his terse reply.)

After World War II Jesselson had built his fortune by investing in mineral rich underdeveloped countries. Now he agonized that Arab hostility toward the Jewish state of Israel was preventing his people from similar participation in the emerging oil rich Arab countries. Uppermost in his mind whenever we met was the question, "How can we get Middle East peace?"

On the first day of the 1967 War I agreed to meet Jesselson for lunch. Ludwig, who was one of Israel's largest financial benefactors, made no attempt to disguise his fear that the combined Arab forces, led by Egypt, would destroy Israel. "You know the Arabs," he said. "What do you think?"

"I can assure you that little Israel is far superior in military might to all the Arab armies combined," I replied. Still anxious, he accused me of telling him what he wanted to hear, and insisted on my honesty.

"The war will be over in ninety-six hours on Israel's terms," I predicted. "Israel has state-of-the-art military hardware, and personnel who are fully confident and trained to use it. This cannot be said of the Arabs, who in terms of mental outlook and technical capacity are still lingering in an earlier century."

As it turned out, I was too optimistic. The war ended on Israel's terms in 120 hours. Three months later Jesselson again invited me to lunch, this time to discuss his recent trip to Israel. Again, he professed to be worried about his people.

"What are you worried about?" I asked. "You should be proud."

"No, I am not proud," he replied. "I'm worried. I saw so many of our young men. You know, they look and act like Nazis!"

This time my response was not comforting. "You shouldn't be surprised," I told him. "They are living in a war culture, and many of them *are* German in temperament and efficiency. Remember where they came from."

Israel itself is no longer an attractive haven for refugees. In recent years the government has gone so far as to solicit immigrants from Eastern Europe and the former Soviet Union—immigrants who have talents sorely needed in their native lands, as those countries emerge from Communism. In Israel, they face unemployment and hardship in the limited labor market, and a housing shortage. If they find housing in one of the new settlements in Gaza or the West Bank, their lives are in danger on a daily basis. Having faced these realities, many of them end up in New York. In spite of this, some zealots continue to be hellbent on expansion of population and territory.

Arab response to this has been to use their oil revenue to purchase the latest weaponry and to hire foreign mercenaries. Of course, the Arab leaders' demonization of Israel has also served to divert public attention from their own shortcomings. In the oil-rich countries of the Persian Gulf, these rulers preserve for themselves and their own clan the privileges of wealth, creating an ever-widening gap between rich and poor. Democratic institutions are unknown, and the general population cannot identify their self-interest with the regimes of these strongarm dictators and newly created royalty. U.S. policy has consistently ignored the inhuman discrimination in these countries, unless our oil supply is threatened. (During the recent Gulf War, the State Department made much of Saddam Hussein's mistreatment of his own people, but said nothing about the institutionalized mistreatment practiced by the Saudi and Kuwaiti royal families).

Soon after returning from the Middle East, Dadourian Corp. directed me to return to Athens to secure the sale of war surplus materials, shipped to Greece on consignment (delivery to destination without prior payment). These materials were stored in the customs warehouse at the nearby port of Piraeus. At the time, Greece was in the midst of a bloody civil war between the Greek Monarchy and pro-Communist guerrillas, supported by Tito's Yugoslavia and the Soviet Union. Athens itself was spared combat, but gunfire could be heard just to the north.

The civil war had caused extreme inflation, robbing Greek currency—the drachma—of much of its domestic purchasing power, and rendering it worthless in foreign exchange. Under these circumstances the Government was very strict about preventing drachma holders from converting them to foreign currency. Legally, hotels could only accept drachma. When I paid my hotel bill, I would carry a suitcase to the bank to buy drachma with my dollars. The official exchange rate was one U.S. dollar for 15,000 drachma, and the largest bill printed was 1,000 drachma. To pay for my weekly rent and meals I needed 5,000 drachma bills of 1,000 each—a suitcase load.

The Grand Bretangia Hotel was the meeting place of the

"wheeler-dealers" of Greek business. As the Civil War raged throughout the country, it paralyzed normal business. Censorship and curfews were imposed. Critical information was not generally available and was exchanged, by word of mouth, at the Grand Bretangia Bar.

With Greek industry largely shut down, the major cash flow available was U.S. Aid, supplying hundreds of millions of dollars under the Greek-Turkish Relief Program. Much of this aid was funneled through private business; even direct Government procurement included the participation of local agents. In the fight against this Communist takeover, the U.S. Congress and Administration naively assumed, as did the American public, that U.S. funds were committed totally to strengthen the Greek government in its struggle against the guerillas.

The boys at the G.B. Bar—at least a dozen of them—every evening conspired to divert part of this huge cash flow of U.S. Aid into their own pockets. Conditions were optimal for this type of corruption. The market was awash with drachma, easily available to anyone with a "deal," and the best deal in town was to "buy" the U.S. foreign aid with drachma. To cash in, the Greek importer or agent for direct government purchases would insist that the U.S. exporter increase the amount of the invoice by at least ten and as much as fifty percent over the actual seller's price. The deal, of course, would require more drachma, easily obtained. The excess over the exporter's actual price would, by prearrangement, be paid in U.S. dollars and deposited in the Greek importer or agent's bank account, in Switzerland or another haven country.

This method of fraud is known as a "kickback," and can be detected only by a post-audit of the transaction. The practice is illegal in politically accountable nations, but in less developed countries, especially the rich oil producers, it is institutionalized as a means of transferring wealth to members of the ruling class. Great fortunes have been amassed through this process—without any contribution by the recipients to the community, and always at the expense of the local treasury. In the case of the Greek-

Turkish Relief Program, this graft was also at the expense of U.S. taxpayers. Years later our General Accounting Office estimated this diversion of U.S. funds into private pockets at between fifteen and thirty percent of total U.S. Aid.

After a few days in Athens, I was convinced that the Greek merchants had conspired to boycott buying our war surplus materials until customs officials seized them, at which time the merchants could acquire them at a forced auction at a fraction of their actual value. The materials were billed at $500,000, but my instructions from Dadourian were to take anything I could get for them before they were seized.

During this period of frustration, I was fortunate to be invited to a U.S. Embassy party where I met an American, Mr. Charles Patterson, who was advising the Greek government as a member of the Currency Committee of the Central Bank. I learned that formerly he had been employed by the U.S. Treasury, and we immediately found common ground with my service in the Bureau of the Budget. The Bureau and Treasury always worked closely in matters of budgets and sources of funds.

I told him of the problem I was having, a problem he immediately understood, for it was commonly created by Greek merchants. He invited me to his office the next morning and told me that the Queen's Relief Fund needed the materials and had the local currency. The drachma would be converted into dollars with his committee's approval. Thanks to his intervention, the Director of the Queen's Fund met with me the next day and inspected the materials. The following day he made payment of $250,000 for one-half of the cargo.

That evening, at the bar of the hotel, one of the Greek merchants, almost screaming at me, demanded to know, "Who did you pay off to make the deal?"

"No one," I replied.

"Impossible!," he shouted. "This is Greece! NO WAY without payoff!" After a pause he quieted down and pleaded, "It's important in my business to know who takes the baksheesh in the Palace."

"Sorry," I replied, "I can't tell you, because there was no baksheesh."

As he became almost convinced I was telling the truth, he grew *more* furious. Was it possible someone could beat the system? After he calmed down, I said, "I'll give you 48 hours to put up $250,000 for the other half of the cargo, or else the Queen's Fund will buy it."

"I'll buy it," he meekly replied.

"Do you have the drachma?," I inquired.

"Of course!" he said emphatically.

I looked at him severely and said, "My question, more specifically, is—do you, personally, own that much money?"

After struggling to fudge a satisfactory answer he finally exclaimed, "My answer is no! I am a business man, not a banker! *Any* damn fool can do business with his own money. A businessman does business with *other* people's money!"

Benefitting from this Greek Realism, I amended what I had learned about business at NYU and Columbia. He promised he'd have the full amount of payment within four hours, and he did.

Many Greek businessmen, including Aristotle Onassis, got rich during the years of the Greek-Turkish Relief Program. Is it any wonder why "the boys" at the G.B. Bar were so outraged when they learned that a half-million dollar deal had gotten past them without 50 to 250 thousand going into their own pockets? On my last night at the bar, I told one of them, "It takes two Armenians to trade equally with one Jew, and three Jews to out-trade one Greek."

With a wry smile, the Greek replied, "You have that story backwards."

On my return from Athens, my connecting flight necessitated an overnight stay in Geneva. At the Hotel Russie (later torn down and replaced by the Hotel Presidential), I shared the elevator with a very tall girl, obviously an American, who looked ill and troubled. When I asked if she were all right, she replied, "I think I can make it home tomorrow, if I don't starve from hunger before then".

As she got off at her floor, I blurted out, “Meet me in the lobby in ten minutes.”

She did, and I took her to a nearby restaurant, famous for steak. While consuming two large ones, she told me that she had run out of money while working to rebuild a railroad in Yugoslavia—a project sponsored by Geneva University, which she had attended as a one-year exchange student from Barnard. She could not ask her family for money, she explained, because they disapproved of her helping Tito’s country. That evening we said goodbye and went our separate ways. More later on this girl, whose name was Anne Aldrich.

Upon my return to New York, I reported to the head of the firm the details of my successful encounter with the Greeks. I expected congratulations and a bonus. Instead his response was, "“Did we make a mistake in not sending more goods?” Disappointed, I felt taken for granted and began to wonder about the wisdom of staying with the firm.

A short while later, in early 1948, I received a call from Cooper, asking me to come to Washington, where he had joined Eric Kohler to help set up the Economic Cooperation Administration (ECA), better known as the Marshall Plan. Having seen the devastation in Europe and especially in Greece, I was excited that I might play some part in the recovery of this wartorn region.

Cooper warned me that Kohler was duty-driven and difficult to please. “He doesn’t tolerate mediocrity and frequently demands more than people can produce.” Then he went on to say, “But if you can get his respect and confidence, you will be associated with one of the country’s great men.” I assured him that I was delighted to take on the challenge. Kohler had stopped by our Connecticut Avenue apartment several times during World War II, and those initial encounters had made a significant impression on me. The next day I was in Washington.

6
The Marshall Plan

WHILE IN PRIVATE PRACTICE I had followed with interest the country's debate over postwar aid to Europe. After five years of war, Americans were tired of shedding blood and money, and the prospect of assuming the additional burden of financing the recoveries of Europe and Japan was not an appealing one. The Marshall Plan was the result of a concerted effort by President Truman, General Marshall—his Secretary of State—and a host of assistants, to win the support of Congress and the American public. This effort had very nearly failed. The House Appropriations Bill for the first year of the Plan passed by a mere one vote. I realized even before starting my new job that those of us entrusted with administering the aid program would have to prove ourselves within that first year.

Bill Cooper occupied a corner office next to Eric Kohler's on the top floor of the newly-built Miatoco Building, across the street from the U.S. Chamber of Commerce, and across Lafayette Park from the White House. As soon as I walked in, he made it clear there was no time for small talk.

"We have an hour before Kohler meets you. Let me quickly give you the setup in this place: the ECA is in the process of staffing. Congress has exempted the Agency from personnel and administrative statutes, and authorized super-grade compensation. The Senate, with its Republican majority, has confirmed a prominent Republican, Paul G. Hoffman—President of Studebaker and Chairman of the Committee for Economic Development—as Administrator. He was hand-picked by Senator Vandenburg, the

Chairman of the Senate Foreign Relations Committee. The extraordinary thing, and I think Vandenburg should be credited with this, is that Hoffman reports directly to the President and to Congress. In spite of the fact that two of Truman's favorites—General Marshall and Robert Lovett—are Secretary and UnderSecretary of State, the State Department has clearly been bypassed. I suspect that the Foreign Relations Committee didn't want a repeat of the Greek-Turkish Aid fiasco, which as you know was the responsibility of the State Department.

"The ECA's Deputy Administrator is a prominent Democrat named Howard Bruce, of the Maryland Bruces. The other people in top echelon positions are the guys who wrote the State Department position papers explaining the need to assist Europe in recovering from the devastation of War. These fellows are now in charge of Program and Operations. Richard M. Bissell, whose official ECA title is Assistant Administrator, is the head, and Harlan and Van Cleveland—two brothers—are his deputies. Hoffman inherited this 'team'." I could tell from Cooper's expression and tone of voice that he didn't think much of them.

"Chief Counsel," Cooper continued, "is Alex Henderson, from Cravath, Swaine, and Moore. He was outside counsel for Hoffman at Studebaker. Hoffman also recruited Kohler to be his Controller, and Kohler reports only to him. Kohler's branch is already largely staffed, with procedures in place for prompt payment and accounting."

"What about the overseas setup?" I asked.

"A regional office has been created in Paris, headed by Ambassador Averill Harriman. The Paris office coordinates the aid missions of the participating countries—former allies and enemies alike—and reviews their requisitions for aid prior to Washington approval. Mission Chiefs are chosen by ECA and function independently of U.S. Embassy staff."

I nodded. "So where do I come in?"

Bill grimaced. "You've got a tall order to fill. The ECA's primary function is to supply dollars for imports that cannot be purchased in local currency. Section 202 of the Appropriation reads,

Above: Eric L. Kohler
Right: Bill Cooper

'No funds made available under the authority of this act shall be used for the purchase in bulk of any commodity at prices higher than the market price prevailing in the United States at the time of purchase, adjusted for differences in the cost of transportation to destination, quality, and terms of payment.'

"Kohler will expect you to put that section into operation, and it won't be easy. Bissell and his bunch say that it's self-contradictory and impossible to administer, and should be disregarded. The ECA Appropriations Bill stipulates that we must use private channels of trade, and Bissell's argument is that if we do that, there is no way to ensure that we will always be paying competitive prices.

"Kohler has the notion that 202 can and should be applied, and wants you to figure out how to do it. He knows that you were a price/cost economist for five years during the war, and no one else in the Agency has your experience.

"You can count on a major policy battle with Bissell, and really it's about a lot more than just 202. You're stepping into the middle of a turf war. Hoffman has given Kohler a lot of power, and Bissell resents it. Program and Operations wants the Controller to be an accountant and nothing more—simply recording the numbers of how the $6.5 billion is spent. But giving the Controller authority to decide what the numbers should be, on each of thousands of supply contracts, is unprecedented in a government agency. If 202 is implemented, that enlarges the Controller's function at the expense of their own authority.

"I told Kohler that when Hoffman listens to the opposing arguments, *you* will be more knowledgeable and persuasive. Once you convince Kohler of your position, he will support you throughout. And when the showdown comes, you'll be glad to have him on your side."

This was going to be more of a challenge than I had imagined. Just then I saw Kohler signaling me to come into his office. Bill smiled. "Good luck, Sam."

Standing elegantly erect at 6'4", Eric Kohler was an imposing figure, with a bass voice befitting his persona. Handsome and always impeccably groomed, he was gracefully cordial with everyone he met. His choice of vocabulary flawlessly conveyed his thinking and message. To me, he seemed the embodiment of perfection.

A bachelor, Kohler had chosen the life of a workaholic. At the social level conversations were minimal, and I had the impression that close personal relationships were a low priority for him. His whole life seemed dedicated to one goal—elevating accounting from its traditional role of bookkeeping to a higher professional status, by incorporating principles and standards that would enable both public and private organizations to function more responsibly. With the fervor of an evangelist—in words, deeds, and in print—he constantly bombarded management with the moral imperative of accountability and fiduciary responsibility.

Kohler's penetrating blue eyes seemed in constant search for information and also for imperfections in those around him. From personal experience, I had no doubt that he lived up to his own high standards. Near the end of the the war, on one of Kohler's infrequent visits to the apartment Cooper and I shared, he mentioned that he wanted to sell a car that he owned. He had purchased the Buick new in 1941, but placed it in storage immediately after Pearl Harbor. As he put it, "I could get along without it and save gasoline for the Military. I hoped more people would put the country's need ahead of personal enjoyment."

"Now I should sell the Buick," he added. "I find I can get along without it and should avoid storage costs."

Quickly I replied, "I would love to have it! It would be my first car."

"All right," Kohler decided. "I will sell it to you at a fair price. I paid $850 in 1941. I'm going to deduct a depreciation rate of 8% for the four years, totaling 32%, which brings the price down to $570, but I will add the storage cost of five dollars per month for 48 months. I believe $818 is a fair price."

I was stunned. The automobile industry was just now reconverting from tanks and airplanes back to automobile production. People ordering new cars were waiting two years or more for delivery. Prices were now double the prewar levels for old as well as new cars. I felt compelled to interject that he was offering to sell the car, with hardly any mileage on it, at less than half the present market price!

"So be it," he replied. "I am not in the car business. I don't want to make a profit."

Enough that I made the point. I did not challenge his personal computation by pointing out that he had not figured in four years interest on his $850 outlay. (The irony is that later, when I wanted to sell the car, I felt inhibited by Kohler's standard of fairness. How could I sell the car at its fair market value and make a profit, when Kohler had steadfastly refused to do so? As long as Kohler was around, I couldn't. It wasn't until 1951, just after he'd left the Agency and Washington, that I finally sold the Buick, then ten years old.)

Kohler greeted me most cordially and asked how the Buick was running. I never had any doubts that my relationship with Kohler, friendly and mutually respectful, was derived from my friendship with Cooper. As I indicated earlier, Kohler and Cooper were close mutual admirers—patron and protege. It was clear that Cooper measured up to his high standards; others, including myself, were conditionally accepted.

The meeting was brief, probably less than an hour. Kohler accepted Cooper's judgment that I was the man to deal with Section 202, but he wanted to assess my reaction to such an assignment. "Given that the Act directs that aid be supplied to the maximum extent possible through private channels, how zealous will you be," he asked, "in administering this limitation on suppliers of goods and services?"

I recited the record aired by Congress on the failure to control waste and fraud in U.N. and Turkish Aid, and highlighted the one vote margin of passage on the Appropriations bill. After acknowledging the difficulties of administering Section 202, I sought to reassure Kohler by stating emphatically that it "must be vigorously enforced by ECA as the fiduciary of the $6.5 billion of taxpayers' money. The one-vote margin is a clear message that Congress might well refuse additional funds if fraud and waste are not controlled."

Kohler warned that powerful groups in the Agency had staked out the position that we should bypass Section 202. "I don't know where Hoffman stands on the issue," he added. "He will make the final decision. I will rely on you to make the case for compliance with the intent of Congress. You must take the initiative in drafting the regulations to implement 202. Other people here are either hostile or somewhat indifferent." Finally he asked, "Can you start right away?"

"Yes," I answered.

"You'll have the office next to mine. As you know, Bill is returning to Carnegie to teach. I will arrange a super grade of CAF-17 for you. That's one level below mine, which is the highest. In the meantime you will serve as a consultant."

After the meeting with Kohler concluded, I returned to Bill's office for more briefing. "Within Program and Operations," he continued, "is the Industry Division, headed by an industry man, Sam Anderson. This division has several branches—Capital Goods, Consumable Goods, Transportation, Agriculture, and Energy. The opposition to you in completing your assignment will include the heads of these branches. They will present themselves as practical men who understand business. An argument you may expect from them is that to control private business in the prices they charge constitutes interference with 'private channels of trade,' the language of the ECA Act. However, they will rely on Bissell to take the responsibility for bypassing Section 202.

Alex Henderson, a close friend of Hoffmann, can be counted on to be open minded. In addition, Hoffman has a Special Assistant for Congressional Relations, Tyler Wood. You can rely on him to support any reasonable effort to prevent price gouging and fraud."

Cooper went on. "As a preview of what you're in for, consider this. Just recently I circulated a memorandum to department heads. I questioned why, with our resources, the ECA should purchase marine cargo insurance, when it can afford to be self-insured and save millions. This was the first indication that the Controller intended to control payments as well as keep the books. It stirred up a hornet's nest of opposition from Bissell and his industry branches. They got the picture. If the Controller is prepared to save a few million here, what can they expect from him when he senses an opportunity to save hundreds of millions? The marine insurance issue is 'high on your immediate agenda,' even as you fit Section 202 into regulation."

Before Cooper left for Pittsburgh, we initiated a meeting with top officials of the Government Accounting Office, which had conducted the post audit of U.S. Foreign Aid programs and reported to Congress their findings of inept management, waste, and fraud. Any thoughts Cooper and I had that GAO would make suggestions helpful to us were dashed when we were told, "Sorry. GAO limits its function to post audit of operations."

"As we draw up the regulations," I pleaded, "can't you informally give us some clues as to how to avoid a disaster like the Greek-Turkish Aid scandal?"

Their curt reply was, "Frankly, we don't know what you can do to avoid being criticized when we conduct our post audit of your operations."

As we left, Cooper eyed me sympathetically and said, "You got the message—you're on your own!"

Soon after this, notice was officially served that marine insurance would not be purchased by ECA. In my first meeting with Hoffman, he asked if I could attend a meeting requested by a Mr. Burns, President of the Marine Underwriters Association. By the time of that meeting, Kohler and I had briefed Hoffman. His understanding of marine insurance was immediate and his decision unequivocal.

"Mr. Burns," he said softly but firmly, "I must make crystal clear (his favorite expression) that I represent you as a tax payer and *not* as an underwriter of insurance. We are not going to make payments for goods and services we don't need."

As it turned out, Hoffman's decision was not the last word on the subject of Marine Insurance. Later in the year Mr. Burns's association of underwriters lobbied Congress to put into the next ECA Appropriations Bill a provision authorizing the payment of marine cargo insurance. Tyler Wood and I made several appearances before the Senate Appropriations Committee engaged in writing this amendment, and we thought that we had settled the matter in favor of ECA by persuading the Committee against such a provision.

To our surprise, when the Appropriations Bill came up for a vote on the Senate floor, Senator McCarran of Nevada offered an amendment which included language authorizing ECA to make payments for marine insurance. Nevada not being known for marine insurance companies, McCarran apparently was acting on behalf of some Eastern senators. The amendment was proposed at a late night session of sleepy senators, who gave it a favorable vote. This amendment then survived the Senate-House

Paul G. Hoffman

Conference Committee and became law.

The language was general. With the help of Tyler Wood, we wrote into the ECA regulation that the exporter could choose to insure the risk on his cargo in ECA dollars. In the event of a loss, the indemnity would be payable to ECA. This removed the exporter's incentive to insure the cargo. If the importer chose to insure the cargo in local currency, this was of no concern to us. Little if any dollar insurance was paid over the next two years, and an estimated twenty million dollars was saved on marine insurance alone.

My battle with the marine insurers was only the first of many controversies in which I became embroiled. Early in my ECA tenure, while Section 202 was still being debated, I ordered payment withheld on a cargo of Saudi crude oil shipped by Esso (now Exxon) to its refinery in Le Havre, France. Esso had presented us with an invoice for $2.23 per barrel FOB (free on board—title passing to the importer at the point of embarkation) plus freight, from Ras Tanura, Saudi Arabia to Le Havre. To understand just how inflated this price was, a little background is in order.

Most of the $6.5 billion in aid was spent in the United States. Crude oil was the major exception. In that case four American companies owned petroleum sources in Saudi Arabia, and another American company had a source in Kuwait. These companies were adamant that they would not supply crude oil without payment in dollars. They refused to accept German marks, Italian lira, French francs, etc., despite the fact that they were delivering crude oil to their own subsidiary refineries. Technically this was an internal transaction—normally ineligible for ECA funding.

However, since these were American companies, and since this was the only way to get much needed oil to the rebuilding countries of Europe, we made the petroleum industry an exception to the rule.

My assistant, Howard Morrison—a former student of Cooper's at Carnegie—and I conducted a quick analysis of crude oil supply and pricing, which revealed some telling facts. By late 1947, Saudi Arabian production and loading facilities had reached a capacity of more than a million barrels a day, most of it shut in for lack of a dollar market. A comparably large supply of crude was available in Kuwait.

Both Saudi Arabia and Kuwait had huge crude oil reservoirs at shallow levels—less than 7000 feet—confirming many billions of barrels in reserve. Fewer than a hundred wells had been drilled by the few existing drilling rigs. Each well would produce more than 20,000 barrels per day. By our calculations, the cost of finding, producing, and loading tankers for export could not exceed ten cents a barrel, plus another fifteen cents in royalties to the local rulers, a finding comparable to that of congressional committee investigators.

Regardless of what we thought the oil companies should be charging, that same congressional committee inquiry had revealed that Aramco of Arabia, an American subsidiary, had made hard-sell efforts to the U.S. Navy, offering crude oil for $1 per barrel. A price of $2.23 a barrel would be a record high for crude supplied from that source.

The morning after I stopped payment on the shipment, George Kegler, General Counsel for Esso, stormed into my office in a state of rage. "By what authority do you order no payment for that crude cargo now in Le Havre?" he almost shouted.

"The price is more than we can pay because we cannot justify it," I replied calmly.

Kegler's rage intensified. "Who are you to decide what price we should charge!?"

As he went on in the same vein, it became clear to me that the purpose of his unannounced visit was not to discuss pricing, nor to seek an understanding of our decision, but rather to intimidate me. Finally his harangue became unbearable. Exercising considerable constraint, I said quietly, "Mr. Kegler, you will either change your tone and attitude or I must ask you to leave." He leered at me, turned, and stalked out the door.

This was a Friday. I took my scheduled flight that afternoon to Cape Cod to spend a weekend with friends. While there, my secretary called to say that Mr. Hoffman expected me to meet with him early Tuesday morning, to prepare for a meeting with Eugene Holman, Chief Executive Officer of Esso, later that day.

This was Hoffman's first exposure to the oil industry, and I gave him a comprehensive briefing. He saw that Esso could set any price it chose and that price would be followed by the other four exclusive suppliers of crude oil under the program: Chevron, Texaco, and Mobil in Saudi Arabia; and Gulf in Kuwait. Most of the crude would be delivered to their subsidiary refineries in Europe, which allied forces had left standing while destroying those of European ownership.

At the meeting with Holman, George Kegler was conspicuously absent. I wondered if Holman had disapproved of Kegler's strongarm tactics with me. In Kegler's place was an assistant of Holman's, Luke Finley. Hoffman and Holman had previously served together on the board of the prestigious Committee for Economic Development, and it was clear they were old friends.

Holman, a Texan of huge physique (Esso's board had a strong preference for the tall man), was warm and cordial. He exhibited an air of great disappointment that Mr. Hoffman had relied on his staff, who did not understand the oil industry. "We are shipping crude from the Middle East because it is much cheaper than if we shipped it from the Western hemisphere," he patiently explained.

Holman went on to expound on why the $2.23 FOB price was a competitive market price, laying out a watershed theory—somewhat new to me as well as to Hoffman—that clearly sounded like a species of the more familiar basing point system of fixing prices to avoid competition. It was a gallant try, but the fact remained that Esso and the three other companies were joint owners of ARAMCO, the Saudi operating company. It was tacitly understood that Gulf would follow their lead in establishing the market price. This was, in effect, a monopoly.

In the first break for Hoffman to speak, he said, "Gene, let me make this crystal clear. I represent you as a taxpayer and not as the head of an oil company." From the tone of finality in Hoffman's voice, Holman knew immediately that he would not get his price. Hoffman then turned to me and said, "Sam, what do you think the price should be?"

"Sir," I replied, "I'm not capable of naming a competitive price because there is no competition. The closest I can come to a reasonable price would be on the basis of costs. I suggest we apply the test that the price under our program should not exceed the price of Esso's shipments to other markets. To reach a comparison of the netback FOB price realized, we would need to adjust for freight to the different destinations. I refer to the East Coast of the United States where the presence of independent companies supplying crude and refining it there constitutes a substantial measure of competition. Our research shows that the average netback price of Esso's cargoes from the Middle East to the East Coast is $1.43 per barrel."

Holman quickly countered by claiming that only a few sporadic shipments of Saudi crude were made to the East Coast, and therefore it was not a regular market. In fact, we had evidence that Esso was shipping increasing volumes of Saudi crude to its East Coast refinery, but before I could challenge his statement Holman suggested a compromise price of $1.75. I detected pleasure in Hoffman's eyes as he turned to me and asked, "Sam, what do *you* think?"

There was a long silence. I realized that Hoffman liked the offer, but I still thought the price excessive. Finally I replied, "I can't recommend that we arbitrarily fix the price at $1.75. I must emphasize, sir, that Saudi crude, in my opinion, will be flowing to the East Coast at a netback price of less than $1.50 per barrel.

This will be a program of several years duration, and I would have great difficulty justifying a regular price of up to 32 cents per barrel over what Esso charges in the free market."

Hoffman nodded and frowned in apparent concentration. Of course both of us were aware that a savings of almost 50 cents a barrel over that same period of time was considerable. To gain this sort of concession from one of the most powerful companies in America was most unusual, and I could tell Hoffman wanted to accept it. Feeling that I would be on thin ice if I remained intransigent, I suggested a compromise that had been in the back of my mind.

"Sir, since there seems to be a difference of opinion regarding the volume and price of Saudi crude delivered to the East Coast, I believe we could accept Mr. Holman's offer of $1.75, subject to the following arrangement. We would not give up the $1.43 netback price; rather ECA would set up a contingent claim fund. The fund will accumulate a claim of 32 cents per barrel (the difference between $1.75 and $1.43) on all oil purchased with ECA dollars, payable upon verification that our statistics are correct."

Holman agreed on the spot. "My assistant here, Luke Finley, is available to meet with your staff to pursue this inquiry."

"Good," said Hoffman. "Luke and Sam should meet as soon as possible."

As the meeting was breaking up I overhead Hoffman say to Holman, "Gene, I recall you offered to sell large quantities of that same crude last year for a dollar a barrel."

Holman turned to Hoffman and said with a smile, "Paul, do you think you could keep this out of the press?" Honoring his friend's request, Hoffman chose not to make this meeting a "newsmaker," and I resisted the temptation to leak it to the press.

As agreed at the meetings, Luke Finley and several of his assistants met with Howard Morrison and myself at Esso's offices at Rockefeller Center, and also in Washington. Walter Levy, the chief of ECA's energy branch, never attended these meetings, but as we argued about how to arrive at a competitive price, he was actively propagating the watershed method Luke was proposing.

My Columbia background—two years of PhD study, with a major in Industrial Organization—plus Morrison's highly developed math skills, appeared equal to the best talent Esso could muster. These meetings were serious engagements, but they failed to move Esso to a lower price. The Agency seemed content to accumulate a claim against the oil companies at the rate of thirty-two cents per barrel, which after three years amounted to $72 million plus interest. The oil companies also seemed content with this arrangement, perhaps figuring that their argument might impress a federal judge more than it did us. In the meantime they were enjoying the opportunity to supply Middle East crude to the European market at the inflated $1.75 price.

My confrontations with the oil and marine insurance industries took time and energy away from my main job, which was to draft ECA Regulation 1 so that we could implement Section 202. This turned out to be as difficult as predicted by Cooper, whose appraisal of the battleground proved highly accurate.

Without a doubt Richard Bissell was my primary adversary. A tall, good-looking, New England blueblood, he came from the culture of Government and Academia. Although he claimed to be an expert on the workings of business, in fact he had no first-hand experience as a businessman. Still, I could not deny that he was an articulate wordsmith, with a penchant for creating a context favorable to his arguments. In our meetings with Hoffman to discuss the implementation of Section 202, he was always pompous and condescending to me. As he saw that I would not retreat from my position, his resentment grew. Bissell and his supporting staff dared not attack Kohler, so they focused on me as the malevolent influence.

As a result, I became the target of accusations within the Agency and leaks to the press. I was described as an ideologue and an OPA Price Controller, bent on preventing the Agency from accepting private channels of trade. Personal attacks went to the extreme. Someone within the Agency planted leaks with two columnists—Earl Wilson of the NY Daily News, and Wanda

Jablonski of the Journal of Commerce—labeling me a Communist. Ruth Montgomery, a personal friend who also happened to be a senior columnist at the Daily News, was outraged over this libel, and demanded that Wilson retract the accusation with an apology, which he did. I was less concerned with Jablonski, who was largely ignored. Also publisher of a weekly newsletter called the "Petroleum Intelligence Weekly," she was generally regarded as little more than a sycophant for the major oil companies.

As if all this wasn't enough, I now had conflict in my personal life as well. Long separations due to my business trips with Dadourian—including one over the Christmas holidays—had put a strain on my marriage. During these periods Pat had become closer to her mother and more estranged from me. Her mother had always felt that Pat had married beneath her, a feeling that was not shared by Pat's father, with whom I got along fine. I often wondered if the marriage would have been happier if Pat's mother had accepted me as her son-in-law.

When I took the job with ECA, Pat reluctantly moved with me back to Washington. Soon afterwards she became ill, requiring surgery that left her unable to bear children. I very much wanted a family and was willing to adopt, but she was not. As 1948 wore on, this issue caused increasing friction between us.

Without the obstacles that Bissell and his crew threw at me, I could have completed ECA Regulation 1 in a week. As it was, it took me nine months. During this period I relied heavily on Kohler's support and encouragement to sustain my efforts. He proved to be as loyal to me as I was to him. After I had been on the job for several months, Cooper visited the Agency and spent some time with each of us. Before he returned to Pittsburgh, he said, "Sam, it appears that you and Kohler get along famously well. Don't you ever disagree?"

"Occasionally," I replied, "I find myself taking a position on an important matter and realize that Kohler prefers a different approach. Demonstrating a greater knowledge of the facts, or of the implications of a certain course of action, might not be enough to change his mind. If he does finally yield to my argument it's usually because I have persuaded him that my way is not only more efficient than the alternatives, but also more virtuous. I wouldn't call Kohler 'pious'—not at all. However, he consciously stakes out a 'high moral ground,' and if he's convinced someone is standing on still higher ground, he'll change his position." This capsule summary of Kohler's character belied his pragmatism, complexity, and capacity for surprises, but when these latter traits came into play it was never at the expense of his moral convictions.

Aside from Tyler Wood, I had only one ally outside the Controller's office. After an early "knockdown" battle with Bissell in Hoffman's office, I was surprised when, after the meeting, I felt a hand on my shoulder. When I turned around, there was dignified, elderly Howard Bruce, the Deputy Administrator. "Young man," he said, "I am not sure I fully understand all aspects of your course of action, but you may be sure that I will support your recommendations. I am confident that you are sincere and dedicated to doing what's right." What a boost to my morale! Obviously, Mr. Bruce was aware of the concerted effort by others within the Agency to do me in, and understood his support would be useful encouragement.

ECA, as did its predecessor agencies—Greek-Turkish Aid and the U.N.—supplied goods and services which presumably could not be purchased in local or any other non-dollar currency. The importer was required to deposit with his government an amount in local currency equivalent to the dollar-cost of the exporter's invoice. As had been the situation in Greece, local currency was abundantly available throughout Europe, with little exchange value, and relatively no burden to the importer. The profit expected from the import would be in local currency. Participating countries enforced as best they could prohibitions against exchanging abundant local currency for scarce dollars.

In supplying aid through private channels (rather than by direct government procurement), terms of procurement were decided mutually by importer and exporter. The latter was paid by ECA against his invoices and shipping documents. The importer was free to choose among available exporters and to set conditions important to him in making the purchase. Under these circumstances many—perhaps most—importers would attempt to take advantage of the procurement process in one of three ways: by demanding that exporters inflate the prices on their invoices—the situation I had encountered in Greece; by demanding that exporters price their goods at a higher level of quality than the goods actually shipped; or by claiming fictitious or excessive agent's commissions. The kickbacks thus obtained would then be deposited in the importer's personal third-country bank account. These kickbacks were the primary reason why commodities were purchased at higher than market prices, and it was this practice I was seeking to stop.

Despite the allegations of my detractors, I was careful not to place undue burdens on the businessmen we would be dealing with. I made a conscious distinction between regulating and controlling. Regulation, in the form of a set of bureaucratic rules to follow, I regarded as unneccessary and undesirable. Control, on the other hand, could be devised as a clear guide for self-enforcement.

Hence, as finally drafted, ECA Reg 1 was really quite simple. To achieve the self-enforcing feature, I proposed that the exporter affirm, in a simple sworn affidavit, that the unit prices in the supply contract were not in excess of prices charged private customers. In addition, he was to name any agents involved in the transaction, and the amount of commissions paid them. Misstatements on the part of the exporter left him open to charges of perjury. All this information was readily known to the exporter and would be put on a 5×7" card, known as ECA Certificate 100, which would accompany the sales and shipping documents.

By the time of the final meeting to decide the fate of ECA Reg 1, Hoffman had already sided with us on the marine insurance and crude oil issues, and had seen firsthand the value of the expanded function of the Controller. At the meeting, Bissell realized early on that he would lose on the issuance of ECA Reg 1, so he focused on the Supplier's Certificate. I regarded this certificate as indispensible to self-enforcement under the regulation.

With pretentions of knowing the businessman's mind, Bissell argued that no exporter would sign such a document. "You're asking legitimate businessmen to tell you they are not crooks!" he said to me dramatically. This was a disingenuous line for Bissell to take, given his distrust of business, but I feared it might be an effective one with Hoffman, who was a businessman himself. Kohler looked shaken as well.

Rather than debate the point with Bissell I replied, "Why do we spend our time speculating about what businessmen will or will not accept? The exporters themselves can tell us. Mr. Hoffman, I propose we convene a cross-section of exporters and then review the certificate with them. I will ask them to approve, disapprove, or amend it."

Before Bissell could respond, Hoffman exclaimed, "Good idea, go ahead!"

Within a week twelve industry representatives convened in our board room to review the certificate. After some deliberation I said, "I'd like the benefit of your advice. Should we use this certificate or not?" The voice vote was unanimously in favor of it. Bissell was unfortunately absent from this meeting. I would love to have seen his face when he learned of his misjudgment.

As I told Kohler, the vote came as no surprise to me. The Supplier's Certificate took the initiative away from importers to demand kickbacks. I expressed my opinion that businessmen would prefer to conduct their affairs honestly, rather than compete by secret and illegal arrangements—an opinion that is not generally shared by federal regulators, or social and political "experts," whose inherent presumption is that dishonesty and corruption is the warp and woof of business.

In real life, business transactions are essentially decisions based on maximizing gains and minimizing detriments, with due regard for both short and long term consequences. Good business is founded on honesty and trust between buyer and seller.

When the government enters the marketplace to buy or sell, or to guarantee property, normal free market restraints against corruption are undermined by the absence of detriments. Absent the fiduciary role of government, and taxpayer awareness, what's to lose by cheating the government? In the Marshall Plan some of us understood the reality that government spending can actually *induce* business corruption.

With ECA Reg 1 and Supplier's Certificate 100 approved, Bissell had been vanquished, and I could breathe easier. After it was all over, I remember saying to Cooper, "You know, Bill, someday that guy's going to get this government in a helluva lot of trouble." Cooper just smiled. This offhand remark turned out to be quite prescient. Over a decade later Bissell, now with the CIA, was put in charge of a top secret operation, which after the fact became known as the "Bay of Pigs."

1949 brought a greater measure of peace both on the job and off. After accepting my offer to share equally all our savings and property, which by then were not insignificant, Pat went out of state to get a divorce. I thought that was the end of it, but as it turned out, divorcing Pat was just as complicated as marrying her had been.

Not wanting the stain of a divorce on their daughter's good name, her family decided to petition the Catholic Church for an annulment. I was advised by the Church's legal counsel to cooperate by confirming that I had known our marriage was illegal within the canons of the Church at the time of the wedding. Supposedly, the priest who married us had been retired and without capacity to perform the ceremony, and the site of the ceremony was beyond the geographical jurisdiction of the priest who had given his permission.

In good conscience I had to reject these allegations. This was all news to me. At the time I had been assured that the marriage was properly authorized by the Church and I knew it to be legal under state law.

The matter did not end there. The Archbishop in Washington was then invoked to persuade me to cooperate. Implications of damage to my personal reputation and other not-so-disguised threats were used, but I refused to make admissions that were palpably false. I was so disturbed by the Church's high priest and legal advisor going after me in this way, that I never inquired whether the annulment was granted after all that effort and (I'm sure) considerable expense.

Once more a bachelor, I resolved that I would put my marriage behind me and enjoy a social life. No longer naive, I could now indulge without guilt in the intimacy of attractive women and not carry the ulterior motive of marriage. For the next couple of years that's exactly what I did.

By the time ECA Reg 1 and the Supplier's Certificate were approved, my staff was already in place to administer them. Kohler had given me carte blanche to hire whomever and as many as I needed. Howard Morrison, who had been recommended by Cooper, was the first of a professional staff of ten, chosen primarily for their analytical capacity and, whenever possible, some experience in their industry niche. They were instructed to analyze the nature of their industry, the principal players in exporting, and any special practices, and to review the supply contracts under their purview. My staff prepared memos for me as well as sharing thoughts and experiences in personal briefings. As a result, I accumulated enough evidence to prove, at least to my satisfaction, that the Agency could function through private channels of trade and in compliance with Section 202.

To the horror of personnel and management experts, I chose not to give myself a deputy, preferring that each staff member have direct access to me, and me to them. Our office performed remarkably well: morale was high, with sick leaves and vacations rarely taken. There was no time for leisure in the office, as a sense of urgency and importance prevailed. In the second year, when I was required to make periodic trips to Europe to meet with the mission staffs of the participating countries, one of my senior staff would fill in and keep things running smoothly in my absence.

I don't recall by what channel Thelma Burdine came to me in 1948 to be interviewed as my secretary. From what she soon told me, she would not have gotten past the Government's personnel office, and she wisely did not apply there. At my request she recounted her personal history. All went well until I asked, "What was your last permament job?"

Suddenly her expression changed to one of gloom and she answered, "That's where I have a problem. I was secretary to Mr. Hunt for a year, before he had to close his office last week. You must have seen the headlines about the Five Percenters Scandal. I'm afraid that I could be an embarrassment to anyone who hires me".

My curiosity was aroused. Of course I had heard of the scandal, featured in big headlines in the New York Herald Tribune above the byline of Washington Bureau Chief Bert Andrews. Supposedly small companies wishing to do business with the federal government had to pay five percent in "tribute" for the privilege. The details had never been adequately spelled out. The whole thing looked to me like a tempest in a teapot, stirred up by the Republicans as election year ammunition against Truman.

I asked Thelma to give me the details of Mr. Hunt's operations and her role in them. What I heard seemed quite normal to me and I told her so, disclaiming any authority to be the judge. She was amazed when I offered her a job as my secretary, to start immediately.

One afternoon earlier in the year Hoffman had telephoned me, asking if I would receive William P. Rogers, Counsel for the Senate Oversight Committee (later Attorney General under Ike and Secretary of State under Nixon). "He needs some help in unraveling a kickback scandal involving the Export-Import Bank," Hoffman explained. "I told him that you were the man to figure it out if anyone could."

Rogers left Hoffman's office and immediately came to mine. He had been recently discharged from the Navy. Prior to the war he had served as Governor Thomas Dewey's Assistant D.A. in New York, and Dewey had been instrumental in getting him the job with the Senate Oversight Committee.

An anonymous tip had directed Rogers's attention to a large payment to an individual. From a cursory review of the documents he showed me, it appeared that the insurance premium included in the total amount was conspicuously exorbitant. In effect, the Export-Import Bank had made an excessive payout, resulting from a conspiracy between a bank client and a third party, with the kickback hidden in the insurance premium.

Rogers thanked me for my insight, and stayed on to chat a while. Bill and I hit it off as friends, and thereafter he frequently visited me at my office.

When the 5%er scandal broke, Rogers announced to the press that the Oversight Committee would hold hearings on it. After that nothing much happened. Rogers's excuse to the press was that he could not begin the Senate hearings until he located Hunt's two secretaries, who were key witnesses.

Now one of these "key witnesses" was working for me! Rogers continued to stop by my office almost every week, and never failed to exchange pleasantries with Thelma. He knew very well that she had been Hunt's secretary, yet never raised the 5%er issue with her or with me. After Truman defeated Dewey in the election of 1948, the 5%er "scandal" vanished—no hearings, and no discovery of Thelma Burdine's whereabouts.

During her three years with me, Thelma kept my staff working in high gear, in the spirit of team cooperation. From her outer office she managed the entrance to mine, treating each staff member equally as they sought access to discuss problems and seek guidance. By the time I left ECA, she had established a reputation as a super human being and an outstanding assistant. When I left the Agency, Hoffman's successor as Administrator, William C. Foster, chose Thelma as his assistant.

(A couple of years later I happened to hear the true story of the Five Percenters Scandal from the man who had broken the story, Bert Andrews himself. We were at a Washington dinner party, and alcohol had loosened his tongue.

"Amazing what you can do in this town," he bragged. "Take the 5% scandal that I put on the front page of every newspaper in the country. You wanna know what that was really all about?" Immediately Andrews was surrounded by everyone within earshot.

"My cousin from out of town comes in to see me before returning to New Hampshire," he began. 'What are you here for?' I ask him.

"He tells me, 'I wanted to register my company to receive tenders from the Defense Department. I've got some products they could use. The procurement officer asked me if I had an office in Washington, and I told him no, my company was too small. He handed me a list of a dozen names and said that these guys were registered agents and for a 5% commission they would screen the tenders and let me know when anything came up for me to bid on.

"I didn't know any of the names so I just picked a guy named Hunt. I was very impressed with him. He's got an autographed picture of Truman on his desk. We hit it off real good, so he's going to go to work for me.'

"'For 5% of any sales he makes for you?' I ask.

"'That's right,' my cousin says. 'Plus a retainer of $1,000 up front. It sounds very reasonable to me. I told him I'd send him a check tomorrow.'

"Suddenly I get a flash. I had a grand in my desk, so I take it out and give it to him. 'Here,' I say to him, 'take this $1,000 to Hunt and get a receipt.' He does, he brings me back the receipt, which is the smoking gun...and that's it! That's all there was to it. The next day I wrote the story and every Republican in the country jumped on the bandwagon. Rogers helped, by saying he was going to hold hearings. I'm damn glad he didn't, or the whole thing might have backfired on me!" Andrews laughed. "We got a lot of mileage out of nothing on that one, but old Harry won anyway."

Obviously Andrews had no qualms about using Hunt and Thelma as pawns in his game. It was a sobering lesson in political ethics, or lack thereof. I said nothing to him in response. I had just returned to private practice and the last thing I needed was for Bert Andrews to come after me.)

Attempts to circumvent Section 202 continued, of course,

even after the issuance of ECA Reg 1 and Supplier's Certificate 100, and it was the job of my office to monitor compliance. In the case of agricultural products such as wheat, corn, and cotton—which are graded and sold according to quality—this meant an all-out effort to prevent the common practice of "shipping shy," in which the exporter prices a shipment at a certain grade but actually delivers an inferior grade. The price differential between the higher and lower grades could amount to a very substantial amount of money—in this case, ECA money, which came directly from the U.S. taxpayer.

This practice, which involved collusion between the exporter and importer, existed long before World War II and was well established. It served the purpose of increasing the importer's costs for tax purposes and diverting funds into his personal account, beyond the reach of his own government. For the exporter, such a prearrangement was usually a prerequisite for getting the importer's business.

With the help of statistical experts W. Edwards (Ed) Deming and David Rosenblatt, formerly our wartime colleagues in the Bureau of the Budget, we determined that the only way to deter the practice of "shipping shy" was to institute a sampling system, whereby all shipments under the program were sampled for quality at both the ports of embarkation and debarkation. Any price discrepancy between the two points would be recovered by ECA or the total payment could be disallowed. When word of our plans leaked to the dozen or so U.S. companies that did the bulk of the business, they expressed outrage, and pressured members of Congress to prevent us from imposing the sampling system. Fortunately their efforts were unsuccessful.

Soon after the sampling system went into effect, Anderson Clayton Company, one of the largest exporters, "shipped shy" a cargo of cotton to France. My office served notice to refuse payment. The following day Will Clayton, founder and president of the company and formerly UnderSecretary of State, called me from National Airport and said, "I arrived in Washington this morning for the sole purpose of meeting with you. What time would be convenient?"

Out of courtesy for this distinguished public servant, I decided to rearrange my schedule and told him, "You may come in right away if you wish."

Within the hour Mr. Clayton arrived at my office. Very politely he asked the reason for my decision to stop payment. My reply was very simple: "The cotton you shipped is invoiced at a price higher than the quality you proposed to deliver. Our sampling process undercovered the discrepancy." He sat there nodding, with a look of concern on his face. Before he could reply I then asked, "Mr. Clayton, knowing your contribution as a public servant for many years, I would appreciate your opinion. Are we doing the right thing by exercising this kind of control?" Without hesitation he replied, "Yes, you are. If I had your job and responsibility I would do the same thing."

We immediately figured out the price differential, which came to more than $100,000. "I will authorize payment on the revised price," I assured him.

We shook hands and Clayton looked at his watch. "Thank you for your kind attention. I can be home in Houston by day's end." I admit to being flattered that I was the only person he met with that day. Finally he asked, "Will this matter reach the press? It would embarrass me personally."

"So far as I know," I replied, "the only two people in the Agency who know about this are my analyst McFeeters and myself. It would make a great story," I said, smiling. "However, I can resist the temptation to make myself a hero at your expense. If you haven't spoken to anyone else in Washington, I don't believe that it will leak to the Press." That was my first and only meeting with Mr. Clayton.

Many years later, Mr. Clayton's oldest daughter, seeking affirmation of her father's role in launching the Marshall Plan, came to Virginia to visit with me. Mrs. Norwood had become a national figure in her own right with the recent press discovery that she had given Colonel Oliver North $1 million to assist him in his fight against the Contras.

I arranged a meeting at the University of Virginia's Miller Center of Public Affairs with its Director, Ken Thompson, and Chairman, Wilson Neuman. Mrs. Norwood's younger sister flew in from Baltimore for the meeting. Mrs. Norwood's interest in having a biography written of her father and his role in the Marshall Plan did not produce any noticeable enthusiasm on the part of Mr. Thompson. If it had, I'm sure Mrs. Norwood would have offered a grant for that purpose.

Before she flew home to Austin, she asked me if I would write the biography, since I was familiar with the Marshall Plan. The job would have been on the periphery of my competence but I could have undertaken it, and my effort would probably have been well rewarded financially. However, given Mrs. Norwood's perception that her father was the father of the Marshall Plan, I could not in good conscience accept. It was true that Will Clayton, in his role as UnderSecretary of State, had been a staunch champion of postwar aid to Europe, but so were others.

Within a few weeks Mrs. Norwood engaged Stanford's Gregory Fossedad, of the Hoover Institute, to write her father's biography. He titled it, "*Our Finest Hour—Will Clayton, the Marshall Plan, and the Triumph of Democracy*," and made a valiant, scholarly effort to maximize Clayton's achievements. Fossedad did properly credit Clayton's contemporaries for their respective roles in winning passage of the Plan, but his book is conspicuously silent on how the job was done. He ignored the fact that after the initial ECA Appropriations Bill passed by only one vote, Congress approved funds for subsequent years by ever-increasing margins. European recovery was achieved beyond all expectations because of the successful management of this $25 billion. The name Paul G. Hoffman—the administrator of this miraculous accomplishment—appears nowhere in the book.

In my three years at ECA, I encountered only two instances of businessmen seeking to exploit their relationships with government officials to circumvent generally applicable rules. The first involved approval of a large shipment of pharmaceutical products to Austria. A careful examination of the shipping documents by one of my staff revealed that these pharmaceuticals had originated in Hungary and could have been purchased by the Austrian importer with local currency. Realizing that he could make a great profit on the transaction if paid in dollars, the exporter had purchased the pharmaceuticals in Hungary, shipped them by air freight to the United States, and then reshipped the cargo to Vienna out of New York.

My office refused to pay for this cargo. It was then that we received telephone calls from the office of Secretary of Commerce Sawyer, pleading the hardship of the supplier. We made no exception in this case and affirmed that our regulation would be strictly enforced. Neither Austria nor ECA paid for the cargo, and the exporter—later identified as a relative of the Secretary—was stuck with it.

In the other incident, Thelma advised me one day on the intercom that a man had just called saying, "This is the White House calling. Mr. X (I don't remember his name) wishes to talk with Mr. Nakasian." Curious, I took the call immediately.

Mr. X came on the phone, speaking broken English with an accent I recognized as Middle Eastern. He was extremely cordial and respectful and hoped that I might receive him for a few minutes. I consented, and set a time late that same afternoon.

Mr. X was a big man. The name on his calling card was Turkish, and when asked he admitted that he was a citizen of Turkey. As is the business custom in his part of the world, the purpose of the meeting was only revealed after prolonged preliminaries. Like a German sentence, the verb is at the end and then you know what is meant. As the conversation progressed, I noted to myself that this was a novel experience—a Turk currying favor from an Armenian refugee from Turkey, whose father had been massacred by Turks. I almost felt sorry for him as he tried to establish a personal relationship based on our common origins.

When he decided that he had created a favorable atmosphere,

he said, "I know that you are the most important man in charge, and you can give me approval of my deal. I can buy 500 Missouri mules and sell them in Greece. My problem is, I don't want to buy these mules until I am sure that I can get paid." Obviously he had gone through our regulations and understood that the normal procedure was to seek payment after the supply contract had been completed, and delivery made.

Something was wrong here, and I had an idea what it was. The Turk had a CIF (cost-insurance-freight: title passing to purchaser at point of delivery) agreement with his Greek importer. Having seen burros and donkeys working the mountainous terrain in Greece, I had a difficult time imagining the huge, Missouri flatland mules making it in this environment. In addition, an ocean voyage was always stressful on animals, who often got sick or died enroute. The importer might refuse payment when he saw the mules, which would leave Mr. X holding the bag—unless he had already received his ECA dollars. I politely advised the Turkish entrepreneur that I would not approve *any* transaction in advance, and that an exception for the purpose of reducing his risk of doing business could not be justified.

I gathered that Mr. X had been well briefed not to mention his White House sponsor(s). Was his contact one of President Truman's aides? It struck me as quite a coincidence that Clark Clifford, General Vaughan, J.K Vardaman, and Donald Dawson were all from Missouri, as were the mules.

Sometime later, in examining documents of supplies to Austria, one of my staff noted a remarkably consistent pattern. For each of dozens of transactions, the Supplier's Certificate 100 identified a Swiss company as agent. This company received 5-10% of the ECA payouts as commission. After investigating, we identified the owners and directors of the Swiss firm to be Austrian. A further effort revealed that they were high officers and directors of the Kreditanstalt, Austria's State Bank and the largest holding company of Austrian corporations.

At the time, Austria was still occupied by the four major powers, including the Soviet Union. A general election was underway, and the Communist party was competing for Chancellor. The danger I sensed was that if the Communists found out about this corruption within the capitalist elite, it might tip the election in their favor. On the other hand, if the government acted to clean this mess up before the Communists learned of it, the publicity value to the Communists would be minimal. In putting the picture together to *my* satisfaction, I decided that my staff member and I would keep this knowledge to ourselves.

I decided on a course of action which would not directly involve our government, but I realized I needed support from several key players, even though they would remain passive. I asked Jim Cooley, ECA Deputy General Counsel, to invite a trusted CIA friend of his to a meeting in my office on Friday. I invited Eleanor Dulles, Chief of the State Department's Austrian desk: I knew her.

At the meeting I told them what we had found. Mrs. Dulles was visibly distraught that her cherished friends in the Austrian elite would engage in this fraud. The CIA operative suggested further action they might take. Cooley looked to me for a suggestion. I replied that I had initiated this meeting only to share this sensitive information, and not to seek action on their parts. "Our interests are best served if we keep out of it. I have a plan that will almost keep us out completely and still get the job done." To the CIA man I said, "I would suggest you do nothing."

I suggested to Mrs. Dulles that she cable our Ambassador in Vienna and request that he set up an appointment on the following Thursday with Chancellor Figl, for the purpose of my making a courtesy call. "Please do not disclose what you learned today!" I warned. Then I filled them in on the rest of my plan.

"Tomorrow morning, even though it's Saturday, I have arranged to meet with Mr. Queenan, head of the New York accounting firm of Haskins and Sells, at his office. I will ask him to assign two investigating accountants to meet me at Idlewild Airport and accompany me to Vienna. We will leave Monday on the four o'clock Pan Am Clipper Flight to London, and from there go to Paris. As a courtesy I will meet privately with Tyler Wood (now ECA Ambassador in Paris) on Tuesday afternoon. If all goes well with our travel plans, the three of us will arrive in Vienna on Wednesday.

I would expect that after Figl gets the facts from me, he will ask what we're going to do. I'll tell him that our two experts will be his employees, and will conduct the investigation in utmost secrecy. Then, when they have presented Figl with the facts and documentary proof, he will be in a position to take whatever action he deems appropriate. We will have no further role in this matter."

Cooley, his CIA friend, and Mrs. Dulles all looked relieved. The meeting was not recorded, and no action had been requested of them. Clearly I was sticking *my* neck out—not theirs.

The following morning I met Queenan in his office high above the streets of New York. There was a hurricane that day—most unusual for the city—and as we discussed my plan, chaos reigned outdoors. Through his picture window we could see windows in other buildings shattering and showering the streets below with glass. Water towers toppled over and billboards blew off their scaffolding. It seemed a fitting metaphor for what might happen in Austria if word leaked out as to the purpose of our mission.

Checking in at Vienna's Bristol Hotel on Wednesday, a message was waiting for me from our Ambassador. It read: "Please come to my residence on your arrival." As I traveled to meet him, I became aware of the tension in the air, with United States, British, French, and Soviet forces occupying their respective quarters of the divided city.

At his residence, the Ambassador told me that Chancellor Figl expected me to come alone at four PM to his office in the Chancery. I presumed that Mrs. Dulles had advised the Ambassador that I would not discuss with him the content of my message to the Chancellor. Accordingly, he did not ask, and I didn't volunteer the information.

The Austrian Chancery represents the grandeur of the Hapsburg Monarchy's Austro-Hungarian Empire. Gatekeepers, doormen, the Chancellor's adjutant—all were elegantly attired in brilliant uniforms. As I was escorted up the regal marble staircase, I tried to focus on how to behave and what to say to the Chancellor. After all, it had been only fifteen years since I had landed at the Newsboys Home, jobless and homeless. Now I was walking into this castle for a private audience with the King, as it were. In these few seconds, I admit the thought crossed my mind that perhaps I was in over my head.

Figl and Foreign Minister Gruber received me formally, as a foreign diplomat. Since they were clearly apprehensive about the purpose of my visit, I spared them further suspense by getting quickly to the point: "Your Excellencies, the information I give you today is well documented and its import, we believe, is so serious as to justify your personal attention. We are mindful that in your upcoming elections the Communist candidates would greatly benefit at the polls—quite possibly dealing a fatal blow to your candidates—if this information were made public. We have taken every precaution to keep it secret, as I expect your Government will wish to do."

"In the due course of administering Marshall Plan aid to Austria, we discovered that a large amount is regularly charged with a commission of 5-10%, payable to a Swiss company as agent for the Austrian importers. This Swiss company appears nowhere as performing a function, either for the American exporters or the Austrian importer. Further inquiry by my staff identified the persons who own this Swiss company. They are high officers and directors of Kreditanstalt. These men, national figures in your country, publicly support the anti-Communist candidates."

Having exploded the bomb, I observed the visible shock and dismay that my revelation had elicited. Almost simultaneously the two men exclaimed, "My God! What are we going to do?" Of course the unspoken question on both their minds was, "What are *you* going to do?"

"Your Excellencies," I reassured them, "We regard this as your internal problem. Involvement on our part we believe would denigrate your integrity. We believe, however, that you should take immediate remedial action and thus defuse the potential damage before the Communists find out about it."

"Yes, of course!" Chancellor Figl replied, "But how can we act on this information without it leaking to the press? Many of our government people are pro-Communist!"

"I have anticipated this situation by arranging to provide you with two expert American investigators. You can rely upon them for competence and secrecy. They will provide you with the documentation you need to take appropriate action."

Their faces lit up with hope. "Who are they? When can we bring them to Vienna?"

I reached in my pocket and said, "They are now *in* Vienna. You will find them at the Bristol Hotel." Then I handed them a slip of paper with the accountants' names and made a slight movement to leave. I understood that protocol dictated that the high official at a meeting stand up first.

As the bearer of bad tidings I was prepared to be resented as much as appreciated, so it came as a bit of a surprise when their goodbyes expressed heartfelt gratitude and graciousness.

"Please stay in Vienna a few days," Gruber offered sincerely.

"Thank you but I must decline," I answered. "Early tomorrow I will drive to Bad Gastein for a weekend of relaxation. Then on Monday I must return to Washington."

"Will you be in touch with me again?" Figl asked.

"I hope not," was my reply. "I think it's best that I leave the scene completely." I smiled as we shook hands. "Thank you again for permitting me the honor of making this courtesy call."

I did not feel it was necessary to follow up on my visit. Clearly it was in their own best interest to act responsibly on the information I had given them. A few months later I happened to see Mr. Queenan at a social function, and asked him about it. He confirmed that the Austrian government had cooperated fully with his accountants.

As fate would have it, I had recently begun dating another Patricia— Patricia Prochnik— whose father had been Austrian Ambassador to the United States. Patricia had just returned to Washington from Europe, where she had served in the Army and

Red Cross. Before long, notions of continued bachelorhood melted away, and I asked her to marry me.

Less than a year after my Austrian adventure, Patty asked me to join her and her father at an Austrian Embassy reception in honor of Foreign Minister Gruber. As the three of us proceeded down the receiving line, Patty's father introduced me to Kleinwechter, the current Ambassador, who then repeated my name to Gruber. Gruber, a big man with a big voice, almost shouted, "I *know* this man—a *great* man. He saved my country from Communism!" Those within earshot gasped in amazement. Of course, no details were offered by Gruber, as the secrecy lid was still on.

Later that evening I explained Gruber's statement to Patty and her father, lest they exaggerate further what they had heard. Soon after this Patty accepted my offer of marriage. I never believed this embassy event had any influence on her decision to take the vows.

There was only one non-European country receiving aid under the Marshall Plan, and that was Nationalist China. (Aid to Japan was included in the Army Appropriations Bill.) By the end of the second year, Chiang Kai-Shek's forces were being driven out of one port city after another by Mao's revolutionary army. Chinese currency—the yuan—was depreciating so fast that by the time Standard Vacuum Oil delivered a shipment, the amount deposited in local currency was no longer enough to cover the cost of the cargo. As a result, the company could no longer comply with the Agency's regulations.

Lloyd (Shorty) Elliot, Chairman of Standard Vacuum, along with his general counsel Art Tripp and Washington lobbyist Hap Sites, met with me and requested an alternative procedure to the regulation so that they could continue to supply petroleum to the evaporating Chiang Kai-Shek Government. In this case I was happy to make an exception to the rule. Henceforth the importer's deposit at the time of the deal was sufficient for us to make payment, regardless of what happened to local currency between the time the deal was struck and the oil delivered.

Troubleshooting like this captured my interest, but my daily routine had ceased to be challenging. Designing a modus operandi to put an act of Congress into effect; bringing together the staff to execute it, and inculcating in them values and esprit de corps—this had been a challenge of the highest order, demanding courage and innovation. Now I was simply adminstering a government function, enforcing regulations and conducting post audits. I began to grow restless.

In spite of this, I stayed on another year. The job's perks were undeniable. Each year I made several trips to Europe aboard the Queen Mary or Elizabeth, or another luxury liner. Upon arrival I was always received by the Embassy Secretary and driven by limousine to my hotel. ECA missions and embassy staff in each country showered me with respect and every possible convenience and hospitality. In fact, frequently I found this attention too intensive and incursive of my freedom, and would evade my chaperones by changing my schedule at the last minute, so that I could go it alone and choose my own social companions.

Also, admittedly, the job was a constant ego trip. Besides the one-on-one with Austrian Chancellor Figl, I had regular, private meetings with ECA Ambassadors Averill Harriman and Tyler Wood, as well as the ECA mission chiefs in each European country. State Department bigwigs might criticize my decisions, but they had no power to overrule me.

As 1950 turned the corner into 1951, Hoffman and Kohler resigned to return to private life. In spite of the VIP life-style I had come to enjoy, I too was ready to move on, and tendered my resignation to Paul Green, Kohler's successor. He urged me to stay on, but I successfully argued that I wasn't needed. A senior member of my staff could replace me very competently. I briefly considered a consulting arrangement, but rejected that as possibly showing a lack of confidence in the staff I had recruited and worked with for three years.

So on April 1st, 1951, I reentered private practice by opening a three-room office in the Tower Building, at 15th & K Streets NW, in Washington. Ironically, a short while later I met Shorty

Elliot at a party. He thanked me again for helping him on the Chiang Kai-Shek deal and offered me a retainer, remarking that I was a man of action and imagination, which Standard Vacuum could use. He seemed surprised when I told him that I was still identified with a multi-million dollar ECA claim against his parent companies (the case had not yet gone to trial), and it would be a conflict of interest for me to accept. I seriously regretted not being able to take him up on his kind offer, and recalled for his benefit the old adage, "No good deed goes unpunished."

I look back with pride on my accomplishments with the ECA. Today the Marshall Plan is hailed as a miracle for its successful restoration of the postwar economies of Europe. Throughout the world it is spoken of as "the way to go" to solve economic and social needs. Years later, with the help of Cooper and other knowledgeable participants in the program, I estimated the numerical savings attributable to the functions my office performed. Following is a quotation from page 11 of *Eric Louis Kohler, Accounting's Man of Principles*, published by Reston Publishing Company, a subsidiary of Prentice Hall:

> The estimates prepared in my office indicate that crude oil costs were reduced by 20 percent, for an annual total approximating $40 million; grain and cotton costs were reduced by some 10 to 20 percent; and against the marine insurance premiums saved of $20 million, there were almost no offsetting losses on shipments. Assuming that all costs were reduced by 10 percent, the Controller's office might then lay claim to savings of $2.5 billion on the $25 billion program as a result of Kohler's "before" and "after" effects. This savings effectively increased the volume of shipments to Europe by 10 percent and avoided the necessity of asking Congress for still larger appropriations.
>
> More important than the savings, perhaps, was the fact that ECA would probably not have survived much

beyond the first year, or been allowed to operate as it did, if the Controller's office had not kept the program credible. This performance was critical to the continuing annual appropriations by Congress for the rapid recovery of Europe (and other parts of the world). If the program had been aborted by a less diligent administration, we can only speculate what would have been the fate of Western Europe and, indeed, the security of the United States.

In the three years of Kohler's tenure, 1948-1951, congressional committees and the GAO conducted no hearings or investigations, and, in fact, none appeared necessary regarding the prices paid in a program of some $25 billion. Full accountability was maintained and the GAO and congressional committee staffs were kept fully informed on all aspects of the vigilance that the Controller's office was seeking to maintain. Our internal vigilance of audits, analyses, and self-directed enforcement assured compliance with our policies and regulations on thousands of transactions involving hundreds of business firms and a dozen or more governments.

ECA was probably Kohler's largest assignment, whether measured in terms of money, multiplicity of transaction, international scope, or urgency. The remarkable fact is that Kohler's administration of this function was performed by a relatively small staff of no more that 100 to 150 persons. My part of the staff numbered 10 professionals to cover transactions involving some $6 billion annually. Finally, as a result of this diligent fiduciary administration of Marshall Plan funds, the program was substantially completed six months ahead of schedule and at a cost nearly $5 billion less than the 1947 estimate made by Hoffman and Commerce Secretary Harriman.

Prominent among my memories of that period is an unscheduled visit to my office in 1950 by Drew Pearson, the nationally syndicated columnist famous for exposing wrongdoing in government. My initial apprehension upon seeing him was soothed when he extended his hand and said, "I just came by to meet you, and to congratulate you for the great job you're doing."

I believe his informant about our program was Rogers, who, by virtue of his role with the Senate Oversight Committee, had in common with Pearson the task of disclosing irregularities in government. Through his own frequent, informal visits, Rogers was very aware of my efforts. Pearson had excoriated the government for the waste and corruption in Greek-Turkish Aid, and no doubt had inquired of Rogers whether the Marshall Plan was a similar debacle.

As Pearson departed, he said to me, "You won't be reading about yourself in my column. I need all my space for the bad guys."

In 1968 I met privately with David Rockefeller, Chairman of Chase Manhattan Bank, in his private suite in Rockefeller Plaza. Knowing of my work in the Marshall Plan, he asked me, "Do you think our foreign aid today is helping third world countries develop economic self-reliance?"

"The simple answer is no," I replied. "For the past 15 years our direct aid has been spent largely to buy the support of foreign governments for whatever policy the State Department happens to be pursuing at the moment. In the Marshall Plan our highest priority was the economic development of the countries involved. We were frequently at odds with State's diplomatic aims, but Paul Hoffman reported directly to Truman, bypassing State according to the will of Congress at that time.

In late 1951, the Democratic majority in Congress replaced ECA with the Mutual Security Agency as an arm of the State Department. Once the Dulles brothers (John Foster at State and Allen at the CIA) came to power in 1953, with foreign aid now under the control of the State Department, everything changed. In the context of the Cold War, foreign aid was used to support diplomacy and treaty negotiations aimed at mutual security. Foreign governments quickly realized that foreign aid from the United States was a bargaining chip, not only in negotiations with *our* government, but between two foreign governments under our sponsorship as well.

The stated foreign aid goal of economic development has become a thinly disguised sham! Under the Marshall Plan, most of our aid funded capital goods, which restored the productive capacity of the manufacturing and agricultural sectors. Today, direct aid to third world countries is spent largely for consumable goods—food and petroleum especially—in effect fostering an ongoing dependency upon us. Agricultural products available for free under our aid programs actually compete with local production! Local energy sources are also being replaced by imported oil.

Indirect aid, through the World Bank and regional banks, is targeted for development projects, but these banks, as well as the United Nations, are excessively bureaucratic and politically driven by member countries. Accountability is woefully lacking, and administrative costs are outlandish, usurping funds desperately needed for third world development."

Rockefeller listened carefully to my tirade, then asked, "So, if foreign aid is as ineffective as you say, why does Congress continue funding it?"

"Lobbyists," I replied. "Not only the State Department, but the U.S. industries that benefit from our largesse: wheat, corn, cotton, milk, oil, aircraft, armaments...they are the true beneficiaries of foreign aid—not the recipient countries. It amounts to a hidden subsidy of these industries by the U.S. taxpayer!"

"So what can be done about this?" he asked, frowning.

"Until someone in a leadership position bucks the lobbyists and elevates the issue to public attention, nothing will be done," I stated flatly.

A quarter century after this conversation, foreign aid as then described is now rigidly institutionalized and even more powerfully supported by these same vested interests. Foreign aid has become a virtual entitlement for Israel and Egypt (a combined $8 billion a year), Jordan, Turkey, and now potentially Syria, if they sign a treaty with Israel and accept promised U.S. aid.

In the half century since World War II Congress has appropriated one *trillion* dollars for foreign aid. The Marshall Plan spent only $25 billion, or two and a half percent of the total. The countries benefitting became self-sufficient again, and this self-sufficiency enhanced their stability. What do we have to show for the rest of the trillion spent? The "New World Order" promised by President Bush is nowhere on the horizon.

7

A New Life: Marriage and Private Practice

AS I PREPARED TO RETURN to private practice, I was optimistic about my prospects. I perceived a new era of major international expansion by American firms and felt that few American lawyers had more experience than I in the international realm. I could have lined up clients while still in government service (common practice nowadays), as several of my colleagues in ECA had done, but I didn't feel comfortable doing that. Instead I chose to resign without advance notice to anyone inside or outside the agency, and therefore commenced private practice without a single client.

So, on April 1st, 1951, I opened the door of my single-practioner law office in the Tower Building at 15th & K Sts. NW, in Washington. Henry Glassie, partner in the neighboring law firm of Weaver and Glassie, reminded me that this was April Fool's Day, implying that single-lawyer practice was foolhardy. Patricia Prochnik, now my fiancee, joined me as a part-time secretary while she attended the Foreign Service night school at Georgetown. She had recently completed an assignment as co-Director of the Orientation Center established by the American Council of Education.

For the first several weeks I wondered, "Where are the clients?" I had hoped that some of the companies whose CEO's knew of my work in ECA would call, at least as a courtesy, if not to seek my advice on their international business. Bill Rogers, who had left his Senate post around the same time to open a Washington office for the New York firm of Royal and Patterson, was busier than I, but not by much. In those early days we commiserated with one another about our lack of business over many a long lunch.

My first client was referred to me by Charles Stewart, husband of my ECA secretary Thelma and a vice president of the Machinery and Allied Products Institute. Stewart advised the Pulp and Paper Machinery Association that my services could be useful to its member companies in complying with the price regulations imposed for the duration of the Korean War. The twenty or so family-owned companies in this industry were located mostly in New England, except for a couple in the Midwest. I enjoyed my trips to Beloit, Wisconsin; Rockford, Illinois; and Pittsfield, Massachusetts to observe family management in action, but for the most part it was humdrum work.

As it turned out, the expansion of American companies abroad did not happen as quickly as I'd anticipated. I needed to find other work that suited my talents. Fortunately, several short-lived but interesting jobs came my way. One took me to Carnegie Graduate School, where Professor Herb Simon had launched a program of instruction in decision-making, with Cooper as his sponsor. I was invited to conduct seminars on identifying management's range of choices. For his pioneering work in Economics, Simon was later awarded the Nobel Prize.

On another job I found myself working with Kohler again. Before the war, Kohler had been engaged by Prentice Hall to write a dictionary for controllers and accountants. He intended this dictionary to better equip them for an expanded role in management decisions and operations. After leaving ECA, Kohler undertook the deferred project with Cooper's assistance. They requested me to prepare the content having to do with cost, prices, trade, and management actions, defined in both legal and practical terms. When I completed my text Kohler asked me to clear it with a number of economists, including George Stocking of Vanderbilt and Corwin Edwards of Harvard.

As a visiting professor at Columbia, Edwards had been on the Ph.D. Committee for my oral examination in 1941, where he threw me a curveball of a question: "Is a single large drugstore in a small town a monopoly?" Posed as a simple yes-or-no question, it stumped me. I waffled like an ignoramus, with the result that he failed me. My ego bruised, I realized too late that I should have discussed public policy relative to monopoly practices in an industry, and avoided his mischievous entrapment. Afterwards, J.M. Clark, Chairman of the Ph.D. Committee, apologetically told me, "We have passed many candidates less impressive than you. However, Professor Edwards was adamant that you should fail, and I did not feel I could oppose him."

Now, a decade later, we met again, and again I was seeking his approval of my work. Edwards received me in the spacious private office provided him as Chief Economist for the Federal Trade Commission. He had read my text beforehand, and questioned me about a term I had used: "administered prices," which I had defined as, "selling prices fixed by a company without regard to market forces." This was common practice in companies that dominated their industry, or in government agencies selling goods or services.

"What is your authority for introducing this term?" he inquired somewhat condescendingly.

"By authority do you mean a publication?" I asked.

"Of course," he replied. "You must identify its source."

"I used none," was my answer.

"Well where did you get it?" he insisted.

Angered by his assault, I replied defiantly, "I *invented* it!" Realizing that I was not the intimidated youth he had badgered ten years ago, Edwards backed off, and the rest of the meeting passed without similar incident.

When I later reported this to Cooper, his response was, "I'm not aware that Edwards has a monopoly on invention." Kohler's, *Dictionary For Accountants,* was published in 1953, and has gone through six editions, crediting me for my contributions, including the term "administered prices."

When I met Patricia in 1950, I felt that, after eight years of government service, I had a pretty good understanding of how Washington worked. My friends were government professionals, lawyers, members of the press, and other capital functionaries. However, I had had very little contact with the society world of old Washington families, whom we termed "the cave dwellers."

All that changed with Patricia's entrance into my life. Her grandfather had served as personal physician to Emperor Franz Joseph during the last decade of the Austro-Hungarian Empire. After the fall of the empire, his two daughters, Stephanie and Valerie, remained in Vienna, sharing the same apartment for many decades. (Later I had the pleasure of meeting these two dignified and gracious ladies, and from them got a sense of Vienna's glorious past.) But his only son, Edgar, continued the foreign service career he had chosen. Following the 1st World War, Edgar became Austria's first Minister to the United States, eventually becoming dean of the diplomatic corps. Just prior to Hitler's annexation of Austria he had renounced the Fuehrer and accepted President Roosevelt's invitation to remain in the U.S. with his Bostonian wife and three children, one of whom was Patricia.

Reared at the Austrian Embassy on Massachusetts Avenue, Pattie had attended the exclusive Holton-Arms School, and in 1939 had attracted considerable attention—including a feature in Life Magazine—as Washington's "Debutante of the Year." She sang professionally with the Meyer Davis Orchestra, which performed at charity balls and blue blood weddings from Maine to Florida, and also performed at night clubs in Washington and New York. Hence she was very prominent in this world of the "cave dwellers."

When we married, in 1951, her mother arranged a reception at the most fashionable women's club in Washington, the Sulgrave Club. It was *my* understanding that the numbers would be modest, but the event soon grew to immodest proportions. French champagne and caviar were plentiful, and since Pattie's father had been without a post or regular income since Hitler came to power, I caught the bill. The champagne alone cost one thousand dollars, staggering my farm boy's sense of frugality. (Thirty-five years

Above left: The Hon. Edgar L.G. Prochnik and daughter Patricia
Above: Mother Prochnik, supervising
Below left: The reception at Sulgrave Club
Below: Patricia and Sam on their wedding day

Left to right: James Clark, Parr Johnson, Melva Coulter, Jack Evans, Pattie and Sam, Bill Cooper, Jack Corbett, and William P. Rogers

later we celebrated Patricia's birthday at the Sulgrave Club with many of the same people. The cost on that occasion was much higher, but less difficult to cover.)

The primary haven of the cave-dwellers was the Chevy Chase Country Club, where we enjoyed summer privileges. Pattie's parents had been members for many years, and in her youth she of course had been also. Largely for the WASP elite, the club had begun admitting non-white foreign ambassadors for membership, so I decided to apply. The exclusive club was not ready to admit a private American of Armenian ancestry, and chose to exclude us. The admissions committee had probably assumed I was an Arab or Jew. In those days Armenians were few, and our history as early converts to Christianity was rarely known.

After My marriage to Pattie, my name appeared with hers in the Social Register, which served as an invitation list for embassy parties and other social functions for the "elite." The embassy parties, at which the Ambassador would make a very predictable speech to his two or three hundred guests about the wonderful relationship between his country and the United States, were generally boring, and we increasingly chose not to attend.

But some of the smaller parties were quite interesting. Bazy

McCormick, who had been a classmate of Patricia's at Holton-Arms, hosted both small and large parties at "Al-Marah," her world famous Arabian horse farm of several hundred acres, on River Road in Bethesda, Maryland. The favorite niece of newspaper tycoon Robert McCormick, Bazy's social invitations were in great demand. The high and mighty, both in Congress and in the Eisenhower Administration, were among the invited guests. It was at these parties such as these that I met the Guggenheims, Kay Filene Shouse, Eugene Meyers, David Lawrence of *U.S. News and World Report*, Al Friendly of the *Washington Post*, Supreme Court Justice William O. Douglas, and other influential Washingtonians.

Vehemently anti-communist, Bazy was very taken with the junior Senator from Wisconsin, Joseph McCarthy, who in the early days of the Eisenhower Administration dominated the headlines with his reckless crusade against alleged Communists in the government, universities, and Hollywood. Aware of Bazy's connections with her uncle's powerful newspaper chain, which included the *Chicago Tribune* and *Washington Times-Herald*, McCarthy spent much of his free time at Al-Marah as her guest.

One evening Patricia and I were invited to a small gathering at Al Marah featuring the Senator. His swarthy, tough-guy persona appeared to fascinate Bazy as well as most of the other guests. Pattie and I were less impressed. The Senator drank heavily throughout the evening, then stood up after dinner and recounted how he had taken his starchy, seniority-dominated colleagues by storm.

It all began with a bit of Irish luck, as he told it. "On July 4th, it's customary for the party regulars to spread across the country and make patriotic speeches. I asked the Senate Republican leadership for my speaking assignment and, since I was a first timer, they assigned me to a small town in Tennessee.

"'Any suggestions as to what should I talk about?' I wondered. Somebody got the idea that since I was a war veteran I could talk about the threat of communism to our country. 'Is there any documentation that I could use?' I asked. The person in charge of the Republican Speakers Bureau told me that there was an old memorandum about alleged communists in the State Department, but that no one took it seriously.

"I made the speech before a couple of hundred people. I accused the State Department of harboring communists and when I got to the climax I waved that memorandum. These country folk didn't seem to give a damn. When I got finished they gave me a polite round of applause and that was it. I thought, 'Oh well, at least I did my duty to the party.'

"The next morning the New York Times printed a wire service report summarizing my speech and mentioning my accusation about communists in the State Department. All day my phone rang off the hook with calls from the press wanting more details. My Republican colleagues and I immediately realized the political value of this. Most of them were convinced, as I am, that during the last two decades of Democratic rule there have been *many* government employees and officials who were at least sympathetic to the Soviets, and a few who were active participants in espionage. But until I made that obligatory speech in that one-horse town it was never an issue. That speech made me the most important first-year Senator in the history of this country!"

McCarthy's startling admission was greeted with laughter and applause. Pattie and I looked at each other in disbelief. Eventually his dishonest tactics caught up with him. Still, Bazy remained loyal to him until the end, even after the Senate formally censured him, drawing the curtain on his political career.

8
Iran

THANKS TO PATTIE'S SOCIAL PROMINENCE, I had gained some needed exposure in Washington's diplomatic and political circles. At one reception, Patricia and I met a short, rotund gentleman named Mohammed Nemazee, whose card identified him as "Honorary Counselor, Embassy of Iran." I gathered that "honorary" meant "unpaid." Following a brief conversation Mr. Nemazee invited me to lunch the next day.

At lunch Nemazee outlined a most interesting background. Born in Shiraz, Iran, he had arrived in Washington two years earlier from Hong Kong, where he had been a trader and owned several cargo vessels. Previously he had lived for many years in India. Despite spending much of his life abroad, Nemazee emphasized that he regarded himself first and foremost as Persian (Iranian). Besides English and his native Farsi, he spoke the other major European languages as well as certain Chinese and Indian dialects, and enthusiastically conversed about all the important issues of the day.

Nemazee was impressed by my experience in the Marshall Plan. "On a private basis," he said, "I have in mind to provide my hometown of Shiraz, to the glory of my ancestors, with a modern medical center and a piped water system. Right now there is neither in the whole of Iran. I appreciate that more than money is needed. Transfer of technology and know-how is just as vital." He went on to mention that he had created and funded the Iran Foundation for just that purpose, with the help of an NYU professor, Leland Robinson.

Robinson had succeeded in organizing a board of prestigious doctors from every branch of medicine. Doctors from NYU, Columbia, Penn, and Johns Hopkins had committed time and energy to this distant project, with the goal that by establishing a model facility they might raise the level of care in all Iranian hospitals from the deplorable standards then existing. These doctors were hopeful of persuading their graduate interns to spend a year or two in Shiraz before commencing practice in the United States.

Nemazee was in the process of drilling water wells and installing plumbing for the 100,000 residents of Shiraz. He hoped that revenue from the water bills would be a permanent source of income for the hospital's operations. After outlining his ambitious plans, Nemazee offered me a retainer for my time and advice.

Every month Nemazee hosted dinner parties for at least fifty people at his spacious home and gardens in Bethesda, Maryland, and Patricia and I were always on the guest list. Among the frequent attendees was Justice Douglas, who had a sincere and long-standing interest in the people of the Middle East. At that time he was spending his summer recesses in Iran, Iraq, and Turkey, and writing a book about their Kurdish natives. Other famous regulars at these dinners

Professor Leland Robinson

included Senator William Fulbright, World Bank officials, Assistant Secretaries of State, and numerous ambassadors.

Nemazee also regularly entertained members of Iran's royal family when they came to Washington. I remember one party attended by a large, imposing gentleman named Gholam, who Nemazee informed me was the Shah's brother. Gholam was sitting on a couch, flanked by a pair of attractive women. Nemazee and I were engrossed in conversation directly in front of them, Nemazee's back facing the Prince. At one point I told Nemazee a joke. Nemazee burst spontaneously into laughter and, to my shock, his pants suddenly dropped to his ankles. In a flash, he pulled them up before his guests (especially the Shah's brother) might notice. One guest who did notice was an official of the World Bank, who told Nemazee seriously, "You know, Mohammad, you should wear suspenders." I immediately sought the washroom, fortunately vacant, to release the belly laugh that had been building inside me.

By the summer of 1951 Iran was a hot topic in the world. The Majilis (Iranian Parliament), which up until then had rubber stamped the policies of the Shah, had elected as Prime Minister a rabidly anti-British populist named Mohammad Mossadeq, who came from a long line of wealthy central Iranian landowners. Self-educated without the benefit of travel, Mossadeq had had little contact with foreigners other than the British, whom he despised. Upon taking office Mossadeq led the Majilis to nationalize the property in Iran of Britain's Anglo-Iranian Oil Company (AIOC).

Following the discovery in the early 1900's of the Majid Sulieman oil field, the British had decided to replace Iran's ruling Khajar Dynasty with an authoritarian leader they could control, in order to protect their newfound wealth. The current Shah, Reza Pahlavi, had succeeded his father, who had been hand-picked for the job from the ranks of the Iranian army. Now, seeing the popularity of Mossadeq and his anti-British rhetoric, Pahlavi had left Tehran and gone into exile in Baghdad (and later Europe).

Obsessed with ridding Iran of the British, Mossadeq had acted impulsively in nationalizing the oil industry without considering the consequences. AIOC immediately shut down Iran's Abadan Refinery (the largest in the world) and repatriated its British nationals. Although Iranians had been employed by AIOC in manual jobs and as junior technicians, none had management experience. Hence, the Iranians were severely handicapped in their attempts to operate the refinery after the British left.

In addition, England declared an embargo on Iranian oil exports. This embargo was made totally effective by support from American oil companies, which replaced AIOC's lost Iranian oil from their own sources in Saudi Arabia, Kuwait, and Iraq—thus preserving AIOC's share of the world market and reducing the necessity to negotiate with Mossadeq's government. AIOC paid dollars for American crude oil but sold the products for sterling as usual, creating a dollar drain that caused a British monetary crisis. Help came from Averill Harriman, then Director of the U.S. Mutual Security Agency, who arranged for a special grant of $300 million to the British Treasury so that they could pay for the oil. In effect, American taxpayers underwrote the cost of Britain's embargo on Iran.

Although Nemazee's main preoccupation was the building of his hospital in Shiraz, he was quite naturally concerned with the embargo and its effect on his native country. From the outset of my relationship with him, he was eager for me to brief him about the major American oil companies, the cooperative relationships between them, and their role in supporting AIOC in the embargo.

In late August 1951, the man Nemazee had picked to be his Medical Director—Dr. Torab Mehra, an Iranian who had studied and was practicing in the United States—was scheduled to leave Washington for a visit to Tehran. Recognizing the isolation of Iranian government officials, and their ignorance of the workings of the international oil industry, Nemazee commissioned me to prepare a briefing report on what concessions to AIOC Iran might make to get the embargo lifted. My report would be translated into Farsi, and personally delivered to the Prime Minister by Mehra.

"How long do I have to put the report together?" I asked.

To my consternation, Nemazee replied, "Mehra leaves in one week." Before I could object, he offered me a fee too generous to refuse. For the next week I worked day and night at the office to finish it. Patricia skipped classes at Georgetown to type and edit the manuscript.

In the report I pointed out that Iran's oil had been replaced by other Middle East sources, and these sources would have to cut back their production if Iran's oil were restored to world markets. Therefore, companies owning these other sources were irreplaceable players in any restoration plan Iran might undertake.

Of even greater importance was the fact that, under international law, Iran was obligated to compensate AIOC for seizing its property. Regardless of the alleged unfairness of the original agreement with the British company, in practical terms compensation was an essential element of any plan to end the embargo. Iran did not have the cash reserves required to pay the British; therefore some agreement would have to be reached whereby AIOC would be compensated from the proceeds of Iran's future oil exports.

I turned in my report and never heard anything about it again. I feel sure that Mossadeq saw the report and rejected its conclusion that AIOC could not be excluded from any plan of restoration.

I had expressed these same views in an article I had submitted for publication in the *Washington Post*. It was accepted, and I soon found myself in an ongoing dialogue about the Iranian situation with the *Post*'s Managing Director, Al Friendly, as well as Robert Esterbrook and cartoonist Herb Block of the OP-ED page. Up until now Iran and most of the Middle East had been *terra incognita*, as far as the American press was concerned. If you knew something about the area, it wasn't hard to get published. At first my friends at the *Post* were not sympathetic to Mossadeq's position. As time went on, their commentaries were somewhat influenced by my advice that the U.S. should work with him to arrive at a solution. Several more of my articles appeared in the *Post* over the next two years.

In early 1952, Allahyar Saleh was sent by Mossadeq to Washington as Ambassador. Since I was known as an advisor to Nemazee, Saleh frequently called me for advice and suggestions as he struggled to adjust to an unfamiliar assignment in a strange country. It soon became evident that Saleh was in "diplomatic exile." He rarely heard from Tehran, and was given no instructions as to what policies he should pursue as Ambassador. With plenty of time on his hands, he often invited Patricia and me to dine with him and his family, either at the Embassy or on a picnic in the surrounding countryside.

Saleh was a man of good will, and uncomplicated—a rarity amongst Iranian high officials. He shared with us his dream of a democratic Iran, with the United States as its model, and spoke eloquently of Washington, Jefferson, and Lincoln, all of whose memorials we visited together. Obviously pro-Mossadeq, he lamented the history of autocratic rule in his country, yet expressed no overt enmity for the Shah, perhaps sensing that his days in power had not come to a permanent end.

Soon after Saleh's arrival in Washington, Mossadeq's Foreign Minister, Fatime, arrived uninvited in Washington with several other Iranian ministers. The State Department all but ignored them, sending only Bill Roundtree, the Iranian desk officer, with a simple message of American solidarity with England: "10 Downing Street is in charge of your problem."

Since their visit was unofficial it fell upon Nemazee to host Fatime and his ministers. He had never met them and was anxious to know their politics. Who among them were pro-Shah? Who was a member of the virulently anti-Shah Tudeh Party? Who was a Communist? And who was simply an opportunist taking advantage of Mossadeq's popularity? Nemazee was generally perceived, correctly, as an apolitical patriot interested in the welfare of his country no matter who was in power.

As part of Nemazee's agenda as host, I was asked to escort the group to visit Nemazee's dairy farm in Rockville, Maryland.

Nemazee's prize dairy cattle were unsurpassed. After the visit to the farm we all gathered for dinner at the Colony Restaurant, across from the Mayflower Hotel in D.C. For Nemazee's benefit, I asked each of the visitors for his impression of Nemazee's cows. My idea was that their opinions of his cows would more or less mirror their opinion of Nemazee, and that is exactly what happened. Several of the visitors were ecstatic, others offered limited compliments, and a couple said they had seen *bigger* cows than Nemazee's. Fatime himself, who was identified with the Tudeh Party, was one who didn't think too much of Nemazee's cows.

Although the State Department showed little interest in the Iranian ministers, the CIA, I strongly suspected, was another story. Fatime had driven to the restaurant with Patricia and me in our new convertible, with the top down. When we arrived at the restaurant Fatime put his attache case in the trunk and we turned the car over to the parking attendant. When we returned to claim the car after dinner, the attendant searched for it and finally declared that it had been stolen. Endless apologies were offered and the police were notified. At no time did Fatime mention the attache case.

Early the next morning the police called and informed me that the car had been recovered in Philadelphia. They delivered it to me that evening and I drove immediately to the embassy to meet Fatime. When we opened the trunk, there was the attache case. Fatime seemed relieved that his papers were all there. I did not volunteer my opinion that the CIA had photocopied them and returned them to the case before abandoning the car.

Nothing came of the ministers' visit, and I doubt they had expected anything more than a vacation abroad—always valued highly by officials of underdeveloped countries. But later in 1952 Mossadeq himself arrived with the purpose of persuading Washington to intervene in the British-Iranian stalemate. He arrived with one personal aide, and checked into a two bedroom suite at the Shoreham Hotel. Why he chose not to stay at the spacious Iranian Embassy, I never heard him say.

Similarly uninvited, Mossadeq encountered the same cold

shoulder from the State Department that his ministers had. Each afternoon Roundtree and George McGhee, the Assistant Secretary for the Middle East, paid a courtesy call; other than that his visit received no official recognition.

During Mossadeq's ten-day stay at the Shoreham, Nemazee and I would visit him for two or three hours every morning. During these visits I tried to convey, with Nemazee translating, my understanding of the realities Mossadeq faced in attempting to restore Iran's oil to the world market. Mossadeq did not share with us the content of his exchange with State's representatives. Nemazee and I assumed that Mossadeq had repeated his stated position that the British must stay out of Iran, to be replaced by Americans and other nationalities. We had no doubt that State had firmly reiterated its support for the British claim that until Iran compensated them for the property nationalized, British rights of ownership were preserved and the embargo would continue. This British stance would force Iran to compromise, if not totally give in.

In my talks with the Prime Minister I too told him that the British must be compensated, and suggested that AIOC could join American and French oil companies in a consortium that would restore Iranian oil production and exports. A portion of the oil revenue would go towards compensation. Mossadeq budged slightly in this direction by asking, "Can we find out how much we would owe the British?" I suggested Kohler as someone who could at least outline how this figure might be determined. "Bring him!" replied Mossadeq.

I contacted Kohler and he agreed come with me to meet the Prime Minister. When we entered Mossadeq's suite, Kohler—a giant of a man next to the frail Iranian—was surprised to find him in pajamas lounging in bed, as was his habit. "I hope your excellency is not ill," was Kohler's first remark.

"Not ill at all," answered the Prime Minister. "I choose to recline in bed most of the day, as well as night, in order to conserve my energy." Pointing at me, he added with a twinkle in his eye, "Just the opposite of Nakasian, who has so much energy that the bed serves him for special purposes only."

Ignoring the sexual innuendo, the proper Kohler went on to explain to Mossadeq how he might arrive at a figure for compensation. Kohler's visit was apparently wasted, as it soon became evident that Mossadeq was set on simply convincing Washington to intercede with the British on his behalf—a miscalculation of the strong ties between England and America, and between the British and American oil companies.

Every afternoon Nemazee and I would wave to McGee and Roundtree in the lobby as they entered and we departed. Finally the day came for Mossadeq's departure. At National Airport we said our farewells and I presented the Prime Minister with a gift—a miniature oil rig, which I assured him would run on Persian current.

In early 1953, following Eisenhower's inauguration, Washington softened its hardline stance against Iran to the extent of authorizing relief shipments of agricultural products that made food supplies more abundant in Tehran. The oil embargo continued.

In midsummer of 1953 Nemazee became increasingly concerned when a large quantity of equipment for the medical center was repeatedly denied entry at the Iranian port of Khoramshah. Torab Mehra had tried and failed to obtain the cargo's release, and could not ascertain from the officials in charge the reason

Dr. Mossadeq, Prime Minister of Iran, Bill Roundtree from the State Department, and Sam

for refusing entry. It looked as though someone in Iran didn't want the hospital to be built. But why? Nemazee was beside himself. Reasoning that since I was known to Mossadeq and Fatime, I could probably enlist their aid in releasing the cargo, he arranged for my first visit to Iran.

Nemazee also suggested that I take whatever documents I might need if the government requested my help with the oil situation. This made me nervous. A few years earlier a Sinclair representative had journeyed to Iran for the purpose of acquiring oil rights and been murdered, and there had been a similar incident before that. If I aroused suspicion that the Shiraz Medical Center was not the sole purpose of my mission, I could very well be the third victim. I took with me only a few sources on oil and buried them deep in the bottom of my suitcase.

The day before I left Washington for New York (all international flights in those days left from New York), I opened my morning newspaper and was shocked to read that Mossadeq had been overthrown and jailed. A General Zafrollah Zahedi had been installed as the new Prime Minister, and the Shah was on his way back to Tehran from Europe. Despite this turn of events, I determined to go ahead with my trip.

Later that day Ambassador Saleh called and asked if I would be willing to meet with W. Alton Jones, who was at that moment in his office. I knew that Jones was the CEO of Cities Service—one of several large independent oil companies in the U.S.—and a frequent golfing and bridge partner of President Eisenhower.

I also knew that Jones had visited Tehran within the past year, accompanied by a team of his top managers. The press had reported that Jones was willing to break the British-Iranian deadlock by taking over management of the industry vacated by AIOC. Whether Ike had encouraged his friend to make the trip was not known, but it was apparent that he had not discouraged him. In any case, Jones's golf/bridge relationship with Ike proved to be nothing more than an annoyance to the combined players of the five major oil companies, who had their own powerful friends in Congress, as well as the Dulles brothers at the CIA and

State. After a short news blitz, Jones's ambition seemed to have died. Perhaps now he had a plan to resurrect it. I was very curious to find out what he had to say.

At his request I met Jones at National Airport's Butler Aviation and flew alone with him to LaGuardia in his DC-3, where we sat in the plane on the tarmac for another hour. Jones did most of the talking, reiterating his willingness to run the Iranian oil operation. Jones could glean from my comments that I was sympathetic to the independents' eagerness to obtain some direct access to cheap Middle East crude, and apparently Saleh had given him the impression that I might be persuasive with the Iranians to work toward that mutually beneficial end. Of course, with the Shah's return most of my contacts would no longer be in office. Jones did not offer me a retainer, and I didn't suggest it. We parted with, "Let's keep in touch."

I had arranged to meet Leland Robinson, who was on a world tour, upon my arrival in Tehran, and the next morning we set out by car for Shiraz, some 500 miles to the south. Torab Mehra accompanied us. The narrow dirt road traversed valleys and the east-west ribs of low mountains. We forded many streams and often had to yield the right of way to herds of sheep or goats.

After a long day's drive we arrived at Isfahan, the ancient capital of Persia. Its renowned "Blue Mosque," an exquisite 14th century structure featuring native azure tiles and imposing minarets, dominates one end of the Royal Mall. The Royal Palace of earlier Shahs stands nearby. From its fourth floor balcony the Shahs addressed their subjects gathered below on the mall.

Mehra reminded me that Isfahan had a large colony of Armenians that had immigrated to the city centuries earlier at the invitation of Shah Abbas, one of Iran's benign Islamic autocrats, who had guaranteed their security and freedom of Christian worship. Over the years these Armenians had contributed much to Iran, particularly as craftsmen (e.g. carpetmakers and masons) and merchants. Unfortunately our schedule did not permit me to visit with these people during our overnight stay.

Departing early the next morning, we reached Persepolis by late afternoon. I found the ruins in Persepolis, the Persian capital during the reign of the great Emperors Cyrus and Darius, as impressive in size and architectural splendor as the Greek Acropolis in Athens or the Roman ruins of Septis Magna and Sebrata in Libya and Balbek in Lebanon. Tragically, the expansive valley in which Persepolis rests, once a lush center of agricultural production, was now largely barren—almost a dust bowl. As we headed south, my parting thoughts focused on the dual capacities of Man: to create works of magnificence, and to destroy through neglect and exploitation Nature's endowment of resources and beauty.

Arriving in nearby Shiraz before sundown, we were startled by the abundance of trees, shrubs and flowers cultivated by its proud residents. Roses were everywhere, and I was not surprised when Mehra told me that Shiraz was famous for them.

My mission in Shiraz was twofold. Nemazee had instructed me to meet with the city leaders to explain the economics of their newly operational pipewater system. Reflecting the experience of the Western world, I explained that, given adequate capacity (as Nemazee had provided), the total cost was largely fixed. The cost had to be covered by revenue whether use of the supply was total or less. Therefore, larger users could be offered a reduction in the price per liter. In a country where water, like all resources, had been scarce and hence sparingly used, this was an impossible concept for the city fathers to grasp. Despite my attempts, they could not be shaken from their conviction that more use should cost more. The idea of fixed and variable costs belonged to a century they had not yet entered.

My second mission had come as a surprise to me. Upon my arrival in Tehran, our Ambassador Loy Henderson had requested a private meeting with me, in which he reported that the U.S. Information Agency building in Shiraz had been ransacked by persons unknown. "While you are in Shiraz," he asked, "would you do what you can to discover the source of this hostile action?" I replied that I would consider it my duty. He introduced the CIA person on his staff, who provided me with the meager details he had garnered from informants. When he had finished his briefing he asked, "Would you feel more secure if we fitted you with one of our bullet-proof vests?" Intuitively, I declined the offer. When I thought about it later I was glad that I had. The Medical Center and the water project identified my purpose in Iran. Accepting the vest would risk exposing me as on a clandestine mission. Any one of a number of Iranians working in our Embassy might leak this information to anti-American factions, placing my life in jeopardy.

When I saw the half-completed medical center in Shiraz, I could not help but wonder anew, "Who was blocking the release of hospital equipment from customs?" I did not expect to find the answer in Shiraz. However, by the end of my brief stay I felt I had the answer to that question as well as the question of who had vandalized the USIA building.

The medical center was being built on land adjoining the beautiful gardens and palace of Khorsrue, ruler of the Gashgai, an ancient nomadic tribe of Turkeman origin. Each year the self-sufficient Gashgai covered 500 miles of rugged terrain in central Iran, traveling by foot (except for the leaders, who traveled on horseback) and living off the sheep and goats that traveled with them. The tribe wintered in Shiraz, enjoying the warm prevailing breezes off the Persian Gulf, and headed north in springtime to graze their herds on vegetation nourished by the melting snows. Their livestock provided them with fresh meat, and the hides were used to make portable tents as well as a few carpets and other woven fabrics for sale. Given their minimal subsistence and relative isolation, the central government in Tehran accepted the autonomy of the Gashgai.

Khorsrue had inherited both civil and religious rule of his people, yet lived most of the year in a regal residence in England, returning to Shiraz once a year to reaffirm his right to a tithe equal to about one dollar from each member of the tribe. With several million subjects, this amounted to an enormous annual income, affording him the opportunity to live in the lifestyle of the British Royalty, a world apart from his impoverished subjects.

Sam and Dr. Leland Robinson tasting Shiraz piped well water—the first in Iran

I had no hard evidence who destroyed the USIA building, but I had a strong hunch that Khorsrue was behind the attack and was also responsible for preventing the release from customs of medical equipment for the Shiraz Hospital. I reasoned that these two very visible manifestations of a modern Western lifestyle would be regarded by Khorsrue as hostile to his personal interests. Perhaps local Gashgai leaders would make demands on Khorsrue to share some of his prodigious wealth with his tribe in similar projects.

During our two days in Shiraz, the city fathers showed Robinson and me the town. The tour included the "poor house," a square, four-story loft building surrounding a central courtyard. Standing in the yard I surveyed the lofts—open living spaces without interior walls—teeming with people in rags. I estimated some one hundred occupants of all ages. "How are these people fed?" I inquired.

"A wagon delivers soup and porridge twice daily," was the reply. "These people come down from their lofts with their pans to get their meal." I did not inquire as to the disposal of their

Sam at Persepolis

excrement: the stench was the obvious answer.

Thanks to Nemazee, the inhabitants were spared having to get their water from a "jube"—an open sewer carrying surface water used for all purposes. "If the water flows, it is fit to drink," reads the Koran. Judging from their appearances, I doubted these people had ever bathed their bodies, or would even now. The parent of a ten year old boy, witnessing the flow of pure water from Nemazee's spigot, asked that I thank Mr. Nemazee, on his behalf, for this blessing. Putting my hand on his son's head, I replied, "The best way to thank Mr. Nemazee is by bathing this boy every day." When my remark was translated, the stunned child bolted off into the crowd.

After two days in Shiraz, Robinson and I took a pre-war DC-3 back to Tehran. I made my report to Ambassador Henderson and took a room at the Park Hotel, where I reflected on what I had seen. Most astonishing to me, the city officials in Shiraz had appeared totally oblivious to the deplorable conditions in the "poor house," which rivalled any one might see in Bombay or Calcutta. It was a revelation to me that, even though the Koran was founded in part on the Bible's New Testament, Moslems clearly rejected, in practice at least, Jesus's teaching that the rich must share their wealth with the poor. It wasn't long before I had another vivid lesson in the Moslem attitude toward personal wealth.

Before I left Washington for Tehran, Nemazee had asked me to meet privately with his cousin Mehdi Nemazee, co-owner with him of a company in Tehran that sold and serviced all General Motors cars, trucks, and other products. This exclusive distributorship, probably arranged by the internationalist Nemazee years earlier, was by this time very profitable. "What I would like you to do," Nemazee requested, "is what I have so far failed to do: try to get Mehdi to fund a school for nurses in honor of his parents and our common grandparents. To assist you Mehra will serve as translator. You will find this task impossible, but for Mehdi's sake in the eyes of God," he pleaded, "we must try!"

In Tehran, Mehdi and I had three separate meetings of several hours each. Despite my passionate invocation of every ethical, humanitarian, and religious principle I could think of, I could not budge Mehdi from his position: "My

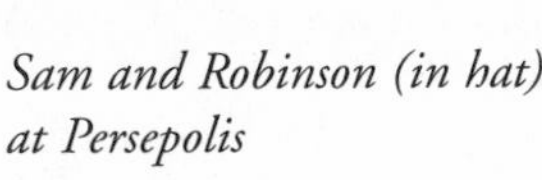

Sam and Robinson (in hat) at Persepolis

wealth is personal possession. I will not give a rial to strangers."

"Nurses are not strangers," I argued. "They serve you, your family and your countrymen! Join your cousin Mohammed in his great contribution to Shiraz!" Mehdi remained obstinately negative, and even questioned his cousin's motives. Finally I had to give up. It came as no surprise to Nemazee.

Mehdi Nemazee's attitude lay strictly within the mainstream of rich Moslems. Traditionally, neither Persian nor Arab Moslems share their wealth with the poor, either directly or by paying taxes for public works which benefit the poor. Wealth of the deceased passes entirely to the male heirs or, in some special cases, to named beneficiaries. Death and estate taxes are non-existent. One exception is the conveyance of wealth to support Moslem mosques and clergy, accomplished by a well established system of trusts, called Wafq.

In my attempts to convince Mehdi of the virtue of charity, Dr. Mehra had been no help beyond his role as translator, and I soon understood why. In spite of his Western education, his thinking on social issues was very traditional. This was brought home to me one day in Tehran when I was with Mehra in his Buick. After running a red light at a busy intersection, he was forced to the curb by a police car. In a rage, Dr. Mehra got out of the Buick and accosted the officer, who immediately shrank in subservience, bowing and begging Mehra's forgiveness. As Dr. Mehra drove off without a citation, I asked him what he had said to the policeman. Mehra answered without a trace of embarassment. "I told him, 'How dare *you* stop *me*! Never do that again! Your mother must be a donkey!'" (This was the Iranians' worst personal insult.)

"How *could* you!" I admonished him. "After twelve years in the United States, after college and medical school...how could you destroy that policeman simply for doing his duty? You ought to be ashamed! What hope have you for your country if you don't respect your people for doing their duty?"

"Sam, you don't understand," Mehra replied evenly. "This is the Iranian way."

That all men are equal in the eyes of God was obviously not shared by Mehra, or by the other wealthy Moslems I observed in Iran. Servants (even public servants) and workers are treated as inferiors—almost as animals. As the master would summon his animals with the word "Byia", which means "Come", so he would summon his servants and other employees with that command, spoken in the same tone.

Nemazee alone stood as proof that not all Iranians treat the poor as subhuman. Later, in Tehran, Mr. Nemazee would receive poor people who wished his audience. Approaching him they would invariably attempt to kiss his hand or feet, often with great fervor. Nemazee, uncomfortable with this tradition, would not let them do so, yet always managed to divert them without making them feel rejected.

With the Shah's return to the throne in September 1953, an 8 P.M. curfew was imposed in Tehran, and strictly enforced. My fellow guests at the Park Hotel included the international press corps, and I generally spent my evenings talking with them in the hotel bar. Jim Bell and Carl Mydens (a photographer) from *Time* Magazine, Robert Doty of the *New York Times*, and Don Schwind of the Associated Press were all there, as well as the Sunday Editor of the London *Times* and a half dozen other reporters from London, Paris, and Washington. Arnaud de Borchgrave, a dashing young reporter for *Newsweek*, did not stay long at the Park. His charm with one of the Shah's sisters landed him more regal housing. Sometime later Wanda Jablonski, who had accused me of being a Communist in my Marshall Plan years, appeared at the hotel, and had the nerve to ask me to introduce her to the principal government officials. I declined, not so much for revenge as out of concern for her lack of integrity, as she was still a panderer for the major oil companies.

After dinner we all gathered at the bar, tended by an Iranian everyone called by his first name—Nagy. The native drink of Vodka and lime was low in price and powerful in impact. Consumption was heavy—too heavy for some. One evening the gentlemanly Bob Doty took offense at one of the British reporters and knocked him down with a punch to the jaw. Everyone converged on the two combatants to restore peace in this normally unpugilistic society.

The bar and dining room at the Park were also the "in" place for prominent local men and their Westernized ladies. These women had shed the shadour (total covering of the face and body), and sought plastic surgery to emulate Hollywood's stars, adding to flat chests and straightening their Iranian hook noses. Their plastic surgeon was a local hero to these rich ladies. He frequently dined at the hotel among members of the press, who dubbed him the "nose-clipper" or "tit-puffer."

As a rare, unofficial American in Tehran during this crisis, I was often asked, "What are *you* doing here?" I easily satisfied the inquirer's curiosity by outlining my role in the Shiraz project. This held very little interest to the press. For them Mossadeq—this rural populist who had twisted the tail of the British lion and caused the Shah to flee the country—was *the* story, and the burning question was, "Would he be executed for treason?" His Foreign Minister Fatime, whom I had gotten to know on his visit to Washington, had already met this fate, and soon Mossadeq's trial would begin.

How the removal of Mossadeq from power had taken place was also a subject of lively speculation. Several versions of the bloodless coup were circulating, most prominent that of CIA agent Kermit Roosevelt, Theodore Roosevelt's nephew. He went public crediting the CIA under *his* leadership for executing the coup, and conjured a tale of drama and excitement that later served to impress Congress during their hearings on CIA appropriations.

George Carroll, another CIA agent, who had befriended me shortly after I returned from Shiraz, told me a somewhat different story. In his version, a scheduled parade of athletic clubs attracted thousands of onlookers, who soon became rowdy. Some shouted pro-Shah slogans; others anti-Shah. The parade turned into a mob scene. While this was going on, Carroll himself made his way to the hideout of General Zahedi, where he convinced him of U.S. support and urged him to have his personal guards take control of the radio station and Prime Minister's office, and then arrest Mosssadegh at his home. The plan was the brainchild of the CIA, but he made no mention of Roosevelt.

Both Jim Bell and Don Schwind, basing their very similar versions on reports from their respective "stringers" (local Iranians employed for their contacts and knowledge of what goes on at critical centers of the Government, Army and Police), told me, in essence, that the parade-turned-mob was an accident that occurred to everyone's surprise. General Zahedi had made a timely move against Mossadeq, whose false confidence in his great popularity left him unprepared to deal with such an event. Asked about Roosevelt, both newsmen replied that Kermit was indulging in unfounded self-aggrandizement.

Bell and Schwind filed reports daily to their respective editors back home. As is common practice, editors add to or delete from these reports based on other information available to them. Back in Washington, Roosevelt circulated his own account to the editors, who published excerpts and created a public eager for the book Kermit would write.

Following his return to the throne the Shah avoided public appearances and any display of celebration, and an atmosphere of uncertainty pervaded everyday life in Tehran. Fortunately for the monarch, the challenge to his rule was confined to the urban area. Iranians outside the "beltway" of Tehran were largely indifferent to events in the capital.

The Shah placed his hopes for staying in power on the U.S., in particular Ambassador Henderson, former Assistant Secretary of State for the Middle East and a great favorite of General George C. Marshall when Marshall had been Secretary of State. With British colonial rule crumbling around the globe, the days of British hegemony in the region were clearly drawing to a close, and the Shah hoped that Henderson could arrange for American leadership in its place, much as Mossadeq had wanted.

In the climate of the Cold War, Iran's security against aggression from its Soviet neighbor was of paramount importance to our State Department. To keep the Shah on the throne became the top priority. Hence, notwithstanding—or perhaps because of—the Shah's lack of popular support, Washington launched a military, police, and intelligence buildup, providing training and modern equipment for what would become one of the most dreaded secret police forces in the world—the Savak. Our Embassy staff was beefed up, and CIA personnel increased. In spite of these efforts, both Henderson and the Shah realized that Iran could be destabilized by either harsh treatment of the popular Mossadeq or by repeal of the hugely popular Oil Nationalization Law, which the people now regarded as their sovereign right.

Through his Prime Minister, General Zahedi, the Shah selected his ministers. Among them was Ali Amini, a prominent figure in Tehran by reason of his wealth and his family ties to the Khajar Dynasty. Since the British had ended the Khajar Dynasty when they had installed the Shah's father on the throne, it was generally believed that Ali Amini's loyalty to the Shah was suspect. Focused on the Mossadeq trial, the press lacked interest in these local events.

Immediately after Amini's appointment as Finance Minister, I met with him on the subject of the detained medical equipment for Shiraz. He promised that the equipment would be released immediately from customs and ordered an unexpectedly favorable rate of exchange for the dollar invoice amount. My primary mission was now accomplished, and I was very grateful.

Apparently Amini had heard of my knowledge of the oil industry, because after we had settled the issue of the medical equipment he sought my advice on restoring Iran's oil industry. I expressed my willingness to help him, as I assumed that, as Finance Minister, he would be in charge of negotiations for his Government, and would take steps to formalize our working relationship.

The following day, as I waited to hear from him, I was surprised by a visit from the Minister of Planning, Dr. Panahi. After stating that he was speaking for both General Zahedi and the Shah, he asked me to stay on for three months as adviser to the

General and his Cabinet. He would arrange for me to be paid a retainer of $10,000 as compensation. A ministerial task force would be headed by Dr. Entezam, to whom I should report. Ali Mansour, his aide, would be second-in-command. I was curious about why Amini was kept out of the briefing process but said nothing at the time.

The next day Henderson invited me to his office to assure me of his endorsement. When I asked about Amini, he explained that the Shah was not comfortable with any enhancement of Amini's prominence, and advised me that Amini "will be pumping you for information. Please keep your responses general. It's best that you try to avoid seeing him, even when invited." I felt unhappy about complying with this request after Amini's help with the Medical Center equipment.

Panahi arranged for Arteshir Zahedi, son of the General, to provide me with security in traveling to and from the Prime Minister's office and to the meetings of the ministers. "He will also be your translator in the exchange of English and Farsi. His command of both is fluent."

Arteshir was a tall, dashingly attractive bachelor who had recently returned home after graduating from the University of Colorado. At this time he was courting the Shah's daughter. Later he married her, divorcing her soon after. In spite of the divorce, he remained a favorite of the Shah's, serving as Deputy Foreign Minister and in a long tenure as Ambassador to the United States.

I met three times a week with the five Ministers and privately with the General. The General's office was on the top floor of the Officers' Club. The elevator stopped at the floor below, requiring Arteshir and me to walk up the narrow staircase, lined on each side by a dozen young, gun-readied soldiers. To get through, we actually had to brush against them. They were nervous and jittery, and their lack of confidence frightened me. Later I learned that they were naive country boys devoid of any political opinions, recruited for their unswerving loyalty to the General.

In contrast, the Ministers met in the Building of Foreign

Affairs and were easily accessible. These meetings were hosted by either the Foreign Minister or his deputy, Ali Mansour. Mansour was definitely a superior, professional, official—multilingual, intelligent and attractive. I established a very favorable relationship with him over the three months of these meetings.

After several meetings with the Prime Minister and the Ministerial Commission, it became clear that I needed a secretary to take dictation and type reports. Finding no one with the needed skills in Tehran, I cabled Patricia to join me and to bring a typewriter. Two or three days later I received a cable: "Arriving Friday on PanAm."

The day before Patricia was to arrive, Henderson called and invited me to a reception he was giving for several congressmen visiting Tehran. "May I bring Patricia along?" I requested. "I expect her to arrive tomorrow morning."

To my surprise, Henderson replied, "I doubt very much Pattie will be here. I have advised the State Department that I am sending all American wives and children home, and have requested that no more women or children come to Tehran until the situation stabilizes and the curfew is lifted."

Incredulous, I answered, "But only yesterday I received a cable saying she was arriving on PanAm's flight!"

"Well, if she gets here, of course, bring her," he conceded. Patricia arrived as scheduled. The following night at the Embassy, as we moved along the receiving line, Henderson greeted us warmly, then asked Patricia to step aside. "I want to *talk* with you." When they were out of earshot of the other guests, he asked her sternly, "How did you get past my instructions that no women were to travel here at this time?"

Patricia replied, "Well, I did have some trouble at the Passport Office in Washington when they asked me where I was going. When I told them I was going to Tehran the officers stated flat-out, 'No women are allowed in. Women are being sent *out*.' I protested vigorously and asked the officers to take a note to Miss Shipley, the head of the Passport Division and a social friend of my parents.

"No sooner had they done so than the Miss Shipley burst through the huge doors of her office waving my note. 'Patricia, what are you up to *now*?' I respectfully voiced an explanation and she said, 'All right, I'll make an exception.'" Patricia shrugged her shoulders innocently.

Henderson, baffled, asked, "What did you say in that note?"

"I merely stated," said Patricia, "that I *had* to go to Iran to consummate my marriage."

At once impressed with her ingenuity and frustrated by how easily she'd evaded his orders, Henderson looked at Patricia for a long moment before finally muttering, "Well, I'll be *damned*!"

Patricia and I were treated as distinguished persons by government officials and other upper income Iranians, as well as by Ambassador and Mrs. Henderson and their Embassy staff. Especially friendly were the CIA agent George Carroll and his wife, who seemed to turn up everywhere we went in Tehran. He knew of my advisory assignment with the government, yet didn't inquire about it. I assumed my meetings with Iranian officials were bugged, providing the Agency with a complete transcript.

Privileged Iranians as well as foreigners lived in Shimran, a suburb of Tehran in the foothills of the perenially snowclad Albourz Mountains, source of Tehran's water supply. Remember that Tehran still did not have piped water. Water was carried from its mountain source throughout the city by a system of jubes—the same open ditches that, thanks to Nemazee, were a thing of the past in Shiraz. The jubes ran along both sides of the primary roads. Houses along these roads diverted water into catch basins, where it was stored until the sediment settled, thus clearing the water for household use. By the time the jubes reached the southern sections of Tehran, the water was syrupy from the sediment and included human and animal wastes. (There was no sewage system in this metropolitan area of one million people.) Those people with disposable income (e.g. *all* residents of Shimran) purchased bottled water—labeled "sans Microbe"—for drinking, but for most city dwellers, the foul jubes supplied their potable water as well.

To avoid Tehran's squalor and oppressive summer heat, the rich lived high above the grimy city in Shimran, where the water of the jube was cleaner and the air mountain-fresh. Homes here were spacious, with modern appliances. Some even had swimming pools. During our time there, there were several hundred residents in this favored area.

Despite the 8 P.M. curfew, the upper classes were able to obtain curfew passes. Wealthy Iranians loved to entertain and were most gracious hosts among their peers. Social life was active, and foreigners were invited rather quickly into the social circle of the Iranians.

Several times a week we were invited to dinner parties. The cuisine ranged from the best of the local dishes to those of other Middle Eastern countries and sometimes France. Patricia and I became accustomed to meals of fresh caviar, lamb and chicken kabobs, fish from nearby lakes and the Caspian Sea, vegetables, and several different rice dishes (Caspian-grown rice is the world's largest and most succulent grain), topped off with a variety of delicate pastries, and accompanied of course by plentiful wine, beer, and imported hard liquor.

The evenings began with the guests assembled in the drawing room to greet one another and enjoy champagne and entertainment (now and then featuring a famous bellydancer). After an hour or so, doors opened to a large dining room featuring a buffet table heavily laden with the entire menu. Guests dashed in and filled their plates and remained standing two or three deep as they savored the food. Patricia and I always avoided the rush and took whatever remained. On one occasion our host was embarrassed that all the food had been consumed by the time we took our turn at the table—only ten minutes after the doors had been opened—and hurriedly went to the kitchen to personally serve us.

After dinner more drinks and cordials were served. In social situations with foreigners Iranians liked to quote Iranian poetry and stories. The writers Hafez and Saadi were particular favorites. I enjoyed most the story of the poor villager Hassan, who knocked on the door of the village mullah (local cleric) and asked for the use of his donkey. "My donkey is not here. Abdul has it," replied the Mullah, to avoid lending it to Hassan, whom he disliked.

At that moment, a large bray came from the Mullah's back yard. In anger Hassan shouted, "You are lying to me. Your donkey is here; I know his sound."

Calmly the Mullah asked Hassan, "Whom do you believe, the donkey or me?"

At one such party someone, knowing that Patricia had been a professional singer, asked her to sing one of her favorite songs. Patricia decided to treat the company to a popular ditty, "The Persian Kitten"—funny, and a little bawdy. Instead of the laughter and applause she expected, the song met with total silence, punctuated by a few grunts. I suppose the metaphor of the Persian Kitten "getting screwed," as it were, was a little hard for the Iranians to take, particularly coming from the mouth of a blonde European. We didn't repeat that mistake again.

Every week the ladies of Iranian high society gathered for bridge. Mrs. Henderson frequently joined them, often choosing Patricia as her partner. Patricia was at first astonished to see the ladies stand up when Mrs. Henderson entered the room, and remain standing until she was seated. They also stood up and remained standing when she left the room. Eventually Patricia got used to this unusual show of respect for the Ambassador's wife. We speculated that it had been introduced by the British Embassy during their years of prominence in Iran.

In mid-November I decided to return to Washington to take care of some office affairs. Before I left Tehran for the States, the Minister to the Court of the Shah called me and requested a meeting. When I met with him he expressed two "wishes" of the Shah. The first was that I bring back with me a nationally known American newscaster. The Shah's second wish was that I persuade Nemazee to return to Tehran, where the Shah needed his help. I replied that I would do my best to fulfill both wishes.

As soon as I arrived in New York I telephoned Cedric Foster, whose primetime radio newscast was broadcast every weekday over some 400 WOR-affiliated stations. From the moment the Shah's minister had put the idea in my head, I was convinced Cedric was ideal for the job. Born and bred in Boston, his dramatic, on-the-scene descriptions of the major news events of the past decade had captured a wide audience while also earning him the respect of his peers. Tall and elegant, with a moustache waxed to sharp tips, he was equally impressive in person. I was also aware that—in keeping with his aristocratic persona—Cedric admired royalty. When I presented him with the idea of doing live broadcasts from Tehran, he jumped at the chance.

Nemazee was quite a bit more reluctant to comply with the Shah's request. He feared that by getting involved with people he deemed of limited capacity—a category in which he placed most Iranian officials, as well as the Shah's palace aides and others in positions of power—he would wind up embroiled in chaos. Ultimately, his sense of duty to his native country overcame his doubts, and he agreed to return within a matter of weeks.

While I was in the U.S., I was also eager to meet with "Shorty" Elliott, who had recently been named Director of Exploration and Production for Esso's global operations. I was sure he remembered the help I had given him when I was in ECA and he headed Standard Vacuum Oil Company, and I felt I could communicate frankly with him and gain his confidence that I was guiding the Iranian officials toward a sensible position on foreign involvement in their oil industry. Elliott did not hesitate to meet with me but steered the conversation away from Iran. After an hour of this I was convinced that, in spite of his new title, Elliott was outside Esso's decision-making loop regarding Iran. I assumed this meant that my old adversary George Kegler, General counsel of Esso, was in charge. If Kegler had wanted to meet with me I'm sure he would have had Elliott arrange it. I judged it useless to seek a meeting directly.

This turn of events clarified an odd occurrence Patricia had reported to me upon her arrival in Tehran. I had asked Patricia to advise W. Alton Jones that she would be joining me in Iran and could deliver any message from him. Jones had invited her to dinner on her overnight stopover in New York, and she had accepted.

Patricia had just arrived at the Pierre Hotel in Manhattan when she was surprised by a telephone call from Donald Dawson, a lawyer who had been a White House Aide to former President Truman. He too urged her to join him for dinner. She declined with regrets. Although Dawson had been only a casual acquaintance in Pat's hometown of Washington, D.C., he talked at length with her on the phone both before and after a pleasant dinner with Jones.

The next day, Jones sent his private limousine to take Pat to the airport. Just as she was checking out of the Pierre, Dawson entered the lobby and began helping her load her luggage into the limo. Then, to her greater surprise, he suddenly jumped into the back seat with her as the chauffeur was pulling away. Patricia was both "puzzled and amused" by Dawson's attention.

I had wondered how Dawson even knew she was at the Pierre. I knew that one of his post-White House clients was Esso, and had suspected that he might be acting for, and upon information supplied by, them. Obviously they were threatened by the prospect of the independents gaining access to the lucrative Iranian oil fields, and saw my relationship with Jones as inimical to their interests. My meeting with Elliott seemed to confirm my suspicion that a plan was underway to get me out of the picture. I felt sure Kegler was the planner.

In order to keep appointments in Washington, I resisted Cedric's urging to spend the night before our journey to Tehran in New York. He was concerned that I might miss the 4 P.M. PanAm flight out. On the day before our departure I phoned Mr. Jones from D.C. and told him I would be available to meet breifly with him in New York the next day. He invited me to lunch with him in his private dining room atop his company's skyscraper in the financial district.

Jones's palatial penthouse, featuring a cathedral ceiling and spectacular view of downtown Manhattan, took up the entire top

Patricia talking with World Court Judge, Zafarollah Khan (of Pakistan), and Cedric Foster

floor of the building. Jones and I sat alone at the end of a very long mahogony dining table, designed to seat fifty. We talked almost exclusively about the Iranian situation. I expressed my view that the independents should share in any reopening of the Iranian oil fields, and that lessening the control of the majors and gaining direct access to the refiners and marketers was in the best interest of Iran. Jones had heard about the Dawson episode from his chauffeur and was outraged that a former Presidential Aide would stoop to spying for his next employer.

The luncheon ran almost to 3 P.M. I hopped into a cab and instructed the driver to get me to Idlewild Airport and to *hurry*. Preoccupied with afterthoughts of the meeting, I paid no attention to his routing until I realized in shock that we were in the Battery Tunnel instead of the more direct Midtown. To make matters worse, the cab stalled dead in the tunnel. That morning I had left my luggage with Cedric at the St. Moritz before meeting with Jones, so I got out of the cab and hitchhiked out of the tunnel. With the help of police at the toll booth in Brooklyn, I took another cab to Idlewild, arriving almost an hour late. As I jumped out of the taxi in a state of frenzy, a uniformed PanAm steward appeared and asked, "Are you Mr. Nakasian?"

"Yes, Yes!!" I replied.

"Don't rush," he said soothingly. "We're holding the plane for you."

You can't imagine my embarrassment as I boarded the plane. All eyes focused on me as if to ask, "Who the hell is this guy?" When I reached my seat next to Cedric's (VIP seats, courtesy of PanAm founder Juan Trippe, a friend of Cedric's), he glared at me and muttered, "You son-of-a-bitch!" I knew better than to try and explain my ordeal to Cedric in his livid condition. Neither of us said anything for some time, then finally he turned to me and demanded through clenched teeth, "Do you have any idea what I went through to convince the Captain to hold the plane? Let history record that no one has ever been described as so indispensible as I made you: the Shah's personal representative, without whose presence my trip to Iran would be aborted and my broadcasts cancelled, outraging my millions of listeners. When none of that worked I threatened to call Juan Trippe himself on his private phone!" Moustache twitching, Cedric shook his finger at me. "Don't *ever* do that to me again!" Then he sank back into his seat. Not until we landed in Shannon, Ireland the next morning did Cedric lose his florid complexion of anger.

For the next two weeks people back home heard Cedric open with: "This is Cedric Foster, reporting to you from Tehran…" Cedric had the time of his life and our airplane misadventure was forgotten. The Shah was greatly pleased by Cedric's efforts to educate Americans about Iran and even more pleased when Cedric reported that the Shah had the enthusiastic support of his people. (He had made sure that Cedric was exposed only to those who *did* support him.)

As Cedric prepared to leave Tehran, the Shah's Minister to the Court called us in for a visit, during which he advised us that the Shah had granted Cedric and me a private audience the next day. Our excitement was quickly tinged with nervousness when he went on to outline the formalities we must observe in the Shah's presence: "First, you must not extend your hand to the Shah. If His Majesty extends his hand to you, accept it with a bow, noticeably from the waist. That is all that is expected of an American.

"During the audience you will talk about whatever the Shah wants to talk about. You are not to introduce any subject unless His Majesty specifically requests. You are expected to accept whatever he says without question. Do not challenge or amend any statements he makes.

"You are to address the Shah as Your Majesty or Royal Highness. Do not look away from him, but dedicate your attention totally to him until *he* decides to end the audience. He will signal this by rising. You will follow immediately. Do not remain seated once he rises!

"Finally, express your gratitude for his indulgence and proceed to leave. As you depart continue to face him, walking backward to the exit door. Do not turn around until you pass through the door and it is closed behind you. Then you may exit the building walking forward."

As Cedric and I were trying to take all this in, he warned us once more with emphasis: "Never turn your back on the Shah!"

The next day the Minister escorted Cedric and me into a large reception room in the Shah's Palace. Elegant Persian carpets adorned the floor and walls. His Majesty was seated at the far end of the room. As we approached, he rose and extended his hand. We each took his hand gently and bowed from the waist. The Minister then departed, leaving us alone with the Shah.

At the outset the Shah asked rhetorically, "So, have you enjoyed yourselves in my country?" Pleased with our enthusiastic responses, he turned his attention primarily to Cedric, first complimenting him on his broadcasts and then expansively outlining his plans for Iran's future, with the implication that Cedric would do a newscast on this after returning home. The Shah spoke of a modern Iran who would take her place among the most advanced nations of the world. "I will provide universal education for my people with an emphasis on science so that we can develop a high-tech workforce to attract foreign companies. To reward their investment I will guarantee them a profit of 6%." He concluded by stating imperiously, "This is my personal blueprint for Iran's future." Then His Majesty stood up, and Cedric and I took our leave, strictly obeying the ritual of departure. I'm sure it is the longest distance I have ever walked backwards in my life.

Back at the Hotel, Cedric and I reviewed the audience, trying to regain our footing after our brush with royalty. Cedric was more smitten than I. I pointed out that the Shah had spoken in conclusory terms of end results, offering no reasons, methods, facts, or expert opinions. He had spoken with apparent sincerity, yet I could not forget the vast chasm between his lifestyle and what I had seen at the poor house in Shiraz.

I recounted to Cedric a story I had heard a few days before: An Iranian educator was hosting a visiting American school superintendent on a tour of Tehran's elementary schools. The Iranian bragged, "Perhaps *our* schools are the best in the world." When the American educator responded with an expression of disbelief, the Iranian challenged him: "Go ahead. Ask this fourth-grade student any question you wish."

Not wishing to embarrass the boy, the American asked him, "How much is two plus two?" The boy looked blank and remained silent. The surprised American looked at his Iranian host. "He should know the answer."

"How could he answer?" replied the Iranian. "You didn't tell him whether he was buying or selling!"

When Nemazee returned to Iran, he was widely perceived as the savant who could end the oil embargo. At the airport he was met by a reception committee of high government officials, and was immediately appointed Minister of State. He also joined the Ministerial Committee to which I reported, which made my task much easier. With his knowledge of both Farsi and the oil industry, he made meaningful translations of my briefing papers and at the meetings themselves. With his help we were able to achieve a consensus of committee members on a prospective plan to end the embargo.

Briefly stated, they accepted the consortium concept. This would break the monopoly of the British by including the other major producers of MidEast oil, who would cut back oil production elsewhere so that oil from Iran's Abadan Refinery could be returned to market without a drop in the price per barrel. AIOC would be the largest shareholder in a consortium with Esso, California, Texas, Mobil, Gulf, CFP (a French Company) and Shell, with the larger U.S. independents—Sinclair, Cities Service, Atlantic, Getty, and perhaps others—included for a combined share of ten percent of the production. AIOC, as the most knowledgeable about Iran's oil industry, would manage the refinery and its exploration and production.

Although AIOC made a big issue of the illegality of the Nationalization Law, the Iranian people regarded the Law as their Declaration of Independence from the yoke of British control, and the Committee steadfastly refused to repeal the law or even amend it. I explained, to the relief of the Shah and his ministers, that the Iranian Government need not sell its land to the oil companies; instead they could accommodate them via contractual lease agreements that would satisfy the companies' tax obligations in their home countries.

AIOC was adamantly resisting *any* revision of its concession payment of fifteen cents per barrel, which had remained constant since its inception decades earlier despite rising market prices. In one of my briefings I explained to the ministers how, during World War II, the U.S. had cooperated with Venezuela in revising its method of payments. Instead of paying a fixed amount per barrel, the oil companies would share their pre-tax profits fifty-fifty with Venezuela. The U.S. government had helped by passing a law that the 50% share paid to Venezuela would qualify as a credit against U.S. taxes. As a result, no U.S. taxes would be paid by the oil companies, and henceforth they would receive 50% of all profits, free of *any* taxes. This was agreeable to both the oil companies and the host country, and a similar arrangement might work in Iran.

The Committee readily understood that the taking of AIOC Property required payment of compensation to AIOC; the matter of the rate of payment and the time period would be a matter of negotiation.

In early January of 1954 Secretary of State Dulles sent Herbert Hoover, Jr. to Tehran on what Hoover described as a fact-finding mission. Hoover and I met privately several times and Patricia and I also lunched with him on occasion. I briefed him on my meetings with General Zahedi and the Ministers, and outlined the agreement on which we had reached a consensus. Anything I shared with Hoover I believe he could readily affirm from transcripts of the bugged meetings. Hoover's visit was the long-awaited signal that finally the United States would get directly involved, if not actually take the lead, in resolving the oil crisis, and I was elated. Yet, my elation was tempered by the realization that Esso was calling the shots, as the hand in the diplomatic glove of our State Department.

Two weeks later I received an urgent call from Nemazee, informing me that "Tex" Reiber and his attorney had arrived in Tehran, and were meeting with the Ministers that afternoon. I had heard nothing of this, and had not been invited to the meeting. Nemazee convinced me to come anyway.

Reiber headed an investment company which was largely vested in oil stocks—Esso in particular. His office was in Rockefeller Plaza, where Esso was also headquartered. Senior in age, he had retained the bombastic style of the legendary Texan. Before World War II he had gained notoriety by announcing his support for Hitler, an action that led to his dismissal as President of Texaco. Given his history, I'm sure he would not have been the State Department's first choice for the job, which further demonstrated to me just how much power Esso had with them. I went to the meeting with a great deal of curiosity and some trepidation.

At the meeting, the usual formality of introductions was bypassed. To my surprise, Ali Amini introduced himself as in charge of "oil negotiations" and announced that Reiber would be his "oil advisor." Reiber had never met me and I am convinced he did not realize that I was present.

Immediately he sought to discredit me, without using my name. "How can anyone suggest," he thundered, "that the independent American oil companies are large enough to participate in this market? Such a person is either stupid or an undisclosed paid agent for these companies!" Feeling confident that my briefings to the contrary had been well understood by the Ministers, I responded by admonishing Reiber for his attempt to mislead the committee and his arrogant assumption that they were ignorant of the facts.

"As an American," I told him face-to-face, "you ought to be ashamed of yourself for perpetrating this deception! You know damn well that the American independents on the east coast control thirty percent of the world's largest refined products market!"

Reiber appeared shocked by this attack on his integrity. Apparently he had assumed he would be talking only to Iranians. I suspect that he had guessed my identity by now. (If he hadn't, he would discover it later from Amini.) In any case he abruptly abandoned his attack and remained silent. Amini quickly adjourned the meeting.

As I left the meeting Amini pulled me to one side and asked me to come to his office the next day. There he apologetically reaffirmed that Reiber would be his oil advisor, adding, "I would like you to stay in Tehran to assist Mr. Nemazee."

"This is Iran's problem, not Nemazee's," I replied. "If my presence would be helpful, I should be assisting you and your government." When no such offer was forthcoming, I advised him that I would leave for home as soon as I had said my goodbyes. Ironically, Reiber's tenure as oil advisor was a short one. In seeking to destroy my credibility, he had destroyed his own. Had Esso's plan succeeded, Reiber would ostensibly have been acting for Iran but in fact negotiating according to his own economic self-interest, since his company owned a large portfolio of

Esso stock. This unseemly picture fortunately did not materialize, as Reiber soon left Tehran for good.

In the final negotiations, which took place after I had left the country, the veteran Howard Page of Esso spoke for the oil companies. The Iranians negotiated without American help, and did a pretty good job of it, with Amini assisted by Engineer Reza Fallah and a couple of his colleagues, notably Bagher Mostofi. Fallah later became a major player in the oil industry as the Shah's personal oil advisor.

The consensus reached by the Ministerial Committee was largely adopted. The principal change was that the independent companies' share of production was reduced from ten percent to five, an obvious concession to Esso. The ministers stood firm on their demand for a Venezuela type of profit sharing. As a result, Iran's oil revenues increased from fifteen to more than fifty cents per barrel. Moreover, under this formula, Iran would directly benefit from any increase in oil prices in future years. This ushered in a new era for the Iranian economy, with oil revenue now the predominant source of the Nation's export income.

Since I'm sure that Esso had access to transcripts of my meetings with Zahedi and the Ministerial Committee, I'm also sure that they held me responsible for the Iranian consensus on major terms. The last thing Esso wanted was for me to become known for this achievement. With such a reputation I would likely be engaged by other oil countries, who might demand renegotiation of their contracts. Up to this time the major international oil companies had pretty much written their own terms in negotiations with local governments who had little or no knowledge of the oil industry.

Patricia and I left Tehran for home in March of 1954. Amini saw me off at the airport, along with Nemazee and several of the other ministers. As a present, Amini handed me a very large can of caviar.

In Geneva Pattie and I parted. She went on to Vienna to visit her elderly aunts Stephanie and Valerie. Born in the Court of Emperor Franz Joseph, they had survived two World Wars that

Sam in meeting with General Zahedi, Prime Minister and the Cabinet with Nemazee (on the far right)

had brought down the Austro-Hungarian Empire, yet they had never lost their imperial dignity.

In the air back to America I had plenty of time to think—about my own future and that of the country I had just left. The Shah certainly had imperial pretensions, but I had great misgivings about his leadership qualities and the future of his reign. I couldn't help but compare him with Mossadeq. In spite of Mossadeq's own background of wealth, there was no doubt in my mind that he was closer to and more beloved by the Iranian people, and had their interests more at heart.

Mossadeq had come to power with the support of Tehran's sophisticated and politically powerful merchant class, who were positioned to benefit if the iron grip of AIOC could be broken and Iran could share more equitably in the revenue generated by its own oil fields. They couldn't have cared less about the people in the countryside, and were pleasantly surprised by Mossadeq's great popularity with them.

The merchants were risking little: if Mossadeq failed, his life was at stake, not theirs. And when he was unable to end the embargo, they deserted him. As it turned out, it was only his great popularity with the common people of Iran that saved him from the same fate as Fatime. A short time after I left, the Shah freed him from jail with the understanding that he would never again leave the village from whence he came.

Upon my arrival in New York I was met by a friend, Frank Kluckhohn, formerly an ace reporter for the *New York Times*. After I related some of my Iranian adventures to him, Frank telephoned Abe Rosenthahl, the Editor of the *Times*, and suggested that I could could provide a lively first-hand report on events in Iran if he called me at the Drake Hotel, where I was spending the night. Rosenthahl did phone and questioned me for half an hour. I answered his questions in detail and in depth, from my recent personal experience. Not a word of this interview appeared the next day, or ever. When I asked Frank about it, he surmised that Rosenthahl had called Esso to see what they had to say, and been pursuaded (probably by Kegler) not to print.

"Esso could teach Tammany Hall a thing or two about power," I thought to myself. But I was left with no public acknowledgement of my contributions to the Iranians or the oil industry, or to my country. My efforts in Iran would remain a secret, I realized. At that moment, I felt defeated and helpless.

Instead of dwelling on the negative, I decided to give an impromptu cocktail party at the Drake, and to invite Kegler himself. I wanted people to see that I was alive and well and back in the country, and I wanted word of this to filter back to Kegler even if he didn't come. To my surprise, he came—out of curiosity, I suppose. Many old friends came also, and by the end of the evening my joie de vivre was no longer feigned. I'm sure Kegler wondered what I would do next.

One other thing troubled me. Back in December, my CIA friend George Carroll and his wife had told us they were being reassigned to Washington. Knowing that our apartment there was vacant, they had requested we rent it to them. Patricia and I talked it over and agreed. Carroll paid us two months rent and we gave him the keys as he departed Tehran.

I had thought it odd that we did not hear from them after

that. Now, upon my return to Washington, there was no evidence the apartment had even been lived in. This confirmed my suspicion that Carroll's sole reason for renting it was to conduct a thorough search for his bosses. It also cast doubt on our social relationship in Tehran. It seemed obvious now that our "friendship" had been just another assignment to Carroll. Tapes of my official meetings were not enough for the Agency: they wanted access to my private thoughts as well. All this was depressing and disillusioning. (I never saw or heard from George Carroll again.)

I had been involved with Nemazee and the Iranians for so long that when I returned to my Washington office there was little work to occupy me and my associate lawyer, Anne Aldrich—the starving exchange student I had taken to dinner in Geneva some years earlier. Anne had gone on to finish second in her class at NYU Law School, and was working for Davison Summers, General Counsel for the World Bank, when she paid me a visit in 1953 at my office in Washington. After hearing about my role in developing Iran's first waterworks and first modern medical center, she startled me by saying, "I want to work with *you*."

"But, why?" I asked. "I would think your job at the World Bank is both interesting and lucrative."

"It's *dull*," she sighed. "I spend all my time reading and reviewing loan agreements other people negotiated. *They* have all the fun." As for her salary, she was willing to take a cut to work for me. It was an offer I could not refuse.

It occurred to me that this lull in business might be a good time to fulfill my promise to Father Lucey that I would write an article for the *Georgetown Law Journal.* Recently the World Court in Hague had refused to hear the Iranian Oil Nationalization case, claiming that the case did not fall within its jurisdiction. As this was within my area of expertise, I undertook an article on the World Court's action, using source material gathered by Anne and Barbara, my secretary. With their help, it didn't take long, and when the next issue of the *Journal* came out, it was the lead article.

One morning Bazy McCormick telephoned and said that she and her husband Tankersley needed my advice on how to handle a very sensitive problem. That afternoon I met them in their living room and Bazy explained the situation. "When my uncle was visiting Saudi Arabia recently, King Ibn Saud gave him a prize Arabian yearling, which he was going to give to us. Tank and I went to Idlewyld to pick it up and were flabbergasted when they unloaded a common work horse so emaciated it required quarantine. What should we do?"

"It's obvious," I replied, "that the Saudis who were entrusted with transport of the animal stole the yearling and replaced it at the last moment with one of their nags. If the King learns of this, it will be a great embarrassment for him. Hands and heads will be severed, so that he will not appear weak.

"I suggest that you replace the nag with one of your own yearlings. If you don't have one that's suitable, then buy one. Then invite the Saudi ambassador and his entourage to a ceremony celebrating the King's gift. If secrecy is maintained, only the three of us will know what really happened."

Relieved, Bazy accepted my idea and immediately put it into action. Her first thought had been to consult the State Department. Now there would be no leaks through the government bureaucracy. A few weeks later she threw a party with the Saudis as honored guests. The beautiful Arabian stallion elicited the admiration of all present, and the Saudi ambassador beamed with pride.

Bazy and Tank seriously tried to understand the rapid emergence of the Middle East and its importance to the United States, and occasionally I would overhear them quoting me to support *their* opinions about this distant and unfamiliar part of the world. Having had first hand experience in the Middle East, it was rewarding to me when some of the notables at their parties would break the stranglehold of Washington's conventional wisdom and ask me for information about Iran (or later, Iraq, Pakistan, or Libya).

Soon after I completed my article for the *Georgetown Law Jour-*

nal, a law school classmate of mine invited me to visit Chile, Argentina, and Brazil with him. At this time, there seemed to be a window of opportunity for the American independent oil companies to become involved in Argentina and Brazil. As the son of a prominent Chilean family known throughout Latin America, my friend would be willing and able to introduce me to key figures in those countries. Since I was looking for work, I gladly accepted his invitation.

In 1954, Argentina was dominated by Peronistas and xenophobia was sweeping the country. Negotiations with foreign oil companies had been stymied by Argentina's insistence that they lease oil fields from their National Oil Company (YPF) rather than purchase them outright as the companies demanded. My friend arranged a meeting with the top management of YPF and also served as translator. When I told YPF of the arrangement I had negotiated for the Iranians, they expressed great interest in coming to similar terms with the American independents. I explained to them that this would lead to an increase in production and hence oil revenue. However, in the current political climate, even leasing domestic resources to a foreign company would be a controversial move, and as time went on they seemed to be getting cold feet. When, after several meetings, no official relationship for the future had been established or even suggested by YPF, I traveled on to Brazil.

There I met with officials of the Brazilian National Oil Company, but the situation was much the same. It appeared that a second, and probably third, trip would be needed before anything concrete materialized. I knew I would not be able to return for several months, and so chose not to pursue opportunities in either country. Perhaps it's just as well. Forty years have gone by and Brazil is *still* closed to foreign oil companies.

The reason I would not be able to return was quite simple. In August Patricia gave birth to our first child, Stephanie. This miraculous event made up for all the recent frustrations I had endured, and gave *me* a new lease on life as well. More on family life later.

9

The Iraqi Dam Project

IN LATE OCTOBER OF 1954 Tommy Tompkins of Tompkins Construction Company, a prominent builder in the District of Columbia, engaged me to supervise the negotiation of a contract with the Government of Iraq. Tompkins was part of a consortium including J.A. Jones Construction of North Carolina, Tecon (owned by the Murchisons of Dallas), and a German company, that had underbid its competitors for a contract to build the 600-foot high, rock-filled, Derbendi Khan Dam—the first project of anywhere near this magnitude in the Persian Gulf area. The general terms of the contract called for the consortium to be paid $25 million to complete the dam within 1,000 days. Only the details remained, but none of the companies had any experience in the Middle East, and Tompkins was understandably apprehensive. I agreed to the assignment, provided I could return to Washington for the holidays.

I met Mr. Jones in Paris and together we flew to Baghdad, where we checked into the Metropole Hotel, a decades-old, three story walk-up on the banks of the Tigris River. Each of its thirty rooms contained only a hard bed, small table and chair, and a place to hang one's clothes. At least ours had a small window overlooking the Tigris. Sharing one shower, sink, and toilet with the ten other guests on our floor took some getting used to, but Jones and I adjusted. There was one telephone—in the manager's office.

The Hotel did have a dining room and bar, which served as a gathering place for locals as well as foreign visitors. Almost every evening a group of us would assemble at the bar for a social hour and history lesson with Jesus—the bearded, charismatic hotel manager and bartender. Jesus escorted us from our distant Western view of the region to a more intimate understanding of the area, and made our stay enjoyable in spite of the lack of amenities.

As we sipped our drinks, Jesus would regale us in fluent English with his own history, as well as his encyclopedic knowledge of Iraq and ancient Mesopotamia. "I am a descendant of the Chaldean tribe you read about in the Bible," he began. "Although Semitic, we converted to Christianity long before Muhammad came."

Jesus went on to outline a brief history of the region: "After the Eighth Century, Muhammad's Islamic crusade targeted Mesopotamia for conversion. Mesopotamia was prosperous; it was one of the world's great agricultural producers, using the waters of the Tigris and Euphrates to create a sophisticated irrigation system. When the Moslems took over they were very tolerant of the diverse ethnic groups living here: Arabs, Jews, Kurds, and other local tribes—some nomadic, others sedentary. As long as they were not politically hostile, the Moslems allowed them to practice their own customs and religions. After the Turks invaded, they too tolerated the non-hostile confessional and ethnic subcultures, as have the British, who in effect replaced the Turks after World War I. Largely isolated from the world beyond, our country has lived in relative peace to this day. Now, with the Western powers' creation of Israel in our backyard, and the exodus of Palestinian refugees, I fear this peace will not last. So far the racial conflict to the west has not reached our polyglot community. We have been lucky."

During my month in Baghdad, I found Jesus's description of an ethnically diverse population living in harmony to be largely accurate. The Kurdish Tayib family, for example, was college educated. One son was a certified public accountant and the other a fabricator of steel products. It impressed me that their father had been Mayor of Baghdad for many years, elected several times by a citizenry in which Kurds were a relatively small minority. Baghdad University, established by the Jesuits in the mid-1920's—the first university in the Persian Gulf area—attracted Moslems as well as Christians seeking higher education.

As an Armenian-American in Baghdad, I easily established a rapport with Arabs as well as Christians, just as I had in Jerusalem some years earlier. The history of the Christian, politically weak Armenians, in many respects paralleled the history of Jesus's Chaldeans. Jesus and I became fast friends, and even though I stayed at the modern Baghdad Hotel on subsequent trips to the city, I always returned to the Metropole for an enriching hour at Jesus's bar.

On that first trip, I couldn't help but compare what I learned about Iraq with what I knew about Iran. Iran was considerably larger in population, it's thirty million including two multimillion nomadic tribes (the Bakhtiars and Khasgais), as well as Kurds, Arabs, and sundry peoples from the Caspian Sea and points north. Iraq claimed only seven million, including many descendants of ethnic clans identified in the Bible, who shared the country with Kurds, Arabs, and other minorities mentioned earlier—most of them immigrants.

Whereas Iran had a long history of internal autocratic rule, Iraq had for centuries been a satrapy (local province, ruled by a "satrap") of the Turkish Empire. After World War I, each country faced the daunting challenge of inculcating its disparate ethnic groups with a sense of common national interest. In Iraq this challenge rested upon a king imported by the British into a country with no tradition of royalty; while in Iran the British replaced a royal dynasty with *its* choice of a military strongman as *the* autocrat.

Each country's oil history differed as well. Whereas the British had been in sole control of Iran's industry until Mossadeq's nationalization decree, in Iraq—thanks to a Turkish Armenian named Gulbenkian—French (CFP) and American (Esso and Mobil) companies had participated in a consortium with the

British since the beginning. In the final days of the Turkish Empire, Gulbenkian had been granted an oil concession for Iraq. In gratitude for his service to their government during World War I, the French had helped him to retain his oil rights after the empire had crumbled. In the 1920's Gulbenkian had assigned these rights to the consortium in return for a five percent share for himself, in perpetuity—making him one of the world's richest men.

The huge Kirkuk Field in northern Iraq produced millions of barrels for the consortium, known as the Iraq Petroleum Company. IPC had built the first international pipeline, carrying that oil to Mediterranean ports, where it was then shipped to its refineries in Europe. During the Iranian oil embargo, IPC had replaced a good part of Iran's lost production.

Iraq, however, had yet to nationalize, and was still subject to the old colonial arrangement, whereby IPC owned the oil fields and paid a set price per barrel to the Iraqi government. This still amounted to a great deal of money, but, as in Iran, several decades of petroleum revenues were not noticeable in community improvement. The Baghdad of 1954 appeared unchanged from the days of the Turkish Empire.

Nonetheless, on the surface Iraq appeared stable under the constitutional monarchy established by the British. In my five months in Iran, I had sensed that the Shah was incompatable with his subjects, and hence depended for his security on a large military and police force. In my brief stay in Baghdad a smaller and less obtrusive military and police presence suggested to me that the King, after several decades on the throne, was being accepted as sovereign.

The stability of the Iraqi government quickly became an underlying issue in contract negotiations on the dam project. Neither Jones nor the Iraqi officials had any precedent for such a major international project, and both needed to be educated about what was required. One provision in particular, proposed by the Iraqi Government, disturbed me. It provided that payment be made in Iraq's currency of dinars. Jones did not appreciate my concern about this currency issue. "You are inconsistent," he charged. "You advised us that Iraq was the most stable country in the Middle East!"

"Relatively speaking," I replied, "that's true, but no one can guarantee there will be no change in this government. If there happens to be a change for the worse, the value of the dinar might be adversely affected." Currency exchange rates were new to Jones, so I tried to make it more concrete for him. "Look," I told him, "you estimate that ten percent of the cost to complete the dam will be in dollars, to purchase U.S. equipment and for shipping. You also estimate a ten percent profit, and this amount you want in dollars. If the dinar is worth less, possibly as much as twenty percent or even more relative to the dollar, you will have lost your profit and possibly suffered a substantial loss!"

This shook up Mr. Jones, but only for a moment. He accused me of "nitpicking" and worried aloud that I would kill his deal. "Not at all," I assured him. "I can convince the Government that it doesn't make good sense for Iraq, as a matter of general procurement policy, to impose a currency exchange risk on foreign contractors. If foreigners assume that risk they will raise their prices to cover it." When I posed the issue in terms of Iraq's interests, Jones dropped his objections.

When I broached this same argument to Mr. Nelson—an American serving as advisor to Iraq's Economic Development Board—he quickly agreed. "Frankly," he said, "I should have thought of that myself. I will speak with the Finance Minister and arrange for you to meet with him."

The Finance Minister understood the merits of my suggestion but had a legitimate concern: "If we price our contracts in U.S. dollars rather than in Iraqi dinars, how do we escape the implication that dinars are worth less than the dollar? You must propose some contractual language that avoids this inference."

By the next day I had solved the problem by providing that the dinar price of the contract be adjustable with the dollar at time of payment. Should the dinar rise relative to the dollar, the government would pay fewer dinars, and if the dinar declined relative to the dollar, then the government would pay more. Exempted from this adjustment would be local expenses incurred *in* Iraqi dinars. The Finance Minister promised that the Council of Ministers would approve this amendment in their first meeting of the new year. Confident that I had covered all the bases, I returned home for the holidays, promising to return if needed. Jones spent the holidays in Baghdad. Tompkins was very pleased with my performance. Since no request was made for my return, I assumed the currency issue was settled as I had suggested.

In early 1958, just as the dam was on the verge of completion, I received a phone call from Tompkins. He was in a rage: "The King has been murdered in a coup! The dinar has collapsed, and we owe Morgan Bank five million dollars, borrowed against the contract! If we repay them by exchanging our present installment of dinars, we'll not only lose our profits: we won't even be able to recover our costs! What happened?!!"

I was flabbergasted. "I thought that issue was settled," I told him. "The dinar price should be adjusted according to its present exchange rate."

"I called Jones," Tompkins replied, "and he told me that the ministers did not reach the currency issue on the agenda of the scheduled meeting. He volunteered to waive the amendment so that we could get on with the job. What do we do now?"

"My advice," I responded, "is that you postpone exchanging your dinars for dollars as long as you can. If Iraq continues exporting oil, which I believe it will, the dinar *will* recover some and possibly all its loss."

Tompkins followed my advice and avoided a disaster. From then on Mr. Jones avoided me as if I were a bad memory. I remained in Tompkins' high esteem, but our relationship ended abruptly with his untimely death in an auto accident soon thereafter.

10
Pakistan and Libya

AFTER OUR EXPERIENCE TOGETHER IN IRAN, Cedric Foster remained a valued friend of mine in Washington. He made it clear that he respected my abilities and would keep me in mind if he learned of any foreign oil opportunities. This paid off in early 1955 when Amjad Ali, Pakistan's Ambassador to the United States, told Cedric that his government was eager to attract American oil companies. By coincidence Nelson Bunker Hunt, the 29-year old son of legendary Texas oil tycoon H.L. Hunt, happened to be in Washington, and Cedric arranged a meeting with Ali. After the Ambassador assured Bunker of his government's cooperation, they decided to proceed toward a formal agreement, and on Cedric's recommendation, Bunker hired me as negotiator.

As the first of the independents to undertake oil exploration abroad, Bunker established himself as a courageous pioneer, but at the time most of his peers viewed his decision as reckless. The conventional wisdom was that foreign operations were a "White Man's Burden," conducted by the majors only because our government insisted upon it. In 1950, when I was enroute to England aboard the Queen Mary, the Chairman of Caltex himself regaled me with this message, which was widely propagated by the majors.

The primary reason the independents believed this to be true was that they believed they would be taxed twice on their profits—once by the host country and then again by the United States. In those days the majors kept their foreign tax credit, which meant that they paid *no* U.S. taxes, a closely guarded secret. But I was aware of it, and after I briefed Bunker I was greatly impressed by his swift and decisive action in undertaking this major investment some 6,000 miles from his home base of Texas.

Bunker engaged me on a monthly retainer to negotiate and write the concession agreement, with a stipulated fee upon completion. Ed Guinn, a Hunt oil-lease lawyer from rural Texas, would accompany me, along with one of Hunt's geologists, charged with mapping out two adjacent concession areas: ten thousand square miles for Bunker, and ten thousand for his wife, Caroline.

Soon afterwards, Guinn and I flew to Pakistan. Arriving in Karachi was a depressing shock. As a desperately poor city—as poor as cities in Iran, if not more so—Karachi was ill-prepared to receive the hundreds of thousands of Moslems fleeing India after British decolonization. Tens of thousands lived in makeshift huts on the banks of the local river, which was the only source of water. Guinn and I stayed at another ancient Metropole Hotel with very meager accomodations. All items on the menu were prepared with gee (the local animal fat) and guaranteed to produce dysentery. The country did, however, possess an educated, English-speaking civil service, developed by the British over several decades.

To escape the squalor and health hazards of Karachi, the substantial British colony had organized the private Sind Club, where they grew their own vegetables and meat. As visiting VIP's, Guinn and I were introduced to the manager of the Club, and given dining and social privileges. At our first dining, the manager of the Club introduced us to one of its distinguished members. When I extended my hand in friendship, he refused to accept it, and responded with an unfriendly grunt. This, I later discovered, was a rather typical British colonial resident.

It astounded me that, even after the liberation of Britain's colonies, including Pakistan itself, these colonials maintained their fanciful sense of superiority over not only the local populace but any foreigners who might be visiting their domain. As servants of Her Majesty in the subcontinent for generations, these Britains, few in numbers relative to their multitudes of subjects, had developed their own distinctive dress, style and manners. As if in uniforms, the men dressed in similar baggy tweeds, had walrus or waxed-end moustaches, smoked crooked, oversized pipes, and carried a riding crop. In manners, they deliberately expressed rejection or indifference toward persons outside their circle.

In their isolation, they hadn't yet realized that the sun had set on the British Empire, and that they were more laughed at than respected, even when they visited England, where they were as conspicuous as they were in Pakistan or India. I recall a story told me by a Londoner, about a colonial on sabbatical in London. As the colonial approached Piccadily Circus, he was addressed from a doorway by a "lady of easy virtue."

"Good evening, Colonel. Would you like to come home with me?" she inquired seductively.

The Colonel looked around and saw that the woman was as black as ebony. Hesitating and clearing his throat, he replied, "Go *home* with you? All the way to *Africa*?"

I found the atmosphere at the Sind Club so depressing that I chose *not* to return, and resolved to endure the lack of hygienic standards at the Metropole. It was a challenge. I thought perhaps fresh fish, which had been popular with the Moslems in Iraq and Iran, might pose less of a health hazard than the local meats, but I was amazed to learn that Pakistanis would not eat fish, despite their abundance in the rivers and Indian Ocean. The Metropole chef wouldn't even cook fish.

On one of my first weekends in Karachi, the Counselor at the U.S. Embassy invited me to fish with him in the Indian Ocean. This thoughtful gesture offered me an escape from the doldrums of the hotel. Early Saturday morning we made ourselves as comfortable as possible in his 20-foot lorry and headed out into open waters, where I was informed that we would trawl for mackerel at a slow speed.

Our equipment consisted of handlines of 30 pound gauge: there were no stanchions. When I told my host that this was my first deepwater fishing, he instructed me as follows: "You will have lots of line to use in landing your strike; don't fight him—keep the line braked but free enough to let him run. He'll tire, and then as he calms down start reeling him in. He'll take off again, and when he calms down again, reel him in some more; you may have to repeat this several times." He didn't tell me that my hands would so tire from such an exercise that I would wish the mackerel had his freedom.

Still, I managed to catch a tuna and five mackerel—one weighing more than fifty pounds. After two hours we put in for shore after catching a maximum load, which my host estimated at more than a thousand pounds. "What will you do with all this fish?" I asked. "The Pakistanis won't eat it."

"All of it will be eaten," he proudly assured me. "The Embassy staff and foreign visitors appreciate the delicacy of fresh fish. But most of it, I clean and freeze. I brought in a big freezer to feed an orphanage of Pakistani children. We taught them to eat and like fish." I felt even better about my catch after hearing that.

I took a smaller twenty pound mackerel back to the Metropole and bribed the Chef to cook it. Unfortunately, he insisted on using gee to cook it, masking the wholesome flavor of the fish. Nevertheless it was one of the best meals I had at the hotel. Guinn and I shared the fish with Senator Bricker of Ohio, who had stopped over in Karachi on a world tour.

Karachi was also a change-of-crew stop for PanAm's daily, round-the-world flights. The top two floors of the Metropole were leased exclusively to PanAm, and contained a private dining room for them. Each day a PanAm Clipper would drop off its crew of six or eight (including two or three beautiful hostesses) for a twenty-four hour layover, and take on a rested crew for the continuing flight.

Karachi was not an uncomfortable rest stop for the crew. They would go fishing, or play tennis at the Embassy, and their meals consisted of the same choice meats, vegetables, and desserts that were served to PanAm passengers. I was frequently invited for tennis or dinner. Romantic indulgences with the lovely stewardesses were common, and often a source of frustration for the younger male crew members, since the Captain and his superior officers had priority. As an outsider I had no chance whatsoever.

With the signing of the Pakistan concession agreement Guinn and I had crafted, Bunker issued me a check for the agreed fee. After depositing it, I made a trip to New York and stopped in at the Children's Aid Society. Arthur Huck, who had reluctantly honored Mr. Brace's promise to me of a college tuition loan, was still the Executive Director. I presented to him my idea of starting a trust fund in honor of Miss Comstock, and offered a donation of $2,500 to launch it. I felt sure that some of the other two thousand boys she had worked with would want to contribute as well. My objective was two-fold: to repay the $1,600—with interest—and to call attention to that singular person who had meant so much to me as I was growing up.

Although Clara Comstock had retired from CAS prior to World War II, I had always stayed in touch with her. Whenever I had visited her modest home in Hornell, N.Y., I found her as active as ever. Besides heading both the Womens' Society at her Methodist Church and the regional chapter of the Womens' Christian Temperance Union, Miss Comstock spoke frequently to community groups—not only about her work with homeless boys, but also about the teachings of Jesus as a foundation for moral values and purpose in life. In addition to the Bible, she was an avid reader of *National Geographic, Readers Digest*, books on American History, and of course her beloved Ralph Waldo Emerson. After I took a job in the federal government, she added the *Congressional Record* to her reading list, so that she could talk intelligently with me about events in Washington. She was a strong supporter of Congressman Cole—a Republican from her state—and kept abreast of happenings in New York City as well. In her eyes, the rich had obligations and the poor needed inspiration. Whether rich or poor, any person had her respect if they led wholesome, God-fearing lives. Undaunted by either poverty or wealth and power, Miss Comstock made certain that both groups got her attention and message.

Hunts Sign $42-Million West Pakistan Exploration Deal

Nelson B. Hunt, Dallas oil man, and his wife, Caroline L. Hunt, will conduct a $42,000,000 search for oil in West Pakistan under two concession agreements signed in Washington. Seated, left to right, are John A. Goodson, who signed for Mrs. Hunt; Nelson B. Hunt; and Syed Amjad Ali, Pakistan ambassador to the United States. Standing, left to right, are Zahiruddin Ahmed, financial advisor to the Pakistan embassy; Samuel Nakasian, who negotiated the 60-year agreements for the Hunts; and Horace Hidreth, U.S. Ambassador to Pakistan. Hunt is the son of H.L. Hunt, president of Hunt Oil Co., Dallas. The concessions cover 20,000 sq. miles (The Oil and Gas Journal, September 19, page 102).

With charitable gifts deductible against 1950's income tax rates as high as 80%, the Children's Aid Society was doing very well. Salaries were competitive with government and private industry, and social security was augmented by a pension plan. Miss Comstock had retired too early to benefit from any of this, and barely subsisted in Hornell. Confident in the awareness that she had "done right" all those years, and aware also that I had achieved a rather good income level, she had for some time accepted modest monthly contributions from me, or her situation would have been even worse.

When CAS employee Nora Johnson, who had worked with Miss Comstock, heard about her plight she was appalled, and devised a program whereby the Society would re-employ Miss Comstock, now in her late seventies, to research its files and locate and communicate with former CAS wards. This employment made her eligible for Social Security and resulted in a number of contributions from "Comstock boys" to the trust fund I had established.

When the Society's Board of Trustees heard about this, they decided to honor Miss Comstock with a luncheon at the Harvard Club in Manhattan. At that time the Board included several members of the city's "Who's Who"—names like Wheeler, Osborne, and Lord. They attended, along with some of the top staff. Several including Wheelock got up to speak. None of them had ever met her, but all found her service to the Society of great inspiration and value.

Then they asked me to say a few words. I began by recounting our first meeting some thirty years earlier, and talked about our relationship through the years. In conclusion I spoke of her character. "No doubt you have the impression she was mild and benign, and made no waves. The reality is that she was tough and refused to compromise what was right. She was determined to get the best out of her boys. She pulled and shoved me along the way, but she also held a star over my head which she challenged me to reach. Perhaps you can imagine the impact on an orphan boy of her frequent enthusiastic approval of diligence, and her rebuke of unjustified performance.

"Miss Comstock's service was an expression of the Biblical virtues of love, trust, and hope. She participated in the lives of her boys and shared with them her faith and strength. This extraordinary lady is truly one of the greats."

Clara Comstock then rose to her feet without invitation, to say "a word or two." There followed the most beautiful articulation of living a useful life that I have ever heard. Quoting from Emerson and the Bible, she reduced the complexities of life to the simplest of time-honored values, and clearly defined the high road to travel. She closed by saying, "All of my two thousand boys were good boys. Some had more capability than others, but each according to his gifts will do good works, I am sure. I thank the Children's Aid Society for making it possible for me to have lived my cherished life."

After the formalities it seemed to me that the board members were ill at ease. To them the luncheon was a perfunctory exercise to put an appreciative gesture on record—a kind of atonement for previous neglect, not only of Miss Comstock, but of all their faithful servants during hard times that they had forgotten. Now that they had done their duty it was time to get on with business. They clearly preferred to relate to others like themselves, and had no real experience or interest in either the boys their organization was helping, or the workers who were helping them. It was the same isolation from the rank and file that I had observed in business executives.

I frankly don't think that seeing one of their boys make good was of any importance to these people. Following this luncheon, I never again had any contact with the Children's Aid Society. Had the board or its top managers asked me to serve the Society in a voluntary role, I would gladly have accepted. It strikes me as greatly ironic that they apparently did not feel comfortable including an Armenian orphan in their elite company.

Before the Pakistan deal was consummated, Bunker had given Guinn and me a second assignment. His interest piqued by recent press reports of American oil companies applying for concession rights in Libya, Bunker asked us to stop off in Tripoli on our trips to and from Karachi, and investigate the Libyan prospects as well.

At that time Rome was a stopover on flights from the U.S. to Karachi, and Alitalia had one daily flight from Rome to Tripoli, via Silicy, Malta, or Catania. This was Tripoli's only air connection to the outside world. The airport was makeshift—a single landing strip of steel mesh laid atop the silt (courtesy of the U.S. Air Force), and a shack-like temporary structure for check-in, baggage, and Customs. Our plane approached over a vast desert, barren except for patches of vegetation—compounds of twenty or thirty acres of citrus, olives, nuts, and vegetables, cultivated by the remaining prewar Italian settlers.

Tripoli was thirty minutes east of the airport. As we drove along the rutted road, people dressed in rags stared out of their crude huts at us. The city itself was surprisingly attractive. With its picturesque narrow streets lined with small shops, its simple Catholic church overlooking the central square, and its seaside promenade, Tripoli looked much like the coastal cities of Italy or Sicily. A primary tourist attraction was the fort of the Barbary Pirates, nemesis of the American navy during Jefferson's presidency. Things were quite a bit more civilized now. The city had a modern water and sewer system, and two charming and well-appointed hotels—the King George and the Uadden. In the early evenings we frequented the cafes off the main square, where the city's Italian population congregated to socialize.

Libyan independence thus far hadn't amounted to much. World War II was over but the Allies and their arms remained, along with thousands of land mines, threatening all travel along the 700-mile Mediterranean Coast and as far as 100 miles inland. Only the coastal road connecting Tripoli with Benghazi and Tobruk was mostly clear of mines.

The British Army continued to provide a domestic police force, and the U.S. had a military presence at the massive Wheelus Air Force Base near Tripoli, with planes taking off and landing constantly, around the clock. The Libyans were passive observers, waiting for something to happen.

Then, in 1954, American oil companies had moved in, braving the land mines as they used their seismic instruments to find subsurface structures capable of holding petroleum. The Libyans found this remarkable, since the Italians, during their decades of rule, had never seriously investigated this possibility. If the Americans were risking the lives of their technicians to find oil, common sense told the Libyans that a fortune lay beneath the desert sands. From that point on, Libyans saw dollar signs when they saw an American.

When Guinn and I arrived in Tripoli, one of the first things I did was to call on Ambassador Jack Tappan, our first Ambassador to Libya, who had earlier served with me in the Marshall Plan. As good friends, we played tennis and spent a great deal of time together socially. This relationship established my credentials as an important person, with Americans as well as Libyans, but it yielded little in the way of useful information.

That information came mostly from Al Lager, a former U.S. official who now represented the independent oil companies Marathon, Conoco and Amerada, known as the "Oasis Group." That the independents had any access to Libyan oil at all was largely due to Lager, who had established an inside position with the Idris Palace in Tobruk and advocated "The Open Door" to all companies. The Libyan pie was big enough for everyone to get a sizeable slice, and since I represented Hunt, another independent, Al generously shared with me the inside scoop on how business was done in Libya.

The King's palace in Tobruk was hardly an executive establishment. It was essentially a household. Neither the King nor his advisors had any staff to assist in the decision-making process that they reserved to themselves. For many years the King's chief advisor had been his brother-in-arms, a desert warrior known as Sheili, who had three sons. King Idris, with little experience outside his native Cyrenaica, had relied entirely on his close friend and aide, until Sheili's death by an assassin's bullet meant for the King himself. In gratitude for Sheili's saving his life, the King appointed Sheili's eldest son, Bushir, to succeed him. Bushir, who had grown up in the palace, was the Kingpin at the time I was in Tripoli. He and his younger brothers had all gone to school in Cairo. The next oldest, Abdul Azis Sheili, had gone to the military academy there, and the third and youngest son, Omar, was in Cairo studying law.

There was amazingly little contact between Tobruk and Tripoli, 700 miles apart. The King hated Tripoli and rarely visited. Proposals made by the Prime Minister and his government in Tripoli were subject to the King's approval in Tobruk, as were laws and regulations. Government and agency heads were chosen by the Palace as particular individuals, and not as representatives of political constituencies. There were no organized political parties. Under these circumstances, it was obvious to us that the Tripoli bureaus had no real power. In order to get *anywhere* in Libya, a company needed the patronage of a Libyan who was close to King Idris's palace.

Historically the major oil companies would be supported by their respective governments in acquiring concessions in foreign lands. Normally, they would have preempted Libya for their exclusive domain, especially since British and American forces were so visible in the country. But Lager's open door policy made sense to those few Libyans who stood to personally profit from their services as patrons of the oil companies. The more companies, the more kickbacks.

Most prominent in this service was the King's cousin, Sayad Abdallah Senussi, known as "The Black Prince" because he clearly exhibited the color of a Sudanese parent. The Black Prince was ambitious; he accepted retainers and promises of royalties from a number of oil companies, even though they were competitors. It was not difficult to arrange a meeting with him.

When he walked into the room in his flowing Arabic robe I was momentarily dumbstruck. The Black Prince was enormous—as tall as he was fat. His English was poor, but we had no trouble understanding one another's interests. The mechanism for deciding which companies would get oil concessions had not been determined yet, but Sayad Abdallah assured me that he would be our patron.

To provide some semblance of administration in Tripoli, an English-speaking Palestinian Arab had been brought in as Libya's Administrator for Oil. He had no oil experience, and no real authority. The oil company representatives persuaded him that a petroleum law and regulations were needed to clarify the obligation and rights of the companies selected for concessions.

I was on the committee formed to draft the new law and regulations in accordance with accepted practice in other countries. Over several months we hashed out the details concerning payments to the government, taxation, land rents, and relinquishment. However, there were no provisions included with respect to how and which companies would be selected, nor were there any stipulations as to size of royalties, specified work obligations (e.g. how many wells must be drilled), or the offering, on a competitive basis, of bonus payments for exceptional production. It was understood that the companies chosen would remove land mines from their respective areas at their own expense and risk.

Once the new laws and regulations were drawn up, the oil companies filed formal applications and lined up like race horses at the starting gate, awaiting the selection decision from King Idris in Tobruk. Late in the filing process, the most creative applicant proved to be Texas Gulf Producing Company, a medium sized oil producer from Texas, controlled by the Reed brothers. They employed as their agent Wendell Phillips, an archeologist with years of experience in the Middle East. Phillips spoke Arabic and was known to a number of Sheiks in the area.

Phillips arrived in Tripoli in a U.S. Air Force plane, accompanied by Secretary of the Air Force Talbot, and the very next day the same plane carried them to Tobruk for a meeting with King Idris. Naturally, all of the other company representatives cried "foul," but the Libyan government ignored them (though later, back in Washington, Talbot faced a congressional inquiry that resulted in his resignation).

Not all would-be applicants were granted participation. A couple never got in the door. One of the rejects was William Buckley, Sr., the President of Pantepec Oil, who stopped off in Libya following negotiations in Israel. The other was Abe "Tex" Feldman, owner of Feldman Oil. He arrived in Tripoli and identified himself as Episcopalian. The Libyans didn't buy it; he was still a Jew to them. Although largely isolated from world events, Idris and Sheili were aware of, and influenced by, Abdul Nasser's hostility to Israel.

Phillips and Talbot succeeded in obtaining for Texas Gulf Producing what was generally regarded as the choice concession in central Libya's vast Sirte Basin. Oasis, Esso, Caltex, and Mobil were also granted concessions in the basin. Royal Dutch Shell received a large grant in the Fezzan Province, and Hunt got the big surface anticline in Cyrenaica, some 300 hundred miles south of Tobruk.

Within 5 years, all of the oil companies except Shell had made major discoveries and had built, or were building, pipelines to the Mediterranean coast. Esso was the first of the large producers, followed by Oasis, Texas Gulf, Caltex, and finally, Bunker Hunt. Soon Libyan crude oil exports exceeded one million barrels a day.

Overnight the few Libyan insiders—the "patrons"—became multi-millionaires, and paraded their newfound wealth in Tripoli and Benghazi. The Black Prince was the most conspicuous as he drove his Silver Cloud Rolls through the narrow streets of Tripoli, honking aggressively to get pedestrians out of his way. (There were no sidewalks). Taking advantage of my friendly relations with him I cautioned that he might be incurring hostility from his many less fortunate countrymen.

"Why," I asked him, "don't you take your Silver Cloud to Geneva? You have a home there, and you could be among others with wealth such as yours."

"Heavens *no*," he replied emphatically. "Here I am noticed; in Geneva everyone has a Rolls Royce."

My favorable relations with Bunker had turned sour and terminated when, after the Pakistan deal was completed, I requested we agree on a completion fee for Libya. He flatly refused, stating that he had paid me enough for Pakistan to include Libya as well.

When Bunker finally struck oil in Libya, the Sarir Field turned out to be the largest in that country. Originally more than seven billion barrels, it remains one of the ten largest oil reservoirs in the world. The oil was paraffinic base, meaning that at the surface it would cool rapidly and solidify. Unless kept heated to liquidity, the oil in the 300-mile pipeline to the sea would solidify into one long candle. Sea transport was possible only in special thermal tankers. This peculiarity did not prevent Bunker from becoming fabulously wealthy.

The story of the deal that made Bunker known as "the richest man in the world" was told to me by Monte Pennell, Director of British Petroleum, who personally negotiated with him to acquire for BP part of Bunker's concession in the Sarir Field. I had met Monte in New York in the early 1960's, when BP and Sinclair were involved in the Prudeau Bay venture in Alaska and

I was on retainer by Sinclair. Later we spent time together in Tehran (where Monte was for a time Managing Director of the Iranian Oil Consortium), and also in his native London.

Monte epitomized the sophisticated Britisher. His beloved Pims cocktails unleashed a devastating charm, enhanced by skillful employment of understatement. If you didn't know better, you'd think Rex Harrison had joined you. During a personal exchange I once asked him, "Monte, as Managing Director of BP you've reached the pinnacle of success. Is your training in geology, or engineering, or what? I never knew."

"Not anything really," he replied modestly. "I was one of the army chaps BP took in after the War."

I wouldn't let him off so easily. "That doesn't explain your success," I continued.

"Quite right!" he answered. "I believe I succeed because Lady Bridgeman rather fancies me." Lady Bridgeman was the Chairman's wife.

Monte knew that I had been engaged by Bunker some years earlier, so he volunteered to tell me about the deal *he* had negotiated with him. "We each had our supporting chaps nearby," he reported, "but it was mostly one on one.

"My Chairman was adamant that we control Bunker's huge Libyan reserves because they were so close to the European refineries who are *our* customers. Our reserves are further away, in Kuwait, Iraq, and Iran; lower priced Sarir crude could have raised hell with us.

"We knew that it would cost two or three hundred million dollars to gather the crude from the wells and pipeline it 300 miles to the ocean. It would require a large diameter pipe and a terminal with large storage tanks for ship loading. Whether Bunker could raise that amount of money was seriously questioned, but we dared not risk that he could. If he succeeded in the financing, then the price of buying him out might well have been prohibitive for us. The consensus of our management and board was that we try to make a deal with him before he acquired the financing.

"We estimated that he had spent only a couple of million

dollars on the project, and felt confident that offering him more than a thousand percent on his investment would be irresistible. Bunker bought the deal—the equivalent of ten cents per barrel in cash for one-half of his reserves. In return we would provide the financing needed to get the crude from the ground to the sea. In addition, we got the marketing rights to Bunker's half of production, which gave us another source of revenue to recover our investment. BP got what it wanted: control of seven billion barrels in reserves. Bunker got what he wanted: a half a billion dollars.

"After the signing," Monte concluded, "Bunker was so excited that, on the spot, he went shopping in London and bought Jaguars for Ed Guinn and his aides. This was quite a surprise, you know, coming from Bunker. After all, this is the same gentleman who'll ask a friend, 'Would you share a coke with me?' and then open a single can!"

11
Mr. Sam

1955 WAS A BUSY YEAR for me. In addition to my work in Pakistan and Libya for Bunker Hunt, I had two memorable jobs stateside as well. Despite the absence of publicity, a few within the oil industry recognized my knowledge and experience in that arena. One of these people was Ray Shaffer, a geologist and petroleum engineer who managed the oil investments of Sam Bronfman, founder and CEO of Seagrams Whiskey. Thus far Bronfman had only invested his own money; however, he was so impressed with Shaffer's success that now he had decided to invest Seagram funds as well—through Frankfort Oil, a subsidiary which Shaffer would manage.

This made Shaffer nervous. Honestly and realistically, Ray knew that no matter how successful he was at finding oil, state and federal limits on production would hold revenue to a fraction of drilling costs. When he tried to explain this to Bronfman, his warnings fell on deaf ears. Knowing that both Bronfman and I came from humble backgrounds, Ray hoped that we might "hit it off," and that I might convince him to embark on a less ambitious drilling program. And so, in the early summer of 1955, I was introduced to "Mr. Sam."

Seagram's U.S. was headquartered on the 17th Floor of the Chrysler Building. I got off the elevator and walked to Mr. Sam's corner office at the other end of the hall. Our first meeting went surprisingly well. From what I had heard of his intimidating manner, I expected him to put me on the defensive with a curt greeting—"What can I do for you?" perhaps, or more likely,

"What can you do for me?" Instead, he received me openly and seemed genuinely interested in establishing a rapport. After bantering with him for a few minutes I felt I could ask him a direct question.

"Mr. Sam," I ventured, "why do you want Seagrams to get into the oil business? In liquor you're the dominant company. You largely control how that industry functions. But in the oil business you would be playing in a system dictated by the majors. You would have no voice, and in all likelihood you would be resented as a possible threat!"

Mr. Sam was impatient, intense and dynamic. His slim five-foot frame was always in motion. Pacing the room, he replied animatedly, "I'll level with you—I want to be a Rockefeller, high class. Liquor is good business, but so what? I'm a nobody."

At that moment came a knock on the door. Annoyed by the interruption, Mr. Sam shouted, "Come in!" It was his general counsel. "What do you want?" Mr. Sam barked.

"Mr. Sam, we have a problem!"

"So? Fix it! That's what I pay you for."

"I need your approval on this, I'm afraid."

"Alright, alright, what is it?"

The counsel explained that a Seagram's vice president had recently attended a political rally in Chicago, where he found himself seated on the dais next to Senator Estes Kefauver. He had promised the Senator a sample of all Seagram's goods, which the Senator had been delighted to accept.

"Just now, Mr. Sam, our truck is outside the Senator's home in Washington, and through a mistake at the warehouse, it's loaded with a *case*, not a sample, of everything we make. The driver asked the Senator where he wanted the truck unloaded, and the Senator told him, 'bring in a bottle of each and put the rest in a warehouse for me to draw on.' What should we do?"

Mr. Sam snorted contemptuously. "That's a *problem*? For Christ's sake let him draw on it!" He dismissed his humbled servant with a wave of his hand and looked down at his watch. "It's twelve o'clock. Let's have a drink!"

Seagram's had their own bar on the 17th floor and at noon sharp each day all the executives dropped in for one cocktail. The men chatted with one another, each of them hoping for some positive attention from their boss. That day Mr. Sam was in a good mood and the atmosphere in the bar was jovial. We did not lunch together, but he invited me back the next week.

Shaffer was ecstatic that I had hit if off with Mr. Sam. He urged that at next meeting I come sharply to the point: Seagrams must cut its drilling budget 50% for the next year to avoid a disastrous effect on Seagrams' Annual Report. "Why didn't the company's treasurer make this clear to Mr. Sam?" I asked.

Ray threw up his hands in frustration. "Either Mr. Sam didn't listen to him," Ray replied, "or he was afraid to tell him Mr. Sam what he wouldn't want to hear." I decided not to tell Ray that Mr. Sam wished to be a Rockefeller.

At my next meeting with Mr. Sam, I did as Shaffer suggested. As advertised, Mr. Sam was a poor listener. When I tried to explain the effect of the current system on his production, he just shrugged and said, "So what's the difference—barrel of whiskey, or barrel of oil? When I have the goods I *sell* them!"

Again there was a knock at the door. The general counsel entered in a state of anguish. "Mr. Sam! The police will not let the trucks unload the steel for the new building."

Mr. Sam was furious. "Why do you tell me this!? Go down to City Hall and tell that f—ing do-nothing Mayor that if he doesn't get that steel unloaded *today*, the money I gave him to get him elected—I'll *double* to get his ass beaten next election!"

The lawyer nodded and quickly exited. Mr. Sam turned to me with a sigh. "I pay these guys *big* salaries and they won't make any decisions! They just bring all their problems back to me." Suddenly he pounded his fist on the desk. "That steel will be unloaded if I have to go down to City Hall in *person* and kick that dead-head Mayor where he deserves it!"

Still angry, he turned to me and added: "I'm building the highest class office building in New York. It will be set back from the street with fountains at the entrance. The copper skin of the building will shine like gold!" That must have triggered another association, for he abruptly looked at his gold watch. It was noon. "Let's have a drink!"

Then Mr. Sam turned to his handsome son Edgar, who was sharing his father's office to learn the business. He was always so quiet that it was easy to forget that he was even there. "Come Edgar, join us for a drink." (That meant *one* drink only!)

Mr. Sam was still seething over the problem with unloading his steel. Edgar and some twenty executives picked up his mood and sat in deathly silence, each sipping his drink. I was very uncomfortable in this strange atmosphere, so I decided to break the silence with a duck hunting story, making the hunter who brings down a *lone* duck a Seagram's drinker. When I began, Mr. Sam appeared not to be listening, but after I delivered the punchline—"Nothing to it, when you shoot into a flock of them"—he roared with laughter.

"Sam, tell that to Edgar!" So I repeated the story for Edgar and all the executives that had not heard it the first time. At the end, Mr. Sam laughed with as much gusto as before, and believe me, twenty cowed executives laughed also.

Mr. Sam did not take me out for lunch that day either, and in fact I never saw him socially in the whole time I worked for him. In what appeared to be a division of labor within the family, he left that up to his brother Edgar (for whom he had named his son), whose office was across the hall. A man of great charm, Edgar invited Patricia and me, along with the Shaffers, to several elegant dinners. At work Edgar never joined in the business discussions and never appeared at the noon cocktail hour.

On my next visit with Mr. Sam, he asked if I had ever procured a lease on government land from the Department of the Interior. I told him I hadn't but was interested in trying. He went on to explain that he had paid option money to someone who had filed for a lease, and the option would expire soon. Apparently "the guy" wasn't making much progress. I promised to look into the matter and get back to Mr. Sam in a day or so.

I met directly with this man, whose name was McKenna. He

explained that he had filed a lease application for oil exploration as an agent for Amoco, but after months of considerable effort and expense Amoco had given up, permitting McKenna to pursue the effort for himself. The lease application was for 20,000 acres in the Lacasinne Waterfowl Refuge in Louisiana, which at the time was under the supervision of Interior's Fish and Wildlife Department. "What are you doing to get the lease issued?" I asked.

"I have Congressman Boggs and Senator Long working on it," he replied. "Up to now we can't get Salyer, the Director, to budge from his negative position."

I reported to Mr. Sam what I had learned and he said, "So, what would *you* do?"

"If you permit me," I told him, "I would tackle this in a different manner. You can hardly afford to get this lease through political pressure on Congress or the White House. Amoco would cover its own failure by claiming you used "whiskey money" to buy the lease."

"You got a point there," he acknowledged. "So how do we do it?"

"I would try to get the lease on the merits without any influence," I replied.

Mr. Sam made a face and exclaimed, "The merits? What the hell is *that*?"

"I won't know 'til I investigate further."

"Do you really believe this'll work?" Mr. Sam asked skeptically.

"I'd like to find out," I replied.

"I *want* that lease, Sam! 20,000 acres is thirty square miles. On three sides there are very productive wells. This could be a bonanza! So whatever you have to do, *do*!" It sounded like an ultimatum. I relished the challenge.

" Mr. Sam, I know that one of your directors, Mr. Slater, is a close friend of President Eisenhower. Can we have a clear understanding that he is not to get involved in any way?"

Mr. Sam took a deep breath. This was not his usual way of

doing business. "OK, Sam, you can tell him in my presence," he finally conceded. Slater was called into his office for these instructions and was, I think, relieved that he would not be called upon to use his influence in this case.

My approach to a meritorious application involved understanding the reasons Fish and Wildlife had given for rejecting the original application. I found that Amoco's application had not overcome the burden that exploration would be harmful to the purposes of the refuge. My challenge was to submit an application that might provide for exploration while making possible the improvement of the refuge.

At my invitation a petroleum engineer and an Ecology professor at Louisiana State met with me in a suite at the Ambassador Hotel in New York. I asked the professor if the refuge was currently in perfect condition for its intended purposes. His answer was an emphatic, "Heavens no!" He explained that the area was not a natural wetlands. Water had been impounded to maintain a certain water level, turning the marshes into a lake. At the present time invasive weeds were choking off life in the lake, which was too large to drain and clean.

"Is there a way to improve it?" I asked.

"Yes, definitely," was his reply. "If it were compartmentalized into units, each one could be drained and cleaned."

I then asked the petroleum engineer if it would be possible for the drilling equipment to have access and operate from the banks of compartments rather than from floats.

"Very practical," he answered, "and not excessively more costly."

I asked him to prepare, as quickly as possible, an exploration plan based on this idea. Then I prepared a new lease application, attaching a brief that described the exploration program as the first stage of improving the refuge.

Prior to formal submission, I met with Fish and Wildlife Director Salyer for his comments. At the outset he was cool and formal. He read the plan with apparent interest. When he had finished he questioned me as to how I come up with the compartment idea, and I explained that it had grown out of my inquiry as to how to improve the refuge. He nodded and continued. "I ask you this question because we have proposed a very similar plan for budget approval." I was elated when he approved the application and submitted it to Secretary of the Interior McKay.

In spite of our good intentions, when news of its approval was made public, the press immediately turned it into a *cause celebre*, implying that Mr. Sam's "whiskey company" had bought the lease. Particularly disturbing was Drew Pearson's assertion in his column that Slater had gone to Denver Hospital, where the President was recuperating from a heart attack, and gotten Ike's approval as he lay sick in bed. Slater called me in Washington and asked if I had seen the column. When I told him I had, he worried, "This is very embarrassing. I feel it will ruin my relations with the President!" I reminded him of our understanding that he was to keep clear of any semblance of involvement in the matter. "I have been most careful," he objected, "not to even talk about it."

"Well, in that case," I told him, "I wouldn't worry about your relationship with the President. Who knows better than he that you never spoke to him about it?"

Around this time Senator Neuberger from Oregon died. Secretary McKay, also from Oregon, was rumored to be the Republican candidate to fill his seat. Neuberger's assistant, whom I knew well socially, was spearheading a Senate committee hearing on the issuance of the lease. The battle pitted the Sierra Club on one side, attacking issuance and suggesting improprieties, and the Fish and Wildlife Department on the other. Salyer testified as to the similarity between the plan I had submitted and his own improvement plan for the refuge, which he had tried unsuccessfully to include in the Department's budget. At the end of his brief appearance he stated simply, "My decision was in the best interest of the refuge."

Nonetheless the committee continued to make headlines. Much was made of Slater's personal friendship with the President, and alleged direct contacts by Seagrams with McKay. All during this period I begged my friend to put me on the stand. "I know the whole story," I pleaded. "My appearance would enhance my reputation as well as put the record straight!"

"No possible way!" he replied. "Your testimony would kill the investigation!"

Two years later, Salyer called me to say that one of the majors was at loggerheads with him over a FWLR lease. "Can you arrange to represent them? You could fashion a program workable for them and probably acceptable to us." I declined with regret, explaining that I felt it unthinkable to solicit a client.

McKay did run for Senate the next year, and the Sierra Club led the attack against him, using the slogan, "McKay is Lacasinne and making it sound obscene." In the end the Sierra Club prevailed, gained added stature for its "principled defense of the natural environment." I knew better.

As predicted, Seagrams' profits as reflected in its next annual report were not up as usual, but substantially down—all because of "spending on oil." The outcry of institutional stockholders was, "What the hell is Seagrams doing, spending our money on oil drilling!?"

Seagrams hired a so-called "oil expert" from Loeb Rhodes, Inc. to get the company "out of its mess" and restore the confidence of its investors. Shaffer was immediately replaced as manager of Frankfort Oil, and since I was identified with him, I never heard another word from Seagrams.

A short while later, the Seagrams Building was completed. As I passed by, a man waved to me from near the entrance. It was Mr. Sam. His greeting was enthusiastic—"Come, let me show you our new building and our offices"—so I got a personal tour from Mr. Sam himself.

Seagrams continued to pursue Mr. Sam's dream of making it—"like Rockefeller"—in the oil business, and within twenty years they became a significant player, by gaining control of independent companies as well as through their own drilling efforts. Big S created a sensation on Wall Street when it nearly acquired control of Continental Oil, a prestigious independent with world-wide operations. In the struggle Dupont came to Conoco's rescue and acquired majority control. Seagrams maintained a large share of Conoco stock, and wound up with more than 20% of Dupont. Unlike his father, Edgar had no trouble listening to others, so he was able to honor his father's memory with a presence in the chemical industry in addition to oil and alcohol.

In the late sixties I met Edgar at a party at the Rockefeller Estate in Pocantico Hills, and we had a warm exchange of memories about his father. In my mind, Mr. Sam stands out as the most original man conceivable. I doubt he had any heroes. I know he had no models.

12
The Marshall Plan Oil Case

NOT LONG AFTER I FIRST met Mr. Sam, I received a telephone call from Warren Burger, who was at that time Assistant Attorney General for the Civil Division of the Department of Justice.

"I'm calling you at the suggestion of Deputy Attorney General Rogers, who's told me that you are most knowledgeable about a Government suit against the major oil companies. This claim is for overcharges they made on oil supplied under the Marshall Plan. I'm sure you're familiar with the case, since you prepared the original complaint for filing in the U.S. District Court in New York in 1952. As the Justice official in charge of civil litigation, I would like to reengage you as Special Assistant to prepare this case for trial and, if need be, to try it. Can we afford you?"

"I believe my rate of $250 per day is in the mainstream of current compensation," I answered. Burger agreed immediately and asked when I could start. With a tone of regret I said, "Unfortunately, I leave tomorrow morning for Pakistan to complete a negotiation. When I return in two weeks I will be free to devote myself to the case."

"No problem. There's no emergency," he replied. "Have a good trip and call me when you get back so that we can get started."

In 1952 Holmes Baldridge, Assistant Attorney General for the Civil Division, had engaged me as a Special Assistant to the Attorney General to prepare the Government's case against the major oil companies, claiming that they had overcharged the government by $72 million for crude oil supplied to ECA countires. On the day the lawsuit was filed, the Assistant Attorney General for Administration asked me to appear at the Justice Department to conduct a press conference. When I arrived, the press room was crowded with eager reporters. As I was about to make my introductory remarks, the Assistant A.G. stunned me with an off-the-record announcement: "Mr. Nakasian will answer all your questions. He will be acting for Attorney General McGrannery. His answers to your questions and his introductory statement is for attribution to the Attorney General, and not for attribution to Nakasian." I had never met the Attorney General and to my knowledge he knew nothing about the case. Quickly I gathered myself and began the press conference.

The next morning the story made the front page all across the country. Sure enough, everything I said was attributed to the Attorney General. Nowhere did my name appear in print. My disgust was only equalled by my distrust—"What else is there about my Government's practices that I don't know?"

When I hung up the phone after talking to Burger, I was on cloud nine. Finally I had a second chance, not only to obtain the recognition that had eluded me the first time, but to bring to justice the major American oil companies that, in my opinion, had taken advantage of the Marshall Plan program. At the outset of the program it was accepted without question that crude oil would be supplied by American majors from their Middle East sources, and shipped to their own refineries in Europe—virtually the only ones left standing after the war. The majors were compensated for refined products in local currencies of francs, sterling, marks, gilders, etc.—all deeply weakened relative to the U.S. dollar—so they were quite eager to obtain ECA dollars in payment for their crude.

At that time (1948-51) the majors' crude costs amounted to about 35 cents per barrel—25 cents in royalties to foreign governments; 10 cents for production costs. At a sale price of $1.75 per barrel, this meant that their profit margin was $1.40 a barrel. During a congressional investigation of the majors in 1947, before foreign aid funds were available, it was disclosed that Aramco was offering crude to the U.S. Armed Forces for one dollar per barrel. This was obviously an attempt to acquire dollars, but it was also an effort to relieve the huge surplus of crude that had accumulated since the war's end.

All of these facts were known to me, as well as to other observers of the oil industry. In legislation for a European recovery, Congress made no effort to deal with profits but it did include provisions to prevent the waste and corruption that had existed in previous foreign aid programs. While affirming the desirability of strengthening private channels of trade, Congress relied on competitive pricing to keep ECA costs down, specifying that suppliers under the Marshall Plan could not charge higher prices than they charged to purchasers in the private sector. This simple and self enforcing limitation was effectively complied with by all suppliers except the major oil companies.

It was obvious to me that applying the competitive price test had no relevance in the absence of competition. The majors could charge anything they wanted, but the congressionally mandated competitive price limitation challenged them to rationalize the price they would charge on Marshall Plan shipments. Naturally they sought to base their prices on the highest cost alternative sources in the Western Hemisphere, and introduced basing point and watershed theories ad infinitum to justify this.

In September of 1948 the issue of pricing Middle East crude had come to a head following my refusal to accept an invoice for Esso crude at the outrageous price of $2.23 a barrel. During Hoffman's subsequent meeting with Esso chairman Eugene Holman, a compromise price of $1.75 was accepted for that and future shipments, subject to verification as to whether Saudi crude was in fact being supplied to the Western Hemisphere at less than $1.50 per barrel, as I maintained. In such an event the price on shipments to Europe would be reduced to my suggested price of $1.43. An escrow account to record the difference of 32 cents per barrel was established in the comptroller's office, and by the end of the Marshall Plan that account had recorded about $72 million dollars in overcharges, for which the government was now suing the oil companies. These were the background facts of the case.

When I returned from Pakistan I called Burger as we had agreed. Imagine my surprise when I was told by his aide that Mr. Burger was not available, and was further advised that the Mutual Security Agency (ECA's successor) was now handling the case! A lawyer named Milo Olsen was now in charge, and I could expect to hear from him soon.

This all seemed very strange to me: that the Justice Department could divest *its* responsibility as legal representative of the Government. My first impulse was to call William Rogers for an explanation, but I decided against it, figuring that Burger had responded to White House pressure over Rogers' head. Vice President Nixon was well known to be readily accessible to the major oil companies. It seemed very plausible to me that the majors had persuaded Nixon that I was hostile to them and that the government should replace me with a "neutral person." Milo Olsen, from California, had no knowledge of the oil industry, and therefore could be "neutral." I never found out exactly how the change had occurred, but there was no doubt *why* it had.

Within a week I received a call from Asst. Attorney General Barnes, of the Anti-Trust Division, asking me to attend a meeting. Present were Barnes, Milo Olsen (now appointed Special Assistant to the Attorney General—the position I was to have), a lawyer from Burger's civil division, and one or two other Justice Department lawyers, but no one from the Mutual Security Agency.

From the outset I sensed a hostile atmosphere and this was confirmed by the loaded questions from Barnes and others, who were seeking to discredit me in support of their own undisclosed, preconceived notions. At one point I reminded the attorneys that I wholeheartedly supported the Government's case and wished to be as helpful as possible. This did not diminish their hostility. When they questioned my integrity by suggesting that I harbored a devious design, I rose to leave. "Considering what has happened today," I said, "recourse to me hereafter will be formal and you will be on the record."

The next action occurred the following year when I was subpoenaed for a deposition by the oil companies' attorneys: Proskauer, Cahill and Webster of New York. In a deposition setting, the companies could establish the parameters of the inquiry. I had to respond to their questions; I could not pose any of my own. The defense counsel asked me questions about legal administrative procedures, competitive pricing, rule-making, and publication in the Federal Register. Implicit in the line of questioning was the presumed right of the oil companies to charge whatever price they chose in the absence of fraud.

After the first morning session, Milo Olsen, who was observing, whispered in my ear, "Would you have lunch with me?"

"Shouldn't you ask opposing counsel for permission? They ought to know."

Olsen did ask them and their answer was, "No objection at all." At lunch, Olsen pleaded with me to support the fact situation he had relied on in his amended complaint, which departed substantially from the complaint which I had prepared. I believed he had fatally weakened the Government's case, and told him so.

Webster was not happy with my answers, which in spite of his leading questions did not help his case. "May I remind you that you are under oath?!" was his frequent admonishment. At one point, irritated by his intended intimidation, I added to my answer, "Let me remind you that *I* am under *oath*!"

During the two day deposition, defense council never referred to the Hoffman-Holman meeting of September 1948, and of course I could not bring it up myself. Later I examined Olsen's brief and the opinion of defense counsel—no mention there either! Olsen agreed to a bench trial (no jury) before Judge Thomas Murphy. I was not among the witnesses called. Olsen never once referenced the meeting between Hoffman and Holman in which, at our insistence, Holman had addressed the netback price of $1.43 on shipments of Saudi crude to the Western Hemisphere. Agreement had been reached at that meeting that if Saudi oil was being shipped in volume to the West, F.O.B. prices to Europe should be reduced to that level. The considerable evidence that such shipments—in volume, at lower prices—had occurred was rendered useless without evidence of such an understanding.

A short while into the proceedings the defendants moved to dismiss the case, supporting their motion with a 79-page Opinion Brief. Judge Murphy dismissed the complaint, entered a judgment for the defense "on the merits," and closed the case with: "This opinion is filed in lieu of findings of fact and conclusions of law pursuant to Rule 52 of the Rules of Civil Procedure. Thomas F. Murphy, USDJ, dated July 17, 1957, New York, N.Y." It should be emphasized that Judge Murphy totally accepted the opinion of defense counsel and found it unnecessary to make his own findings of fact and conclusions of law.

The next day, as I was walking down the staircase of the Bar Association, I saw Proskauer and Webster ascending, arm in arm. They had the nerve to greet me with, "Sam, you saw we won the case!"

Bitterly I countered with, "Did you *win* the case or did the government lose it?" We kept on walking our separate ways.

13

From Washington to New York

IN 1955, WHEN OUR SECOND child was born, I paid $20,000 in cash for a small, semi-detached, three bedroom house in Georgetown, near the C&O Canal. In retrospect I think this was a mistake. When clients paying me substantial fees saw my modest home, they might have assumed they were overpaying me.

I was starting to become a bit frustrated doing business out of Washington. I felt too dependent on referrals from out-of-state companies and law firms, and wanted desperately to meet one-on-one with the heads of international companies, many of which were headquartered in and around New York City. I began to think seriously about moving there myself.

In the presidential election of 1952, Bill Rogers had invited me to join him in the Dewey organization, which was working to elect General Eisenhower. I felt strongly that Washington's war bureaucracy should be dismantled, and I thought that Stevenson was more up to the task than Ike. When I informed Bill of my decision to support Stevenson, he smiled and shrugged. "One of us will be on the winning team," he said.

By the end of Eisenhower's first term, it seemed that Washington was going in the direction I favored, in spite of the General's lack of commitment to this course. It was my conviction that Americans would never tolerate a large federal bureaucracy in peacetime, and I anticipated that Washington's federal reach would continue to narrow rather than expand. I never dreamed that Ike's successors would get us into a new war and simultaneously launch the Great Society domestic programs, elephantizing the federal government. When this happened, global corporations began to headquarter in metropolitan Washington. Had I foreseen this, Pattie and I would probably have settled permanently in Washington.

Instead Pattie and I made the decision to move our family of four from Washington to New York. After careful research we finally decided on the Westchester County village of Bronxville. It was only thirty minutes from midtown Manhattan, and had an excellent public school. Home to many corporate CEO's, the town of approximately one square mile featured large, attractive houses set in lush, manicured gardens.

We were aided in our search for an affordable home by our very competent real estate agent, Mary Woodhull. A longtime resident of Bronxville, she assured us that we would be welcomed by the community in spite of my Armenian origin. Soon afterwards I purchased a house from Mr. Clifford Marshall, then President of Standard Vacuum Oil Company. Deploring any debt, I paid for it in cash, just as I had done in Washington.

The day that we closed on the house, I was preparing for a trip to D.C. In late afternoon I realized that I needed to cash a check. Mary phoned her friend Mr. Chambers, Chairman (and son of the founder) of Gramatan Bank, told him I had just purchased a house in town, and asked if he would cash my personal check. He agreed to meet with me at his office.

After grilling me for a half-hour about my family and occupational history, Chambers announced that since I didn't have an account at Gramatan, he couldn't cash my check. Stunned, I began to wonder whether Mary had been overly optimistic about our reception in Bronxville. At a party sometime later, after Pattie and I had become prominent in the community, Chambers met me at a social function and asked why I did not have an account at his bank. Realizing that he did not remember our previous encounter, I smiled and said, "I have a long memory," and excused myself.

It was obvious that Bronxville was not generally receptive to minorities. In our twenty years there, not one Afro-American family lived in the town, and there was only one Jewish family. Every year, the New York Times featured a full-page article on Bronxville, referring to it as a "tight little island" of wealthy white cave-dwellers, hostile to minorities. Although we stood out as the only Armenian family, Chambers's bigotry proved to be the exception in our case. When curious neighbors asked me how we were being treated, I could honestly reply, "Very well."

Our new home on Sunny Brae was only five blocks from Dr. Fosdick's retirement home. Whether by design or coincidence, his street name was The High Road and his house number was 4—for the high road. When I called to tell him that we were neighbors, his greeting was enthusiastic. "You and your wife must come to tea this afternoon." We accepted his invitation.

Full of gratitude and nostalgia, I was prepared to update him on my sixteen years in the nation's capital, but no sooner had I launched into my prepared saga than he cut me off sharply. "Never mind the past. I'm sure you've done very well. Now that you're here, what are your plans for the future?" Even in old age he was always looking ahead. He listened politely while I outlined my private practice, but he really perked up when I told him that Patricia and I shared an interest in community service. In his retirement Dr. Fosdick attended the Bronxville Dutch Reformed (Presbyterian) Church, and we joined the church as well. It soon became a focal point for our family activities. It was there that our children took bible study and learned to sing and perform in front of the large congregation, accompanied by the great church organ. Later they became much involved in a church-sponsored program in East Harlem, where they tutored younger children in remedial reading.

Pattie and I would see Dr. Fosdick from time to time at church functions. He would always greet me warmly, but no more so than others he had met relatively recently. It didn't bother me, but it upset Pattie that he was so "impersonal." Knowing what a crucial role he had played in my life and the lives of many others, I always came to his defense.

Bronxville was remarkably close to old ties in Washington. General William Knowlton, former aide to General Eisenhower and a friend of Patricia's during his private schooling and cadet years, was then Superintendent of the U.S. Military Academy at nearby West Point. Every fall he invited fifty special guests to the first Army home football game, and Pattie and I were included amongst cabinet members, ambassadors, and high military officers. Cocktails would be served at his residence, prior to a luncheon served in the cathedral-like dining hall at the Academy. Each of his guests would be assigned a seat at a table of eight cadets. I treasured my conversations with these polished gentlemen and future officers, and pride in my country ascended to new heights.

After lunch, the guests took their seats with the General on the fifty-yard line to watch the cadet band and colorful parade before the kickoff. Following the game Pattie and I would return home with the keen sense of being specially privileged.

Thanks to Pattie, we integrated into the life of the community immediately. Since we managed on my income alone, she was able—after her first priority to the children—to devote her time and talents to community projects. Beginning with only two friends from the past, she soon became known to everyone. At various times during our years in Bronxville, she was President of the 1,000 member Women's Society of the Church, President of the League of Women Voters, head of the Mariner Girl Scouts, and she initiated an ecumenical movement that brought together the community's different denominations for social purposes and understanding. When one of our Washington friends inquired as to how my life had changed since the move, I replied, "In Washington I was known as Patricia Prochnik's husband; in Bronxville I am known as Patricia Nakasian's husband."

By her grace, charm, and leadership in the community, Pattie identified us as belonging socially among its prominent residents, which included the presidents or CEO's of AT&T, IBM, Citicorp, New York Telephone, and many other Fortune 500 companies.

Most everyone in the village had a corporate title, or were doctors at nearby Lawrence Hospital, or lawyers for some well-known firm.

I was different, and perhaps a puzzle for many. I had no familiar nameplate. At social gatherings I discovered to my chagrin that my high-powered neighbors seemed restrained in relating to me. I knew that if I had been identified with a prestigious company or university I would have been engaged immediately.

The thirty minute rail commute to midtown Manhattan and back played a big part in my overcoming this unspoken obstacle of identity. Casual conversation with my Bronxvillian seatmates soon led to friendships. Among my fellow commuters were public television's Robin McNeil, Brendan Gill of the New Yorker, Fred Kappel of AT&T, Tom Vaughn of Freeport Minerals, Hans Stauffer of Stauffer Chemical Company, and James D. Miller, trustee of several foundations. We all looked forward to these one-on-one exchanges of information and experience as a way of breaking out of our own niches and enriching our lives.

When I arrived in Bronxville I found one friend from Washington, John Walstrom, head of one of Shell Oil's subsidiaries. He introduced us to his friends in the village and offered to sponsor my joining the prestigious Siwanoy Country Club, which had a membership of less than 200. "I might have some trouble getting you admitted," he acknowledged. "The people in this town are not accustomed to strange names like yours, but we'll give it a try. Would you send me some written information that I could give to the Committee on Admissions?"

I sent John a copy of the current "Who's Who in Commerce and Industry," which contained a lengthy commentary about me. To his relief as well as mine, I was accepted into the club. At the cocktail party welcoming new members, John confessed to the committee chairman that he had been a little worried about my being accepted. The chairman replied, "How could we keep out a man with an eight inch 'Who's Who'?"

Siwanoy was strictly a golfing club, with no other athletic

facilities, so instead of playing tennis I soon became an avid golfer. If you wished to play you were required to hire a caddie, whether or not you took a golf cart. Hence the caddie shack was always well attended, with caddies ranging in age from teenagers to middle-aged men. As a new member I was of course unknown to them. That changed rather abruptly following a certain unusual and unforeseen event.

The night after my return from a trip to the Middle East, Patricia awakened me at one a.m. and asked me to come to the phone. A policeman had told her that our black maid Alma's brother, a boy of eighteen or so, was in a Mt. Vernon jail, charged with assault with a deadly weapon. I told the officer that I would come down to see the boy first thing in the morning. The next morning I went down to the jail and identified myself as the boy's attorney, despite the fact that I had no experience in criminal cases. I was then escorted to the boy's cell, where I found him slumped over in dejection and fear. I asked the boy one simple question. "Do you like it in here?"

"No sir!" he replied emphatically.

"I'm here to help you on one condition," I told him. "That you tell me the truth, and I mean *all* the truth. Otherwise you can just stay here in jail. Now tell me what happened."

The boy told me that he had come from South Carolina to live with his sister only a week before. He had gone to Playland, an amusement park in Rye, and won a hara-kiri type knife about six inches long at one of the games. When he returned to Mt. Vernon that evening and showed off his prize to some of his new friends, a neighborhood bully had tried to take it from him. He was running away from the bully when a policeman came from across the street and arrested him.

In court later that morning, with the boy at my side, the judge asked, "How do you plead?"

"Not guilty," I responded, and followed by asking the judge to place this boy in my custody. "We employ his sister, and I can vouch for his appearance."

The Italian-American judge leered at me and called out, "Not guilty, you plead?"

"Yessir!" I replied.

"$1,000 bail!" he retorted triumphantly. "Next case!"

Having just returned from overseas, I had traveller's checks, but when I went to the bailiff's window to give them over to the court, I was promptly reminded that I could not post bail for my client. Alma and I went around the corner and cashed the checks and she put up the bail money.

While still in Mt. Vernon, I went to the County Attorney's Office, told him the story, and requested he dismiss the case. He refused to do so, and told me that if the arresting officer would not drop the charges, the case would go to trial. I contacted the policeman and he refused to drop the charges, so a month later the trial took place.

After I listened to the arresting officer describe the alleged assault, I began my cross examination. I fixed the spot from which he had observed the incident from across the street, and established that the defendant was positioned to the north of the "victim." I then asked the officer if the two boys were standing still or moving. "They were moving," he responded. "As a matter of fact they were running!"

"In which direction were they running?" I queried. He pointed north up Gramatan Avenue. Suddenly it dawned on him that the boy with the knife was running *away* from his alleged victim!

I knew the case against Alma's brother had been destroyed, but I wasn't sure how to terminate it, so I turned to the Attorney for the County and asked, "Will you move to dismiss this case, or should I make a motion?"

Obviously displeased with this turn of events, the judge scowled and announced, "Never mind, *I'll* dismiss the case. But if I had my way I'd give this boy five years!"

"Your Honor," I replied angrily, "it's obvious that you don't approve of people carrying knives. You should know that *this* knife was won by this boy as a prize at Playland! If you feel so strongly about knives, why don't you use your prestigious position to do something about their casual distribution?"

Unaccustomed to being admonished by a defense attorney, the judge merely grunted and banged his gavel for dismissal, thus bringing to a successful conclusion the only criminal case in my long legal career. The experience was an eloquent reminder that prejudice against Afro-Americans can be as extreme in the North as it is in the South.

That weekend, as I appeared at Siwanoy Country Club to play golf, I was met by a standing ovation from the caddie shack. The trial had been reported in the local paper, including my final remarks to the judge, who was not popular with the caddies, half of whom were black.

By coincidence, a week later, the caddie assigned to me was none other than arresting officer in the case. In amazement, he said, "Mr. Nakasian, I didn't know you were a member here."

"So what?" I responded.

"Well," he stammered, "if I had known, I would have taken a different position."

"What difference does it make whether I was a member here or not?" I asked.

"I'm sorry," he mumbled.

"I'm not," I said vehemently. "I want you to drop my bag, and I will see to it, to the extent that I have any influence, that you don't caddie here anymore. As a police officer, you ought to be ashamed of yourself!" This was overheard by the Caddie Master and a good number of the caddies. My status in their eyes was further elevated, and the policeman, known as "Red," never moonlighted as a caddie at the club again.

Unlike most golf clubs, where the players arranged their foursomes from amongst their friends and associates, Siwanoy had the tradition that you played with whomever was available at the time. As a result, I eventually got to play with most of its 200 members, and I established some treasured friendships. One of my friends was Jim Hagerty, President Eisenhower's Press Secretary. Jim was a fervent golfer with a handicap of 5 or 6, and he and I would often team up in a foursome. He was a seasoned golfer and I was a beginner, but I made up for my inexperience with my long drives. Jim would say, "The best place to know the quality of a man is on the golf course. In the way he relates to his partner, to his opponents, and to the rules of the game, he reveals his character and values, and you can make an assessment." That observation has been confirmed by my own personal experience many times.

My friend Bill Rogers, who was at that time Deputy Attorney General, believed it unwise to practice law in New York without joining an established firm. Calling upon his close association with former Governor Dewey, he volunteered to introduce me to the firm of Dewey Ballentine Bushby Palmer & Wood, and called one of the partners, Dewey's long-time personal aide Burdell Bixby, to set up an appointment for me to meet with Dewey himself.

I carried to my meeting with Dewey a perception, gleaned from the press, that he was a cold and indifferent man. I had expected him to treat the appointment as perfuctory, but to my astonishment and delight he seemed genuinely interested in my capabilities, and in me as a person. Originally scheduled for a half hour, the meeting lasted all afternoon, and he requested that I return the following day. Bixby could not believe that Dewey had spent four hours alone with *any*body, much less extended the meeting into the next day.

I made my case to the Governor (as he was still fondly known) that American businesses were now poised to internationalize their operations into the newly accessible European market. The Common Market, fostered by the Marshall Plan, offered companies in one country freer access to markets in other countries. These companies would need reliable legal counsel to adjust to foreign jurisdictions, and at this time, only one or two American law firms had ventured to establish European offices. I felt that with my experience abroad I could help Dewey's law firm tap into this new and lucrative market.

At the Governor's suggestion I was circulated throughout the firm to meet all the partners. As my confidant Bixby told me, several of the senior partners were apprehensive about expanding the firm's services beyond what they had done traditionally.

In spite of these objections, I was asked to meet with the managing partner, Charles McClain, to negotiate a partnership agreement.

As these discussions progressed, John Foster Dulles died, and there was speculation that Dewey would replace him as Secretary of State. The reluctant senior partners convinced McClain to put my negotiations "on hold," since the Governor might be leaving the firm. This succeeded in effectively killing my chances for partnership, even though Dewey was *not* named Secretary of State.

Several months later I heard from Bixby that the firm had accepted a major retainer from the Turkish Government, and a short time after that the firm opened an office in Brussels. Once again I had to assume that it was my Armenian heritage that had disqualified me from joining this silk-stocking, WASP organization.

When it looked as though I might become a partner in Dewey's firm, I had suspended my search for an office of my own. With those prospects dashed, it became imperative that I find one. A couple of years earlier I had met international businessman Charles Koons in the elevator of the Bristol Hotel in Buenos Aires. He had recognized me from a meeting I had chaired in 1949 to review Marshall Plan regulations. We chatted briefly and he invited me to call him whenever I came to New York.

As I was hunting for an office, I came across Mr. Koons's business card and decided to pay him a call at his offices on the top floor of the British Empire Building, facing 5th Avenue in Rockefeller Center. Before I could relate my needs to him, he launched into an explanation of an urgent problem of *his*, which he thought I could help him with.

Koons's major business was importing Italian pipeline for water and sewer systems in the rapidly growing communities on Long Island, but recently he had purchased, with the financial assistance of Pamela Woolworth, a controlling interest in International Products Corporation (IPC), which traded publicly on the American Stock Exchange. As he outlined the Company's operational and financial condition, it was clear that IPC was nearing bankruptcy—a condition reflected in the low price of its stock that made *his* purchase of controlling shares possible.

IPC owned thousands of acres in Paraguay. Its principal operation was raising and processing cattle for the export of canned corned beef. To make earnings look good, the prior management had deferred maintenance for years. Thus production facilities were not only dilapidated but obsolete. Koons's problem was that banks would not lend him the working capital he needed, requiring him to borrow from factors against the pledge of his production. Factors, generally marketers of the same product, charge up to twice as much as a bank, and receive marketing rights to boot. Hence they are truly lenders of last resort.

"Would you be willing," Koons asked, "to take on this situation and do what you can to better this company's financial condition?" Koons perceived me as knowledgeable about international finance and was not seeking to retain my legal services. (He already had a competent lawyer in Joe Flom, a young Jewish lawyer, who later became the major domo of Skadden Arps etc.) With his irrepressible promoter's pitch, it was hard to say no, particularly after he offered me a beautiful private office that opened onto his roof garden. We agreed that I could pursue my own practice as long as I worked on his IPC problem. In addition to the office I would receive a comfortable retainer and secretarial services. I accepted his offer and we shook on it. "If you succeed," he added, "you will be due a commission, and I will grant you the option of becoming President of IPC."

As I further explored the fact situation at IPC, I learned that Koons had destroyed his welcome at the banks, except for limited help from Chemical. Plant improvements were a necessity if IPC was to make a go of it. Factors were too expensive a source for working capital. I needed to find other sources of loans for IPC.

Over the past couple of years, the newly established Inter-American Bank, funded largely by the U.S. Export-Import Bank, had made a number of loans to South American governments.

Although the bank was also chartered to make loans to the private sector, they had not yet done so. I decided to apply to the Inter-American Bank for a loan of three and a half million dollars, for IPC capital improvements. The intergovernmental loans the bank had approved thus far were relatively simple undertakings, and the bank's staff was understandably tentative about dealing with the multiple conditions essential to a private loan contract. By suggesting appropriate contractual language their concerns were lessened, and I gained their confidence.

Mr. Waugh, President of the Export-Import Bank and Chairman of the Board of the Inter-American Bank, was in the position to either approve the application or turn it down. Fortunately I had established a friendly relationship with him from his State Department days, and he readily agreed to meet with me. Koons and I arrived at his city block-long office, first occupied by Jesse Jones of Texas when he was head of the Reconstruction Finance Corporation. To my amazement, Waugh came to his outer office, told Koons to wait outside, and asked me to come in. Later I learned that Koons had burned his bridges to Waugh in prior acrimonious dealings with the State Department and the Export-Import Bank.

Noticeably embarrassed by his extravagantly large office, Waugh led me to a seating area in one corner. "Actually, Sam," he said, "I'm impressed by your efforts to forge your own instrument to serve IPC." Adding that it might serve as a model for other private loans, he assured me of his support. IPC's capital financing was now secured. Koons, still outraged by his exclusion from the meeting, was mollified by the good news.

In spite of my success, however, he failed to keep his promise about offering me the Presidency of IPC, suggesting instead that I accept the office of Executive Vice-President, and become a board member. Evidently he had decided to keep all the power himself. I reluctantly agreed, and tried to quell my own sense of betrayal.

By this time I had become acquainted with William I. Spencer, a Vice President (and later President) of Citibank. He was upset that the Bank's new branch in Ascuncion, Paraguay, was denied IPC business. "IPC is Paraguay's biggest company. We *need* them. Can you help us?"

When I asked Koons about this, he replied vindictively, "Why should I give them any business? When I asked Citibank in New York for a loan, they wouldn't give me a dime!"

I reported Koons's negativity back to Spencer, but added, "If we can create a new frame of reference for him, I think there's a good chance you'll get IPC's bank business."

Spencer looked at me curiously. "What have you got in mind?" he asked.

"IPC has just received a loan from the Inter-American Bank for capital improvements," I explained, "but the company still needs three to four million in working capital at bank rates, rather than the factor's. It would save the company close to a half a million dollars annually, both in lower interest rates and higher prices for its products. With your branch in Asuncion, you could head a consortium of banks to loan the money to IPC. You would administer the funds and control the receivables to liquidate the loan. Your Argentine bank could join in, and I believe Chemical and perhaps another bank would be interested as well. If we can pull this off, I'll bet Koons will give you his business."

Spencer brightened immediately. "Our Argentine bank manager is in town now. I'll have him work with you to set this up."

The next day the Argentine expert and I laid out the prerequisites of such a loan, which included insurance against war and political risks that would have to be provided by the U.S. Foreign Investment Guarantee Program. His lawyer from the prestigious Sherman & Sterling firm was attending the meeting, and when he heard this, he arrogantly rose to leave. "I'm wasting my time here," he asserted. "This loan will never be approved for a government guarantee."

Annoyed by his presumption, I said to the bank officer, "Tell your lawyer to listen to what I am about to propose." The lawyer from S&S reluctantly sat back down. "I know that the guarantee program requires at least a five-year loan, and I am aware that

Citibank will not commit to five years. I propose that Citibank makes a five-year loan with the stipulation that if they encounter a change in circumstances they have the right to terminate the loan at annual intervals. This will provide the safeguard Citibank requires for their involvement."

"You can't get away with that kind of shenanigans," the lawyer interjected disgustedly. I asked his client, the bank officer, if this was a course of action he could endorse, and when he assented I asked him to insist that his attorney travel with me to Washington, which he did. I was optimistic about getting approval for my plan because it made sense, especially since the half-million dollar annual savings would strengthen the payback ability on the three and a half million dollar capital loan. And I knew it wouldn't hurt that Charles Warden, the government's Guaranty Officer, had been on my staff in the Marshall Plan.

Recognizing that this was a win situation all around—for the Government, for the Bank, and for IPC—Warden approved the plan in our first meeting, much to the surprise of the lawyer from S&S. The Paraguay deal was the beginning of a long relationship between Spencer and me as I watched him climb to the Presidency of Citibank.

A short time before this, Pamela Woolworth ejected from IPC by selling her shares to two Dutch partners. Whereas Pamela's role had been a passive one, the Dutch were actively concerned. The company was now postured to make money, and they and Koons owned the controlling shares.

This was a difficult time for all concerned. As a trader, Koons was interested in being bought out at a handsome profit. Apparently his strategy was that if he caused the Dutch enough problems, they might buy him out. A heavy drinker, Koons's alcohol consumption became even more excessive during this period. Friction between Koons and the Dutch developed into open hostility and, as Director and Executive Vice-President of the company, I was caught in the middle.

Finally, before a board meeting, Koons advised me that he would resign, and ordered me to vote in favor of accepting his resignation. I believe he expected the other board members to refuse his resignation and beg him to stay, thus strengthening his hand. Much to his surprise, the majority of the board *accepted* his resignation. The next day, Koons changed his mind and ordered me to manipulate the board to call him back and reinstate him as CEO.

I had had enough. Resentful of his using me in this fashion, I resigned from the board and from the company, to the hostility of Mr. Koons. Sometime later IPC was sold to the Odgen Corporation, at a considerable profit to Koons and the Dutch.

Shortly after my IPC adventure, I found a nice three room corner office on the 32nd floor of 30 Rockefeller Plaza, which became my station for the next decade of law practice. Although the Dewey Firm hadn't taken me in, I had developed a close relationship with Burdell Bixby, and despite the Dewey firm's Brussels office, Bixby recommended me to several of the firm's clients with problems in their overseas businesses.

Senator Ken Keating hosts Pat and Sam, Senate Dining Room

One of these clients, a Jewish family with a large printing enterprise, had acquired, on a trip to Karachi, some gorgeous illustrations depicting scenes from the Koran. Their problem was obvious. As Jews, how could they publish and market these masterpieces without running up against the Arab boycott? I suggested that they set up a Swiss company with a non-Jewish name, and ship the prints from there to markets in the Arab world. They took my advice, and encountered no further problems.

Occasionally I was called back to Washington by our government. This happened in 1962, around the time of the Cuban missile crisis. Informed of my Senate testimony on Soviet oil trading a decade earlier, New York's Republican Senator Kenneth Keating called me before the Security Committee to update them on these practices.

I began by citing statistics that were a matter of public record. The Soviet Union was the world's largest energy producer, producing twelve million barrels of crude oil each day and a volume of natural gas equivalent to another seven million. In addition, its vast petroliferous regions gave it the potential to double that production. Half of this enormous output was exported, primarily to Japan and the industrialized countries of Europe, but also to less developed countries.

Then I went on to explain that these were not reciprocal markets in the conventional sense of independent buyers and sellers of consumer goods. Few of the Soviet imports found their way to the civilian population. Instead the Soviets were trading oil for—in the case of Japan and Western Europe—technology and hardware they needed for their military-industrial complex, or—in the case of countries such as Cuba—other strategic military advantages. My testimony was printed in the *Congressional Record* and widely distributed.

In preparing for the hearings, I was assisted by Esso director George Piercy and his assistant Lauren Kahl. George and I became good friends, and we continued to lunch together from time to time until his retirement in 1970. During this time Esso vacated its headquarters ten floors above my office in 30 Rockefeller Plaza, and moved to its own skyscraper on the Avenue of the Americas. In my first visit to the executive floor in the new building, I was awed by the twenty-foot ceilings and massive doors of equal height, but it fit the magisterial bearing of Esso's executives. I assumed that Piercy knew the story of my stormy relationship with George Kegler, but we never spoke of it.

14

A Candidate for Congress

IN 1958 NELSON A. ROCKEFELLER had defeated Averill Harriman's bid for reelection as Governor of New York. Rocky impressed me with his positive attitude and infectious dynamism. He had an affable personality and a common touch—street smarts, really, despite his privileged upbringing. (His brother Winthrop, later Governor of Arkansas, shared these qualities, but his other brothers—John, David, and Lawrence, did not.)

Politics had always interested me, and not long after I moved to Bronxville, I had asked Dr. Fosdick if he would introduce me to Nelson, assuming that since Nelson's father John D. Jr. had funded the building of Riverside Church, he must know him. I was somewhat taken aback when he objected that he "didn't do that sort of thing." Later it dawned on me that in all the many times I had used my A-1 pew card, I had never seen any Rockefellers there, and it occurred to me that perhaps Fosdick did *not* know Nelson and his brothers.

Burdell Bixby turned out to be my entry point into New York politics. Campaign manager for Rocky in all three of his gubernatorial efforts, Bixby brought me onto the political team as manager of the Speakers' Bureau during Rocky's campaign for reelection in 1962. If Rocky could not attend an event, it was my job to solicit a spokesman appropriate to the occasion. John Lindsay, a dashing young Republican congressman, and Rita Hauser, an attractive New York attorney and community activist, were both excellent speakers and eager to help. Rocky later repaid Lindsay with huge financial support during his successful 1964 campaign for Mayor of New York City, for which I donated the services of Mike Keating, a young lawyer from my office.

The younger Rockefellers—Nelson's son Rodman and Laurence's son Larry—were also eager to help, but much less adept as speakers. They received invitations to speak independent of my bureau (sometimes, I suspect, from people who simply wanted to meet a Rockefeller). I was struck by the fact that the invitations they accepted were usually in the lower-income areas of New York, rather than the silk-stocking districts with which they were identified. But their speeches to blacks in Harlem and the poor of the Lower East Side were often patronizing in both tone and content. Larry in particular was a problem. Just out of college, the burden of establishing rapport with these voters was almost insurmountable for him. Bill Pfeiffer, who was managing the campaign with Bixby, asked me to talk with him. "I don't think he's helping us," he confided.

I asked Larry to pay me a visit and he accepted. "How well do you know your uncle Nelson?" I inquired.

"Very well," he replied, with a puzzled look.

"I suppose you meet at family gatherings," I persisted.

"Yes, of course," he answered.

"Do you ever meet with him alone—one-on-one?" I asked.

"Of course I do. All my life, whenever I've had a question about anything—intellectual, personal, whatever—I always call Uncle Nelse, and he always makes time for me. He's been so generous with his wisdom and understanding and sensitivity. He really enjoys helping people. That's why I want to help him now!"

"Larry," I told him earnestly, "in my opinion you can be *most* helpful to your uncle if you would tell your audience just what you've told me—what kind of man Nelson Rockefeller is. Keep it personal and detailed and relevant. What is Rocky really like? That's what people want to find out. You know him better than almost anyone in the campaign. Tell them!"

Larry seemed relieved. He really preferred to talk about what he knew, rather than an unfamiliar social program some pundit might have suggested to him. After our conversation his speeches improved immeasurably. He spoke eloquently and informatively about his uncle and would always close with, "I hope you will vote for my Uncle Nelse!"

I soon discovered that a political campaign, even when managed by top professionals like Bixby and Pfeiffer, functions more or less chaotically. Many of the volunteers are unknown quantities, with high expectations of gain but limited abilities. Discipline by those at the top is required to prevent these eager beavers from doing more harm than good.

The campaign staff is organized to perform specific functions, most of which are known to the public, but there are certain common practices the average voter is probably unaware of. Many of the letters to the editors printed in the scores of daily and weekly newspapers were written at campaign headquarters and sent to supporters' residences for them to sign and then mail to their local papers. Sizeable cash distributions to local leaders of churches, clubs, and unions are also a well-kept secret. I doubt that Rocky himself knew the nuts and bolts of this part of his campaign operation.

Rocky essentially financed his 1958 campaign with family money. For his second campaign Bill Pfeiffer organized the Governor's Club, which required an annual membership fee of $500. I was the eleventh member of this club, which soon counted nearly one thousand members—substantial money for those days. Rocky was ecstatic when he realized that he wouldn't have to finance his political career out of his own pocket, and could avoid the accusation that he was buying the office with his own money.

After his successful campaign in 1966, Rocky asked me to organize a citizen's committee for "The Transportation Bond Issue." Using the Speakers' Bureau technique to promote the idea, we got it accepted by referendum. Ostensibly this bond was for public transportation, but later I became aware that it was actually used, in lieu of a tax increase, for general budget support. The public quickly caught on, and defeated similar bond issues in two future referendums. I chose not to be involved after the first effort.

Rockefeller was canny enough to recognize that, as a Republican candidate in a heavily Democratic state, he needed the support of organized labor. He secured the support of New York's populous building trades by launching the most ambitious construction program imaginable. In addition to public housing, the state capitol in Albany was totally rebuilt, to a new elegance and grandeur. Major new campuses in Albany, Buffalo, Binghamton, and Stonybrook were added to the state university system, and many new community colleges were built as well. (Rocky appointed me a trustee of the State University at Binghamton, where I served during its construction and evolution into a fully functioning institution.)

Rocky's goals were laudable, and if he wanted to get something done, he found a way to do it. Sometime later I asked Joe Persico, Rocky's longtime friend and speechwriter, how he would characterize him. Joe reflected for a moment and then said, "Nelson aspires to the morality of St. Thomas Aquinas, but in practice his methods are Machiavellian."

In 1966 I made a belated attempt to gain the Republican nomination for the House of Representatives. A letter to Bronxville residents brought in several thousand dollars, which I returned when I failed to gain the nomination. A politician returning campaign contributions to donors? Unheard of, was the townspeoples' reaction! Although I had returned the money as a matter of honor, this gesture unwittingly paved the way for more generous support two years hence.

Today congressional representatives have annual salaries of $130,000, with generous health and pension benefits, a large office staff, and a liberal expense account. In addition their wives are given preference for employment in government or in lobbying firms. Real family incomes for elected officials can exceed a half million dollars a year, which is more than competitive with the private sector. But at the time I ran for Congress in 1968, the salary was less than $20,000 a year, and health and retirement benefits were modest. My incentive to seek public office was to serve the public, and I was willing to take a substantial cut in pay

Photo for Sam's 1966 Campaign for the House of Representatives

to do so. Of course, if one were already independently wealthy, the compensation was a moot point.

The Democratic Representative from the 25th Congressional District was Richard Ottinger, heir to a large fortune, who had unseated the Republican incumbent in the Democratic landslide of 1964. In that election his lack of political experience had worked to his advantage, as his highly paid consultants had successfully created a public persona of Ottinger as the dedicated public servant, untainted by involvement in the seamy world of politics. To magnify his image, Ottinger methodically hacked away at Rocky, whose family compound of Pocantico Hills was in the 25th District.

Though Ottinger represented more of an irritant than a real challenge, by 1968 the Governor was fed up with his attacks and pleased to hear that I was available to run against him. Being more robust in appearance and decisive in manner, I contrasted favorably with the slight and thin-voiced Ottinger, who wore platform shoes to enhance his stature. Rocky was running for President that year, and I was thrilled by the prospect of being on the ticket

Sam with then House Minority Leader Gerald Ford

with him. He was a great vote-getter, especially in Westchester County.

As New York's Republican leader for over a decade, Rocky's choice was always decisive, so I was nominated by acclamation at the Westchester Community Center—an event attended by both Rocky and Richard Nixon, his rival for the Presidential nomination. To my surprise—and the delight of the visiting dignitaries—my daughter Stephanie and twenty of her classmates celebrated my nomination with banners and song. A short time later, at a campaign kickoff dinner at the Tarrytown Hilton, House Minority Leader Gerald Ford delivered the main address, and opera star Melva Barborka, our former next door neighbor in

Bronxville, electrified the ballroom audience with her rendition of the National Anthem.

Against a weak opponent, Ottinger had reportedly spent more than $200,000 in the last election. For this contest, which would cost more, he had his family fortune to fall back on, whereas I had to raise funds from my supporters. Rocky and his brothers each contributed about $15,000, and Pompeo and Phoebe Maresi, friends of Patricia's brother (and later my clients) contributed $30,000. But the largest individual contributor to my campaign turned out to be Robert Abplanalp, a Bronxville neighbor I had never met until my nomination. Abplanalp, founder of Precision Valve Company (maker of the aerosol valve) and a close friend of Richard Nixon, supplied manpower as well as cash, and imaginatively dealt with my lack of name recognition by employing skywriters. One Sunday afternoon the wind carried his "NIXON-NAKASIAN" message over the Polo Grounds, where the Giants were playing football. A Texas friend of mine, entertaining a group seated on the fifty yard line, looked up and asked facetiously, "Who is that guy with Nakasian?"

The 25th District extended from the Bronx north to Dutchess County, a distance of seventy miles, encompassing the western half of Westchester County and all of Putnam. The major city was Yonkers. From April to November, I dedicated eighteen hours a day to making speeches, and shaking the hands of commuters in dozens of train stations. I visited the workers at Otis Elevator in Yonkers and General Motors in Tarrytown, and quickly learned that one-on-one contact was more effective when they were on the way to work rather than on their way home.

Despite its physical toll on me (I dropped 20 pounds from an already-lean physique), I found the campaign invigorating and enlightening. When I paid a call on two black ministers in Yonkers, I was impressed when one pleaded, "Would you *please* not promise my people an easy lifestyle on Welfare?"

The other quickly chimed in. "On Sunday I preach self respect through useful work, while six days a week you politicians offer the alternative of Welfare. In most cases, Welfare destroys the human being!" When the ministers learned of my humble origins, they were convinced that I sincerely shared their belief.

Patricia was a great asset throughout the campaign, often as a charming and eloquent speaker. At one prestigious gathering, after the Governor, Patricia, and I had all spoken, someone in the audience was heard to remark, "The wrong member of *that* family is a candidate." Rocky looked at me and grinned.

My golfing buddy Jim Hagerty was also a great help. It was he who suggested the rallying cry for my campaign, "Enough is enough!" But Ottinger's voting record was so vacuous that I had little opportunity to use it against positions that he strongly supported in the campaign.

The most vexing obstacle I confronted was Ottinger's inconsistency from speech to speech, which was ignored by the press. For instance, in Yonkers he spoke in favor of gun control, whereas in rural Putnam County he favored the NRA position strongly opposing it. He also painted me as "pro-Arab" to his Jewish audiences, playing on their ignorance of Armenian history and culture. Of course, it was understood that he, as a Jew, was pro-Israel.

After Ottinger did this in front of a large audience in the Mt. Vernon Synagogue, I was furious. Shortly thereafter I found myself seated next to him on a speaker's platform in Yonkers. Before the event started I turned to him and said in disgust, "You ought to be ashamed of yourself, if you *have* any shame." Fearing that I might pursue the attack, Ottinger began to shake and stutter, at which point I turned away and ignored him.

This was Ottinger's third election, and by now he had ingratiated himself with the major newspapers and radio stations in the area. I too visited the media centers, hoping to impress the writers and broadcasters that I was the worthier candidate, but I left these meetings firmly convinced that they had already committed to Ottinger. Traditionally, the *New York Times* invites major local candidates to come in for an interview, but when it came my turn, a lone member of the editorial staff received me and questioned me for a half an hour in a "gentlemanly" and perfunc-

Sam's nomination for Congress
Attending were Governor Rockefeller and his wife, Happy, with Richard Nixon

tory manner. In their ensuing editorial I was mentioned as a credible and impressive man, but their endorsement still went to Ottinger, whose family had long ties with the Sulzbergers, owners of the *Times*.

The 25th District had no television stations of its own, but it was well served by New York City's. Each of the major networks scheduled one debate between us. ABC was the first. After a long and frustrating campaign, I looked forward to this opportunity to nail Ottinger on his inconsistencies. On television he would have to address all the district's voters at once. I was determined to expose him as a phony, without using this harsh label.

Ottinger began the debate with a well-rehearsed, self-serving, and characteristically vague statement. When it came time for my reply, I faced him and said, "Congressman, it's clear from your record that you sing like a Republican in Westchester County, but you dance like a Democrat in Washington."

Roger Grimsby, the moderator, turned to Ottinger and said,

"Your turn, Congressman. Will you sing or dance?"

Unable to improvise, the wooden Ottinger stammered in frustration. Without a script, he was lost. After this debacle, Ottinger realized that the debates would help me, and immediately cancelled the remaining two.

Unfortunately for my campaign, my triumph in the debate was too little, too late. I had known I was in trouble from the moment Rockefeller dropped out of the Presidential race. Nixon was not nearly as popular in the district. At that time Rocky had sent me two of his campaign operatives, George Humphrey and Persico, but they had not been the boon I had hoped for. Humphrey was spending my campaign money for his girlfriend, visiting from Georgia, to do some studies of questionable relevance to my effort. Joe had written some speeches for me, only to discover that I could not credibly deliver a speech someone else had written. Both were on Rocky's payroll, but their considerable expenses were paid from *my* resources.

When polls in mid-October showed me losing to Ottinger by 10-12%, Rockefeller contributions stopped. Under the circumstances, I didn't feel that I could ask my other friends and supporters for still more money, so in order to keep the campaign going I personally borrowed $50,000 from the Yonker's branch of Citibank. Most of this money went toward a last-ditch mailing effort to get my views out to the voters.

Most congressional campaigns are waged on a single, or at most three or four issues, but I believed that the voters should know where I stood on all the major issues Congress was likely to address. For almost five months I had worked on a brochure that comprehensively stated my positions on these issues. The cost of printing and mailing the brochure to 50,000 households was enormous, but it represented my last hope for overtaking Ottinger.

Two weeks before the election, my office manager delivered the brochures, in large bundles, to the Yonkers Post Office, not far from my headquarters. When we detected no upsurge in my support as a result of the mailing, we made a quick check to make sure voters had received them. To my horror we found that only a few thousand had been received, mostly in areas that already supported me. The conclusion was odious, but obvious. In their loyalty to the incumbent Ottinger, some of the postal employees had dumped the brochures in the trash. In view of Ottinger's pandering to the unions, I should have anticipated this possibility and had my manager deliver them directly to local post offices throughout the district. Now, with the election only days away, there was nothing I could do to rectify this error.

Ottinger's final margin of victory was 17,000 votes. Pride prevented me from going back to my supporters to pay off the debts of my failed campaign, as is the custom, or from defaulting on the bank loan—despite my knowledge that banks rarely take action to collect on campaign debts. To this day, I doubt that anyone—including the Rockefellers, Maresis, Abplanalp, or Citibank President Spencer—knows that I repaid every penny of the $50,000 loan, plus interest, out of my own pocket.

In retrospect I can see the mistakes I made. I always felt that the voters could better relate to a self-supporting candidate who had succeeded against the odds, than to a candidate whose wealth had shielded him from hardship. Yet out of concern that highlighting this difference in our backgrounds might expose Rocky to similar criticism, I let Ottinger off the hook. I should have forcefully drawn the distinction and, when necessary, defended Rockefeller as an outstanding public servant whose record—unlike Ottinger's—proved him an exception to the rule.

I also erred when I refused the support of the Conservative Party (CP), whose leaders had come to my home and enthusiastically offered their endorsement. This would have put me on the ballot twice, like Ottinger, who also ran as the Liberal Party (LP) candidate. Instead, knowing the war Rocky was waging against this splinter party, I declined. Thus rejected, the CP nominated for the third time DeVito, who attacked *me* rather than the Democrats. As it turned out, Devito garnered—you guessed it—17,000 votes, which, if mine, would have made my race with Ottinger at least a dead heat. Looking back, I believe that Rocky, as a political realist, would have understood my decision to accept the CP nomination as necessary for victory.

Thus ended my political ambitions. Two years later, in the New York Senate race, CP candidate James Buckley defeated Ottinger and a Republican in a three-way race. To prepare for his campaign, Buckley came over to my house and picked up two file cabinets of material on Ottinger that I had accumulated during mine. I wished him well.

During my campaign for Congress, I was introduced to Dr. Broderick, a surgeon and the Director of St. Joseph's Hospital in Yonkers. The old hospital, located in downtown Yonkers, had been founded by the Sisters of Charity at the turn of the Century. In recent years it had struggled to stay solvent and to remain open. Following the election, Dr. Broderick reported to me that the hospital was now on the brink of bankruptcy, and asked if I would join the Board and help save it. Being on the Board of Directors of a hospital was a status symbol (like being an Elder in the church), and I knew plenty of men that served in this capacity for wealthier hospitals. They were always trying to expand their hospitals beyond all demonstrated need—a version of keeping up with the Jones's—and I had never had any desire to join them in this endeavor.

But St. Joseph's was different. I knew that the hospital was needed to serve the nearby ghetto area, and other low-income neighborhoods in South Yonkers. St. Johns, the only other city hospital, was located in North Yonkers, and was not convenient to these areas of need. So I accepted the invitation, and became the only outsider on a board composed of Broderick, two other doctors from the hospital, and several sisters of the charity order.

Dr. Broderick had apparently told the Board that I was close to the Governor and could bring Albany to St. Joseph's rescue. At my first meeting with them I suggested that public assistance would more likely be granted to a community hospital under the direction of representatives of the population it served, rather than under a religious order. Speaking candidly I told them, "We need blacks, Jews and Protestants, reflecting the ethnic diversity of

Yonkers. They should be the majority of the Board." I then proposed the names of people I had met and gotten to know during the campaign.

All were approved and joined the Board by the next meeting. I was chosen Chairman and elected President. My function was to direct the Board in choosing policy and program options, and to support the Executive Director, Sister Mary Lenihan, in their execution.

The onus was clearly on me to deal with the urgency the hospital faced. Its revenue *barely* covered its expenses, and it had been condemned for not conforming with existing health codes. Fortunately a temporary waiver had been granted, giving the hospital a short grace period to replace the old facility.

Cost estimates for replacing the facility ranged from forty to sixty million dollars, a daunting sum to raise in the limited time available. The State's lending authority had the funds, but its strict terms required an equity contribution of ten percent to support such a loan. The Sisters of Charity, who owned the property, were also broke. It looked like it would take a miracle to save the hospital.

As it happened, the miracle we were hoping for was right next door, where the U.S. Vitamin Company, a subsidiary of Revlon, occupied four and a half acres. Revlon President (?) Revson decided to vacate the property, and kindly offered to sell it to the Sisters for $750,000. For only $10,000 he would grant an option to purchase. Sister Lenihan was worried about finding the $10,000, to say nothing of the $750,000. I assured her that we would find $10,000 if I had to put it up myself. With that, the Board accepted my proposal to buy the option.

With the option in hand I engaged an appraiser—a devout Catholic, who worked pro bono—to value the property "for the highest density permitted under code." On that basis he came up with an appraised value of several million dollars. I then took his appraisal to Mr. Revson and suggested that Revlon would be better off donating the property to St. Joseph's and taking a tax deduction. This would save the company far more in taxes than the amount of the purchase price (which, incidentally, we had no hope of coming up with by the expiration date on the option). Revson needed no persuasion.

Now we could claim the added assets. How best to proceed? Sister Mary thought that a geriatric center might be built on part of the old property. She had convincing evidence that it was critically needed and would be fully occupied immediately upon completion. It would cost $20 million, but the cashflow from the new facility would be substantial, and would be available to support the replacement hospital. The State agreed, and granted St. Joseph's a loan to build the geriatric center.

Now the loan application for replacing the old hospital could be supported by the original property of some four acres, yielding a substantial cashflow, and the adjacent U.S. Vitamin property—creating a single block of nearly ten acres. A $60 million dollar loan was soon approved for the construction of the new St. Joseph's Hospital.

During the several years of my tenure as Board Chairman, I became known to Cardinal Cooke, who took a keen interest in our progress, and praised and blessed me no end. I think the Cardinal was fascinated by my knowledge of a financial world alien to him. In his eyes, I *was* a miracle worker. "Your Holiness," I once told him, "I am not a Catholic."

"That's good," he replied. "The Church needs help from non-Catholics!" It surprised me to discover that the Catholic Church gave no support—beyond the Cardinal's token distribution of profits from the annual Alfred E. Smith Dinner—to the thirteen Catholic hospitals within the Cardinal's diocese.

When we moved to Virginia in 1977 I resigned from St. Joseph's. The next year I received an invitation to attend the dedication of the new hospital. Under the tent my daughters Stephanie and Suzy and I took our seats in the large audience. On the dais sat Cardinal Cooke, several Bishops, and the incumbent Board. Halfway through his commemoration the Cardinal paused, pointed to me and said, "I see Sam Nakasian out there. Come

Dedication Ceremony

County Executive Alfred DelBello (left), his Eminence Terence Cardinal Cooke, Sister Margaret Dowling, President of the Sisters of Charity of New York and Bronxville resident Samuel Nakasian, president of the Board of Trustees of St. Joseph's Hospital attend the ribbon cutting ceremonies at the Friday, April 9 dedication of St. Joseph's Hospital Nursing Home in Yonkers. Nakasian and others stand at the entrance of the six story 200 bed facility. The home is a first step of a major construction and renovation program designed to replace the present facilities of St. Joseph's Hospital.

up here, Sam." As I made my way to the dais he added, "This great man made all of this possible." As my daughters watched proudly, the Cardinal warmly embraced me. I was on cloud nine.

I had a similar experience with the Cardinal the last time I saw him, shortly before his untimely death from cancer. Patricia and I were attending the annual Alfred E. Smith Dinner at the Waldorf-Astoria, as guests of Blanka Rosenstiel, a major church benefactor. The Cardinal headed the receiving line, which included Governor Carey and other dignitaries. When we got to the Cardinal, Blanka started to introduce me when his face suddenly lit up. After greeting me he held up the receiving line several minutes to tell the Governor and all within earshot how we had accomplished the miracle of St. Joseph's Hospital. Afterwards Laurence Rockefeller greeted me and said, "I wish you would run again for Congress. You have my support!"

Had Nelson asked me to run for the same House seat in 1970, I might have considered it, and undoubtedly would have won. But by then I had become involved in an important business deal in Korea that needed my full attention.

15

Back to the Middle East: Turkey and Libya

DURING THE TIME I WAS in New York I made many trips to the Middle East in connection with various business ventures. In fact, in mid-1960 I very nearly visited my long-forgotten birthplace in Turkey. I was advising an executive of a Houston oil company looking to move into that country. At the time, Turks were trying to make up to Armenians for executing the genocide against us, and the oil company accepted my prediction that my presence during their meetings with Turkish government officials would be advantageous.

The Turks I met were over-solicitious in extending the hand of friendship to me, and claimed me as one of their own when they saw from my passport that I had been born in Turkey. Still, I could not bring myself to reciprocate. Although I knew that the Germans and British had provoked the genocide, I also knew that the Turks had been willing executioners and plunderers of victims' property, and my own family had suffered at their hands. I found that I could not truly forgive this, even though I had managed to forget everything I had experienced in that country as a child.

When the company's local Turkish lawyer graciously invited me to join him on a trip to my family's homes in Marsavon and Samsun—an easy day's trip from Ankara—to his surprise and puzzlement I declined without explanation or regret. I had no desire to dredge up painful memories. When the business meetings concluded, I was very glad to leave Turkey and return home.

My first venture as a business partner, rather than lawyer, had come the year before, in Libya. When it became evident that Esso was going to build their Zelten pipeline there, I contacted friends at the Stone-Webster Construction Company and interested them in bidding on the job. I also brought onto the team the Bledsoe Organization of Tulsa, Oklahoma, builders of a gas pipeline that ran from the Midwest into Florida. Unfortunately, despite a very credible bid on our part, Bechtel got the job.

Esso decided that, in order to save money, they would forgo the building of a terminal on the coast. Instead they would pipe the oil directly out to their tankers in the deep water offshore. First, of course, Bechtel had to build the pipeline, and to build it they had to float the pipe ashore from ocean carriers.

For the arrival of the first ocean carrier, loaded with pipe, Esso arranged the greatest ceremony in Libyan history. There was a grandstand for King Idris and other dignitaries from throughout the region, as well as representatives from Esso and the U.S. government. When the invited guests were all assembled, the Libyan and American National Anthems were played.

Finally, with a flourish of trumpets, the ship started unloading. The ship's crane picked up a string of pipe and lowered it, and as soon as the pipe hit the water it sank, before the waiting motor launch could snare it and tow it to shore. Undeterred, the crew lowered a second string of pipe, and it too sank. After the third also plummeted to the bottom, the effort was disbanded.

The Libyans were shocked. Keep in mind that the American companies, for their achievements in clearing mines and discovering the oil fields, had been viewed by the Libyans as heroes sent by the Gods. This event tarnished their hitherto unblemished reputation. One of Esso's managers came out and explained to the stunned crowd that there had been a miscalculation. In the heat of the blazing Libyan sun, the plugs in the ends of the pipe had not expanded at the same rate as the steel pipe itself, and hence leaked.

The ship turned around and carried the pipes back to London. Esso improved the seals and the pipes were then floated successfully to shore in Libya, without the fanfare that had accompanied the first attempt.

My second business venture also involved Libya. It occurred to me that a central oil field supply operation, that serviced and inventoried equipment for all the drilling companies, could save each of them a substantial sum of money. Avery Adams, CEO and Chairman of Jones & Loughlin Steel Company, heard my presentation and directed several officers of its oil field supply division to go with me to Libya, where they could make an on-the-spot investigation and obtain assurances from the oil companies they would buy these services.

I felt somewhat like a tour guide for these midwesterners, on their first overseas trip. When we settled in at the King George Hotel in Tripoli, the General Counsel of J&L, was particularly fascinated by the bowl *next* to the toilet in the bathroom.

"Sam," he asked "what is that?"

"It's a bidet," I replied.

"What is it used for?"

"For local bathing," I replied.

Within an hour he was back in my room. "These bathrooms all have tubs and showers. Why is this necessary—this what-do-you-call-it?"

"Bidet," I repeated. Finally I graphically explained to him that it was designed to keep the genitals clean, a high priority in European society. He flushed a deep red and nodded, embarrassed more by his question than my answer.

When we returned to the States, the J&L officers wrote an enthusiastic recommendation for Adams and his board. I attended the board meeting in Pittsburgh and sat in the adjoining room to await formal approval. After the meeting Adams called me to his office and said, "Sorry to tell you Sam, the answer is no."

"But why? The economics are all there!" I pleaded.

Without uttering a word, he pulled out of his desk a copy of Life Magazine, which contained a reporter's prediction that Egypt would take over Libya. "That information is good enough for me," he added with finality.

I left his suite with a growing sense of incredulity. "This is the decision-making process in the Executive Suite?" I thought to myself. Adam's officers were no less outraged.

During my visits to Tripoli in those years I spent some time socially with Saad Bughaighis, a young business associate of the Black Prince. In his youth, the self-educated Saad had worked and read in a Benghazi bookstore owned by a relative, and now he kept company with a cadre of young intelligentsia (relatively speaking) headed by General Abdul Aziz Sheili, the middle son of the King's late friend and advisor.

On several occasions, Saad invited me to join the General and his friends at the King's palace in Tripoli (formerly the residence of the Italian Governor). While drinking Scotch, the General and his companions would speak seriously of Libya's future. The General had modeled himself after his idol, Abdul Nasser, the charismatic Egyptian leader. In these unofficial meetings Sheili was intensely patriotic in his position as the ranking officer of the new Libyan army. He was also scrupulously correct in his decorum—influenced, I believe, by his English wife. I attended my last such get-together in 1962, by which time it was clear to me that those present believed that the King was in ill health and would soon retire, naming the General as Libya's new leader.

This was not the way things worked out. In 1969, while King Idris was in Athens for medical attention, a young communications officer in the Libyan army staged a successful coup. Virtually unknown in Libya at the time, his name was Muammar Ghaddafi. General Sheili and other top army and police officers were rounded up and placed under arrest in a military barracks, referred to facetiously as "the Hilton." Ghaddafi secured himself and his family in a barracks outside Tripoli, and quickly organized his own army of young bedouins, who were assigned to be present at all government meetings.

Ghaddafi's coup took everyone by surprise, and the full story behind it has never been made public. My preferred theory is that Abdul Aziz Sheili's time had finally come. King Idris was about to abdicate and turn the government over to him, and chose to make one final trip abroad before stepping down as monarch. I believe Ghaddafi had used his communications post both to intercept conversations regarding the official plan and to secretly organize his own takeover force. He timed his move perfectly, encountering no serious resistance, and relations between Libya and the West would never be the same.

Ghaddafi defied efforts to liken him to other dictators. An ascetic man of the desert, he was not about to change his spartan lifestyle by exploiting for his own use the vast oil revenues available to him. By 1969 Libya was exporting three million barrels of crude a day. Money was pouring into the treasury faster than the ruling elite could spend it, but little of this money was directly benefiting the people. Ghaddafi immediately invested oil revenues in housing, hospitals, schools, and roads, and generously rewarded his newly recruited bedouin army. He quickly became a hero to the Libyan poor and a serious threat to the few privileged rich. (Being out of the country at the time of the coup, the Black Prince luckily avoided arrest and prosecution. In time he was separated from his fortune. I lost track of him until a headline caught my eye a few years later: BLACK PRINCE ARRESTED IN BEIRUT FOR TRANSPORTING DRUGS.)

But Ghaddafi was not content with being a hero in his own backward country. He wanted to be a major player on the world stage—and what better way to achieve that than by taking on the oil companies?

Ghaddafi and Jallud, Ghaddafi's more visible right-hand man, had no knowledge of the oil industry, and few in their government did. An exception was Omar Muntasser, a holdover with limited experience. I doubt that there was any clearly thought out strategy as to how to proceed against the oil producers. The objective was very simple: try to make them pay more revenue, and see what happens.

Under the original and still applicable Petroleum Law, the 50-50 profitsharing was based on the company's realized prices for crude sold, less the cost of producing it. The independent companies, which had over half the market in Libya, competed with the majors by lowering their prices to existing refineries, most of them in Europe. As an alternative, Occidental and the Oasis Group had invested heavily in building their own refineries and in marketing. To reduce their tax liability and finance their investment, these companies had increased production and lowered their prices on crude still further. Their realized prices were lower than that of crude oil exported from the Middle East, despite Libya's generally superior quality and a freight advantage to Europe of fifty cents per barrel. This threatened the majors, and of course adversely affected Libya's profit share.

With this much crude oil loose on the market, the majors needed action to protect their turf. Libya's desire for more revenue and the majors' interest in reducing the cash flow of the independents merged into a common interest. Esso is credited with suggesting to Ghaddafi a redefinition of the realized profit calculation that would work to both their advantages. Ghaddafi decreed that from then on the profit calculation would be based on posted prices, fixed at a higher level than Middle East crude, plus the fifty cent per barrel freight differential.

The new policy achieved the desired effect for both parties. At a considerable loss on facilities it had acquired and would now have to sell at distressed prices, Occidental discontinued its refinery and marketing program entirely, and Oasis immediately curtailed its expansion as well. The revenues of both companies (but particularly Oxy) plummeted, while Libyan oil revenue skyrocketed. Word got out that Ghaddafi had made the oil companies knuckle under, and suddenly he had the notoriety he sought. Jallud was spotted celebrating extravagantly in the night clubs of Rome, while Muammar remained in his army barracks, cultivating his image as a mysterious desert Robin Hood.

This near doubling of Libya's revenue proved so easy that Ghaddafi assumed there must be more available. It didn't take much investigation to learn that Mexico, Argentina, and Brazil owned *all* their production. Why couldn't Libya force the companies to give up some of their concessions, and therefore some of their production share? Oxy was most vulnerable since Libya was its only source of production. Despite pressure from the other producers to resist, Armand Hammer, Oxy's major domo, capitulated to Ghaddafi's nationalization of half its concession. Libya's revenues increased yet *again* and left Oxy with only about *fifteen* percent of its profits. The Oasis Group soon followed, and the Hunt-BP partnership in the Sarir Field was totally nationalized.

The majors of Aramco refused to accept these demands, realizing that it might create a precedent that could be used against them in Saudi Arabia. Eventually Caltex and Mobil abandoned their concessions altogether. Esso was able to strike a special deal, when Libya realized that it could not operate Esso's huge gas-liquidification plant on its own. Once Ghaddafi initiated the revolutionary practice of basing taxes on posted prices, limits on production and price-fixing would soon follow. For thirty years Dr. Alfonso Parra of Venezuela had sought to establish an organization of petroleum exporting countries for just this purpose. As a high-cost oil producer, it was in Venezuela's interest to fix posted prices at higher levels so that it could remain competitive with the Middle East, where production costs were much lower. Now, with Ghaddafi's move, the time was right.

The independents' abundantly available "loose" (on the world market) crude threatened the price levels and market shares of the majors. Standardizing prices would restrain the growth of the independents into marketing and refining, and thus address both problems at once. The majors' support of such a practice was no doubt communicated to their friends in Washington, and so when OPEC was born, during the reign of Kissinger as National Security Advisor and Rogers as Secretary of State, not a peep was heard from the major oil companies or from government officials.

Saudi Arabia, as the largest exporter, was the dominant member of OPEC. As Ghaddafi had done with Esso, the Saudis made a sweetheart deal with their four American companies. The Saudis would nationalize the oil industry and Aramco, the service company. In return, these companies would receive preemptive rights to Saudi Arabia's oil exports at a discounted price, and the former owners of Aramco would receive a generous fee to continue managing the operation. These two benefits became known as the "Aramco Advantage."

OPEC failed to attract all of the oil exporting countries. Russia remained outside, along with Mexico, Norway and Britain in the North Sea, and of course the United States. Companies in these countries chose to benefit from OPEC's higher prices without being members of the organization. The effect on the individual consumer, both here and abroad, was felt immediately in the form of steep price increases on gasoline and other petroleum products.

Our State Department may have remained silent about the birth of OPEC, but they were anything but silent about Ghaddafi himself. When he nationalized BP and the American companies, both the American State Department and British Foreign Ministry responded with a media-blitz condemning Ghaddafi as "an outlaw," even though he compensated the companies in accordance with international law (i.e. for the amount of their unrecovered investment, *not* anticipated future profits). If this strategy was intended to induce Ghaddafi to be more compliant, it backfired badly. Ghaddafi retaliated by issuing the demand (unprecedented in diplomatic relations) that all British and American passports be translated into Arabic before Libya would issue entry visas, which would be considered only after a written invitation to visit the country for a stated purpose.

The hostility escalated from there. The big American aircraft Ghaddafi had purchased and paid for were impounded in Georgia, as was Libyan cash in U.S. banks. Libyan crude oil was denied entry into the United States. Accusations that Ghaddafi was fomenting acts of international terrorism followed, finally culminating in President Reagan's order for an airforce attack on Ghaddafi's barracks in Libya. By then Washington had ordered all Americans out of Libya. As the American and British companies left the country—victims of our government's rhetoric and actions—French, Italian, and Austrian companies moved in.

Almost a quarter century later, Libya has suffered little if any economic detriment, and Ghaddafi himself basks in the publicity and celebrity we have given him. A master of manipulating popular opinion through the media, he remains a hero to his own people and those of many other third world countries. Potentially embarrassing incidents have never received media attention. I personally know of one such incident.

During the 1973 Israeli War, Ghaddafi made headlines in the world press by announcing that he would support the Egyptian Army with his huge mobile artillery carriers. Enroute from Tripoli to the airport the next day, I saw these same vehicles become stuck in the sand as they attempted to make a sharp turn onto the main road from the army base. They never made it out in time to join the fray. The press never reported this because Ghaddafi made sure they never *heard* about it.

On one of my last trips to Libya during the Ghaddafi years, I ran into Arnaud de Borchgrave and his (current) lovely young wife at the Libyan Palace Hotel. During Kissinger's regime as Secretary of State, Arnaud's reports made Newsweek and the Washington Post the most lively and informative source of news about the Middle East. This was because Arnaud chose to pursue his own sources, rather than rely on the briefings of Kissinger himself, who had developed a most effective way of controlling the press.

According to Arnaud, Kissinger regularly invited the VIP's of the press to fly with him aboard Air Force One to his destination in the Middle East, where he would reserve a floor for them at a luxury hotel. Throughout the trip he would brief the chosen press corps, most of them new to that part of the world, regularly and in great detail, but "off the record." Then he would issue a press release to them that left out most of what he had told them in private.

After his first such trip, Arnaud told me, "I had had enough of Henry's captivity." By now Arnaud had spent much time in the Middle East, and had friends everywhere. Thereafter he took a commercial flight and stayed with friends rather than accept Kissinger's hospitality. He read Henry's press releases but wrote his own stories, free to use the best sources.

When I saw Arnaud at the Libyan Palace Hotel, he was beside himself with frustration. "I need your help," Arnaud pleaded. "A week ago, my wife and I met Ghaddafi at a press conference in Cairo. He invited us to Tripoli and promised a private interview, and we changed our plans and came directly here. That was more than a *week* ago! Every day, at about 6 P.M., one of his men comes by the hotel and tells me that Ghaddafi will see me the next day. I desperately want to interview him, but we can't sit here forever! Why is he treating me this way? You'd think he'd never heard of me."

"Oh, he's heard of you all right," I assured him. "And therein lies the rub."

Arnaud looked at me strangely. "What do you mean?"

"I never *met* Ghaddafi," I conceded, "but I believe I understand his mind and his intentions. He wants to impress you with his power to keep *you*, an important journalist, waiting, and thus magnify the importance of the event when it finally happens. I would wager that if you tell his man—tonight, when he visits you—that you are booked to leave tomorrow morning, Ghaddafi will suddenly find the time to see you. Be sure you *are* booked to take the plane," I cautioned. "They will check the passenger list to see!"

The next morning at breakfast, Arnaud excitedly reported, "It worked! I told Ghaddafi's flunky that I was taking the plane out this morning and said 'Goodbye' to him. At midnight he came back to the hotel and took me to see Ghaddafi. I got my interview. Thanks!"

Arnaud's meeting with Ghaddafi was the first ever for a Western journalist. His account in Newsweek was widely read by a public eager for a behind-the-scenes look at the mystery man.

When Caltex, operating in Libya as Amoseas, decided to abandon its concession, I was consulted by Edward Carey, owner of New England Petroleum Company (Nepco) for advice on whether he would be justified in buying crude oil from the Libyan Government that was formerly produced by Amoseas. Nepco was a major supplier of fuel oil to electric utilities in New York and along the east coast. Pollution standards recently imposed required the substitution of low-sulphur fuel oil for coal in the generation of electricity. Nepco, in partnership with California (half owner of Amoseas), had built a large refinery in the Bahamas to process low-sulphur Libyan crude, but now that Amoseas was defunct, California had decided not to purchase anymore Libyan crude, and also not to replace the supply from other sources. I advised Mr. Carey that under these circumstances, Nepco would be justified, as a matter of self-survival, in buying crude from Libya if it were the only available source that would meet the pollution standards. I further offered to help expedite the purchase and delivery of the crude, using my overseas connections.

I was confident that the purchase could be made at a good price, because Caltex had scared away other buyers by threatening legal seizure of their cargo. I suggested that a Nepco tanker be moved to Libyan waters, and without delay Nepco buyer Peter Hunter and I flew to London, and then by private charter to Tripoli. After overcoming visa difficulties, we purchased several large tanker cargoes at a discounted price. "When can you load?" the Libyan official asked. "We want to deliver as soon as possible."

"If you reduce the price another 20%," I quickly offered, "we would be able to start loading a tanker tomorrow." He agreed, and the Nepco "Courageous" docked the next day to take on the cargo.

We had been forewarned that the Libyan crude, destined for a refinery in southern Italy, would be seized by judicial action when it docked. Immediately after consummating the deal I flew to Rome to find an Italian lawyer willing to vacate the seizure for Nepco. It was a discouraging quest. Every law firm I went to rejected my retainer, citing conflict of interest. Caltex had already retained them!

I was desperate. It was late afternoon and the Courageous would dock in Italy the next day. As I walked up the Via Veneto from the Excelsior Hotel where I was staying, I spied a modest plaque on one of the buildings. It read Grazia Dei, Advocato. "The Grace of God," I thought to myself. "That's certainly what

I need right now." I entered the office and was received by a lawyer who informed me that his firm too had been retained by Caltex. Noting my pained expression, he suggested that I return in the morning and speak directly with Signor Dei.

The next morning as I entered his office Signor Dei rose from his desk and asked, "Haven't we met before?" When I replied that I could not remember any prior meeting, he was unconvinced. "This is not your first visit to Rome?"

"No", I replied. "I have been here many times. I was first here over twenty years ago on Marshall Plan business. I was an officer of the Agency in Washington."

Signor Dei's eyes widened and he became very emotional. "*That's* when we met! I was Ambassador Zellerbach's Legal Advisor!" It was true. Although I still could not remember him, I was most thankful that he remembered me. I could hardly believe my ears when Dei turned to his associate whom I had met the day before and said, "This Caltex business—why don't we forget it? We will help this nice man." I surmised that he wanted to make a gesture of appreciation for U.S. aid during Italy's postwar crisis years. I was only too happy to accept, and offered him a generous retainer in return.

Grazia Dei was in southern Italy when the Courageous docked. The cargo was seized as had been expected, but Dei succeeded in securing its release. I left Italy confident that additional cargoes destined for southern Italy would also be released. But for "the Grace of God," my reputation in the industry might have been seriously damaged.

The Libyan story would be incomplete without special attention to the other successful wildcatter (besides Hunt)—Armand Hammer of Occidental. Hammer was a latecomer on the Libyan scene, entering in 1964. Several years earlier he had acquired a modest west coast company, Occidental Petroleum, as the vehicle for drilling several wildcat wells in the U.S. with funding from individual investors. Hammer had been the first American businessman to establish ties with Russia, and had made a fortune selling the fine art masterpieces he had acquired there. Word of the fabulous oil discoveries in Libya whetted his appetite for a piece of that action too.

Hammer entered into a joint venture with the Allen brothers of Wall Street, who claimed to have unimpeachable contacts with King Idris and his advisors. In accordance with the Libyan Petroleum Law, the companies granted concessions in 1955 were obligated to return 25% of their unproductive acreage to the Government within ten years. In 1965 these areas would be offerred again to the oil industry on a selective basis. It was Mobil's surrendered area that attracted the most attention, and that's what Hammer targeted.

Hammer was undaunted by the serious obstacles he faced. Oxy had meager assets reflecting its mediocre record in discovering domestic oil, and no foreign experience whatever. Moreover, Hammer's highly publicized friendship with the Kremlin would not sit well with the anti-communist Libyan King. And if that were not enough to get the door slammed in his face, he was a Jew with close ties to important figures in the Israeli government.

With all this working against him, Hammer relied on the Allen brothers to deliver the concession. Shortly before the deadline for filing an application, Hammer found out that the "unimpeachable" contact persons in Libya were nothing more than con artists, and when he confronted the Allens with his discovery, they admitted that they had been taken in.

In desperation, Hammer searched for another link to Tobruk. Among Hammer's acquaintances was a newsman who knew Wendell Phillips. Knowing of Phillips's role in delivering that choice concession to Texas Gulf Producing Company, Hammer and his newsman friend flew immediately from Los Angeles to Rome to meet him. Phillips agreed to represent Hammer in return for an overriding royalty (ORR) he would share with Hans Kunz and *his* friend Said. Phillips had worked with Kunz on the Texas Gulf deal ten years earlier, and Said was a close friend of Omar Sheili, the King's Chief Advisor since the death of his older brother Bushir in an auto accident.

In order to commit Omar, a large ORR for his personal account would be required. Hammer quickly negotiated a one percent ORR for the three go-betweens to share equally. Omar agreed on a 2 1/2% ORR, stipulating that payment would be made by Oxy to a numbered Swiss bank account. Kunz and his partner Said signed the royalty agreement as fiduciaries of the unnamed beneficiary of the Swiss account.

Omar dressed up Oxy's application to include the development of the King's favorite desert oasis into a lush, park-like area. Other companies protested that Oxy lacked financial resources and exploration experience and that Hammer himself was a Jew. At a critical stage, Hammer wrote a letter to Omar assuring him that he was a "congregationalist," quoting a minister as proof. In the end, Omar delivered the concession.

Hammer drilled two dry wells and nearly exhausted his capital. He was just about to admit defeat when his third well gushed oil from a prolific reservoir that had escaped Mobil's detection (and almost Oxy's). Hammer easily raised the capital for several confirmation wells; now the big money would have to be raised. Many millions would be required for a two-hundred mile large-diameter pipeline from the oilfields to the ocean, a gathering system, and an ocean terminal with storage and loading facilities—and many additional millions for drilling hundreds of development wells. Without refineries and marketing, or committed buyers to provide assurances of revenue, such financing was not available in the capital market.

Undaunted, Hammer persuaded Bechtel, the world's largest and best known construction company, to both arrange the financing and undertake the construction. This achievement shocked the oil industry, especially the majors whom Bechtel had served throughout the world in their biggest projects. I suspect that Hammer's powers of persuasion grew from promises that he would deliver to Bechtel huge state projects of the Soviet Union and other countries with whose leaders he had cultivated personal friendships. In less than three years (record time), Bechtel had Oxy exporting a half million barrels of oil daily, and Hammer was well on his way to stardom. Oxy was now a major player in the industry, threatening the majors.

Whether he had failed to analyze its impact, or whether he simply agreed to the numbers to get his deal, the two ORR's—totalling three and a half percent, off the top—had such an impact on Oxy's net return that Hammer began to search for a way out of his obligation. When Omar received his first quarterly royalty payment in 1969, it was for a fraction of what he had expected. Omar had figured out two and a half percent of the revenue from 500,000 barrels of oil a day and come up with a very large number. Furious, Omar returned the royalty check to Hammer and threatened to have Oxy's concession cancelled. Immediately Hammer sent him a check for one million dollars, with a promise of a one-on-one meeting to iron out all differences. Omar cashed the check, and before his meeting with Hammer, visited Europe. While he was there, Ghaddafi came into power. Omar could never go home again, and all payments to his numbered Swiss bank account stopped.

Hammer also reneged on his deal with Kunz, Said, and Phillips. Kunz and Said took legal action against Oxy and settled out of court. Omar brought action in the Swiss Court against Kunz and Said, claiming *his* royalty payments. Imagine his shock and dismay when they denied that any such royalty agreement existed. The one million dollar payment to Omar was explained as a gift to a friend in financial need. Without anything in writing, Omar lost the case. Years later, in Geneva, he told me, "I did not think it was necessary for me to be named in the ORR Agreement. I was in control of everything!"

In early 1980, the Wendell Phillips Estate hired me to audit the royalty payments and determine the proper amount owed. Over the next several years Captain Gordon Hodgson, the Executor of the Estate, and I met frequently with Hammer's counsel and staff. We narrowed the point of conflict to the amounts of Oxy's deductions against the royalties owed to the Phillips Estate. Then, just when it looked like we had reached agreement on the interpretation, Oxy chose to undermine it.

Finally, after two years of this haggling, we decided to sue in Federal Court. In preparation for the trial, we pursued our discovery rights and, under the Freedom of Information Act, gained limited access to Oxy's disclosures to the FCC, as well as the court records for Kunz vs. Occidental. We discovered that, while Kunz and Said had agreements identical to Wendell's in terms and amounts, Oxy had paid Wendell thousands compared with *millions* to Kunz and Said. These two had been paid handsomely to keep their mouths shut about the deal with Omar.

In all the years of meetings in Oxy's offices in Los Angeles, I never met Hammer until he was subpoenaed to be deposed. During a full day of deposition, it amazed me that Hammer, almost ninety years old, could testify with such precision of memory, and beyond that—when it suited his interest—to claim facts which were *not* true.

Questioned about his meetings and telephone calls with Omar, he repeatedly answered, "I do not recall." When our trial counsel showed him his "Dear Omar" letter, disclaiming his Jewish faith and pleading for help against his adversary companies in Libya, he flushed with anger, glowering at his prestigious lawyer for permitting this surprise. His lawyer promptly requested a lunch break.

After lunch we were all assembled at the conference table awaiting Hammer's return. Hammer's lawyer was standing, regaling us with an anecdote, when suddenly Hammer stormed into the room with a scowl and barked, "Sit down and shut up!" The order was obeyed instantly. Later I restrained myself from asking the humiliated lawyer to finish his story.

The day before the commencement of trial, Oxy offered a cash settlement and, as Executor, Captain Hodgson accepted. This battle gave me some insight into how Armand Hammer had, in the span of thirty years, built Oxy from insignificance into a company grossing twelve billion dollars a year, fighting the majors all the way.

16
Iraq and Algeria

IN 1963 ED STEINIGER, CEO of Sinclair Oil, consulted me as to the wisdom of seeking an oil concession in Iraq. The Iraqis had recently repatriated 90% of the non-producing territory originally granted to IPC, the foreign oil consortium that had controlled Iraqi oil production for decades. However, our State Department had condemned the land recovery, and Steiniger was concerned about the moral and legal issues surrounding such a venture. "Our company has always been interested in the Middle East, but we've never been able to unlock the control of the majors. We were included in Iran's allocation of 5% of their producing territory to independents, but as a result of what *you* did, rather than by our efforts. This appears to be another opportunity to get involved over there. What do you think? Would we be justified in acquiring a concession in Iraq, and if so, would you go to Baghdad and represent us?"

"As for justification," I replied, "Iraq generously recognized IPC's entitlement to all its producing areas and even gave them contiguous land totalling ten percent of the entire rest of the country. The land they reclaimed is untouched by IPC exploration, and under international law the companies cannot claim to have suffered damages.

"What's more, President Kassem pleaded with IPC for some time to program more exploration and production, but to no avail. He complained that IPC partners were dramatically expanding production in Kuwait, Saudi Arabia, and the Gulf, thereby serving the sparce population of those countries and neglecting

Iraq's millions. Under these circumstances," I assured him, "you are amply justified to pursue your course without retribution on legal or moral grounds. However, you should prepare yourself for criticism from Esso and Mobil, and their surrogates in Washington. As for myself, I would be happy to represent your interests in Baghdad."

I was aware that, a short time before, shipping magnate D.K. Ludwig had sent a representative to Baghdad to conduct a preliminary geological survey, and that this man had been arrested for unauthorized possession of oil documents. I was careful to gain the support of Iraqi officials before any surveys would be made.

After touching base with Iraq's Ambassador to the UN, to relay word of our visit to his government, I flew to Baghdad accompanied by Sinclair assistant counsel Dudley Phillips and a geologist. Much had changed in the city since my last trip there in 1956. Two new bridges had been built over the Euphrates and a new palace perched elegantly on its banks. Several high rise government office buildings and the minarets of a new mosque towered above the low, flat buildings of old Baghdad, and the new Baghdad Hotel had become the social center of the city. All these were signs of Iraq's ever-increasing oil revenues.

The Iraqi political situation was very unsettled. The King had been assassinated in 1958. Following British and U.S. condemnation of the act, Kassem had invited in Soviet technicians and workers to build a modern infrastructure for Baghdad. Many of these Soviets were still around, but their government forbade them to mingle with the Iraqis, and they were rarely seen in public.

Then, within the past year, Kassem himself had been murdered and replaced as President by Arif, his co-conspirator in the assassination of the King. Now the army was everywhere, as if waiting for something to happen, creating an atmosphere of tension. All this, in addition to basic culture shock, was too much for the geologist, who took to his bed soon after our arrival.

My first official visit was to the new Minister of Oil, Al-Watarri, a young engineer with no previous government experience. We met in his comfortable office in an older walkup building. He was polite but guarded. It turned out that he had an Armenian mother, but even our common ancestry did not soften his reserve. He gave no hint as to his plans for the oil concessions.

My next step was to call the palace directly and seek a meeting with President Arif. This was easier than I had anticipated. I could see the heavily secured palace—a hybrid of East and West in terms of its design—from my room at the Baghdad Hotel, and I admit to being a bit apprehensive when I entered it the next day. Iraq had an antagonistic recent history with the United States, and I was well aware that I was not walking into a friendly court.

Arif greeted me in military attire. He was short and stocky, and spoke broken English. At first he too was guarded. I knew he was sizing me up: trying to obtain more information than he would divulge. The awkward encounter turned in a more favorable direction when, towards the end of the meeting, he commented, "You don't look like an American." His discovery that I was Armenian led to a discussion of the common history Armenians and Iraqis shared with respect to the Turks. By the end of the meeting he had relaxed considerably, and I felt my efforts would bear fruit.

My friend Nadim Tayib was most helpful in pointing out details that would prove useful in my dealings with Iraqi officials. I was also fortunate in making the acquaintance of a very distinguished lawyer named Shamas, who remained above the political maneuvering in the country.

My increasingly friendly relationship with the President must have influenced Al-Watarri, because after several inconclusive meetings he finally approved my proposal that Sinclair make a geological study of Iraq at its own expense. A geology team was brought in, and while they were at work I began preliminary negotiations toward a concession agreement.

After my second trip to Baghdad, I received a call from Steiniger asking me to come to his office. When I arrived he was in a state of distress. He had just received a telephone call from UnderSecretary of State Averill Harriman, advising him that

Sinclair's activity in Iraq violated State Department policy. "That pretty much shuts us down," Steiniger said despondently.

Gently I suggested that he call Harriman and request a copy of that policy statement so that we would know what we had to comply with. "Good idea!" he responded, perking up a bit. In my presence he then got Harriman on the phone and asked him point-blank for a copy of the State Department's policy statement. Harriman replied, "Oh, I was just calling to give you some friendly advice. We don't have any such statement."

Steiniger hung up and reported to me what Harriman had told him. "Friendly advice," he sneered. "Friendly advice from his friends at Esso and Mobil, I'll bet."

Sinclair's geology team, under the leadership of Dr. Phil Chenowith, took just over a year to complete their basin study. During that time I made several trips to Baghdad, along with Dudley Phillips, to hammer out the terms of the concession agreement with Al-Watarri and his aides.

Knowing that my telephone conversations were taped by the police, I would fly to Cairo to make my calls to New York. On one weekend there, the international publishing house of McGraw-Hill threw a party at the Cairo Hilton, and I was invited. Soon after I arrived, an editor I knew asked me to do him a favor. "The Russian Ambassador has expressed a desire to meet you. Let me introduce you to him." Being seen with the Russian could do me no good and might even endanger the relationship of trust I had established with the Iraqis, but I saw no way I could reasonably refuse.

Ambassador Markulov expressed effusive joy in meeting me. "Doctor Nakasian," he offered, "you must know that we Russians regard Armenians as Russians."

Aware of the many onlookers, I replied loudly enough for all to hear, "Your Excellency, may I assure you that we Armenians do *not* regard ourselves as Russians."

The Ambassador laughed off my retort and turned to those assembled. "You see how clever these Armenians are?" I laughed along with everybody else.

Upon my arrival in Baghdad, I would always pay a visit to

President Arif. He felt comfortable with me now, and began to express his wishes for better relations with the United States. He frequently complained about the presence of the Soviets. "They are building some projects for us with second-rate technicians! Their work is poor, and my people resent them. Not only that—I *know* that their KGB is gathering information and recruiting my people as agents! Can you get a message through to your President that I prefer to get rid of the Russians and bring Americans in to help develop our country?" I had no contact in the White House, but I did I pass this message to the State Department's desk officer for the Middle East.

It was perhaps wishful thinking, but I was hopeful that despite the obstacles—primarily factional strife among the army brass and the hostility of Egypt's Nassar, who wanted to bring Iraq into his sphere of influence—Arif could provide the leadership to rally his people to support him, and would become an ally of the United States. To lend him encouragement I presented him with a Steuben glass memorial of George Washington, with the inscription "Father of His Country" translated into Arabic. He was overwhelmed by the gift, and could not thank me enough. By now the basin study was completed, indentifying several huge reservoir prospects, and the Sinclair Oil Agreement had been finalized. The next time I would see Arif would be at the signing ceremony a week hence. Or so I thought.

The day before the signing, a radio bulletin broke the news that Arif had been killed when his helicopter exploded in midair. His older brother (known to be popular with the military) had been named to succeed him as President. It was widely assumed that Arif had been assassinated, the victim—depending on the theorist—of either Nasser, the secretive Bath Party, or dissident Iraqi generals. I thought it suspicious that his helicopter blew up just as he was about to sign the Sinclair Agreement, but when I voiced this in a meeting with the new President, he was unwilling to speculate on who was behind his brother's death.

I favored the theory that Nasser had engineered it. Seeking to become leader of an Arab superstate—the United Arab Republics—he had no use for another strong leader in the region.

If the Sinclair deal had been consummated, and Arif had entered into an alliance with the U.S., it was Nasser who stood to lose. He would much prefer the maintenance of a chaotic political situation in Iraq, which he could step into as savior.

Several meetings with the successor-brother did nothing to dispel my suspicions. He obviously had no interest in reconciliation with Washington, or in honoring his brother's intentions regarding Sinclair. The deal was dead.

Later the brother was overthrown in favor of another General. Under new President Bakr, Iraq entered an era of courtship with France, which resulted in French oil companies acquiring the rights to prospects identified in Sinclair's survey. The French companies were immediately successful in finding and producing *large* quantities of crude oil. This was heartbreaking for me, since Sinclair had agreed to pay me additional compensation for my original services from their subsequent Iraqi production revenues.

While I was negotiating the concession agreement with Iraq, Steiniger gave me a second assignment. Although Sinclair had not met with a great deal of success in the Middle East, one country where it had done business was Algeria. Now Algeria, which had recently gained its independence from France in a bloody civil war, was seeking to bleed Sinclair of the revenue from its producing oil and gas fields there. Steiniger sent me to Algiers to negotiate with the new government.

Algiers was a lovely French city, situated on a low mountain sloping gently to the sea, and my hotel was equally charming. The concierge made it a point to tell me that my room had been occupied by General Eisenhower when he visited Algiers during the Second World War. There was some evidence in the city of the more recent civil war in the form of damaged buildings, etc.

Abdelsalam, the Minister of Petroleum, was one of many Algerians who had been educated in France during the colonial period. These people, who spoke French much better than Arabic, were now jockeying for power in the new government, and

I suspect tht Abdelsalam's power play with Sinclair was a way of enhancing his own prestige within the revolutionary junta.

During the negotiations it became clear to me that the new rulers had concluded that their self-interest was best served by a socialist economy. The alternative of free enterprise would disperse economic power, making it more difficult to control and personally exploit.

One of the Algerian business insiders, Mohammad Segar, lunched with me on his first visit to New York. We were at my club on the 65th floor of 30 Rockefeller Plaza, and it was a clear day. Segar parroted socialist doctrine, pausing frequently to marvel at the impressive view of Manhattan north to the George Washington Bridge. "Magnifique, magnifique," he kept repeating.

At one point his words of praise followed a particularly impassioned stream of socialist rhetoric. "What you see is all private sector, except the Park," I pointed out. Segar laughed good-naturedly, but we both knew he would never jeopardize his privileged inside position with the socialist junta by embracing capitalism.

The most objectionable of Aldelsalam's demands was that Sinclair repatriate *all* its export profits to Algerian currency and invest it in further exploration in Algeria. I think he expected me to plead that this would be an undue hardship on Sinclair. By doing this I would be tacitly accepting his frame of reference, whereupon he would magnanimously lower his repatriation demand to, say, 50% of export profits, and still essentially get his way.

I surprised him by arguing from an entirely different frame of reference—that he was pursuing a course of action against the best interests of *Algeria*. "You are telling the world oil industry to avoid Algeria because the government will seize the rewards of their success—violating the terms initially agreed upon to induce their risky investments. This is *not* in Algeria's interest and Sinclair will not participate in such policies."

Abdelsalam was clearly frustrated at his inability to outmaneuver me in this or subsequent meetings. Shortly afterwards he met Steiniger at a meeting in Paris and pointedly remarked that he could not understand why it was necessary for a big company like Sinclair to engage an outsider to negotiate for them when it had competent people already *in* Algeria. Steiniger—a nice guy but strategically naive—fell for it hook, line, and sinker. "Perhaps the Minister is right," he reported to me, and the negotiations were turned over to one of his managers in Algeria.

Abdelsalam proceeded to take Sinclair to the cleaners. The demands that I had rejected were now accepted, with the added insult that Sonatrack, the Algerian state company, hired away some of Sinclair's top local managers. Eventually Sinclair lost its reserves in the interior of Algeria, which they had discovered at their own risk and expense.

Sinclair fared much better when Steiniger listened to his own advisors. During the time I was counsel for Sinclair, I became quite close with their Chief Geologist, Fred Bush, who was urging the company to do exploratory drilling on the North Slope of Alaska. Bush's detractors attacked the idea as an irresponsibly wild gamble that would place undue strain on Sinclair's resources.

Bush often asked me to accompany him to meetings with Sinclair executives, in case they had specific questions pertaining to Iraq or Algeria, and for moral support in his battle against company skeptics. I was present when their Executive Vice President pleaded with Steiniger, "Even if we find oil, how can we possibly get it to our ocean carriers? Prudeau Bay is only reachable by sea two or three months a year, and the land route to get there goes over 900 miles of permafrost and mountains!"

Bush replied calmly and confidently, "I understand that transport will be expensive, but I am convinced we will discover a multi-billion barrel reservoir that will provide funding for it." To Steiniger's credit, he let Bush have his way, and the Prudeau Bay venture resulted in the largest oil reservoir ever discovered in America—ten billion barrels—creating more than adequate funding for the Alaskan Pipeline.

In 1968 another business deal took me back to Iraq. This time it was not an oil company that retained me, but Freeport Minerals—the world's largest producer of elemental sulphur (much in world demand for producing fertilizer). Iraq had just announced that it was inviting foreign companies to submit proposals for development and export of its large deposits of elemental sulphur at Mishrak, near the oil fields of Kirkuk. Tom Vaughn, CEO of Freeport, hired me to guide the company's efforts to acquire these rights.

Paul Douglas—Freeport's Vice President (and son of Senator Douglas of Illinois)—and I began negotiations while an impressive team of company engineers and geologists conducted an onsite feasibility study. The investigation explored the mining potential of the deposit, the practicality of surface transportation by the Baghdad-Basra Railroad, and the question of an ocean terminal for access to world markets. Other companies competing for the Mishrak were Pan American Sulphur, Acquitaine (a French company), a Polish state-owned producing company, and a politically well placed Lebanese group. Representatives of all these companies stayed at the Baghdad Hotel.

Freeport was really more interested in keeping the sulphur off the world market than in mining it themselves. Their primary fear was that someone would flood the market with it and depress prices. If Freeport didn't get the concession themselves, they wanted it in either friendly hands, or incompetent hands—i.e. a company without the knowledge or resources to get the sulphur on the market. Acquitaine was friendly: Douglas had close working relations with Chevariat, and I with Alain de Taillac, whom I had met in my Tripoli days. The Polish and Lebanese entries were not viewed as threats due to questionable resources. The one company to be feared was Pan American, Freeport's archrival.

Pan-American was represented by Robert Anderson, a Texan who had been Secretary of the Treasury under Johnson. Anderson's strategy was to magnify his own importance on the world stage. He made sure everyone knew about his contacts in the White House and his directorship of various companies—

especially Pan American Airways, which served Baghdad. Before leaving Washington, Anderson would issue a press release that he had just visited the White House, implying that he had met with the President. Then he would book himself on a plane to Cairo and issue another press release implying that he had met with President Nasser. These press releases, accepted in Baghdad as fact, were misleading if not outright fabrications. Anderson apparently never considered the possibility that his high profile strategy might backfire.

Alain made it his business to find out what the competition was up to and with whom they were gaining influence. One day he called me in a state of alarm to report that Anderson had paid out $200,000 to secure the support of various army generals and government officials. "My company has authorized me to spend only $100,000 for this purpose," he complained. "How much have you laid out?"

"Not a dime," I replied casually.

"I'm amazed!" Alain exclaimed. "Every important Iraqi official believes Freeport is favored. How have you been able to pull this off without spending any money?"

"I too have been offered help by generals and other important people here," I conceded. "My response is always that we would be grateful for their help because our company is the best qualified to undertake the project. When they directly ask me for money, I explain that it is against company policy and that the only Iraqi we pay is Mr. Shamas, for his legal services." Alain was stunned.

When I reported our conversation to Douglas, he looked at me curiously. "You must have some strategy in mind."

"My thinking," I replied, "is that money paid out prematurely creates more enemies than it does friends; no one is mad at us because they didn't get money and others did. That we would rely solely on our superior technology I believe has impressed them as well."

"Does this mean," Paul asked, "that you oppose compensation to those who help?"

"I didn't say that, did I? We haven't reached the stage to make that decision. I believe our competitors are naive in the strategy they are following."

Paul was the ideal company officer to travel with. Unfamiliar with the country and its people, he trusted me to act in his company's best interest, and supported me all the way. I remember one meeting when the government officials began speaking amongst themselves in Arabic so as not to disclose their thinking to us. Apparently they didn't want our lawyer Shamas to understand them either, because something they said in Arabic caused him to jump to his feet and rush out of the meeting. On instinct I turned to Paul and said "Let's Go!" Paul rose without questioning why and followed me to the door. Alarmed, the Iraqis pleaded with us. "Please! Why are you leaving?"

"I believe that you ordered Shamas to leave!" I replied. "As he is representing us, I believe Mr. Douglas and I should also leave."

Immediately one of the Iraqis charged down the stairs to find Shamas before he disappeared. The next day the meeting was reconvened with apologies from the Iraqis for offending us and an assurance that Shamas's presence was welcomed.

My action had been based more on principle than a burning desire to know what the Iraqis had been saying at that particular moment. I remembered Steiniger's weakness with Abdelsalam in a similar situation. I had vowed then that I would always insist on our right to choose whomever we wished as a member of our negotiating team, and to support them when challenged.

As the time neared for the Iraqi government to make their final decision, Douglas and I left the U.S. for Beirut and arrived the following morning, with plans to pick up our Iraqi visas and take the next plane to Baghdad. At the Iraqi Consulate, the officer on duty advised us that he had instructions from Baghdad *not* to issue us visas! After recovering from the shock, Paul and I agreed that there was sculduggery afoot, and that Anderson was behind it. "He's attempting a *fait accomplit*," I reasoned, "and needs to keep us out to pull it off." I decided to catch a plane to Tehran, where I hoped I would be able to get a visa. If I succeeded,

I would arrive in Baghdad the next day. Paul returned to New York.

Fortunately my plan worked. As I checked in at the Baghdad Hotel, Anderson saw me and almost fainted. Unannounced, I went immediately to the Ministry and was greeted with, "How did you get in?"

"Call it American ingenuity," I replied. "My question to you," I added angrily, "is, what are *you* up to?" The question was a rhetorical one: I knew I wouldn't get a straight answer. Leaving them to stew in their own embarrassment, I stormed out of the Ministry and returned to my hotel. I was reasonably certain that my appearance on the scene had foiled Anderson's plans.

I stayed on in Baghdad for several days, until the government's announcement that they would make no decision on the sulphur project for thirty days. As it turned out, before the thirty days was up, the government announced its choice—the Polish Sulphur Company. Freeport was far from displeased. Anderson's company could have threatened Freeport's prices and market share. The Poles, on the other hand, would take years to perfect the mining and transportation facilities needed to put the Mishrak sulphur on the world market.

A month or so later, in the lobby of the Phoenicia Hotel in Beirut, I heard my name called, and turned around to see Pan Am's Baghdad agent. "I feel lucky to be speaking to you," he exclaimed. "I just got out of an Iraqi jail. The police arrested me because of Anderson. Since he's a Director of Pan Am, they thought I was working with him on the sulphur deal. They've been following him for months.

"You wouldn't believe what's going on in Baghdad," he continued. "They've arrested three government officials and some army generals for taking bribes from Anderson. They've already been convicted and may be executed!"

"Is Mr. Shamas all right?" I asked with some trepidation.

"Oh, he's fine and so are the rest of your friends. None of them are in trouble."

I breathed a sigh of relief and thought to myself, "*That's* the way I like to do business!"

I never went back to Iraq after that. A short time later Saddam Hussein came to power, ending a decade of chaos that saw five coups. During this period of chaos, the vainglorious Shah of Iran had humiliated Iraq by imposing *his* terms regarding use of the crucial Shattal-Arab Waterways.

Unlike his predecessor generals—all products of a third-rate military training—Saddam had been trained in Egypt's finest academy and was a protege of Nassar himself. A member of the controversial Ba'ath Party, he had been wounded in a 1959 assassination attempt on Kassem, and lived in exile in Egypt until Kassem was murdered in 1963.

As soon as he took power Saddam began using Iraqi oil revenues to build an impressive military machine, and following the fall of the Shah, took advantage of what he thought would be chaos under the Khomeini regime to launch a long, bloody war against his hated neighbor. That war ended in a stalemate with over a million casualties, and a resounding defeat in Desert Storm followed that, yet despite these two national disasters Saddam remains firmly in power, sharing the notorious status of international outlaw with Ghaddafi. His longevity is due in no small part to an absolute ruthlessness in dealing with anyone he dislikes.

Nadim Tayib was an early victim of Saddam's. Nadim was a Kurd, and the Kurds were the objects of much ethnic animosity in Iraq. Because of this, and to protect his steel business in Baghdad, Nadim was discreetly apolitical, and definitely not a threat to Saddam's power in any way.

Out of necessity, Nadim traveled to Moscow every other year in order to buy steel and equipment from the Soviets. On one of these trips I accepted his invitation to join him. We were met at the Moscow Airport by his business counterpart and another person, whom Nadim identified in a whisper as "KGB."

The two men accompanied us to our hotel—the Excelsior

Hotel, across Red Square from the Kremlin—and invited themselves to a late dinner. Nadim knew what was coming and was prepared. We shared his flask of olive oil to line our stomachs against the vodka that kept flowing long after the food was gone. The KGB man's agenda was obviously focused on *me*. He revealed with great drama that like me he was Armenian, and after several hours of clinking vodka glasses, had me considering a trip with him to Armenia's capital of Yeravan and to Mt. Ararat. Nadim's olive oil allowed me to keep pace with the KGB's drinking volume until finally he succumbed, nearly passing out. That was the first and last time he appeared during my week's stay.

The Excelsior's guests included the most beautiful women in Moscow—English-speaking and as fashionable as any in Europe. To my disappointment Nadim cautioned, "These are KGB—out-of-bounds for both of us!" Even the floor maids spoke English, less surprising when Nadim explained, "They are also KGB. When they clean our rooms they make certain the 'bugs' are hidden in their proper places. Don't make any hostile or derogatory remarks about anything Russian," he warned me. The next time I looked out the window of my room overlooking Red Square, I voiced my wonder at its beauty and majesty. This very true statement came easily.

I later learned that Nadim had been executed, early in Saddam's regime. I knew he had been framed. His trips to Moscow and his Kurdish origins would have made it easy.

I also have a strong suspicion as to Saddam's motive for doing away with him. In his Baghdad home Nadim had a priceless collection of oriental rugs, purchased with profits from his steel business. I wouldn't be surprised if these rugs were in Saddam's personal residence today.

17

The Russians and their Oil

ON MY TRIP TO RUSSIA with Nadim, I had the opportunity to meet one of the high officials in the Soviet oil industry. At that time the Soviet Union was the first or second largest producer of oil and natural gas in the world—producing twelve million barrels of oil daily and a comparable quantity of gas—and the major supplier of fuel to Europe. My meeting was easily arranged with Vladimir Arutunian, Vice Chairman of Sojuznefte, the state oil company.

After we shook hands and sat down, I decided to try and break through the formalities. "You are the first Armenian I ever met with blue eyes," I told him with a smile.

Quickly, and in perfect English, he responded, "I am pure Armenian. That's why my eyes are blue. I notice *your* eyes are brown. You must have Turkish blood." We shared a hearty laugh. Then *he* took the offensive. "Your first name, Samuel, is not Armenian."

"I don't recognize Vladimir as Armenian, either," I retorted.

Laughing again, he answered, "Living in other countries, we must make some compromises, don't you agree?" Before I left he volunteered that he would soon be stationed in London to manage the Soviets' marketing in Europe, and would welcome my visit there.

As it turned out, I did meet Vladimir in London, and again in the United States, during the oil embargo of 1973. As U.S. motorists lined up at gas stations due to the fuel shortage, Soviets were desperate for grain to replace their own drought-induced shortage. Our government, looking for alternative sources of oil, negotiated a deal whereby we would sell the Soviets grain in exchange for their selling us oil.

By the time we delivered the grain, the oil embargo was over and our fuel crisis eased. Nonetheless, when the Soviets declared themselves ready to deliver their crude oil, the State Department invited Sojuznefte executives to Washington. Vladimir telephoned me to announce that he was visiting, along with his Chairman, Vaslij Merkulov, two deputies and two members of the Soviet Central Bank. "No one in our party has ever been to the United States," he explained. "We need your help to make our visit enjoyable. Also," he added, "we do not know which of your refineries on the east coast import foreign crude."

This was public information but I told Vladimir I would Telex it to him. In ten days he called again to tell me that his party of six would spend a weekend in New York before the scheduled meetings In D.C. with the State Department. "We need a good hotel. Would you arrange it?"

"By good, do you mean an average one, or the best?" I asked.

"The best, of course, with a suite for the Chairman!" he replied with some irritation.

Taking no chances on disappointing them, I chose the Pierre Hotel. On the evening of their arrival I took Arutunian and Merkulov to dinner at "21." The Chairman, a staunch Communist, asked me to show him the town—"the good and the bad," as he put it.

"We have nothing to hide," I promised him. "We have both and I will be glad to show you as much as your time allows." The next day we visited Harlem and the East Side ghettos, as well as Park and Fifth Avenues and Wall Street. With time running short, I proposed that we tour the city by helicopter, and they readily agreed.

It was a clear day. The pilot circled Manhattan just above the peaks of the skyscrapers. The Russians seemed to have a special fascination for the Statue of Liberty, and asked the pilot to circle it three times, as they took dozens of pictures. Then, as we headed up the Hudson, Merkulov pointed to downtown and asked, "Which building is David Rockefeller's?" When I pointed to the Chase building, he followed with, "So that is the biggest bank?"

"No, the *second* biggest bank," I corrected him.

"Who is biggest?" he asked.

"Citibank," I informed him. "It has a bigger building," I said, pointing to it.

"Do you know the President?" he asked me.

"Yes, he happens to be a friend of mine."

"Could you arrange for me to meet him?"

"I believe so."

"Please try. I want to meet him!" said Merkulov.

The next day I telephoned Spencer. "Do you want to meet the Russians? They met David Rockefeller in Moscow, after I told them that your bank is bigger than his, they want to meet *you*.

"Yes indeed," Spencer answered quickly. "We're having difficulty getting in there. David has the jump on us."

Spencer ordered a table for ten in the Bank's private dining room. The party included the Soviet Trade Minister and the Economic Minister from the Washington Embassy. I sat next to the latter, who had a Russian name. Imagine my surprise when, halfway through the meal, he leaned over and whispered conspiratorially in my ear, "I must tell you—I am Armenian!"

After ten days of State Department meetings there had been no progress in finding a buyer for the Soviet oil. Apparently State had raised technical questions about Soviet imports that had not been resolved. Arutunian finally asked me if I knew an Atlantic Coast refiner who might be interested in purchasing it. I knew that Ashland Oil purchased crude for its refineries, and personally knew Orin Atkins, their President. When I called and advised him of this opportunity, he was elated and arranged for a private dinner with the Russians at Washington's Madison Hotel, three days hence. At the last minute Atkins announced that he couldn't make it, and that the V.P. for Refining would take his place. The meeting was very important to the Russians. They had already overstayed their scheduled visit and did *not* want to return to Moscow without concluding a deal.

At dinner, Ashland's man was equivocating about quality, price and other alleged complications. Finally, in exasperation Merkulov retorted, "Look, I make it easy for you. At no cost to you we deliver a cargo, you refine it, you tell us what it is worth, you pay us what you want. OK?!!"

What could the VP say, other than, "Fair enough. We will give you an answer in a day or so."

Days passed, and still no word from Ashland. The Russians went home, having wasted two weeks in Washington. I was frankly puzzled by this turn of events. It seemed to me to be in our national interest to buy oil from the Russians, rather than have them gain strategic security advantages by selling it to desperate Third World countries. Ultimately I concluded that pressure on the State Department from ARAMCO shareholders had been behind the collapse of the deal. Soviet crude would compete with its own sources.

18
The Tragedy of Lebanon

DURING MY QUARTER CENTURY OF frequent travel to the Middle East, I always stopped off in Beirut, either going or coming (or both). Beirut's modern postwar Phoenicia Hotel was the crown jewel of Middle East hostelry, and always featured an international cast of guests—Arabs, Kurds, Syrians, Egyptians, Greeks, Armenians, and Turks, as well as westerners from Europe and the United States. Other westerners, including myself and many members of the world press, preferred the classic King George Hotel, which predated the first World War. Built on the shoreline of the Mediterranean, its famous dining room featured a western view of its popular beach, teeming with bathers, and a northern view of snowcapped mountains tumbling to the sea.

It was here that I usually found the Palestinian Abu Said, the resident correspondent for Time Life. Jim Bell of *Time* had introduced me to Abu Said back in the fifties, and there began a long friendship. Abu Said had skillfully established a network of reliable stringers throughout the Middle East, earning a well-deserved reputation as the best informed reporter on that region of the world. Beirut itself was a second home to hundreds of rich Gulf Arabs, who preferred the city's beauty and western culture (including indulgence in alcohol and western prostitutes) to what their native countries offered. Abu Said had ready access to their mansions, and was also welcome in the overcrowded Palestinian refugee camps located throughout Lebanon.

Despite his open support of Palestinian causes, which earned him the trust of his violently anti-Israeli brethren, Abu Said was able to keep his post at Time Life due to the support of Bell, Jim Lennon, and other Time Life executives, who viewed him as indispensable. Regardless of how one felt about the Arab-Israeli conflict, it was impossible not to recognize Said as a remarkably intelligent and dedicated man. My understanding of the Middle East and particularly of Beirut was greatly enriched by knowing him.

Beirut was truly an intellectual and cosmopolitan oasis in that vast area stretching from Rome to the Far East. It had a long tradition of great ethnic diversity, in which its various cultures, languages, and religions fertilized one another and elevated the community through high levels of achievement. American University, which educated Moslems and Christians alike in its beautiful campus overlooking the Mediterranean, was a fountain of science and culture, and intellectual stimulation.

During the first quarter century following the establishment of Israel, Beirut had remained largely aloof from the regional tensions this event precipitated. This changed in the early 1970's. As oil revenues skyrocketed, Ghadaffi of Libya and Hafez Assad of Syria began using Beirut to enhance their international visibility. Oil rich Arabs financed private armies of terrorists, recruited from the manpower surplus of the Palestinian refugee camps.

These private armies, ostensibly addressing the injustice of Israel's dispossession of the Palestinians, began eagerly employing their arms against *all* Beirut property owners, whether they were Jews or not. These owners were offered the choice of paying ransom for protection or having their property destroyed. In the late seventies, after the Phoenicia and King George Hotels had been rendered uninhabitable by the fighting, I stayed at the Bristol Hotel. When I asked the owner—from one of two or three families that owned most of the Hamrah section of Beirut—how he had escaped the bombs, his answer was brief and to the point: "Money!"

At the height of the violence, the Executive Director of UNICEF (United Nations International Children's Emergency Fund) asked me to help raise funds to supplement their inadequate relief budget. I responded to his request by establishing an organization, United States for Lebanon (USFL), to solicit funds. To add credibility to the organization, a board of Lebanese community leaders—Arabs, Armenians, and Druze Moslems, headed by Monsignor Maron—would direct the distribution of children's aid.

Senator Hubert Humphrey accepted the honorary chairmanship and was soon joined by other senators, as well as VIP's of Lebanese origin. I had the pleasure of speaking with Danny Thomas, Dr. Donald Debakey the famous heart surgeon from Houston, Joe Robbie, owner of the Miami Dolphins, and the widow of Elmer Pobst, founder of the Warner-Lambert Company.

The Pobsts had built a research library at NYU, and Mrs. Pobst, a diminutive beauty born in Lebanon, had an office there, from which she directed various philanthropic projects. She took her giving very seriously. In a private conversation with her, she told me candidly that she generally avoided contributing to relief organizations because she believed that very little of the money reached the truly needy. "Usually I contribute directly to the people in need," she informed me. "But in this case I will make an exception."

To launch the relief program, Senator Humphrey convened a meeting in the hearing room of the Senate Foreign Relations Committee. Monsignor Maron and Mr. Hratah Taroukian, representing the Lebanese committee, joined the Senator, the UNICEF Director, and me on the dais. The room was packed with Lebanese-Americans.

To my surprise and dismay the meeting soon degenerated into chaos. The audience bombarded us with one demand after another, all of them in conflict with each other. Each of the warring factions in Beirut was represented in the room, and each sought to manipulate the relief effort for its own power enhancement. To Senator Humphrey's credit, he never lost his cool. When the bell rang for a Senate roll call, the Senator rose to leave, then leaned over and whispered in my ear, "Thank God an Armenian is in charge here."

The Executive Director of UNICEF was visibly shaken by the discord and animosity in the Lebanese-American community, and withdrew UN sponsorship of USFL. The relief effort crumbled soon afterwards.

The Christian Maronites in Beirut had their own Phalangist militia, headed by the Gemayel family. Thanks to Israeli support, the Phalangists were the most heavily armed group in Lebanon, and Bushir Gemayel, son of the founder, was trying to bring the other Christian communities under Phalangist domination. If he succeeded, he felt he could effectively control the country. In return for Israeli arms and money, Gemayel offered the promise of a Lebanon that was friend and not foe to Israel.

This unholy alliance reached its climax when the Phalangists, under cover of the invading Israel army, massacred hundreds in the Beirut refugee camp of Shatila.

In spite of this, the U.S. government blindly followed the wishes of Israel and supported Gemayel for the presidency of Lebanon. In part our government was motivated by fear of Palestinian terrorism, which since the fall of the Shah had been increasingly sponsored by Iran's Shiite fundamentalists. If it took the iron hand of Gemayel to crush them, so be it, seemed to be the philosophy of our government.

After Reagan's election as President, I took advantage of my status as an "Eagle" (a contributor of $10,000 to his campaign) to request a meeting with Judge Clark, his National Security Adviser, or Clark's deputy, General William McFarland. I quickly secured an initial meeting with Deputy Howard Teicher of the Middle East section, in the old State Office Building, which housed the National Security Council.

I expressed my opinion that Gemayel represented a minority within the Christian community, that he was regarded as a gangster by the other Christians, and that his appointment as President would unify the non-Christian minorities against him. In short, we were backing the wrong horse, just as we had done earlier in Iran.

After my half-hour presentation, Teicher understood that my

knowledge of Lebanon was based on considerable personal experience, and assured me that a meeting with Judge Clark or MacFarland would soon be arranged. Before I left I inquired in a friendly manner as to Teicher's own experience in the Middle East, and almost failed to keep my composure when he replied, "I was there once, on a trip to Cairo."

Teicher never called me. I called him twice and received lame excuses as to why a meeting with Clark or McFarland had not yet been scheduled. Eventually I realized I was being given the brush-off and gave up. I felt that Teicher had been genuinely impressed at our meeting and theorized that his superiors had rejected my proposed meeting, but I will never know for sure. Later I came to realize that, without my campaign contribution of $10,000, I would not even have gotten to meet with Teicher. Had I been a $100,000 contributor, I'm sure my meeting with Clark and MacFarland would have taken place.

Soon after Gemayel maneuvered his way into the Presidency, Lebanon's internal chaos worsened. Probably under pressure from American supporters of the Phalangists, the White House agreed to support Gemayel with a "peacekeeping unit of Marines," and the presence of U.S. warships off the coast.

When I learned that the Marines barracks were near the airport, on the road from Beirut, I was outraged. I had travelled that road many times, and knew that was it was within easy reach of mortar fire from the nearby foothills. Later I read that McFarland had personally visited this barracks.

As we know now, the Lebanese opponents of Gemayel had bigger plans in mind than simply sniping at the Marines from the hills. Several days after MacFarland's visit, a suicide bomber drove his truck into the marine compound, killing over 200 of our troops. It took a tragedy of this magnitude for the message get through to the National Security Council and the White House. Now under pressure from the American public, Reagan ordered a complete pull-out. Shortly after the Americans left, Gemayel was forced to abandon his ambitious plans for minority rule. None of this seems to have affected the reputations of Teicher and his colleague Kemp, who still appear frequently on television newscasts, billed as "Middle East experts."

19

Iran Revisited

AFTER LEAVING IRAN IN 1954 I had no further business activity there until the early 1970's. However, from time to time during this period I would stop in Tehran on the way to or from Karachi or Baghdad. I always visited with Nemazee, who continued to develop the Shiraz Medical Center and waterworks, as well as a number of other major projects, e.g. textile mills, cement factories, and the General Motors distributorship. He was always proudest of the Shiraz endeavors, and minimized his considerable achievements in the business world. To the Iranians he was a miracle worker, a stature that he did not feel entirely comfortable with, since he was well aware of the dangers of upstaging the Shah.

On my visits I sometimes stayed at the city's first modern American-style hotel, the Royal Tehran Hilton, built by the Shah's Pahlavi Foundation on the slopes of Albourz Mountain, overlooking the city. The Hilton-trained staff was all Iranian, and performed up to the highest international standards. Dressed in their native costumes, they exuded pride in being Iranian, and loved the American guests.

I had other Iranian friends besides Nemazee. One of them was Parviz Raens. I had first met him in 1953 when he was the Iranian stringer for Don Schwind of AP and Jim Bell of Time. On my occasional visits in the fifties and sixties he would update me on Iran's evolution from a desperately impoverished Third World country to an ostentatious player on the world stage. Most of the ever-increasing oil revenues seemed to go towards maintaining the Shah's obscenely lavish lifestyle. I believe it was Parviz who told me that the Shah secretly gave himself a large annual royalty as compensation for *his* services in the oil settlement.

The old palace where I had visited the Shah in Tehran was no longer good enough for him. He had built a huge new one in Shimron, with a soccer field and all imaginable luxuries. As the years rolled by, he built still newer palaces in southern Iran, on the Gulf, and on the Caspian Sea.

After the Arab-Israeli War of 1967, Washington all but declared its dependence on the Shah, and he became increasingly imperial. Awed by public displays of modern air force planes and the latest in ground equipment (purchased from the U.S. with U.S. aid), the native population began to believe that he really was the "Shah-en-Shah" (King of Kings), as he called himself.

To enhance his image outside Iran, the Shah relied on imperial personal visits to the world's principal capitals, and extravagant spending by his ambassadors. In Washington, the city of embassies, Iran overwhelmed the capital's diplomatic society with extravaganzas unmatched by even the Europeans. Iranian Ambassador from the late sixties into the seventies was my old friend Arteshir Zahedi, who had served as my bodyguard during the oil negotiations. Arteshir had divorced the Shah's daughter shortly after their marriage, but this did not adversely affect his former father-in-law's admiration and reliance upon him.

Arteshir's job was to curry favor with Washington's elected and appointed officials, press, and society elite by means of lavish entertainment. A combination of flamboyant cowboy (reflecting his days at the University of Colorado) and sophisticated diplomat, Arteshir was the ideal host for the Shah's purpose. Tall, dark, and handsome, he attracted Hollywood stars, and was romantically linked with—among others—Elizabeth Taylor, adding lustre to his public image.

By 1970 I was well out of the D.C. social circle. So when I ran into Cedric Foster at Washington's Mayflower Hotel early that year, I was surprised when he greeted me with, "I suppose you're here for Arteshir's party at the Embassy."

"No, I wasn't invited," I replied. A short while later I received a phone call from Arteshir, urging me to attend. Unknownst to me, Cedric had called him to let him know I was in town.

When I arrived at the Iranian Embassy that evening, I found Massachusetts Avenue and the surrounding streets lined with cars for blocks. A thousand guests were in attendance. The reception line extended from the main hall through the lobby and out onto the street. As I reached the lobby, Arteshir saw me, stopped greeting guests, and came to me at the lobby entrance. He proceeded to kiss me on both cheeks (the warmest of Iranian greetings), and take me by the hand right into the main hall, informing his curious guests enroute that, "This man has made great contributions to the Iranian oil settlement, and to the establishment of the Shiraz Medical Center!"

As I circulated among the guests that evening, several times I found Arteshir at my side. Toward the end of the party he insisted that I remain after to talk with him before returning to New York. I did, and in the wee hours of the morning he regaled me at length with boasts of Iran's great wealth, rapid industrialization, and progress in westernizing its people.

Taking advantage of our close friendship in Tehran during the embargo, I spoke candidly, raising doubts about the wisdom of spending so much for opulent parties in view of the country's widespread poverty, and stating frankly that I found such extravagance personally distasteful. He smiled, and told me not to be concerned: with oil revenues and generous American aid, there was plenty to go around. That was my last visit to the Iranian Embassy, although I continued to run across Arteshir in other settings.

In 1971 the Shah reached his megalomanic zenith by staging the greatest extravaganza in the history of the planet. The celebration, held in Persepolis, was ostensibly to honor Iran's great Emperors of antiquity, Darius and Cyrus, but by claiming them as his ancestors (a preposterous falsehood), he in effect became the living honoree. Thousands of the world's leaders were invited to attend—all expenses paid—and many of the world's top entertainers were hired to perform. This week-long event necessitated not only housing, but also infrastructure—water, sewerage, and roads—at an estimated cost of 100-200 million dollars. When I heard of this, I couldn't help but remember the Iranians I had seen crammed into the Shiraz poorhouse. I seriously doubt that *any* of Iran's new-found oil wealth had reached them.

Another Iranian with whom I maintained contact was Reza Fallah, the Shah's oil minister. I had known both Reza and his colleague Bagher Mostofi since the days of the embargo, when they were young engineers suddenly thrust into management of the Abadan Refinery.

The last time I saw Fallah was in 1972, when I stopped off in Tehran to visit Nemazee. Reza heard I was in town and called on me at the Royal Tehran Hilton with a lady friend. After tea and an exchange of pleasantries, he asked if I would like to see his new house in the exclusive section of Shimran. I replied that I would like that very much, and a few moments later we drove off in his Mercedes.

After ascending into the Albourz foothills, we arrived at an ornate gate and guardhouse. Inside we passed through an extensive garden, finally arriving at not a house but a palace fit for a King, with fountains and flowers everywhere. (There were literally *thousands* of roses!) Its walls were covered with the classic blue Persian tile found in famous mosques.

Inside Reza showed off his enormous banquet hall, and followed that with a tour of many of the thirty or so rooms, all furnished in regal splendor. Dumbfounded at first, I finally asked Reza, "Does the Shah come to visit?"

"Oh yes," he answered proudly. "He loves to come here. He has often congratulated me on my good taste. You know, this cost me eleven million dollars."

I knew that Fallah also had apartments in London and New York. "An amazing accomplishment," I thought to myself, "for a man who has always been in the employ of government agencies."

(Fortunately for Reza, he was in London when Khomeini took over. Today Lillie Lawrence, his daughter, is well known in New

York for her fervent support of workers' causes as well as her fabulous wealth, which is explained as coming from her father, "an oil baron.")

By the late sixties the Shah realized that he could up the ante on new oil concessions in Iran, and had Fallah structure a bidding contest for offshore areas, requiring bonus payments and heavy drilling obligations, with no assurance as to the levels at which production would be taxed.

During this period I was on retainer by Sinclair, who sought my recommendation as to whether they should join a consortium to bid on some of these areas. I counseled against it, reasoning that if Iran reserved the unilateral right to fix the tax burden on the participating oil companies, it was unlikely to be a fair one. Sinclair took my advice, and later was glad they had, since all companies that bid on the offshore areas ended up losing money on the oil they produced.

Soon after I left Sinclair I was approached by Leon Hess, CEO of Amerada, who asked if I would act as his Middle East negotiator.

"Why do you need me to negotiate for you?" I asked. "Your own reputation as a negotiator is legendary!"

He smiled. "I guess you heard about my Virgin Islands deal."

"Yes, but not in any detail," I hinted, with genuine curiosity. I knew that he had secured an ideal harbor site in St. Croix for a large oil refinery he planned to build, but that was all I knew.

"A middle-aged widow owned the property," he began. "My men had tried for months to purchase it from her, but they weren't getting anywhere. I have to admit I was getting impatient. So I packed a large suitcase with crisp new hundred dollar bills and flew down to St. Croix in the company plane.

"When I got there I telephoned her and asked if I could drop by and talk with her. I think the fact that I was the CEO made an impression on her, because she sounded enthusiastic when she said that she would love to see me.

"We chatted over tea for a few minutes, and then, without

warning, I said to her 'I am dead serious about buying your property.' At that moment I opened my suitcase. The packs of hundred dollar bills must have looked like they were jumping out at her. Her jaw almost dropped to the floor of her veranda.

"'Just tell me how much you want,' I said. 'Name your price and I'll pay it...*and* I'll leave this suitcase and its contents with you.'

"She gave me a number, we shook hands and agreed to let our lawyers work out the details. And that was that."

I sat there shaking my head. "Leon, no one but you could have done that piece of work. What on earth do you need me for?"

"I'll tell you," he replied. "That one worked, but in Iran, the Shah all but took my hide. I had been negotiating with Fallah on an offshore block, and he was demanding terms that were outrageous. I was just about to leave for home without a deal when I received a gold-embossed invitation for a private meeting with the Shah. Sam, going to that meeting was one of the worst mistakes I've ever made! The Shah flattered me and painted this glorious picture of our future working together. Then he stuck out his hand and said, 'We have a deal!'

"Like a fool I shook it and said, 'Yes'. I don't know what came over me! We found oil all right, but it was lousy—low gravity, high sulphur, low pressure—and with the taxes that Fallah hit me with there was no way I could make any money! It was too late to pull out, so we ended up taking a tremendous loss.

"If I had had a negotiator in Tehran," Hess went on to say, "he could have told his Majesty that the decision was mine, and my decision would have been 'no deal.' Sam, as a Jew, I have great difficulty in negotiating with the Arabs. That's why I need *you*."

"Leon," I answered, "you are mistaken. As long as you have what the Arabs want, they'll negotiate with you. If you don't raise the Jewish question, they won't raise it either."

From the story Leon had told me, I got the impression that he wanted a messenger more than anything. It was clear that he was not going to delegate serious negotiations to *any*one else. Around that same time Leon's friend Ed Carey, of New England

Petroleum, asked me to negotiate the purchase and delivery of a shipment of Libyan crude oil, and I accepted his offer instead. In the early seventies, Freeport CEO Tom Vaughn asked me if I could investigate a suspected source of sulphur in Iran. "We get smatterings of information about a huge deposit, but I can't get any confirmation, even through Admiral (Arleigh) Burke, who's on our board *and* Texaco's. He tells us he can't get *any* information from Texaco about their operations in Iran: it's all very secretive. Do you think you could find out what's going on through *your* contacts?"

I promised to try, and proceeded to telephone Monte Pennell in Tehran. Monte, who was then manager of operations for the Iran consortium, invited me for a visit and said that after our meeting, he might be able to arrange for an official visit by Freeport.

Monte was completely forthcoming about the mysterious sulphur find. "We found sulphur all right, but very nearly created a catastrophe doing it. The Shah was behind it, as you might suspect. No amount of production is ever enough to satisfy him! He had the bright notion that since the Sulieman fields were still gushing after sixty years, that there must be great reservoirs of oil at even deeper levels. I had always believed that the Sulieman oil was produced by gas drive, and gas at those deep levels we don't need.

"But BP wouldn't listen to me, and to appease the Shah they went ahead and drilled a deep test well. Sure enough, the well blew out of control with gas so poisonous as to kill every living being for miles around! We couldn't get close enough to it to cap it, so we set it on fire to burn off the gas and sulphur, and drilled a relief well directionally to intercept the flow of the original test well. *This* well we were able to cap, but soon we faced yet another hazard. The old Sulieman wells suddenly began doubling and tripling their production! Obviously the gas from the deeper structure was pouring into the shallow oil reservoirs. "At first we welcomed the additional oil, but then we saw the overburden rising to dangerous levels. To avoid a blow-off from the old wells, we decided to flare the relief well. This whole thing has been going on for over two years now, with no reduction in the rate of gasflow. The gas reservoir must be *enormous*.

"As it happens, Freeport's interest is very timely. The government has decided to build a chemical plant so that the sulphur and gas doesn't continue to go to waste. The Shah's chemical advisor is Mostofi. I believe you know him?"

"Very well," I replied. "We are good friends."

"Good," Monte answered. "I will arrange for the government's chemical company to invite Freeport over."

When I brought this news back to Freeport, they welcomed me as a hero. Soon afterwards an invitation from Mostofi arrived. In the old days of prop aircraft and primitive hotel accomodations, a journey to Tehran was not particularly attractive, but with modern jet service and the elegant Royal Tehran Hilton awaiting us, more of the Freeport executives wanted to go than the company could take. Finally six men besides myself were selected. Paul Douglas led the group, which included Freeport's general counsel and four engineers.

The day after our arrival, Monte Pennell invited us to a briefing session conducted by BP's chief geologist. The following day, Mostofi arranged for one of the Shah's private planes to take us to the site of the relief well in central Iran. It was an awesome sight—a thousand foot column of fire so hot we could not get closer than several hundred yards.

From there we flew over the route a gas pipeline might take south to the sea. We had lunch at Abadan and viewed the world's largest refinery, and in the afternoon flew east along the coast, past several harbors, finally arriving at the new port of Kharg Island, where four of the world's largest oil tankers were loading aboard crude. Kharg Island could load eight million barrels of oil a day. The facility's gigantic dimensions were accentuated by its isolation in a barren landscape.

To complete the day, we flew back to Tehran. After dark we could see hundreds of wells flaring and brightening the sky, as gas pushed the oil up out of the ground and into fuel tanks, from whence it would go via pipeline to Kharg, and via ocean tanker to all parts of the world.

The next evening Mostofi put on an elegant banquet for us. After dinner he made a speech in which he praised my earlier contributions to Iran, and welcomed Freeport to consider building a chemical plant, using this plentiful high sulphur gas as its source. "Come back to us," he said, "with a proposal for a fruit basket of many products!" Before we left Mostofi assured me that Freeport would have preference over any other company.

We knew what Mostofi had meant by a "fruit basket of many products." He expected such a chemical plant to produce ammonia and a number of other hydrocarbon-based chemicals. But after careful research Freeport concluded that such a "fruit basket" was not economically feasible, and their proposal was rejected as too limited. Soon afterwards Mostofi accepted the bid of Allied Chemical, who did propose a more bountiful fruit basket, and agreed to invest fifty million dollars in the construction of the chemical plant that would produce these "fruits."

Several years later Fred Bissinger, a neighbor of ours in Bronxville and recently appointed CEO of Allied, made the decision to withdraw from the Iran project and forsake the fifty million dollar investment. He lamented to me that his predecessor had succumbed to the urging of J. Howard Marshall, an aggressive promoter of international oil and mineral deals, and committed to the overly ambitious project, which could not be made profitable.

In the early seventies I was also retained by a U.S. manufacturer who had shipped a boatload of pipeline coating to Iran. Although it was made according to U.S. specifications, the Iran National Oil Company (INOC) informed the manufacturer that they were rejecting the shipment as defective, unless a large payment were made to the American company's Iranian agent. This was not uncommon in foreign countries, and was in effect a request for a bribe. At this point I was called in.

I counseled against any payment or attempts at legal action, and asked for an opportunity to straighten out the situation directly with Fallah, who was Chairman of the Board of INOC. I suspected that the U.S. company's agent was an accomplice in this extortion attempt and should not be trusted.

When I arrived in Iran, Fallah greeted me warmly. I was convinced that he had no prior knowledge of the situation, which he promised to look into. A short time later he advised me to go along with the requested payment as the easiest way out. It was obvious he was not about to ring the bell on his colleagues.

I wrung a promise from Reza that if my client, Plymouth Rubber, chose not to pay the tribute, they could take back the shipload without penalty. We shook hands to seal the agreement. Fallah was certain Plymouth would pay, and was very surprised when they repossessed the coating for sale in the U.S. Nonetheless he kept his word and ordered that the ship be allowed to sail with all its cargo. I found out later that INOC had to pay a much higher price to replace the supplies—a price which I'm sure factored in their kickback.

In the 1970's crude oil prices skyrocketed from $3 to $50 per barrel, thanks to OPEC and the collusion of the international oil companies, who realized they too would benefit from the artificially created price hikes. (The major price hawk was the Shah himself, in spite of annual Iranian oil revenues approaching a hundred *billion* dollars.) Oil spokesmen, including managers of large oil companies that knew better, argued that "the supply of oil is finite; we are running out of oil!" And after the very effective Arab oil embargo of 1973, most Americans believed them. A common prediction was that crude oil prices would stabilize at $100 per barrel.

I decided to address this perception in a speech I gave at the 1974 convention of the National Association of Tax Accountants. Invited by Ted Romak, a partner at Arthur Young, I addressed the 2000 accountants in the main ballroom of the Waldorf Astoria in New York. My message was simple and clarion: "The supply of oil is *not finite* as most of you believe; higher price levels will make it possible to put existing technology to work that will produce profitable oil:

1) in hostile arctic environments, transporting it hundreds of miles to sea terminals (e.g. Alaska's North Slope and Russia);

2) in jungles, using equipment flown in to drill sites (e.g. in the Andes, Venezuela, New Guinea, and Indonesia);

3) in the sea at depths of up to a mile (e.g. the Gulf of Mexico); and

4) in ocean waters now deemed too treacherous to explore (e.g. Great Britain, Norway, the North Sea, and China).

"Moreover," I told them, "at current OPEC price levels oil companies will undertake secondary and tertiary engineered production facilities to recover half the oil left in reservoirs after primary production."

Accompanying my address were charts and tables, prepared for me by Dr. Frank Mlynarczyk of City Bank, on the areas in which I predicted production would increase. The ultimate effect of the increased production would of course be a lowering of oil prices to more traditional levels. My predictions were not popular with my audience; evidently they did not want to be shaken from their belief that the oil price honeymoon would go on forever. The press likewise gave my speech short shrift—relegating it to a few lines on the back pages of the *New York Times* and *Wall Street Journal*.

After the price hikes of 1973, the oil industry in the American Southwest entered an era of unprecedented and ultimately disastrous expansion. Within ten years, despite OPEC's efforts to buttress prices at the highest possible levels, oil from the predicted new sources created a surplus, driving prices below ten dollars a barrel. The consequence of this oil "binge," based on the notion that "the supply of oil is finite," was that businesses, and especially banks, went bust all through the Southwest, with the bank bailout ultimately costing U.S. taxpayers many billions of dollars.

OPEC was forced to cut back its production from a high of

forty million barrels a day to below twenty million. In recent years, world oil prices have ranged from fifteen to twenty dollars per barrel. OPEC supplies an average of twenty-five million barrels a day, with the remaining forty-two million barrels of daily world consumption produced by countries outside the cartel.

On one of my last social visits to Tehran, I received a call from my old friend Ali Mansour, who had been Deputy Foreign Minister during my first stint in Iran. In recent national elections Mansour had led a new political party to majority control of the Majlis, and was now Prime Minister, supposedly with the Shah's blessing. He invited me to a private dinner at his home, and I accepted.

Unlike many in politics, Ali aspired to be a true statesman. Although he had been educated in France, Ali was more interested in establishing an American-style democracy in Iran, which he believed would strengthen the Shah's public support. He had delved into the American political process and had many questions for me. His beautiful young wife was fascinated when I told her about Patricia's involvement in the League of Women Voters, and expressed her fervent desire that Iranian women similarly participate in the political process.

Ali also questioned me at length about my experience in the Marshall Plan. He was particularly interested in its efficiency and avoidance of corruption. The evening ended with Ali urging me to remain in Iran for awhile before returning to the States. "Would you tour the country," he asked, "and help me develop a schedule of priorities for expanding public participation in the democratic process?"

I explained that business obligations necessitated my immediate return to New York, but that I would be happy to help him when I was free, in about a month. Ali thanked me profusely, and we shook hands and said good night.

Before the month's end Mansour was fatally shot on the steps of the Majlis. The event saddened me, but it did not come as a total surprise. The "King of Kings" obviously did not share Ali's enthusiasm for democracy, and viewed him as a possible threat. It was not the first time that a popular political leader in Iran had been assassinated, and I doubted it would be the last.

After Mansour's demise, I continued to visit his chief of cabinet, Dr. Karem Bahadouri, a Ph.D. from the University of Michigan, who had joined the royal staff as Minister to the Queen. During our lunches at Shimron Palace, I hoped for inside information on the circumstances of Ali's death, but none was forthcoming. Later I realized that the palace was probably bugged.

On one of my last visits with Nemazee, he told me with a great sense of relief that he had donated the Shiraz projects to the Shah's Pahlavi Foundation. I don't recall whether his gift occurred after Mansour's assassination or before, but I do know that Nemazee was keenly aware that *any* leader who became highly prominent would be regarded by the Shah as a threat. Hence he had, especially in more recent years, shunned the press and the publicity of radio and television.

When I visited Tehran in 1972 I was shocked to hear that Nemazee was dead. According to his son Hassan, he had come down with a minor illness and entered a Tehran hospital, where he was misdiagnosed. Treated for an ailment he didn't have, he died suddenly. Had he gone to his own hospital at Shiraz, he would almost certainly have been treated properly and released. It struck me as a tragic irony that Nemazee, who was responsible for bringing modern medicine to this part of the world, should have met such an end.

Soon after this, in Tehran. I dinned with Hassan, his sister Suzie, and several of their young Iranian friends. Discussion was lively and disagreement heated over Iran's future. Disgusted by widespread corruption under the Shah, Suzie vehemently advocated a return to traditional Moslem values, and championed the idea of Aytollah Khomeini, an exiled cleric living in France.

Hassan, on the other hand, was dispassionate. He was getting out and cashing in. It was the ideal time. The rial was convertible at an historic high of almost five dollars. His plan was to liquidate his father's textile and cement operations, which he had just inherited. The next time I saw him was in Houston, where he was busy building a skyscraper. I couldn't help but wonder how two siblings—close in age, both born in D.C. and educated at Friends School and Harvard—could be so different in their feelings toward Iran.

In the early and mid-1970's the Shah was on a roll. Everything he did made news. Thanks to U.S. aid, both in military hardware and training, the Shah was able to humiliate neighboring Iraq and its new dictator Saddam Hussein, by forcing him to accept onerous terms regarding the common use of the Shattal-Arab Waterway to the Gulf. For the first time Iran was building a naval presence. As a U.S. surrogate, Iran was becoming the regional military giant. How had this happened?

American aid to the Shah had jumped to new levels after the election of Nixon as President in 1968. The relationship between Nixon and the Shah actually started back in 1953, when Nixon visited Iran as Vice President. After that Nixon played a critical role in Washington's replacing 10 Downing Street as the driving force in resolving the oil naturalization dispute.

Later, after Nixon had lost both the 1960 presidential race and the 1962 campaign for the California governorship, the Shah was one of the few heads of state to receive him when he embarked on a world tour. The Shah's reception of Nixon during his darkest days, when most considered him a political has-been, sealed a deep friendship between them.

Henry Kissinger and Bill Rogers, as Nixon's National Security Advisor and Secretary of State, were largely ignorant about the Middle East, but sensed that we needed another strong ally (besides Israel) in the region to counterbalance the growing alienation of the Arab oil states after their defeat by Israel in the 1967 war. Increased aid enabled the Shah to begin his military buildup, which accelerated after Israel's 1973 humiliation of their Arab neighbors led to even greater Arab hostility toward America.

To American security strategists, the rule of the Shah had become critical to securing Gulf oil for the United States and our allies in Europe and the Far East. Iran could also serve as a buffer against threatened Soviet expansion in the region. Iran looked like an ideal ally for many reasons, not the least of which was that its population was greater than the combined populations of all other Arab countries in the Middle East, exclusive of Egypt. What our strategists didn't realize, however, is that most of Iran's large population were indifferent to or hated the Shah.

The Shah's public declarations about turning Iran into an industrial nation had caused an unprecedented migration from the villages to the cities. International companies did build local factories, but jobs were being created at a much slower rate than the migration, resulting in great urban poverty. Living conditions for most were primitive. Tehran was gradually being piped for water and sewerage, but hardly at the pace of the city's skyrocketing growth.

The oil driven economy escalated the prices of goods workers had to buy, while high unemployment rates kept wages fixed. Hence even those with jobs were poor, and the age-old "master-serf" mentality dominated employer-worker relations in the factories. As the urban immigrants struggled with their poverty, they witnessed the wealth exhibited by their "masters"—the Shah and his palace retinue, and those merchants, traders, agents of foreign companies, bureaucrats, and military brass who benefited from the explosion in oil revenues. This new class of super-rich Iranian became ever more flagrant in flaunting their wealth and ignoring or mistreating the urban poor. Meanwhile the Shah accepted the pandering of these sycophants as evidence of his national popularity.

Worker protests were dealt with severely as unpatriotic. The government's response was disciplinary rather than remedial—an easy choice for a military monarchy with a master-serf tradition. Action against protesters by the military and the Savak—the Shah's Gestapo-like secret police, trained by the U.S.—fomented more protests in marketplaces throughout the city, in a downward spiral of chaos and repression.

Carter, like Nixon and Ford before him, also became enamored of the Shah. His State Department, CIA, and military sources assured him that the Shah was the bulwark of Middle East security, and he believed them. Never mind that the Shah had laid claim to neighboring Bahrain, humiliated Iraq, and denigrated other oil monarchs to the south and east, and never mind that his public support (always exaggerated) was at its nadir. All these warning signs were ignored, as was the growing popularity of Khomeini. Convential wisdom held that the Shiite clergy had never been a credible force, and would not be now.

In late 1978, a diplomat in residence at the University of Virginia, asked me what I thought would happen in Iran, where he had served the State Department. My reply was simple: "The Shah will be out of there by year's end."

"How can you say that," he asked with a shocked look, "given his police and military?"

"I say that because the Shah's public support is far lower now than in the Mossadegh days. When so many of his people are looking to an aged, infirm, medieval cleric like Khomeini as their savior, you must assume they are fed up with the Shah. And don't count on the police or military to save the Shah. I suspect they're having their own doubts about him. When the final uprising comes, they will not shoot their own people. That is my prediction."

By the time the Shah's palace command recognized that the police and military were becoming sympathetic to the plight of the workers, it was too late to replace disciplinary action with remedial programs. Iran was in need of an alternative civic leader to address the chaos in the country, but given the Shah's animosity to such a figure, there was none. The Shah stood alone.

Khomeini had depicted him as having betrayed the common man while he pursued his own riches. Finally the Shah could withstand Khomeini's propaganda barrage no longer, and went into exile again—this time never to return. Without opposition Khomeini stepped into the leader's role and the United States went from the frying pan into the fire.

We have only ourselves to blame for the rising tide of Islamic fundamentalism now sweeping the Middle East. Based on our support of Israel and the Shah, Khomeini and his heirs have successfully portrayed America as "the Great Satan," and Iran is now a primary sponsor of international terrorism. Ironically, the billions of dollars worth of military hardware supplied to Iran by the United States came into the hands of the Shiite government after the Shah fled the country, and I imagine much of it still exists even after Iran's decade-long war with Iraq. As I reflect on these tragic developments, I can't help but wonder how events might have played out, had we not turned our backs on Mossadegh in his time of need.

20

Korea and the Weeks Disappointment

TOM HINKLE, A LAWYER IN my office (and formerly an attorney for Esso), had represented Lewis G. Weeks, retired Chief Geologist for Esso, and after Hinkle's death in 1969 Lewis kept in touch with me as he sought new business opportunities in his field. Several years earlier he had induced a large Australian oil company, Broken Hills Proprietaries (BHP), to stop drilling onshore in Australia and concentrate on the Bass Straits, off southern Australia. After supervising a seismic survey, Lewis persuaded Esso to take a half-interest in the large concession. For his services BHP had granted Weeks an overriding royalty of two and a half percent. Fabulous reserves of oil *and* gas were discovered in the Bass Straits. Unfortunately for Lewis, production (oil alone eventually reached 400,000 barrels a day) did not begin until after his death.

Lewis devoted his last years to finding another Bass Straits, and I incorporated Weeks Associates as the vehicle by which we would jointly pursue this goal. The Maresis, who both came from wealthy families (Phoebe Cornell Maresi was heiress to an IBM fortune), loaned us half a million dollars, which served as the bulk of our capital, supplementing the modest cash from the founders' shares Weeks and I had purchased. For Weeks's convenience we rented and furnished an office near his home in Westport, Connecticut, and also engaged a geologist of his choice, named Douglas Klemme.

Weeks was a religious man and frequently attended prayer meetings with Paul Temple, who was employed by ESSO in Spain.

For reasons not clear to me at the time, Lewis urged me to meet Temple in Barcelona, on one of my trips abroad. The meaning of this became evident when Temple told me that he too was retiring from ESSO, and would soon join Weeks. I welcomed him aboard, and upon learning that he had graduated from Princeton—as had Pompeo Maresi—I asked him to join me on a visit to the Maresi family estate, on Lake Como in Italy.

He consented, and the Maresis cordially hosted us and our wives for two days. Temple explained to our financier that he had tired of his role as executive of a giant corporation, and looked forward to the challenge of building an oil company from the ground up.

Soon after our trip to Italy, Temple retired from ESSO and Weeks brought him into the company as President. Temple had already been pursuing additional financing for the company through a Princeton connection at Donaldson-Lufkin, and we were all pleased when this came through. So it came as something of a shock when I then received a phone call from Pompeo, informing me—without going into detail—that he had investigated Temple and wanted nothing to do with him. "Please return my $500,000 loan as soon as possible," he requested. Stunned, I complied immediately. Now *I* had serious doubts about Temple, but since he had Weeks's confidence I could not simply walk away from him, as had Pompeo.

Lewis's questionable judgment was demonstrated by an incident shortly afterwards. Bob Abplanalp, my primary benefactor during my run for Congress, was intrigued by the oil business, and knew of Weeks's exalted reputation. Expressing confidence in both Weeks and myself, he told me that he might be interested in becoming involved with Weeks Associates. Before we could discuss just what form his involvement might take, Weeks called me to say that an inventer friend of his, whom he knew well from his church and as a neighbor, had perfected a remarkable invention. This device could record the density of hydrocarbons released into the atmosphere from oil and gas deposits deep below the surface of the earth. A low-flying aircraft equipped with this device could pinpoint these oil and gas fields. Whoever possessed the device, called "the Black Box," would never have to worry about drilling a dry hole again.

Knowing that Bob funded a modest research lab at Precision Valve Company, I thought that he and his technical people should have a look at this device. Weeks brought his friend, a Yale alumnus from Oklahoma, to Precision's offices in Yonkers, where he gave a persuasive theoretical explanation of his technical breakthrough. However, he was adamant that the Black Box itself could not be inspected. "I will *not* share my secret," he stated emphatically, "but I will use it for my clients." The meeting adjourned subject to further consideration.

Later, while out of the country, I learned that Weeks' friend had pursued a deal with Precision directly, and that the company, without further investigation, had already made an initial payment to him of $50,000. Apparently Abplanalp had authorized the payment on the basis of Weeks's endorsement and my introduction.

When I returned from abroad I found an unsolicited check for $5,000, which was for "expenses." I became even more uneasy when I picked up my phone one day and heard this firend's wife talking intimately with another man *about* her husband. This comical wiring error alerted me that my phone was being tapped, probably by the FBI. Abplanalp admitted that he had used his connections to precipitate an investigation of Owens. The investigation, now completed, had revealed that ESSO had earlier examined and rejected a similar device, and that an application for a patent on it had been turned down.

Despite the fact that I had had no involvement in the fiasco beyond making the initial introduction, and had had no further contact about the Black Box, I realized that my integrity had been tarnished, and immediately sent Bob the check I had received. Precision also demanded return of the rest of the $50,000.

I was surprised that Weeks had not been able to see through the "black box," and it puzzled me even further that he was apparently ignorant of ESSO's history with the device. To ask him directly about it would have come off as accusatory. In retrospect, I attribute these lapses to his advanced age and failing memory.

Fortunately this event did not end my friendship with Abplanalp, but it certainly didn't enhance it, either. When the subject came up in a later meeting with Precision's executives, they insinuated that I had been derelict. "I just made an introduction so you could investigate it!" I objected. "Next time," one of the men retorted, "*you* investigate it before you make the introduction to *us*!"

By the time I made my decision not to run for Congress in 1970, these unpleasant episodes were behind me and an exciting new possibility had opened up for Weeks Associates. I had brought to Lewis's attention a news piece in Platts Oilgram, the daily industry report that I subscribed to. Wendell Phillips had just acquired rights to a huge concession in South Korea, located in the East China Sea south of the Korean island of Chechu. Lewis responded with rare animation. "That's the most promising area in the north Pacific! You know Phillips. Try to reach him and work out a position for us."

Before meeting with Phillips, which would be easy, I found out all I could about Phillips's concession. I discovered that all the offshore areas within South Korea's undisputed jurisdiction had been recently leased to the major oil companies. Despite the fact that parts of his concession area were claimed by either Japan or China, Phillips had determined that South Korea could legitimately claim the entire area (25,000 square miles!), and had taken up residence in Seoul's Chosen Hotel to convince the government to enact such legislation. I later learned that in this pursuit he had engaged two Koreans, Charlie Oh and his sister. Charlie's sister was particularly helpful, as she had enjoyed a close personal relationship with President Syngman Rhee since before the Korean War.

Phillips, Weeks, and I met in the Sky Club, of which I was a member, atop the PanAm Building in Manhattan. Phillips expressed his pleasure at meeting Weeks, and was obviously pleased that the renowned geologist shared his appraisal of the area's prospects. Then, without small talk, he made his position clear. Phillips wanted to assign his concession right to an oil company or companies that had the capital and technology to undertake offshore ocean exploration and drilling. In return he wanted a passive overriding royalty of two and a half percent.

"I did my homework," he volunteered, "and know that Nakasian has the experience to take on this project." Before the meeting ended, Phillips had given us his word that he would work solely with us, and not make any parallel efforts. I had to work fast. By the terms of Phillips's agreement with the Koreans, he had to make a good-faith down payment of $100,000 by a certain date, and that date was fast approaching. Phillips expected the participating companies to come up with it.

The majors all had varying interests in Japan and did not want to jeopardize them by involvement in this project. Phillips had already approached them and received unequivocal rejections, so this simplified the course of action I would pursue.

First I set up a meeting with one of the Hamilton Brothers of Tulsa, who owned an independent company with a history of deep-water exploration and drilling. In the meeting I clearly outlined the problem of Japan's rival claim and suggested that before any substantial expenditures were incurred, we should pursue the possibility of a joint development treaty between Korea and Japan.

"Could this be achieved?" Hamilton asked. I argued that given the almost total reliance of both countries on foreign oil, it was in their common interest. With Japan's capital and technology, combined with Korea's cheap labor, it was very viable from an economic standpoint. I further assuaged his doubts by promising that any agreement I negotiated would provide that drilling be deferred until a joint development treaty was signed. Hamilton agreed to accept a 25% working interest in the project contingent upon my finding other acceptable companies to put up the remaining 75%. Weeks committed company money for another 25%, and for the remaining half I approached—at the suggestion of William Spencer of Citibank—D.K. Ludwig, the shipping magnate, who was eager to invest some of the enormous cash flow from his tanker business, Universe Tankers. Ludwig was ecstatic. Where else could they invest in such a huge drilling area in a pro-American part of the world? The one negative was China, whose claim lay in the western part of the concession area. But even excluding that part there was still ample opportunity for a major find.

With all three companies committed, I made my first trip to Seoul, where I was splendidly received by Charlie Oh. Charlie and his sister had negotiated a share of Phillip's overriding royalty, and Charlie had promised a part of his share to the owner of a local casino. In return the casino owner had given him cash up front, which Charlie spent in Seoul's main kesing houses, lavishly entertaining visitors who were in Korea on the business of this concession.

Phillips's lawyer, Darryl Danker, traveled with me to Seoul but elected not to attend my meetings with Minister Lee, for obvious reasons. Lee was incensed that Phillips was now trying to assign his concession rights. "Phillips deceived us!" he ranted. "He told us that Phillips Petroleum Company would develop the concession."

After a pause for Mr. Lee to cool off, I said sympathetically, "If there *was* deception, *I* was not involved. I came into the picture later, when Phillips chose to assign his interests. It seems to me, your Excellency, that you have two choices. You can plead that you were deceived and endure the incriminations that would result, or you can approve the requested assignment because the interest of your country is better served by the technology and resources of *these* companies." I went on to suggest that the three companies be joined together as the Korean-American Oil Company (KOAM). Lee invited me to return the next day, after he had had time to think over my proposal. The following afternoon he agreed to approve the assignment papers we would prepare and have ready on our next trip.

Back in New York, Phillips was euphoric when I reported my

success, but his euphoria was short-lived. Ludwig's lawyers were trying to change the deal at the last minute, reducing Universe's costs from fifty to forty percent, while retaining a 50% participation in the project. I objected that this was an inexcusable attempt to take undue advantage of their superior financial resources. Universe's reply was, "Take it or leave it!" Phillips, who in the meantime had called his old friend Armand Hammer, shouted triumphantly, "To *hell* with Universe! We don't need them. Occidental has offered to take the whole deal!"

On my second trip to Seoul I was accompanied by Lewis's son Austin. Phillips had arranged for us to stop off in Los Angeles to meet with Oxy officials. Within hours Oxy's executive vice president agreed to pick up Universe's 50% and gave me a bank draft for $50,000, to go along with $25,000 from Hamilton and $25,000 from Weeks. Now all the elements were in place.

A complication arose almost immediately. On our flight to Seoul, who should sit down next to us but Hampers, Vice President of Universe. "We changed our minds," he explained nonchalantly. "The original deal is fine. I have the $50,000 deposit with me."

I was in a quandary. Who should we go with—Oxy or Universe? Although I resented Universe's attempt to renege on their deal, I was also thinking of Minister Lee's resentment of Phillips for similar reasons. What would he think now, if I suddenly introduced yet another player into the game?

I tried unsuccessfully to reach Phillips, and his attorney Danker was unwilling to decide on his behalf. With the decision resting on me, I reluctantly opted to go with Universe. When Phillips found out, he was furious with me. Unknownst to me, he and Hammer had developed a close association, based on his having helped Oxy get the Libyan concession several years earlier. Still, Lee was pleased to see the down payment, and two more trips to Seoul produced a concession agreement ready for the Government's signature.

Then, on the signing trip, a potential disaster arose. When I walked into Lee's office his first words to me were, "Why should

I approve this concession when you can't do the work? Assistant Secretary of State Green told me yesterday that no American company may conduct activity in the East China Sea." Concealing my shock, I replied calmly, "I agree with you. If we can't do the work, you shouldn't give us the concession." Surprised by my reaction, Lee asked, "Is Mr. Green wrong?"

"I believe his position may be clarified," I answered.

"But can you *change* his position?" he asked.

"I believe so."

Minister Lee sighed with apparent frustration, then looked me straight in the eye. "How much time do you need?"

"Give me a month," I replied.

"I will give you *three* months," he announced. "If you can fix this so a seismograph ship can begin work by July 1, I will sign the concession agreement."

I had already fixed an option on a French seismic ship, the Sister Pearl. Hurriedly I returned to New York and put in a call to Bill Rogers, who was then Nixon's Secretary of State. His longtime secretary, whom I knew well, told me that Bill was out of the country but that she would ask Assistant Secretary Green to see me immediately. The next morning I met with Green and opened by telling him, "I've just returned from Seoul, and I find that the Koreans are angry at being treated like the ball in a ping-pong game between the United States and China."

Green explained that Henry Kissinger, as National Security Advisor, had ordered that no American ships or facilities be present in the East China Sea. "This edict is not subject to discussion or review. I believe Dr. Kissinger is concerned that there might be another Pueblo incident, which would harm our attempts to develop friendlier relations with China. Of course you understand that this policy is not law—you can do what you want."

"We have no desire," I emphasized, "to enter into your 'black book' by ignoring it. But can we discuss what the edict means? We have an opportunity here that will be lost if we do not meet certain obligations. I know that you share our concerns. These obligations, I should mention, can be met without American personnel or equipment. Does this edict relate solely to personnel and equipment, or does it encompass American ownership as well?"

"Of course we are not anti-business," Green assured me. "We wish only to avoid seizure of Americans and American equipment."

"In that case," I quickly interjected, "a foreign ship and crew should not be objectionable."

"Yes, I suppose that would be all right," he acknowledged.

I cabled Minister Lee at once with the good news: "Met with Secretary Green. No objections to Sister Pearl, French flag and crew. Work to commence July 1."

Immediately I received a return cable: "Congratulations. You did good work. Concession agreement signed today. Minister Lee."

Now that the deal was completed, Temple reentered the picture, proposing that Weeks grant his principal officers an overriding royalty on its Korean interest. This royalty would be shared on a graduated scale: Lewis, as Chairman, would receive the largest part; Temple, as President of Weeks Associates, would receive the next largest, despite the fact that he had no role in Korea; Klemme and I would share the balance, about one-half the amount Temple allotted to himself.

There was little I could do. Since Weeks had recently assigned me the task of preparing his will and trusts, and establishing Citibank as custodian, I saw my long term interests best served by avoiding any disagreement, either directly, or indirectly through Temple. I stood to benefit enormously as counsel to Weeks's estate, which promised to reach many millions of dollars annually from his Bath Straits ORR.

The series of events that Temple then set in motion explain my separation from Weeks.

Now that Weeks Associates held a 25% share of the potentially lucrative Korean concession, Temple could initiate a public offering of shares in the Company. The underwriters required that all existing shareholders include their shares, to which I was agreeable. To make the shares more attractive, Weeks added a portion of his Bath Straits royalties. Although I was counsel for the Company and for Weeks, Temple chose not to involve me in this undertaking. Instead he brought into the company a long-time friend as his assistant.

Then Temple invited me to lunch with him at the Princeton Club, where he told me—without explanation—that henceforth I would not be included in the management of the company, but might be called upon from time to time as outside counsel. It was immediately clear to me that Temple saw me as an obstacle to taking complete control of the company. When I recovered from my shock, I replied, "I don't wish to be a passive shareholder. Therefore, in view of what you have just put to me, I withdraw my shares from the undertaking and offer them to those of you who will continue in the management."

I believe Temple was prepared for this response, and saw it as a welcome opportunity to create a wedge in my relationship with Weeks. He then persuaded Weeks to buy me out. If Temple expected me to exploit my strategic position, I surprised him with my offer to accept the same price per share that the public would pay in the initial offering.

When I met Weeks at Citibank for the purpose of completing the sale of my shares to him, Temple's next move was to have his assistant produce a document for me to sign, by which I would release Weeks from any and all claims I had against him. At no time had I ever made a claim against Weeks, nor did I intend any. If ever I was caught on the horns of a dilemma, this was it. If I refused to sign the release, Temple might use this as evidence that I *did* plan to sue Weeks. Yet I knew that if I signed the release, Temple would take credit for protecting Weeks against claims I would have made against him. Frustrated and dejected, I signed the document to complete the sale.

As I had predicted to Hamilton and Universe, treaty negotiations between Korea and Japan went smoothly, and the treaty was signed in 1974. However, the operating agreement, a more technical document covering many details of managing an oil exploration, was not signed until 1979. Japan and Korea shared ownership equally, and Japan assigned its concession rights to two Japanese oil companies and Texaco. These companies joined with KOAM to cover the projected $56 million cost of a four-well drilling program. For the difficult offshore conditions Hamilton Brothers, which had been chosen as operator, engaged an expensive drill ship that fixed its drilling position electronically, enabling it to move off site in advance of severe turbulence and return to its precise position after the disturbance had passed.

Weeks Associates, as a founding partner in KOAM, actively participated in negotiations with the Japanese assignees, but Temple, as expected, employed other counsel. During this period I heard nothing from Temple *or* Weeks, and I learned from a third party that Weeks had replaced me as counsel with respect to his will and trusts.

Then one day I got a phone call from Mrs. Weeks, informing me that Lewis was terminally ill with cancer and wished to see me. I visited him alone in his private room in the local hospital at Westport. Despite his weakness and sedation Lewis stood up and shook hands, gazing at me with a warm smile. He explained that he had commissioned his biography to be written by a well-known biographer of VIP's, and wanted me to get in touch with the writer and help him write the section "covering the fifteen years of our close relationship." I smiled and nodded noncommittally. That was the last time I saw him.

After his death, his son Austin told me that in his final days Lewis had engaged in a violent argument with Temple, which Austin believed had hastened his end. I gathered from Austin that Lewis had finally come to a realistic understanding of what Temple was up to. I would like to believe that he also came to understand that I had always been a loyal friend and attorney.

I never contacted Weeks's biographer, and when the book came out it did not surprise me that I was not mentioned. But I think it's significant that, in spite of his long association with Lewis, Temple was never mentioned either, by name or by deed.

Under stockholder pressure, Weeks Associates directors replaced Temple as President with an outsider. The company was finally acquired by an Australian conglomerate in a hostile takeover.

As an epilogue to the story of the Korean concession, I received a call one day from Gordon Hodgson, Executor of Phillips's estate. Hodgson had recently returned from London, where he happened upon my old friend from Sinclair, Fred Bush. Hodgson had told Bush of his frustrations in trying to sort out the estate, and asked if Bush knew of anyone who could help him. Fred had recommended me.

The estate still owned most of the two and a half percent ORR that Phillips had reserved for himself when he assigned his working interest to the KOAM partners. Exploratory drilling was now underway, and Hodgson was considering selling shares in the royalty. He had questions concerning the potential of the concession, and the value of Phillips's ORR relative to his other royalties. After meeting with him I agreed to prepare a detailed report on these subjects, to be available to meet with potential buyers of the royalties, and to arrange the transfer of royalty units from the Estate to the buyers. Peter Lagemann, a respected Wall Street financial advisor, agreed to do the marketing.

When I learned that Lagemann was close to partners of Lazard's of London, I suggested to him that they might be interested in purchasing the initial royalty shares. From the days when their aristocracy funded pirate expeditions (like those of Sir Walter Raleigh), the British had been drawn to high-risk ventures, and since the concession was still in the exploratory stage, that's what this would be. A public offering would necessitate SEC registration and possibly expose "widows and orphans" to risk. "Lazard is active in the North Sea," I argued, "knows Hamilton Brothers, and they and their clients are wealthy and sophisticated risk takers."

Lazard's Joe Fielding and Andrew Clive were interested in the royalties, and employed a prominent New York law firm to investigate all pertinent documents prior to the sale. With my cooperation in supplying the documents, a month was ample time for them to complete the review.

At month's end Fielding and Clive arrived in New York and immediately advised Lagemann that the sale would have to be postponed because of several reservations expressed by their counsel. At my urging, Lagemann persuaded Fielding and Clive to bring their lawyers to our scheduled meeting, where their reservations could be discussed directly with me.

At the meeting the firm's senior partner gravely and pretentiously advised caution and thoroughness in dealing with several imaginatively dire theoretical possibilities. The more he talked, the clearer it became to me, and I believe to Fielding and Clive as well, that the lawyer wanted to spend more of his time (and their money) on the project, despite his admission that they had received copies of all documents in a timely fashion.

At one point Fielding asked his lawyer, "My principal concern is, do we incur any liabilities or obligations by owning these royalties?"

The lawyer proceeded into a lengthy discourse, trying my patience and that of his clients. Exasperated, I finally spoke up. "Counselor, that question can be answered unequivocally—yes or no. What is your answer?"

Somewhat contritely he replied, "I meant to say 'no.'"

After the meeting, Fielding waited until his lawyer departed and then told us, "You've got a deal. We agree to purchase ten percent of the total royalties for two and a half million dollars. Our bank draft will be delivered to you in the morning."

I arranged to include half of my royalties in the offering, along with a small portion of the other outstanding royalties from Weeks Associates. Hodgson ended up selling about half of the Phillips royalties, to Lazard and other prominent banking firms in London, Hong Kong, Switzerland, and the United States. To provide more flexibility and management efficiency for new owners of the royalty, I established, with the help of Winthrop, Stimson, Putnam and Roberts, the East China Sea Royalty Trust. Trustees were William Spencer, Paul Douglas (former president of Freeport Minerals), and William Humphreys (retired chief geologist at Amoco), with me as managing trustee. The new owners exchanged their royalty units for proportionate shares in the newly established Trust, which we registered with the SEC.

As the first exploratory well was about to be spudded, Temple decided to offer some of his royalties, and called Hodgson, whom he knew. Then, for the first time in ten years, he contacted me, to discuss what price he should charge. I referred him to Lagemann, who was handling sales. "I know his price," Temple replied. "I want to have your evaluation."

"Sorry," I answered, "I am not inclined to advise you!"

Through Lagemann, Temple sold half his royalties. "I've changed my mind," he told Lagemann. "That well, I have learned, is a *great* discovery. I want a higher price."

Lagemann was incredulous. "What kind of person is he?" he asked me.

I answered, "You can judge for yourself."

As it turned out, Temple's decision backfired on him. I learned that he held onto *all* his royalties, which turned out to be worthless. Four dry (non-commerical) holes were drilled, at a total cost of nearly $100 million, before the KOAM partners relinquished their concession rights to the Korean Government.

21
Back to the Farm

IN 1975, IN MY SIXTIETH year, Patricia and I appraised our family and financial situation. Three of our four children were off to college: Stephanie to Northwestern, Stirling to Carnegie Mellon, and Suzanne to Barnard. Only our youngest, Stacey, was still at home, and her study habits assured us she would do well in school *anywhere*. Trust funds we had created earlier would cover all their college expenses. With our financial position secure, and our children well on their way to successful and independent lives, we wondered if we should remain in the New York area, or seek a less stressful lifestyle elsewhere.

After almost a quarter century of private practice, I was still a loner in my profession. My experience with the Dewey firm had discouraged me from further efforts to become a partner in an established law firm. I could have joined one of the "nameplate" firms, which essentially operate as storefronts for individual lawyers, who share the rent and pay a percentage of their fees to the owners. But this was not appealing to me either; I didn't need the "storefront" to attract clients, and I didn't like the idea of sharing my fees.

Most of my business consisted of corporate CEO's hiring me for assignments which, because of my experience and expertise, only I could perform. None of my major clients came to my office; I went to their's. I realized that I had achieved considerable recognition as "an international lawyer," and that it was no longer necessary for me to be in New York.

To me, the ideal place to live was on a farm. Frankly, it would not have been Pattie's choice, but she accepted my preference. In considering where we would look for one, I thought about the upstate New York of my cherished youthful memories, where the younger Whites still lived. Then I remembered the long, bitterly cold winters and deep snow, and the fact that it was so distant from international airports, and I ruled it out.

With upstate as a reference point, Pattie and I decided on several prerequisites for our new home: the climate must include four distinct seasons with a mild, short winter; it must have an international airport nearby, as well as a university where I might lecture; and most importantly, it must have a view of the mountains. Patricia had decided she could adjust to a rural lifestyle if it were adorned by prominent mountain views, such as she loved in the Austrian Alps.

I had traveled more abroad than domestically, but one place we had visited stood out in both our minds. Our friends Trudy and Bradley Peyton had a home outside Charlottesville in Albemarle County, Virginia, and more recently Henry Maresi, son of Pompeo and Phoebe, had purchased a farm in Albemarle's scenic Greenwood area. I decided to visit Henry and further explore that vicinity.

Henry and Lala, his exuberantly attractive mate, hosted me for two days while their friend, a real estate agent, showed me a dozen or so country estates. These were all large establishments, which would have required servants and handymen, and a commitment to upkeep greater than I was prepared to make.

On the last day of my visit, I was enjoying cocktails with Henry and Lala on their veranda, when I spied across the valley a wooded hilltop that suggested a hidden residence. When I inquired about it, Henry explained that there *was* a home there, owned by an elderly couple, the Martins, whom he had never met. But he really piqued my interest when he added, "I am told that it has a *magnificent* view."

The next morning I drove up the Martin's long, winding, private driveway and came to the top of the hill. There I feasted on a panoramic view of encircling mountains—looming above me on one side, stretching into the distance and rimming the horizon on the other, with a beautiful valley in between. It was easily the most stunning view I had ever seen from a private residence.

The house itself—of modest size compared to the mansions shown me by Stevens—was a classic Normandy village style dwelling featuring reversed brick, a slate roof and a huge three-funneled stone and brick chimney. An adjoining building, built as a stables, looked like a potential guest house and office. I was tempted to knock on the door to declare my interest, but thought better of it, since there was no indication the property was for sale.

When I returned to the Maresis I telephoned his real estate friend to thank him for his efforts, and told him that I had stumbled upon exactly what I was looking for. "What place are you talking about?" he asked. When I told him, he surprised me by declaring, "If that place comes on the market, *I* will buy it for *myself*!"

As far as I was concerned, that agent no longer represented me, but himself as a competing buyer. Fortunately, Henry Maresi promised to alert me of any evidence that the Martins might sell. We were in no hurry to leave Bronxville. We could wait.

Two years later we received a call from Henry reporting that the Martins had advised their immediate neighbor that they were thinking about selling the property and moving to The Cedars, a retirement home in Charlottesville. Henry had told the Martins of our interest and they were receptive to talking with us. I telephoned them immediately and arranged for my family to visit the following weekend, after attending Stephanie's graduation from Northwestern.

With our three oldest children and a college friend of Stephanie's, we arrived at the Martins in our Bonneville station wagon at noon on a Sunday. Following introductions, I left Patricia and the children to chat with the Martins, while their hired man took me on a tour of the farm. Recently there had been a severe drought, and I asked my guide to show me the water supply. Two wells produced a good flow of water for the house and, to my delight, the stream providing water for the pastures was fed by an underground spring, rather than surface water.

After an hour or so I returned to find Patricia in an animated conversation with Mrs. Martin. The children sat quietly listening, as did the ailing Mr. Martin. No sooner had I sat down than Mrs. Martin turned to me and said, "Mr. Nakasian, Mr. Martin and I would be very happy to have your beautiful family follow us here. We have cherished this place for *seventeen* years."

After quickly caucusing my family, I reported that our answer was a unanimous and resounding "Yes!"

Mrs. Martin smiled and quickly announced, "Junius Fishburne, III handles our affairs. I will tell him to expect your call—shall I say tomorrow?" I nodded and thanked her gratefully, and we began the 350-mile trip back to Bronxville.

"This is fantastic!" I said to Pattie, as soon as we were enroute. "What on earth did you say to her?"

"Well," Pattie related, "of course she knew we were from Bronxville, so practically the first thing she said to me was, 'Before my husband and I came to this lovely mountain place, we lived in Crestwood, just a short distance from you, and worshipped at the Asbury Methodist Church. We loved it there.' "When I told her that the minister of that church had been very helpful to me when I chaired the county's Ecumenical Movement of Churches, her eyes lit up. I think she felt a kinship with us, and that, for her, was more important than getting the highest price for the property."

Mr. Fishburne appeared to be expecting my call the next day. "I understand", he said "that the Martins wish to sell their farm to you, and that you wish to purchase it. Unfortunately, they haven't given me anything to go on in the way of a price, and don't seem interested in engaging a real estate firm to advise them. Perhaps you could suggest a means by which we might set a mutually acceptable price.

I had already given the matter some thought. "The property," I answered, "consists of about sixty acres: half woods in rugged terrain, half meadow and lawns. Suppose we set a price for each of the wooded acres, a price for each of the open acres, and a price for the buildings? I cannot put a value on the view because it would take the price out of my range."

He nodded. "Do you have these prices in mind?"

For each of the three categories I suggested a price. Fishburne added up the amounts and said, "I can submit this total to the Martin's as a purchase price." Within the hour he called and announced, "The Martins accept".

In a state of excitement I called out to Pattie, "We have the property! You did it....or was it an Act of God?"

After the move many of my neighbors told us, "We never knew the Martin place was on the market. How did you get it? We wanted it for ourselves!"

To this I would always reply, "You're right. It was not on the market. We got it through an Act of God!"

When word of our impending move circulated in Bronxville, my popularity plummeted. How could I take gregarious Patricia away from her church activities, her operas and symphonies, her bridge, tennis, and golf, and isolate her on a farm, with all the drudgery that connoted to them? I had to explain that this "farm" was situated amongst historical estates now owned by some of the wealthiest people in America. "Our new home," I told them, "looks down upon Mirador, where Lady Astor, the original 'Gibson Girl' spent her youth. Our lifestyle there will not exclude any of Patricia's favorite activities. We're just ready for a slower tempo."

Within a year of our move, several of our closest Bronxville friends came to visit "Sunny Brae," which we named after our street in Bronxville, and had their concerns assuaged. Over the next several years we purchased an additional 130 acres, built a swimming pool, added two large family rooms to capture the sunrise and sunset over our gardens, and modernized the kitchen. I built a large barn for storing hay, and raised a herd of prize Charlois beef cattle—thirty-five cows and one very distinguished bull. More recently we built a modern dwelling near ours to house personal servants when our age requires them. In the meantime, we rent it to a compatible couple.

Every April, owners of private estates open their homes and gardens to the general public during Garden Week. For several years the garden committee besieged Pattie to include *our* property, but my wife protested: "We have no household antiques. The Nazis took my family's, and the Turks took Sam's. We neglect our gardens. All we have of interest is our view." She finally consented, when the committee kept reminding her that it *was* the view they wished to show off to the visitors.

While I was in Europe on a business trip, Patricia hosted a two day garden tour of 1600 people, who arrived in cars and busses. Both days the sky was crystal clear. Jefferson's Monticello could be pointed out, twenty miles to the east; west of us stands Afton Mountain, made famous by the Waltons TV series; to the south lies a valley, mountains, and more mountains, stretching to the horizon; to the north our intimate 2500-foot mountain rises above the foothills we own, limiting our view in that direction but more than compensating with its vivid hardwood colors each spring and fall.

Patricia circulated among the visitors and heard their comments. More than one exclaimed, "This is a more impressive view than Monticello's!" She reported all this to me when I returned from my trip.

"Thank God," I told her, "we bought the property privately, without a price on the view. Imagine how much view lovers would have paid for it!"

Integrating into the cosmopolitan Charlottesville community was no problem. In our first year here we joined the beautiful Farmington Country Club, which boasts 1200 out-of-town members from across the country and overseas, and made many friends. We also joined a committee that was seeking to upgrade the local symphony, which played to half-empty houses even with prices of two or three dollars a ticket. The effort, spearheaded by Marita McClymonds, Chair of the University of Virginia's McIntire Department of Music, was so successful that a larger

Sam at Sunny Brae in 1995

and more prestigious symphony now performs to perenially sold-out houses at up to *twenty* dollars a ticket, and an expanded UVA music department now commands more attention "on grounds."

Pattie and I were also invited to join a local committee organized to explore the prospect of a summer music festival at Ashlawn, President Monroe's ancestral home near Monticello. The committee successfully bridged the gap between the College of William & Mary—Ashlawn's distant landlord—and the local community, and now both residents and tourists enjoy a full slate of live operas, popular musicals, concerts, and children's programs each summer.

Soon after we arrived at Sunny Brae, Trudy and Bradley Peyton invited us to a black tie gathering at "Seven Oaks," their nearby estate. The thirty guests were served a magnificent dinner at a single table, by uniformed servants. This was our introduction to the gracious Virginia hospitality we have come to love. (In Westchester County this would have been a *rare* event.) I was seated next to Dr. Frank Hereford, then President of UVA. He politely inquired as to why we had chosen to settle in Albemarle County. I explained that it was purely a lifestyle decision to leave New York, and that one of the reasons we had picked this area was its proximity to the University. One of my desires in relocating here was to lecture at UVA. I told him how valuable it had been for me, as a student at NYU, to have visiting lecturers from outside academia, and I felt I had a wealth of real-world experience, both in the government and abroad, to share with the students at UVA. I also mentioned my trusteeship at SUNY Binghamton, and the decision-making seminars I had led at Carnegie Mellon.

Dr. Hereford listened with great interest, then leaned toward me and spoke confidentially. "You must realize that, as President, I have no influence over the faculties of the schools. The most I can do is to send each of the appropriate chairmen a note, with a copy of your vita, and suggest they meet you."

He followed through and before long I had meetings scheduled with the chairmen of the Law, Business, Government, and Commerce departments. Each greeted me cordially but was noticeably unenthusiastic about my offer to lecture occasionally. One of the chairmen, acknowledged as an expert on the Middle East, began our meeting with, "I hear you have been in the Middle East," as if it were a sole recent trip. When I replied, "Many times over thirty years, with an extended six-month engagement as resident adviser to a Prime Minister," he suddenly looked at his watch and said, "Excuse me, I am late for another appointment," and showed me the door. This was the shortest meeting of my long career.

I was stunned at their apparent perception of me as an intruder on their turf. It was so different from NYU, which had actively sought outside lecturers, particularly in Economics and Finance. How could UVA justify this isolationist stance when they had so much talent available to them, both in the immediate community and nearby Washington? In fairness to the chairmen of these departments, I must confess that I did not contact them again after I experienced their obvious disinterest. As time went on, individual professors that I got to know did invite me to lecture in their law, commerce, and business seminars.

By contrast, UVA's Miller Center of Public Affairs, under Professor Ken Thompson, invites both incumbent and retired government, military, and business leaders to the school for a series of lectures and interviews—generally open to the public. To facilitate and encourage this program, Wilson Newman generously donated a beautiful building featuring a large round table for discussion. The material gathered from these visits is then used for meaningful dissertations by graduate students and faculty. This ongoing, nationally-acclaimed program bridges the gap between academia and the real world and enhances the prestige of the University.

About the time Patricia and I settled down on Sunny Brae Farm, Robert H. Rines, a friend and classmate from Georgetown Law School, embarked on a bold and imaginative venture. Bob had inherited his father's Boston law practice, which mainly served the inventive faculty of MIT. Bob's idea was to expand the practice into a new law school, with a curriculum oriented to intellectual property rights. Bob located his new school in nearby Concord, New Hampshire, and named it the Franklin Pierce Law Center, after the state's only President.

I was flattered when he invited me to join his venture as one of the trustees. At my introduction I spoke on the same program with Professor Edgerton of MIT, inventor of the strobe light. Franklin Pierce was quickly accredited and has turned out many talented graduates in the specialized practice of intellectual property rights. By reason of the school's distance from my new home, my contribution was, regretfully, insignificant.

In 1979 Pattie and I received a visit from Anne Aldrich Mooney, whom I had first met as a starving exchange student in Geneva, and who later worked for me in my Washington office. At the time of her visit Anne was a Professor at Cleveland Law School, but she told us that she expected President Carter to appoint her Judge of the U.S. District Court of Ohio, and I should expect a visit from an FBI investigator of her character fitness. A month or so later I had a visit from an FBI agent, who was most pleasant and seemed more interested in our rural setting than in Ann. When her appointment was approved by the U.S. Senate, Ann asked if I would make the customary address upon her induction to the court. "This ceremony," she emphasized, "is a major public event, attended by both U.S. Senators, the local Congressmen, the entire Court, the local bar, and the public." "What should I talk about?" I asked.

"Anything you want," was her reply. "Feel free; you can't be held in contempt."

"Good," I answered, "I have a few criticisms I want to get off my chest."

The packed courtroom was in a celebratory mood, but my speech was more disturbing than joyful. "Your new judge," I told them, "will endeavor to restore to the Court its rightful role prescribed by the Constitution. She will not be one of those tyrannical judges who pursue their own social agenda by extending acts of Congress beyond the legislative intent—as was done, for example, with antitrust laws on overseas operations, and even more egregiously, with the reorganization of the entire telephone industry."

After my speech, Ohio's Democratic Senator Howard Metzenbaum confronted me and complained about the criticism I had leveled at several of his pet causes. His grown daughter, standing next to him, then praised my speech, to the visible discomfort of her father.

In our first ten years at Sunny Brae Farm, I had a full time secretary and an office in the building adjoining our residence. Even so my work involved almost as much travel as when I lived in New York. The Wendell Phillips Estate and its problems required repeated trips to Los Angeles, and the Korean oil concession and establishment of the East China Sea Royalty Trust, among other matters, required weekly commuting to New York, where I maintained a midtown office/apartment. Beyond these activities, which I've already discussed, there were several other business adventures worth mentioning.

Not long after we moved to Virginia, I made a trip to Saudi Arabia on behalf of Freeport. I arrived in Jedda just as the military was engaging a band of rebels attempting to capture the holy city of Mecca. The airport was immediately shut down, and I spent the night on an airport bench. The next evening, dining in Riyadh with a friend of mine—the former secretary to old King Ibn Saud—I inquired if the attack in Mecca had been made by the Iranians?" He shook his head and sorrowfully said, "They were are *own* boys."

From a business standpoint, the trip was a total loss of time and effort. Saudis everywhere, especially in government, were totally preoccupied with what had happened in Mecca, and terrified that such violence might reach them. The Saudi Army was stationed everywhere, including the airport. To my amazement, they stood guard holding their rifles pointed down toward their feet.

On another occasion I received a call from a New York lawyer whose client, a Swiss Bank owner and world trader, was interested in entering the oil business. Several people had recommended me as a knowledgeable person for his client to talk with, and the lawyer was calling to engage me to meet with his client in Geneva. At Citicorp headquarters (whose dossiers on all significant people in business and finance are available to a privileged few) I learned what I needed to know to make the trip.

I arrived in Geneva in the early morning, took a shower and a quick nap, and called the client around eleven o'clock. "Come to my office, if you aren't too tired," was his invitation, which I accepted.

When I entered his office, which overlooked Lake Geneva, he looked up from his desk and said in a single breath, "Glad you could come over. Do you play golf?"

"I do," I answered.

"Then let's go play golf." Before I could reply he was up and ushering me out the door. Within a half an hour I was being outfitted with clubs and shoes at Devon, the ritzy French resort. On the first tee he said, "My handicap is twenty; what's yours?" "Fifteen," I answered.

"Give me five strokes and I'll play you for fifty dollar nassau."

"Normally," I demurred, "I play for only a dollar nassau, so that I lose, at most, four of five dollars."

"Let's play for fifty," he insisted. Finally I relented, realizing I was playing on *his* time and money, and we began the game.

The course was quite hilly and laid out to necessitate hooks and fades off the tee. My client's tee shots were of moderate length, but he one-putted a number of greens for par. I suspected that his handicap of 20 was bogus. Very fatigued after the all-night flight, I was less vigorous and swung slower, and therefore better. Coming to the 18th tee after several Texases (doublings of the bet), he was down to me about $400. Again he challenged me: "Double or nothing." I was in no position to disagree. I reached the green in two; he got on in three. He putted first for par and missed, settling for a five, which with his handicap became a four. I had a downhill putt with a two-foot break for a three. When I dropped it he turned livid. As he peeled off eight one hundred dollar bills, he barked, "What are you—a hustler?"

"No, I told you I hardly *ever* play for more than a dollar nassau."

"You surprise me," he said. "Is this how you treat all your clients? Does that make *sense*?"

"It does to me," I replied. "You should get the impression that I play to *win*."

On the way back to the hotel, he had very little to say and I was half asleep. When we parted company he said simply, "See you at ten in the morning." This relationship lasted for about two years, during which I made several trips to Geneva, Antwerp, and Bangkok in connection with oil refinery deals he was pursuing.

Among the fringe benefits of my association with this banker were invitations to several pro-am golf tournaments. I flew with my client in his G2 jet to the Bing Crosby tournament in Pebble Beach, and to an extravaganza he himself hosted at Deep Dale, a private course on the former Grace estate in Long Island. At the latter Patricia and I had the pleasure of cocktails and dinner with Ray Floyd and Gary Player. Both were charming and lively conversationalists. Player, from South Africa, opposed apartheid and predicted its eventual demise, expressing optimism that the races would someday coexist peacefully there.

A week before the British Open, the banker would assemble a dozen of the top qualifiers to play at Devon for a charity event. His VIP friends, as well as high government officials from all over the world, were invited for the privilege of playing golf with Tom Watson and other renowned professionals. One year John Schroeder and I were paired. The morning fog off the lake was down to the ground, and we reached the fourteenth hole without seeing a single fairway or green. Fortunately our foursome included a local club member who advised us on direction and distance for our drives and approach shots. Incredibly, John shot four under par, and with my strokes our combined best score was 58. We came in second.

After two years the banker acquired from me most of what I knew about the oil business and amicably terminated my services. Thereafter he continued to invite me to pro-ams in Europe, but I chose not to undergo the travel expense. I remain gratefully aware that my inclusion in these celebrity events was a rare fringe benefit for someone in my position.

In these two years I got a pretty good sense of Geneva. Surrounding Lake Geneva on three sides, its pristine, picturesque setting belies the sophisticated corruption that goes on behind the scenes. Besides the legitimate international business transacted there, secret Swiss bank accounts hide untold billions in ill-gotten wealth, deposited by foreigners from across the globe, out of reach of their own governments.

Many of the newly-rich were dictators or VIP's from emerging African nations. It was common practice for Swiss "promoters" to furnish these men with diamonds from the many high-priced jewelry stores, bagfuls of chips for the gambling casinos, and the most attractive white prostitutes from Switzerland and France. Later, bribes given in exchange for special favors in the VIP's home countries would go directly into their pockets. I couldn't help wondering just how much foreign aid, from the U.S. and other countries, winds up in private Swiss bank accounts, a practice which continues unchanged to this day. The lax accountability constitutes a virtual "license to steal."

My last significant business venture took place in 1989, in newly independent Poland. Our Albemarle neighbor Blanka Rosenstiel, the wealthy widow of industrialist Lewis Rosenstiel, asked if I had any ideas that would help Poland develop its economy. Blanka had been an active patron of expatriot Polish artists and academics, and was very excited by her native country's emergence from Soviet domination.

I saw immediately that the opening of Poland's economy created a promising opportunity for U.S. companies. A quick investigation revealed that the Kremlin had used Poland as a market for its oil exports, and hence the country's own potential petroleum resources had been ignored. I reported this to Blanka, and let her know that the technology was now available to readily determine whether Poland's sedimentary basins had oil and gas reservoirs.

Among the dozen or so oil companies I had gotten to know pretty well over the years, I thought Anadarko Petroleum of Houston, which focused almost exclusively on exploration and production, was the company best equipped to help Poland. I knew their president, Robert Allison, who had first been introduced to me by the famous AMOCO geologist, William Humphrey. I met with Allison and explained the situation. Allison believed that central Poland showed promise and expressed interest in drilling exploratory wells there.

After that events unfolded quickly. Blanka called the U.S. Ambassador to Poland, John Davis, who arranged a meeting with Polish officials in Warsaw. Blanka and I then stopped by the State Department and talked with General Ed Romney, who had been assigned by President Bush to oversee Poland's transition. Romney was also very helpful, and called Poland's Minister of Industry, who happened to be in New York at that time. The Minister flew down and met with us in General Romney's office. He was very receptive and, in response to my question, promised that all state records pertaining to Poland's geology would be made available to Anadarko. He also mentioned that the purpose of his trip to New York had been to meet with AMOCO officials, who were also interested in Poland. Following this meeting, the General took us out to dinner and, after the meal, treated us to an improptu concert on his harmonica!

This auspicious beginning unfortunately did not carry over to our visit to Warsaw. In our first meeting there, with the Managing Director of Polish Oil and Gas, we learned that the Minister of Industry had already been replaced. The Director of POG made no objections to fulfilling the former minister's assurances, but was less than enthusiastic. "Ministers come and go," he announced casually. "It doesn't matter. I'm still here." I took this to mean that he expected a kickback for any assistance he might offer.

The Anadarko technicians who accompanied us got copies of relevant documents and took them home to study. Blanka and I stayed on another day or two, visiting the U.S. Embassy as well as Poland's ministries. At this time Walesa was the country's de facto leader, and was awaiting a national election to formalize his position.

Several weeks later, Anadarko was prepared to make a proposal to the Polish government. Allison called and told me that he and his wife, along with his staff, would fly the company jet—a Gruman G3—directly to Warsaw, after picking up Blanka and me in Charlottesville. Patricia was also invited, and readily accepted. At 40,000 feet, well above the turbulence, it was the smoothest plane ride I have ever experienced. We flew non-stop to Warsaw over the North Pole in seven and a half hours—a record which I suspect has yet to be broken.

We all stayed at the modern new Marriot Hotel. Allison reserved a private meeting room, and on the third day Walesa came, accompanied by an aide, who—judging from his size—doubled as a bodyguard. Patricia set up a VHF camera and recorded the whole thing. Blanka served as translator.

Allison proposed that Anadarko drill three exploratory wells, at no expense to Poland. This initial phase of their investment would be completed in less than two years. If production were developed, any oil would be shared equally between Poland and Anadarko. The animated Walesa seemed overwhelmed by what he saw as Anadarko's generosity. At the end of the meeting, he excitedly summarized his understanding: "You offer Poland to do this work at no cost to Poland, and if you find oil and gas you will deliver half of it to us free of charge." Then he declared, "It is done! I agree." Allison promised to put the agreement in formal language and deliver a copy to Walesa in Gdansk within two days.

We flew up to Gdansk in the G3 and met Walesa's aide for lunch. Walesa had business at the shipyards and was unable to join us. His aide promised to carry the document to his boss. Before leaving Poland we also delivered copies to Polish Oil and Gas and the new Minister of Industry.

We returned to the States in a triumphant mood, expecting a response in a few days. When, after weeks, we had still heard not a word, Blanka and I decided to go to Warsaw to find out what was going on. When we arrived we were told that Walesa was unavailable. The Polish Oil and Gas Director was non-commital, as was the Minister of Industry, who was noticeably ill-at-ease. Ambassador Davis also got the diplomatic run-around from Poland's Minister of Planning—an American-trained economist he knew quite well—who claimed ignorance of this matter that was clearly within his jurisdiction. In a state of frustration, Blanka and I returned home.

A short time later, national elections were held and Walesa was elected President. Soon afterwards we learned that the government had employed a British firm of consulting geologists to study Poland's geology. Oil companies would then buy the completed report and on the basis of its findings, prepare their competitive bids. Allison rejected the firm's invitation to make such a bid, pointing out that Anadarko had offered the government all that there was to give.

This process alone consumed two years, and exploratory drilling could commence years later than it would have had the job gone to Anadarko as Walesa had promised. How could this have happened? The answer may be found in the culture of government agencies that were holdovers from the communist regime, or were now headed by newcomers out of academia with no experience in business. Both the old and the new employees were bribe-prone. Poverty level salaries in the highly inflationary free market environment created a desperate need in these people for supplementary income. On more than one occasion I was personally approached by government employees who suggested that if I were responsive to their need they could help win approval of our project. Unconvinced that they had the power to deliver, I declined in each instance.

It should be noted that Poland was also being worked over by the U.S. and international agencies (AID, the World Bank, etc.). These large bureaucracies are affiliated and intertwined with other bureaucracies, primarily consulting firms (employed at public expense) which serve as buffers between the international agencies and the recipient governments. What do these firms do? Well, they take the burden of responsibility off the official agency, and are expected to take the rap if the agency's decisions are criticized. I am sure these same practices are perpetuated everywhere by international agencies as they function with immunity from fiduciary responsibility and accountability.

Poland was set back five years by this invasion of bureaucrats. If these international agencies efficiently used their considerable financial resources, Eastern Europe's transition to a market economy could be both eased and expedited. I can't help but contrast the snail-paced progress toward this goal with the remarkable recovery of Europe after World War II, achieved in three years under the Marshall Plan.

Not long after I had returned from Warsaw, Pattie and I received an invitation from Bill Cooper's wife Ruth to a conference at Carnegie Mellon in Pittsburgh. The conference would feature presentations and seminars on the subject that Bill had devoted four decades to—Managerial Science. Ruth had succeeded in keeping secret from Bill the fact that he would be the Guest of Honor, and asked if I would say a few words about him to the attendees. I replied that I would be most honored to, and promised not to tip Bill off as to the actual purpose of the event.

Bill and I had remained close friends ever since he had left Bureau of the Budget and returned to Carnegie to teach. His contributions to the school were many, and it was natural that they should want to honor him. He had played a major role in securing the grant from the Mellon family that had created Carnegie Mellon, and before that had contributed to the school's enrichment and worldwide reputation by bringing in a wealth of outside talent to teach and conduct seminars. The seminars I had conducted there in decision-making were part of that initiative. Later, when the Saudis emerged on the world scene and a joint venture between Carnegie and the University of Saudi Arabia was contemplated, I was invited to share my knowledge of the country with Carnegie's President, Richard Cyert, and faculty. I was but one of many whose knowledge and expertise Bill drew on in his quest to send his students out into the world fully prepared to change it for the better.

After Carnegie, Bill occupied the distinguished Richardson Chair as Professor at Harvard, and then moved on to the Foster Parker Chair at the University of Texas, where he was teaching at the time of the conference. Besides his teaching, he had an active consulting career for both the government as well as large corporations—Bell Labs, Gulf Oil, and Mars Candy to name but a few. Ever the evangelist, he lectured and wrote widely, both here and abroad, on such topics as linear programing, managerial accounting, and statistical evaluations. He co-authored the "Dictionary for Accountants" (to which I contributed) with Kohler, and after Kohler's death regularly updated it himself. Today Bill's students (disciples, actually) are prominent in academia, business, and government. Literally hundreds of them attended the conference honoring him.

The two-day event was held at Carnegie's new graduate school. Many speakers took the opportunity to speak on new developments in the field of Managerial Science, a subject beyond my expertise. That first evening in Pittsburgh I collected my thoughts on what I should say about this friend of mine for almost half a century. I decided to speak of Bill's consuming drive not only to perfect the science of management, but also to make a positive difference in the lives of all those he came into contact with, be they students, colleagues, or friends. I knew I had to tell the audience about the cherished visits I had made over the years to Pittsburgh, Cambridge, and Austin; the late night discussions with him that remained as intellectually stimulating as those we'd had in college; and the charming rapport I felt with the equally engaging Ruth, a distinguished lawyer in her own right.

When the time came for me to speak I said all this and more. I suggested that Bill's cauliflower ear was a kind of trademark. "He fought through the complexities of ideas and theories with the same fervor as a pugilist meeting a boxing opponent in the ring!" I told my audience. Finally I told them about the generosity of Bill and Ruth in shaping my own career. My speech was well-received, yet still I was not quite satisfied with it. The next morning, after a troubled sleep, I recalled the verse, "Time oh time in thy fleeting flight: I just recalled what I should have said last night!" There in the presence of his many admirers, I *should* have nominated W.W. Cooper for the Nobel Prize.

My third trip to Warsaw in 1990 was the last of my overseas assignments. Pattie does not share my current reluctance to travel. She reminds me that we have not been to Mainland China or Australia, and dreams of seeing Eastern Europe by sailing down the Danube. She offers to pack her bags on a moment's notice.

These past five years I have been quite content living the full life of a "country gentleman." Although my enthusiasm for manual labor has waned, I do enjoy an hour or two on my John Deere tractor, and it's always a special event when one of my Charlois cows gives birth. (On one occasion I successfully served as "midwife," evoking memories of my youth at the Whites.)

I still spend about ten hours a week on the golf course at Farmington. Younger players often include me in their foursomes, and express amazement when I occasionally outdrive them. Another hour a day is allotted to managing our investments and perfecting a plan for transferring our estate to our children, who have started their own families. Pattie and I are typical, doting grandparents, and playfully compete for genetic credit for our grandchildrens' precocity.

Both Pattie and I remain keenly interested in world affairs and especially the domestic and foreign policies of our own government. Every day we monitor developments via radio, television, and newspapers, and by reading books. We often compare journalist's dispatches from faraway lands with our own personal experiences in those places. The Bosnian catastrophe is particularly difficult for us to reconcile with the peaceful and positive impressions formed during our 1969 trip to Zagreb and Belgrade and the countryside in between. I saw no evidence of ethnic or religious strife then or on two previous trips, although I did speculate on whether it might erupt following the death of Yugoslavia's war hero and leader, Marshal Tito.

Especially disheartening to us is this tragedy of "ethnic cleansing," a euphemism for genocide. Our nation's leadership, as well as NATO's, grievously failed to take immediate action to stop the "cleansing," in effect inviting it. The limited and ineffective response of the civilized world to genocidal campaigns waged there and elsewhere remains one of humankind's most inexcusable failings.

In 1984 Lee Iacocca organized a centennial celebration for the Statue of Liberty. The intent was to contrast the despair of static and less humane conditions in the Old World with the continuing promise of hope held out by the New. Our daughter Suzanne joined his planning staff and initiated a program to involve immigrants in the festivities.

Knowing our family history, she attempted to lead the various immigrant groups to adopt an agenda dedicated to preventing genocide throughout the world. *All* immigrants share the strongest desire to prevent these atrocities.

As we monitor our national leadership, Patricia and I are disgusted by the enormous influence of special interests, who through intensive lobbying and excessive spending are threatening to undermine our cherished tradition of participatory democracy. Suzanne herself, after working on the election campaigns of Pete Wilson and Bob Dole, among others, quit her career in politics for the ministry—a decision Pattie and I applauded. As Suzy put it, "This activity is not gratifying. The national interest has become secondary to special interests, who literally buy their privileges through campaign donations and paid lobbyists who provide elected officials with 'expert advice.' Republicans compete with the Democrats, without shame, to amass 'war chests' of millions and millions of dollars. Soon it will be billions. It's insane!"

Public concern that mergers and acquisitions have seriously reduced competitors in the market place could well force our leadership to reactivate available antitrust remedies, kept dormant by Democratic and Republican Presidents alike in these past two decades. During this period we have accumulated nearly five trillion dollars of debt, almost half of it held by foreigners, who are paid 150 billion dollars a year in interest from our Treasury. Our trade deficit has reached two trillion dollars, representing a loss of four million manufacturing jobs in the United States.

As if all this weren't enough, the money taken from citizens has been used by Washington to launch massive bureaucratic systems that invade every facet of life, creating a dependence on Washington that destroys incentive and accountability in families and individuals. Fortunately, our recently elected leaders seem to understand these cause-and-effect relationships, renewing our hope that an aroused public will force the reforms necessary to remove the awesome debt burden our generation has created and placed on our children and grandchildren, and restore the family discipline that guided this nation to greatness.

Pattie and I are gratified that we have been able, from our personal income, to enable our four children to complete college and graduate schools, all free of debt. Three of them have demonstrated their self-confidence and independence of mind by changing their careers to ones more to their liking. Our oldest

The Nakasian Family
Stacey, Sam, Suzanne, Patricia, Grandson Stephen, Stirling, Gundi (Stirling's wife), Grandaughter Sonja, Hod (Stephanie's husband) and Stephanie

child, Stephanie, quit banking to become a widely traveled and critically applauded jazz vocalist. (I can't claim credit for the genes that made *that* choice possible.) Stirling changed his vocation from Sieman's Comptroller to science teacher. As a clergywoman I'm sure Suzy will make a wonderful contribution to society—not in influencing legislation, but in helping to restore our traditional family values. Thus far our youngest, Stacey, seems well satisfied with her choice of Law, which she pursues as a litigator.

When our children were growing up in the Anglo-Saxon enclave of Bronxville, my wife and I frequently wondered how they saw themselves. The question was answered for us one day by a lady whose grandchild attended kindergarten with Stephanie. She reported to us that when her granddaughter asked Stephanie, "What are *you*?," Stephanie replied matter-of-factly, "I'm triple-A."

"What's that?" her friend asked.

"I'm American/Armenian/Austrian," Stephanie answered. To this day, all four of our children see themselves as "Triple-A."

Around the same time as the Statue of Liberty celebration, U.S. District Court Judge James A. Michael, Jr. asked if I would address a group of applicants for citizenship by naturalization in his Charlottesville courtroom. I was greatly honored by this opportunity to tell these people what America has meant to me. Now, a decade later, in spite of the increasing sentiment against immigrants in certain areas of the country, I still feel that my words are as true to the experience of most immigrants as they were to my own experience. Here is what I told them:

To My New Fellow Americans:

Some forty years ago, in a U.S. District Court in New York - a court in the neighborhood of the Statue of Liberty and Ellis Island where I entered America—I applied for American citizenship and received it. In my hand, I hold my naturalization certificate. May I share with you what this certificate has meant to me?

This is my American birthright. I have cherished it above all other possessions for forty years. It means something very special, for no other country in the world offers as much as this certificate guarantees.

If you came here to escape discrimination because you are a member of a minority in your religious beliefs, ethnic origins or political preference, *here* you are guaranteed your religious rights and personal freedom. This Court, and other courts, are here to serve you, to protect your personal rights and property, and to hear your petitions with impartial justice. If you came here to make a better life for yourself and your family, for the opportunity of formal education to the highest level of your capacity, ours is one of the few countries where you can climb the intellectual ladder to the top and achieve economic and cultural benefits as well.

I must now, unavoidably, become personal—to emphasize this point:

I was brought here very young, very poor, by one surviving parent of the Turkish Government genocide of Armenians. Shortly after arriving in the United States, I was orphaned and spent a few years in an orphanage. In my first job, as a farm hand, I had a dream to be a lawyer. By taking advantage of America's opportunities for work and for education I earned my living and the expenses for school. I realized my dream and thereafter I supported a family of four children, each of whom now has a college education at my expense and has employment of his choice. And how nice it is that my wife and I, as we approach the late years, are not financially dependent on our children or on our Government.

Do you know what I hate to hear? "You are a self-made man." I am NOT a self-made man. I am the product of this great country and its generous people. *America* made me!!!

The opportunity to work is here. The schools are here and available, whether or not you can afford the tuition for college or graduate school. If you have dreams and make the effort, *you* can make it—or more accurately—America can make *you*.

The major difference in America is the 200-year old system. I know the difference firsthand, because since World War II I have traveled to almost every country in the world as representative of our Government and as overseas negotiator for American companies. It was my duty to know the systems of these countries. Whatever the country of your origin, people who come to America are remade by our free society system. They become dedicated Americans regardless of their ethnic origins.

Whatever community of your choice, you will find neighbors happy to meet with you and eager to help you in your careers. They will probably invite you to their homes and welcome you to their churches. Your young children will join with theirs in everything from school to scouts to slumber parties. You will appreciate this community spirit as uniquely American. As you may know, in other countries people live within the family circle and rarely invite one another to their homes. What is more, they are secretive about business and technical matters which they do not share even within their own clan.

Before World War II, immigrants were regarded one or two notches below the social level of earlier American families. The greatest social prestige came from having an ancestor on the Mayflower or in the War of Independence. In these times, Americans of several generations reach out to immigrants who choose this country. In social settings today, why it's even possible for immigrants to compete within this framework of ancestor worship. Presumptuously, I've been known to put my oar in, suggesting that my Armenian ancestors originated in the shadows of Mt. Ararat where Noah's Ark, with the help of God, saved two members of every animal and one human family from the Great Flood. This upstaging collapsed on one occasion, when my oar went adrift as a quick-witted Virginian asked me: "Which animal were you?"

Today, all is changed. You are respected for your diligence and honor. It doesn't matter that your skin is darker, eyes more slanted or speech heavily accented. You are respected for what you can contribute to your family, community, and country.

Read the awards of the Nobel Prize; read the list of distinguished scientists; read the election sheets; read *Forbes* Magazine listing the richest Americans today. You will find immigrants in all those records of achievement. However, for the time being, under our Constitution, the only office you cannot hold is that of President of the United States—but your children can.

In recent years immigrants fly in, so perhaps many of you have not had the opportunity to see the Statue of Liberty. Would you, the first chance you get, visit there and read what is inscribed. The statue is the symbol of America's outreach to the world's people. America is great because it is composed of almost every race and religion in the world. It is a community which has been enriched by what immigrants brought here and planted here to flourish in a free society—a society based on government as the *servant* of the people and *not* government as the *master* of people. What you do with your lives is your decision, not the Government's.

For Heaven's sake, and our Country's, don't lose your identity! Don't change your name to Smith, Jones, or White. And, above all, don't melt away—for America is not, as so many have said, a "Melting Pot." Hopefully you will keep alive, through your children, your native language, your songs, your cultural customs and history of your progenitors. In so doing, you will bring wealth to your adopted country.

Finally, let me say this. A popular song goes, "If you can make it (in New York) you can make it anywhere." I believe that. I also believe that if you can't make it in *America*, you were not likely to make it anywhere else.

You will make it here, no doubt, because you came here to work. You will find, as I did, that America's rewards are generous.

God Bless You All.

Samuel Nakasian

The Nakasian Home—Sunny Brae Farm

This Life we seek to balance in,
This world one secon we espy;
So much to catch, to lose or win
So many friends we pass thereby.
This Lord thru Whom we all unite,
This Christ Whose Birthday we employ;
So grand the chance to pause in flight
So dear the thoughts; so sweet the joy!

Patricia Nakasian

Errata

page	*line*	*change*
4	10	southeast replaces *northeast*
4	35	confessional replaces *professional*
28	33	insert coma (,) after milk
49	13	McBurney replaces *McBirney*
52	12	McBurney replaces *McBirney*
53	10	McBurney replaces *McBirney*
76	19	close replaces *boyhood*
76	24	thirty replaces *twenty*
78	16	eliminate *Seymour Raskin*
113	25	eliminate *the*
119	2	Menachem replaces *Menahem*
211	7	eliminate *Abe Rosenthal*
211	10	the editor replaces *Rosenthal*
211	14	the *Times* replaces *Rosenthal*
292	27	eliminate *regularly and*
301	15	Tigris replaces *Euphrates*
322	33	add *to* before *get*
349	31	Bass replaces *Bath*
350	3	Bass replaces *Bath*
352	5	eliminate *recently returned from London where he*
365	34	Divonne replaces *Devon*
367	4	Divonne replaces *Devon*